"No other [...]
a pleasure [...]

". . . Excellently organized [...]
looking for a mix of recreation and cultural insight."
Washington Post

★ ★ ★ ★ ★ (5-star rating) "Crisply written and remarkably personable. Cleverly organized so you can pluck out the minutest fact in a moment. Satisfyingly thorough."
Réalités

"The information they offer is up-to-date, crisply presented but far from exhaustive, the judgments knowledgeable but not opinionated."　*New York Times*

"The individual volumes are compact, the prose succinct, and the coverage up-to-date and knowledgeable . . . The format is portable and the index admirably detailed."
John Barkham Syndicate

". . . An abundance of excellent directions, diversions, and facts, including perspectives and getting-ready-to-go advice — succinct, detailed, and well organized in an easy-to-follow style."　*Los Angeles Times*

"They contain an amount of information that is truly staggering, besides being surprisingly current."
Detroit News

"These guides address themselves to the needs of the modern traveler demanding precise, qualitative information . . . Upbeat, slick, and well put together."
Dallas Morning News

". . . Attractive to look at, refreshingly easy to read, and generously packed with information."　*Miami Herald*

"These guides are as good as any published, and much better than most."　*Louisville* (Kentucky) *Times*

Stephen Birnbaum Travel Guides

Acapulco
Bahamas, Turks & Caicos
Barcelona
Bermuda
Boston
Canada
Cancun, Cozumel, and Isla Mujeres
Caribbean
Chicago
Disneyland
Eastern Europe
Europe
Europe for Business Travelers
Florence
France
Great Britain
Hawaii
Ireland
Italy
Ixtapa & Zihuatanejo
London
Los Angeles
Mexico
Miami & Ft. Lauderdale
New York
Paris
Portugal
Rome
San Francisco
South America
Spain
United States
USA for Business Travelers
Venice
Walt Disney World
Western Europe

CONTRIBUTING EDITORS

Rochelle Goldstein
Judith Harris
Melinda Tang

MAPS General Cartography, Inc.
SYMBOLS Gloria McKeown

A Stephen Birnbaum Travel Guide

Birnbaum's
ROME
1992

Stephen Birnbaum
Alexandra Mayes Birnbaum
EDITORS

Lois Spritzer
EXECUTIVE EDITOR

Laura L. Brengelman
Managing Editor

Mary Callahan
Ann-Rebecca Laschever
Beth Schlau
Dana Margaret Schwartz
Associate Editors

Gene Gold
Assistant Editor

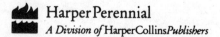
HarperPerennial
A Division of HarperCollins*Publishers*

BIRNBAUM'S ROME 1992 Copyright © 1992 by HarperCollins Publishers. All rights reserved. Printed in the United States of America. No part of this book may be used or reproduced in any manner whatsoever without written permission except in the case of brief quotations embodied in critical articles and reviews. For information address HarperCollins*Publishers,* 10 East 53rd Street, New York, NY 10022.

FIRST EDITION

ISSN: 0749-2561 (Stephen Birnbaum Travel Guides)
ISSN: 1056-442X (Rome)
ISBN: 0-06-278028-X (pbk.)

92 93 94 95 96 CC/MPC 10 9 8 7 6 5 4 3 2 1

Contents

USEFUL WORDS AND PHRASES

THE CITY

Thorough, qualitative guide to Rome. Each section offers a comprehensive report on the city's most compelling attractions and amenities, designed to be used on the spot.

DIVERSIONS

A selective guide to more than a dozen active and/or cerebral theme vacations, including the best places in Rome to pursue them.

For the Experience

For the Body

For the Mind

DIRECTIONS

Ten of the most delightful walks through Rome.

A Word from the Editor

I fell in love with London and Paris at first sight; Rome just took a little longer. That doesn't mean that the romance didn't eventually grow to be deep and abiding; it's just that it took a bit of doing to get past the hurdles that Rome puts in front of folks who try to get to know it.

Roman life proceeds with complete indifference to visitors; governments collapse, strikes cripple services, and citizens disport themselves to tunes that register only on local ears. It all seems — at least at first — as though the casual visitor is an intruder on the rhythm of city life. But the truth is that, once you get the hang of it, Roman life is the easiest to assimilate if you are prepared to do as the Romans do. And since Roman attitudes are the most blissfully self-indulgent and capricious, it is a lifestyle that's pure pleasure to adopt.

So over the years, I've found myself more and more able to ignore the vagaries of daily Roman life, and to accept the unpressured pace of Roman attitudes toward the rest of the world. It has not only increased my overall enjoyment of this singular city, but has meaningfully expanded my ability to enjoy other unfamiliar cities as I roamed the globe. Bravo, Rome!

My own evolution as a traveler (which happily continues) is mirrored by the evolution of our guidebook series. When we began our series of modern travel guides, we logically began with "area" books, attempting to publish guides that would include the widest possible number of attractive destinations. When the public seemed to accept our new way of delivering travel data, we added titles covering only a single country, and when these became popular we began our newest expansion phase, which centers on a group of books that deal with only a single city. Now we not only can highlight our favorite urban destinations, but can really describe how to get the very most out of a visit.

Such treatment of travel information only mirrors an increasingly pervasive trend among travelers — the frequent return to a treasured foreign travel spot. Once upon a time, even the most dedicated travelers would visit distant parts of the world no more than once in a lifetime — usually as part of that fabled Grand Tour. But greater numbers of would-be sojourners are now availing themselves of the opportunity to visit a favored part of the world over and over again.

So where once it was routine to say you'd "seen" a particular country after a very superficial, once-over-lightly encounter, the more perceptive travelers of today recognize that it's entirely possible to have only skimmed the surface of a specific travel destination even after having visited that place more than a dozen times. Similarly, repeated visits to a single site permit true exploration of special interests, whether they be sporting, artistic, or intellectual.

For those of us who spent the several years working out the special system under which we present information in this series, the luxury of being able to devote nearly as much space as we'd like to just a single city is as close to paradise for guide writers and editors as any of us expects to come. But clearly this is not the first guide to the glories of Rome — one suspects that guides of one sort or another have existed at least since Julius began leading his legions north, east, south, and west. Guides to Rome have probably existed in one form or another for centuries, so a traveler might logically ask why a new one is suddenly necessary.

Our answer is that the nature of travel to Rome — and even of the travelers who now routinely make the trip — has changed dramatically of late. For the past 2,000 years or so, travel to any foreign address was an extremely elaborate undertaking, one that required extensive advance planning. Even as recently as the 1950s, a person who had actually been to Rome — to say nothing of Venice, Florence, or Milan — could dine out on his or her experiences for years, since such adventures were quite extraordinary and usually the province of the privileged alone.

With the advent of jet air travel in the late 1950s, however, and of increased-capacity, wide-body aircraft during the 1960s, travel to and around once distant destinations became extremely common. In fact, in more than 2 decades of nearly unending inflation, airfares may be the only commodity in the world that has actually gone down in price.

Attitudes as well as costs have also changed significantly in the last couple of decades. Beginning with the so-called flower children of the 1960s, international travel lost much of its aura of mystery. Whereas their parents might have been happy with just a superficial sampling of Rome, these young people simply picked up and settled in various parts of Europe for an indefinite stay. While living as inexpensively as possible, they adapted to the local lifestyle, and generally immersed themselves in things European.

Thus began an explosion of travel. And over the years, the development of inexpensive charter flights and packages fueled and sharpened the new American interest in and appetite for more extensive exploration.

Now, in the 1990s, those same flower children who were in the forefront of the modern travel revolution have undeniably aged. While it may be impolite to point out that they are probably well into their untrustworthy thirties and forties, their original zeal for travel remains undiminished. For them, it's hardly news that the way to get to the Colosseum is to confront the traffic on the Via dei Fori Imperiali. Such experienced and knowledgeable travelers have decided precisely where they want to go and are more often searching for ideas and insights to expand their already sophisticated travel consciousnesses.

Obviously, any new guidebook to Rome must keep pace with and answer the real needs of today's travelers. That's why we've tried to create a guide that's specifically organized, written, and edited for this more demanding modern audience, travelers for whom qualitative information is infinitely more desirable than mere quantities of unappraised data. We think that this book and the other guides in our series represent a new generation of travel guides, one that is especially responsive to modern needs and interests.

For years, dating back as far as Herr Baedeker, travel guides have tended to be encyclopedic, seemingly much more concerned with demonstrating expertise in geography and history than with making a real analysis of the sorts of things that actually concern a typical modern tourist. But today, when it is hardly necessary to tell a traveler where Rome is located (in many cases, the traveler has been there nearly as often as the guidebook editors), it becomes the responsibility of those editors to provide new perspectives and to suggest new directions in order to make the guide genuinely valuable.

That's exactly what we've tried to do in this series. I think you'll notice a different, more contemporary tone to the text, as well as an organization and focus that are distinctive and more functional. And even a random reading of what follows will demonstrate a substantial departure from the standard guidebook orientation, for not only have we attempted to provide information of a more compelling sort, but we also have tried to present the data in a format that makes it particularly accessible.

Needless to say, it's difficult to decide precisely what to include in a guide-book of this size — and what to omit. Early on, we realized that giving up the encyclopedic approach precluded our listing every single route and restaurant, a realization that helped define our overall editorial focus. Similarly, when we discussed the possibility of presenting certain information in other than strict geographic order, we found that the new format enabled us to arrange data in a way we feel best answers the questions travelers typically ask.

Large numbers of specific questions have provided the real editorial skele-ton for this book. The volume of mail I regularly receive emphasizes that modern travelers want very precise information, so we've tried to organize our material in the most responsive way possible. Readers who want to know the best restaurants or the best places to find inexpensive couturier fashions in Paris will have no trouble extracting that data from this guide.

Travel guides are, understandably, reflections of personal taste, and putting one's name on a title page obviously puts one's preferences on the line. But I think I ought to amplify just what "personal" means. I don't believe in the sort of personal guidebook that's a palpable misrepresentation on its face. It is, for example, hardly possible for any single travel writer to visit thousands of restaurants (and nearly as many hotels) in any given year and provide accurate appraisals of each. And even if it were physically possible for one human being to survive such an itinerary, it would of necessity have to be done at a dead sprint and the perceptions derived therefrom would probably be less valid than those of any other intelligent individual visiting the same establishments. It is, therefore, impossible (especially in a large, annually revised guidebook *series* such as we offer) to have only one person provide all the data on the entire world.

I also happen to think that such individual orientation is of substantially less value to readers. Visiting a single hotel for just one night or eating one hasty meal in a random restaurant hardly equips anyone to provide appraisals that are of more than passing interest. No amount of doggedly alliterative or oppressively onomatopoeic text can camouflage a technique that is essentially specious. We have, therefore, chosen what I like to describe as the "thee and me" approach to restaurant and hotel evaluation and, to a somewhat more limited degree, to the sites and sights we have included in the other sections of our text. What this really reflects is a personal sampling tempered by intelligent counsel from informed local sources, and these additional friends-of-the-editor are almost always residents of the city and/or area about which they are consulted.

Despite the presence of several editors, writers, researchers, and local correspondents, very precise editing and tailoring keep our text fiercely subjective. So what follows is the gospel according to the Birnbaums, and represents as much of our own taste and instincts as we can manage. It is probable, therefore, that if you like your cities stylish and prefer small hotels with personality to huge high-rise anonymities, we're likely to have a long and meaningful relationship. Readers with dissimilar tastes may be less enraptured.

I also should point out something about the person to whom this guidebook is directed. Above all, he or she is a "visitor." This means that such elements as restaurants have been specifically picked to provide the visitor with a representative, enlightening, stimulating, and, above all, pleasant experience. Since so many extraneous considerations can affect the reception and service accorded a regular restaurant patron, our choices can in no way be construed as an exhaustive guide to resident dining. We think we've listed all the best places, in various price ranges, but they were chosen with a visitor's enjoyment in mind.

Other evidence of how we've tried to tailor our text to reflect modern travel habits is most apparent in the section we call DIVERSIONS. Where once it was common for travelers to spend a foreign visit in a determinedly passive state, the emphasis is far more active today. So we've organized every activity we could reasonably evaluate and presented the material in a way that is especially accessible to activists of either athletic or cerebral bent. It is no longer necessary, therefore, to wade through a pound or two of superfluous prose just to find the very best shop or most palatable pasta within the circumference of the ancient Roman walls.

If there is a single thing that best characterizes the revolution in and evolution of current holiday habits, it is that most travelers now consider travel a right rather than a privilege. No longer is a trip to the far corners of the globe necessarily a once-in-a-lifetime thing; nor is the idea of visiting exotic, faraway places in the least worrisome. Travel today translates as the enthusiastic desire to sample all of the world's opportunities, to find that elusive quality of experience that is not only enriching but comfortable. For that reason, we've tried to make what follows not only helpful and enlightening but the sort of welcome companion of which every traveler dreams.

Finally, I also should point out that every good travel guide is a living enterprise; that is, no part of this text is carved in stone. In our annual revisions, we refine, expand, and further hone all our material to serve your travel needs better. To this end, no contribution is of greater value to us than your personal reaction to what we have written, as well as information reflecting your own experiences while using the book. We earnestly and enthusiastically solicit your comments about this guide *and* your opinions and perceptions about places you have recently visited. In this way, we will be able to provide the most current information — including the actual experiences of recent travelers — and to make those experiences more readily available to others. Please write to us at 60 E. 42nd St., New York, NY 10165.

We sincerely hope to hear from you.

STEPHEN BIRNBAUM

How to Use This Guide

A great deal of care has gone into the organization of this guide-book, and we believe it represents a real breakthrough in the presentation of travel material. Our aim is to create a new, more modern generation of travel books and to make this guide the most useful and practical travel tool available today.

Our text is divided into five basic sections in order to present information in the best way on every possible aspect of a Rome vacation. This organization itself should alert you to the vast and varied opportunities available, as well as indicate all the specific data necessary to plan a successful trip. You won't find much of the conventional "swaying palms and shimmering sand" text here; we've chosen instead to deliver more useful and practical information. Prospective itineraries tend to speak for themselves, and with so many diverse travel opportunities, we feel our main job is to highlight what's where and to provide basic information — how, when, where, how much, and what's best — to assist you in making the most intelligent choices possible.

Here is a brief summary of the five basic sections and what you can expect to find in each. We believe that you will find both your travel planning and en route enjoyment enhanced by having this book at your side.

GETTING READY TO GO

This mini-encyclopedia of practical travel facts is a sort of know-it-all companion with all the precise information necessary to create a successful trip to Rome. There are entries on more than 2 dozen separate topics, including how to get where you're going, what preparations to make before leaving, what your trip is likely to cost, and how to avoid prospective problems. The individual entries are specific, realistic, and where appropriate, cost-oriented.

We expect you to use this section most in the course of planning your trip, for its ideas and suggestions are intended to simplify this often confusing period. Entries are intentionally concise, in an effort to get to the meat of the matter with the least extraneous prose. These entries are augmented by extensive lists of specific sources from which to obtain even more specialized data, plus some suggestions for obtaining travel information on your own.

USEFUL WORDS AND PHRASES

Though most hotels and restaurants in Rome have at least one English-speaking staff member, at smaller establishments a little knowledge of Italian will go a long way. This collection of often-used words and phrases will help you to make a hotel or dinner reservation, order a meal, mail a letter — and even buy toothpaste.

THE CITY

The report on Rome has been created with the assistance of researchers, contributors, professional journalists, and experts who live in the city. Although useful at the planning stage, THE CITY is really designed to be taken along and used on the spot. The reports offer a short-stay guide, including an essay introducing the city as a historic entity and as a contemporary place to visit. *At-a-Glance* material is actually a site-by-site survey of the most important, interesting (and sometimes most eclectic) sights to see and things to do. *Sources and Resources* is a concise listing of pertinent information meant to answer a range of potentially pressing questions as they arise — simple things such as the address of the local tourist office, how to get around, which sightseeing tours to take, when special events occur, where to find the best nightspot or hail a taxi, which are the chic places to shop, and where the best beaches and golf are to be found. *Best in Town* is our collection of cost-and-quality choices of the best places to eat and sleep on a variety of budgets.

DIVERSIONS

This section is designed to help travelers find the best places in which to pursue a wide range of physical and cerebral activities, without having to wade through endless pages of unrelated text. This very selective guide lists the broadest possible range of activities, including all the best places to pursue them.

We start with a list of possibilities that offer various places to stay and eat, move to those that require some perspiration — sports preferences and other rigorous pursuits — and go on to report on a number of more cerebral and spiritual vacation opportunities. In every case, our suggestion of a particular location — and often our recommendation of a specific hotel — is intended to guide you to that special place where the quality of experience is likely to be the highest. Whether you seek a romantic hostelry or an inspiring cooking school, each category is the equivalent of a comprehensive checklist of the absolute best in Rome.

DIRECTIONS

Here are 10 walks that cover the city, along its main thoroughfares and side streets, past its most spectacular landmarks and magnificent parks, and into its nearby suburbs. DIRECTIONS is organized thematically; you will find that some routes cross one another, but the sights and sites are viewed from different vantage points. Choose from among those that interest you; many itineraries can be "connected" for longer sojourns or used individually for short, intensive explorations.

Although each of the book's sections has a distinct format and a special function, they have all been designed to be used together to provide a complete inventory of travel information. To use this book to full advantage, take a few minutes to read the table of contents and random entries in each section to get a firsthand feel of how it all fits together.

Pick and choose needed information. Assume, for example, that you have always wanted to take that typically Roman vacation, an eating tour of the city's temples of gastronomy — but you never really knew how to organize it or where to go. Choose specific restaurants from the selections offered in "Eating Out" in THE CITY, in each walking tour in DIRECTIONS, and in the roundup of the best in the city called *Buon Appetito: The Best Restaurants in Rome* in the DIVERSIONS section. Then, refer to USEFUL WORDS AND PHRASES to help you with everything from deciphering the menu to identifying pasta shapes.

In other words, the sections of this book are building blocks designed to help you put together the best possible trip. Use them selectively as a tool, a source of ideas, a reference work for accurate facts, and a guidebook to the best buys, the most exciting sights, the most pleasant accommodations, the tastiest food — *the best travel experience* that you can possibly have in Rome.

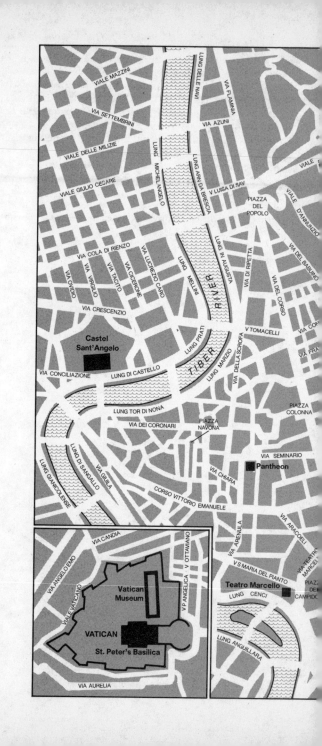

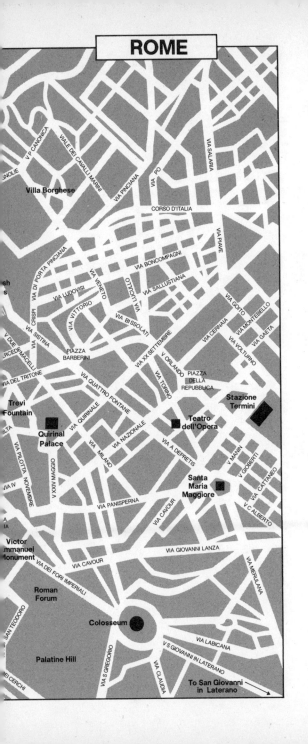

ROME

Villa Borghese

V P CANONICA

VIALE DEI CAVALLI MARINI

VIA PINCIANA

VIA PO

VIA SALARIA

CORSO D'ITALIA

VIA PIAVE

VIA DI PORTA PINCIANA

VIA BONCOMPAGNI

VIA VENETO

VIA LUDOVISI

VIA LUCULLO

VIA SALLUSTIANA

VIA VITTORIO

VIA CRISPI

VIA BISSOLATI

VIA GOITO

VIA MONTEBELLO

VIA CERNAIA

VIA GAETA

VIA SISTINA

VIA XX SETTEMBRE

VIA VOLTURNO

V DUE
MACELLI
RCEDE

PIAZZA
BARBERINI

V ORLANDO

PIAZZA
DELLA
REPUBBLICA

VIA DEL TRITONE

VIA QUATTRO FONTANE

VIA TORINO

Stazione
Termini

Trevi
Fountain

VIA QUIRINALE

Teatro
dell'Opera

Quirinal
Palace

VIA MILANO

VIA NAZIONALE

VIA A DEPRETIS

V MANIN

V GIOBERTI

VIA PILOTTA

V XXIV MAGGIO

Santa
Maria
Maggiore

VIA CATTANEO

VIA IV NOVEMBRE

VIA PANISPERNA

VIA CAVOUR

V C. ALBERTO

Victor
Emmanuel
Monument

VIA GIOVANNI LANZA

VIA MERULANA

VIA DEI FORI IMPERIALI

VIA CAVOUR

Roman
Forum

SAN TEODORO

Colosseum

VIA LABICANA

V S GIOVANNI IN LATERANO

Palatine Hill

VIA S GREGORIO

VIA CLAUDIA

To San Giovanni
in Laterano

DEI CERCHI

GETTING READY TO GO

When and How to Go

When to Go

There really isn't a "best" time to visit Rome. For North Americans, as well as Europeans, the period from April to mid-September has long been — and remains — the peak travel period, traditionally the most popular vacation time.

It is important to emphasize that Rome, like the rest of Italy, is hardly a single-season destination; more and more vacationers who have a choice are enjoying the substantial advantages of off-season travel. Most tourist attractions remain open throughout the year, so travelers do not have to risk the chance of finding an attraction closed during the time they are visiting. During the off-season, people relax and Roman life proceeds at a more leisurely pace. What's more, travel generally is less expensive.

For some, the most convincing argument in favor of off-season travel is the economic one. Getting there and staying there are less expensive during less popular travel periods, as airfares go down and less expensive package tours become available; the independent traveler can go farther on less, too. However, hotel and car rental rates in Rome tend to stay the same throughout the year.

A definite bonus to visiting during the off-season is that even the most basic services are performed more efficiently. In theory, off-season service is identical to that offered during high season, but the fact is that the absence of demanding crowds inevitably begets much more thoughtful and personal attention.

Even during the off-season, high-season rates may prevail because of an important local event. Particularly in the larger cities, and Rome is the major commercial city in the country, special events and major trade shows or conferences held at the time of your visit are sure to affect not only the availability of discounts on accommodations, but the basic availability of a place to stay.

It also should be noted that the months immediately before and after the peak summer months — what the travel industry refers to as shoulder seasons — often are sought out because they offer fair weather and somewhat smaller crowds.

In short, like many other popular places, in Italy and elsewhere, Rome's vacation appeal has become multi-seasonal. But the noted exceptions notwithstanding, most travel destinations are decidedly less heavily trafficked and less expensive during the winter.

CLIMATE: In Rome, average July and August temperatures hover around the low to mid-80s, but a heavy *scirocco* (southeast wind) can push the maximum above 100F. A refreshing breeze often provides relief on summer evenings. Winters are moderate, with temperatures averaging in the high 40s from December through February. The temperature seldom drops below freezing, and snow is very rare, but the *tramontana* (north wind) can be chilly (definitely overcoat weather) and winter rains are heavy.

Generally, Rome maintains fairly moderate temperatures year-round. For example, the average monthly temperature is 49F (9C) in January, 62F (17C) in April, 82F (28C) in July, and 65F (18C) in October.

Travelers can get current readings and 3-day Accu-Weather forecasts through *American Express Travel Related Services*' Worldwide Weather Report number. By dialing 900-WEATHER and punching in the access code for numerous travel destinations worldwide, an up-to-date recording will provide current temperature, sky conditions, wind speed and direction, heat index, relative humidity, local time, highway reports, and beach and boating reports or ski conditions (where appropriate). For the weather in Rome, punch in ROM. This 24-hour service can be accessed from any touch-tone phone in the US or Canada and costs 95¢ per minute. The charge will show up on your phone bill. For a free list of the areas covered, send a self-addressed, stamped envelope to *1-900-WEATHER,* 261 Central Ave., Farmingdale, NY 11735.

SPECIAL EVENTS: Rome is a city of religious festivities. *Christmas* is a season of endless nativities and joyous celebrations throughout the city. It doesn't end until the *Epiphany* on January 6. This has got to be the favorite season of children. A fair takes place in front of the Bernini Fountains, where they receive more gifts after *Christmas.* The *Holy Week* of *Easter* is another major tourist attraction. It starts off on *Good Friday* with a pilgrim procession, which usually comprises at least thousands of people, and the pope gives his blessing on *Easter Sunday* in St. Peter's Square. Meanwhile, hundreds of celebrations and religious ceremonies go on in different neighborhood churches. In mid-July, the *Festa di Noiantri* is a folklore celebration held in Rome's oldest quarter, Trastevere.

Traveling by Plane

Flying is the most efficient way to get to Rome, and it is the quickest, most convenient means of travel between different parts of Italy once you are there.

The air space between North America and Europe is the most heavily trafficked in the world. It is served by dozens of airlines, almost all of which sell seats at a variety of prices under a vast spectrum of requirements and restrictions. You probably will spend more for your airfare than for any other single item in your travel budget, so try to take advantage of the lowest fares offered by either scheduled airlines or charter companies. You should know what kinds of flights are available, the rules under which air travel operates, and all the special package options.

GATEWAYS: At present, nonstop flights to Rome are available from New York's Kennedy Airport.

SCHEDULED FLIGHTS: The following airlines have regular service to Rome: *Alitalia, Delta,* and *TWA.*

A number of other European carriers serve Rome from the US with connecting flights through their main hubs: *Air France* from Anchorage, Boston, Chicago, Houston, Los Angeles, Miami, Newark, New York, San Francisco, and Washington, DC, via Paris; *British Airways* via London's Heathrow Airport; *Iberia* from Los Angeles, Miami, and New York via Madrid; *Lufthansa* from Atlanta, Boston, Charlotte, Los Angeles, Miami, New York, Philadelphia, San Francisco, and Washington, DC, via Frankfurt; *Sabena* from Boston and New York via Brussels; and *TAP Air Portugal* from Boston, Newark, and New York via Lisbon.

Tickets: When traveling on one of the many regularly scheduled flights, a full-fare ticket provides maximum travel flexibility (although at considerable expense) because there are no advance booking requirements. A prospective passenger can buy a ticket for a flight right up to the minute of takeoff — if a seat is available. If your ticket is for a round trip, you can make the return reservation whenever you wish — months before you leave or the day before you return. Assuming foreign immigration require-ments are met, you can stay at your destination for as long as you like. (Tickets generally are good for a year and can be renewed if not used.) You also can cancel your flight at any time without penalty. However, while it is true that this category of ticket can be purchased at the last minute, it is advisable to reserve well in advance during popular vacation periods and around holiday times.

Fares – Airfares continue to change so rapidly that even experts find it difficult to keep up with them. This ever-changing situation is due to a number of factors, including airline deregulation, volatile labor relations, increasing fuel costs, and vastly increased competition.

Perhaps the most common misconception about fares on scheduled airlines is that the cost of the ticket determines how much service will be provided on the flight. This is true only to a certain extent. A far more realistic rule of thumb is that the less you pay for your ticket, the more restrictions and qualifications are likely to come into play *before* you board the plane (as well as after you get off). These qualifying aspects relate to the months (and the days of the week) during which you must travel, how far in advance you must purchase your ticket, the minimum and maximum amount of time you may or must remain away, your willingness to decide on a return date at the time of booking — and your ability to stick to that decision. It is not uncommon for passen-gers sitting side by side on the same wide-body jet to have paid fares varying by hundreds of dollars, and all too often the traveler paying more would have been equally willing (and able) to accept the terms of the far less expensive ticket.

In general, the great variety of fares between the US and Rome can be reduced to four basic categories — first class, business class, coach (also called economy or tourist class), and excursion or discount fares. In addition, Advance Purchase Excursion (APEX) fares offer savings under certain conditions.

In a class by itself is the *Concorde,* the supersonic jet developed jointly by France and Great Britain that cruises at speeds of 1,350 miles per hour (almost twice the speed of sound) and makes transatlantic crossings in half the time (3¾ hours from New York to Paris) of conventional, subsonic jets. *Air France* offers *Concorde* service to Paris from New York; *British Airways* flies from Miami, Washington, DC, and New York to London. Service is "single" class (with champagne and caviar all the way), and the fare is expensive, about 20% more than a first class ticket on a subsonic aircraft. Some discounts have been offered, but time is the real gift of the *Concorde.* For travelers to European destinations other than Paris or London, this "gift" may be more or less valuable as compared to a direct flight when taking connecting flights into account.

A **first class** ticket admits you to the special section of the aircraft with larger seats, more legroom, better (or more elaborately served) food, free drinks and headsets for movies and music channels, and above all, personal attention. First class fares are about twice those of full-fare (often called "regular") economy.

Behind first class often lies **business class**, usually a separate cabin or cabins. While standards of comfort and service are not as high as in first class, they represent a considerable improvement over conditions in the rear of the plane, with roomier seats, more leg and shoulder space between passengers, and fewer seats abreast. Free liquor and headsets, a choice of meal entrées, and a separate counter for speedier check-in are other inducements. Note that airlines often have their own names for their business class service — such as Le Club on *Air France* and Ambassador Class on *TWA.*

The terms of the **coach** or **economy** fare may vary slightly from airline to airline; from time to time airlines may be selling more than one type of economy fare. Coach or economy passengers sit more snugly, as many as 10 in a single row on a wide-body jet, behind the first class and business class sections. Normally, alcoholic drinks are not free, nor are the headsets.

In first, business, and economy class, passengers are entitled to reserve seats and are sold tickets on an open reservation system, with tickets sold up to the last minute if seats are available. The passengers may travel on any scheduled flight they wish, buy a one-way or round-trip ticket, and have the ticket remain valid for a year. There are no requirements for a minimum or maximum stay or for advance booking and no cancellation penalties. The first class and business tickets also allow free stopover privileges; limited free stopovers often are permitted in some economy fares, while with others a surcharge may apply. The cost of economy and business class tickets between the US and Italy does not vary much in the course of the year.

Excursion and other **discount** fares are the airlines' equivalent of a special sale and usually apply to round-trip bookings only. These fares generally differ according to the season and the number of travel days permitted. They are only a bit less flexible than full-fare economy tickets, and are, therefore, often useful for both business and holiday travelers. Most round-trip excursion tickets include strict minimum and maximum stay requirements and can be changed only within prescribed time limits. So don't count on extending a ticket beyond the specified time of return or staying less time than required. Different airlines may have different regulations concerning the number of stopovers permitted, and sometimes excursion fares are less expensive during midweek. The availability of these reduced-rate seats is most limited at busy times such as holidays. Discount or excursion fare ticket holders sit with the coach passengers and, for all intents and purposes, are indistinguishable from them. They receive all the same basic services, even though they may have paid anywhere between 30% and 55% less for the trip. Obviously, it's wise to make plans early enough to qualify for this less expensive transportation if possible.

These discount or excursion fares may masquerade under a variety of names and invariably have strings attached. A common requirement is that the ticket be purchased a certain number of days — usually no fewer than 7 or 14 days — in advance of departure, though it may be booked weeks or months in advance (it has to be "ticketed," or paid for, shortly after booking, however). The return reservation usually has to be made at the time of the original ticketing and cannot be changed later than a certain number of days (again, usually 7 or 14) before the return flight. If events force a passenger to change the return reservation after the date allowed, the difference between the round-trip excursion rate and the round-trip coach rate probably will have to be paid, though most airlines allow passengers to use their discounted fares by standing by for an empty seat, even if the carrier doesn't otherwise have standby fares. Another common condition is the minimum and maximum stay requirement; for example, 1 to 6 days or 6 to 14 days (but including a Saturday night). Last, cancellation penalties of up to 50% of the full price of the ticket have been assessed — check the specific penalty in effect when you purchase your discount/excursion ticket — so careful planning is imperative.

Of even greater risk — and bearing the lowest price of all the current discount fares — is the ticket where no change at all in departure and/or return flights is permitted, and where the ticket price is totally nonrefundable. If you do buy a nonrefundable ticket, you should be aware of a new policy followed by many airlines that may make it easier to change your plans if necessary. For a fee — set by each airline and payable at the airport when checking in — you *may* be able to change the time or date of a return flight on a nonrefundable ticket. However, if the nonrefundable ticket price for the replacement flight is higher than that of the original (as often is the case when trading in a weekday for a weekend flight), you also will have to pay the difference. Any such change must be made a certain number of days in advance — in some cases as little as 2 days — of either the original or the replacement flight, whichever is earlier; restrictions are set by the individual carrier. (Travelers holding a nonrefundable or other restricted ticket who must change their plans due to a family emergency should know that some carriers may make special allowances in such situations; see *Medical and Legal Aid and Consular Services,* in this section.)

One excursion fare available for travel between the US and Rome, but not to the majority of other European destinations, comes unencumbered by advance booking requirements and cancellation penalties, permits one stopover (for a fee) in each direction, and has "open jaws," meaning that you can fly to one city and depart from another, arranging and paying for your own transportation between the two. The ticket costs about a third less than economy — during the off-season. High-season prices may be less attractive. The ticket currently is good for a minimum of 7 days and a maximum of 6 months abroad.

There also is a newer, often less expensive, type of excursion fare, the **APEX**, or **Advanced Purchase Excursion** fare. (In the case of flights to Europe, this type of fare also may be called a "Eurosaver" fare.) As with traditional excursion fares, passengers paying an APEX fare sit with and receive the same basic services as any other coach or economy passengers, even though they may have paid up to 50% less for their seats. In return, they are subject to certain restrictions. In the case of flights to Rome, the ticket usually is good for a minimum of 7 days abroad and a maximum, currently, of 2 months (depending on the airline and the destination); and as its name implies, it must be "ticketed," or paid for in its entirety, a certain period of time before departure — usually 21 days, although in the case of Rome it may be as little as 14 days.

The drawback to an APEX fare is that it penalizes travelers who change their minds — and travel plans. The return reservation must be made at the time of the original ticketing, and if for some reason you change your schedule, you will have to pay a penalty of $100 or 10% of the ticket value, whichever is greater, as long as you travel within the validity period of your ticket. But if you change your return to a date less than the minimum stay or more than the maximum stay, the difference between the round-trip APEX fare and the full round-trip coach rate will have to be paid. There also is a penalty of anywhere from $75 to $125 or more for canceling or changing a reservation *before* travel begins — check the specific penalty in effect when you purchase your ticket. No stopovers are allowed on an APEX ticket, but it is possible to create an open-jaw effect by buying an APEX on a split ticket basis: for example, flying to Rome and returning from Venice. The total price would be half the price of an APEX to Rome plus half the price of an APEX to Venice. APEX tickets to Rome are sold at basic and peak rates (peak season is around May through September) and may include surcharges for weekend flights.

There also is a Winter or Super APEX, which may go under different names for different carriers. Similar to the regular APEX fare, it costs slightly less but is more restrictive. Depending on the airline and destination, it usually is available only for off-peak winter travel and is limited to a stay of between 7 and 21 days. Advance purchase still is required (currently, 30 days prior to travel), and ticketing must be completed within 48 hours of reservation. The fare is nonrefundable, except in cases of hospitalization or death.

At the time of this writing, *Alitalia* offered Super APEX on transatlantic flights to most destinations in Italy during the off-season.

Another type of fare that sometimes is available is the youth fare. At present, most US airlines and *Alitalia* are using a form of APEX fare as a youth fare for travelers up to age 24. The maximum stay is extended to a year. Seats can be reserved no more than 3 days before departure, and tickets must be purchased when the reservation is made. The return is booked at time of reservation, or it can be left open. There is no cancellation penalty, but the fare is subject to availability, so it may be difficult to book a return during peak travel periods, and as with the regular APEX fare, it may not even be available for travel to or from Italy during high season, especially if you have a strict traveling schedule.

The major airlines serving Rome from the US also may offer individual excursion fares in conjunction with ground accommodation packages. Previously called ITX, and sometimes referred to as individual tour-basing fares, these fares generally are offered as part of "air/hotel/car/transfer packages," and can reduce the cost of an economy fare by more than a third. The packages are booked for a specific length of time, with return dates specified; rescheduling and cancellation restrictions and penalties vary from carrier to carrier. At the time of this writing, airlines that offer this type of fare to Rome include *Air France, Alitalia, British Airways,* and *TWA.* Note that their offerings may or may not represent substantial savings over standard economy fares, so check at the time you plan to travel. (For further information on package options, see *Package Tours,* in this section.)

Travelers looking for the least expensive possible airfares should, finally, scan the travel pages of their hometown newspapers (especially the Sunday travel sections) for announcements of special promotional fares. Most airlines traditionally have offered their most attractive special fares to encourage travel during slow seasons, and to inaugurate and publicize new routes. Even if none of these factors apply, prospective passengers can be fairly sure that the number of discount seats per flight at the lowest price is strictly limited, or that the fare offering includes a set expiration date — which means it's absolutely necessary to move fast to enjoy the lowest possible price.

It's always wise to ask about discount or promotional fares and about any conditions that might restrict booking, payment, cancellation, and changes in plans. Check the prices from other neighboring cities. A special rate may be offered in a nearby city but not in yours, and it may be enough of a bargain to warrant your leaving from that city. Ask if there is a difference in price for midweek versus weekend travel, or if there is a further discount for traveling early in the morning or late at night. Also be sure to investigate package deals, which are offered by virtually every airline. These may include a car rental, accommodations, and dining and/or sightseeing features in addition to the basic airfare, and the combined cost of packaged elements usually is considerably less than the cost of the exact same elements when purchased separately.

If in the course of your research you come across a deal that seems too good to be true, keep in mind that logic may not be a component of deeply discounted airfares — there's not always any sane relationship between miles to be flown and the price to get there. More often than not, the level of competition on a given route dictates the degree of discount, and don't be dissuaded from accepting an offer that sounds irresistible just because it also sounds illogical. Better to buy that inexpensive fare while it's being offered and worry about the sense — or absence thereof — while you're flying to your desired destination.

When you're satisfied that you've found the lowest possible price for which you can conveniently qualify, make your booking. You may have to call the airline more than once, because different airline reservations clerks have been known to quote different prices, and different fares will be available at different times for the same flight because of a relatively new computerized airline practice called yield management, which adds or subtracts low-fare seats to a given flight depending on how well it is selling.

To protect yourself against fare increases, purchase and pay for your ticket as soon as possible after you've received a confirmed reservation. Airlines generally will honor their tickets, even if the operative price at the time of your flight is higher than the price you paid; if fares go up between the time you *reserve* a flight and the time you *pay* for it, you likely will be out of luck. Finally, with excursion or discount fares, it is important to remember that when a reservation clerk says that you must purchase a ticket by a specific date, this is an absolute deadline. Miss it and the airline may automatically cancel your reservation without telling you.

Frequent Flyers – Among the leading carriers serving Italy, *Air France, British Airways,* and *TWA* offer a bonus system to frequent travelers. After the first 10,000 miles, for example, a passenger might be eligible for a first class seat for the coach fare; after another 10,000 miles, he or she might receive a discount on his or her next ticket purchase. The value of the bonuses continues to increase as more miles are logged. Once you are signed up for such a program, if flying to Europe on *Air France, Alitalia, Iberia, Lufthansa,* or another Europe-based airline, ask if the miles to be flown may be applied toward your collective bonus mileage account with a US carrier. For example, miles flown on *Alitalia* can be applied to *Continental, United, and USAir* frequent flyer mileage programs.

Bonus miles also may be earned by patronizing affiliated car rental companies or hotel chains, or by using one of the credit cards that now offers this reward. In deciding whether to accept such a credit card from one of the issuing organizations that tempt you with frequent flyer mileage bonuses on a specific airline, first determine whether the interest rate charged on the unpaid balance is the same as (or less than) possible alternate credit cards, and whether the annual "membership" fee also is equal or lower. If these charges are slightly higher than those of competing cards, weigh the difference against the potential value in airfare savings. Also ask about any bonus miles awarded just for signing up — 1,000 is common, 5,000 generally the maximum.

For the most up-to-date information on frequent flyer bonus options, you may want to send for the monthly newsletter *Frequent.* Issued by Frequent Publications, it provides current information about frequent flyer plans in general, as well as specific data about promotions, awards, and combination deals to help you keep track of the profusion — and confusion — of current and upcoming availabilities. For a year's subscription, send $33 to Frequent Publications, 4715-C Town Center Dr., Colorado Springs, CO 80916 (phone: 800-333-5937).

There also is a monthly magazine called *Frequent Flyer,* but unlike the newsletter mentioned above, its focus is primarily on newsy articles of interest to business travelers and other frequent flyers. Published by Official Airline Guides (PO Box 58543, Boulder, CO 80322-8543; phone: 800-323-3537), *Frequent Flyer* is available for $24 for a 1-year subscription.

Low-Fare Airlines – Increasingly, the stimulus for special fares is the appearance of airlines associated with bargain rates. On these airlines, all seats on any given flight generally sell for the same price, which is somewhat below the lowest discount fare offered by the larger, more established airlines. It is important to note that tickets offered by the smaller airlines specializing in low-cost travel frequently are not subject to the same restrictions as the lowest-priced ticket offered by the more established carriers. They may not require advance purchase or minimum and maximum stays, may involve no cancellation penalties, and may be available one way or round trip. A disadvantage to low-fare airlines, however, is that when something goes wrong, such as delayed baggage or a flight cancellation due to equipment breakdown, their smaller fleets and fewer flights mean that passengers may have to wait longer for a solution than they would on one of the equipment-rich major carriers.

At press time, one of the few airlines offering a consistently low fare to Europe was *Virgin Atlantic* (phone: 800-862-8621 or 212-242-1330), which flies daily from New York (Newark) to London's Gatwick Airport. The airline sells tickets in several categories, including business or "upper" class, economy, APEX, and nonrefundable variations on standby. Fares from New York to London include Late Saver fares — which must be purchased not less than 7 days prior to travel — and Late Late Saver fares — which are purchased no later than 1 day prior to travel. Travelers to Rome have to take a second flight there from London, but still may save money. To determine the potential savings, add the cost of these transatlantic fares and the cost of connecting flights to come up with the total ticket price.

In a class by itself is *Icelandair,* which always has been a scheduled airline but long has been known as a good source of low-cost flights to Europe. *Icelandair* flies from Baltimore/Washington, DC, New York, and Orlando to Copenhagen (Denmark), Glasgow and London (Great Britain), Gothenburg and Stockholm (Sweden), Helsinki (Finland), Luxembourg (in the country of the same name), Oslo (Norway), Paris

(France), and Reykjavik (Iceland). In addition, the airline increases the options for its passengers by offering "thru-fares" on connecting flights to other European cities. (The price of the intra-European flights — aboard Luxembourg's *Luxair* — is included in the price *Icelandair* quotes for the transatlantic portion of the travel to these additional destinations.)

Icelandair sells tickets in a variety of categories, from unrestricted economy fares to a sort of standby "3-days-before" fare (which functions just like the youth fares described above but has no age requirement). Travelers should be aware, however, that most *Icelandair* flights stop in Reykjavik, Iceland, for 45 minutes — a minor delay for most, but one that further prolongs the trip for passengers who will wait again to board connecting flights to their ultimate destination of Rome. (At the time of this writing, *Icelandair* did not offer connecting flights to Italy, but *Luxair* has connecting flights from Reykjavik to Rome.) It may be a better choice for travelers intending to visit *other* destinations on the Continent when taking both this delay and the cost of connections into account. For reservations and tickets, contact a travel agent or *Icelandair* (phone: 800-223-5500 or 212-967-8888).

Intra-European Fares – The cost of the round trip across the Atlantic is not the only expense to consider, for flights between European cities can be quite expensive. But discounts have recently been introduced on routes between some European cities, and other discounts do exist.

Recent Common Market moves toward airline deregulation are expected to lead gradually to a greater number of budget fares. In the meantime, however, the high cost of fares between most European cities can be avoided by careful use of stopover rights on the higher-priced transatlantic tickets — first class, business class, and full-fare economy. If your ticket doesn't allow stopovers, ask about excursion fares such as PEX and Super PEX, APEX for round trips, and other excursion fares for one-way trips. If you are able to comply with applicable restrictions and can use them, you may save as much as 35% to 50% off full-fare economy. Note that these tickets, which once could be bought only after arrival in Europe, now are sold in the US and can be bought before departure.

Both *Alitalia* and its subsidiary, *Aero Transporti Italiano* (a domestic airline), offer discount fares for round-trip travel within Italy. These special fares must be purchased with a transatlantic flight on board *Alitalia*.

At press time, *Alitalia* was offering a program called Visit Italy for travel within Italy. Passengers can take two flights to any destinations on board either *Alitalia* or *Aero Transporti Italiano* for $100. Visit Italy must be purchased in the US together with a transatlantic flight, and each portion of the domestic flights must also be booked while in the US. Check with *Alitalia* at the time you plan to travel, to see if this program is still available.

Taxes and Other Fees – Travelers who have shopped for the best possible flight at the lowest possible price should be warned that a number of extras will be added to that price and collected by the airline or travel agent who issues the ticket. These taxes *usually* (but not always) are included in the prices quoted by airline reservations clerks.

The $6 International Air Transportation Tax is a departure tax paid by all passengers flying from the US to a foreign destination. A $10 US Federal Inspection Fee is levied on all air and cruise passengers who arrive in the US from outside North America. Still another fee is charged by some airlines to cover more stringent security procedures, prompted by recent terrorist incidents. The 8% federal US Transportation Tax applies to travel within the US or US territories, as well as to passengers flying between US cities en route to a foreign destination if the trip includes a stopover of more than 12 hours at a US point. Someone flying from Los Angeles to New York and stopping in

New York for more than 12 hours before boarding a flight to Rome, for instance, would pay the 8% tax on the domestic portion of the trip.

Reservations – For those who don't have the time or patience to investigate personally all possible air departures and connections for a proposed trip, a travel agent can be of inestimable help. A good agent should have all the information on which flights go where and when, and which categories of tickets are available on each. Most have computerized reservation links with the major carriers, so that a seat can be reserved and confirmed in minutes. An increasing number of agents also possess fare-comparison computer programs, so they often are very reliable sources of detailed competitive price data. (For more information, see *How to Use a Travel Agent,* in this section.)

When making reservations through a travel agent, ask the agent to give the airline your home phone number, as well as your daytime business phone number. All too often the agent uses the agency number as the official contact for changes in flight plans. Especially during the winter, weather conditions hundreds or even thousands of miles away can wreak havoc with flight schedules. Aircraft are constantly in use, and a plane delayed in the Orient or on the West Coast can miss its scheduled flight from the East Coast the next morning. The airlines are fairly reliable about getting this sort of information to passengers if they can reach them; diligence does little good at 10 PM if the airline has only the agency's or an office number.

Reconfirmation is strongly recommended for all international flights, and in the case of flights to Rome, it is a good idea to confirm your round-trip reservations — especially the return leg — as well as any point-to-point flights within Europe. Some (though increasingly fewer) reservations to and from international destinations are automatically canceled after a required reconfirmation period (typically 72 hours) has passed — even if you have a confirmed, fully paid ticket in hand. It always is wise to call ahead to make sure that the airline did not slip up in entering your original reservation, or in registering any changes you may have made since, and that it has your seat reservation and/or special meal request in the computer. If you look at the printed information on the ticket, you'll see the airline's reconfirmation policy stated explicitly. Don't be lulled into a false sense of security by the "OK" on your ticket next to the number and time of the return flight. This only means that a reservation has been entered; a reconfirmation still may be necessary. If in doubt — call.

If you plan not to take a flight on which you hold a confirmed reservation, by all means inform the airline. Because the problem of "no-shows" is a constant expense for airlines, they are allowed to overbook flights, a practice that often contributes to the threat of denied boarding for a certain number of passengers (see "Getting Bumped," below).

Seating – For most types of tickets, airline seats usually are assigned on a first-come, first-served basis at check-in, although some airlines make it possible to reserve a seat at the time of ticket purchase. Always check in early for your flight, even with advance seat assignments. A good rule of thumb for international flights is to arrive at the airport *at least* 2 hours before the scheduled departure to give yourself plenty of time in case there are long lines.

Most airlines furnish seating charts, which make choosing a seat much easier, but there are a few basics to consider. You must decide whether you prefer a window, aisle, or middle seat. On flights where smoking is permitted, you also should specify if you prefer the smoking or nonsmoking section. There is a useful quarterly publication called the *Airline Seating Guide* that publishes seating charts for most major US airlines and many foreign carriers as well. Your travel agent should have a copy, or you can buy the US edition for $39.95 per year and the international edition for $44.95. Order from Carlson Publishing Co., Box 888, Los Alamitos, CA 90720 (phone: 800-728-4877 or 213-493-4877).

Simply reserving an airline seat in advance, however, actually may guarantee very little. Most airlines require that passengers arrive at the departure gate at least 45 minutes (sometimes more) ahead of time to hold a seat reservation. Some US airlines may cancel seat assignments and may not honor reservations of passengers not "checked in" 45 minutes before the scheduled departure time, and they *ask* travelers to check in at least 2 hours before all international flights. It pays to read the fine print on your ticket carefully and plan ahead.

A far better strategy is to visit an airline ticket office (or one of a select group of travel agents) to secure an actual boarding pass for your specific flight. Once this has been issued, airline computers show you as checked in, and you effectively own the seat you have selected (although some carriers may not honor boarding passes of passengers arriving at the gate less than 10 minutes before departure). This also is good — but not foolproof — insurance against getting bumped from an overbooked flight and is, therefore, an especially valuable tactic at peak travel times.

Smoking – For information on airplane smoking regulations, there is a wallet-size guide that notes in detail the rights of smokers and nonsmokers according to current US regulations. It is available by sending a self-addressed, stamped envelope to *ASH (Action on Smoking and Health),* Airline Card, 2013 H St. NW, Washington, DC 20006 (phone: 202-659-4310).

Meals – If you have specific diet requirements, be sure to let the airline know well before departure time. The available meals include vegetarian, seafood, kosher, Muslim, Hindu, high-protein, low-calorie, low-cholesterol, low-fat, low-sodium, diabetic, bland, and children's menus. There is no extra charge for this option. It usually is necessary to request special meals when you make your reservations — check-in time is too late. It's also wise to reconfirm that your request for a special meal has made its way into the airline's computer — the time to do this is 24 hours before departure. (Note that special meals generally are not available on intra-European flights on small local carriers. If this poses a problem, try to eat before you board, or bring a snack with you.)

Baggage – When you fly on a US airline or on a major international carrier such as *Alitalia,* US baggage regulations will be in effect. Though airline baggage allowances vary slightly, in general all passengers are allowed to carry on board, without charge, one piece of luggage that will fit easily under a seat of the plane or in an overhead bin and whose combined dimensions (length, width, and depth) do not exceed 45 inches. A reasonable amount of reading material, camera equipment, and a handbag also are allowed. In addition, all passengers are allowed to check two bags in the cargo hold: one usually not to exceed 62 inches when length, width, and depth are combined, the other not to exceed 55 inches in combined dimensions. Generally no single bag may weigh more than 70 pounds.

Airline Clubs – US carriers often have clubs for travelers who pay for membership. These clubs are not solely for first class passengers, although a first class ticket *may* entitle a passenger to lounge privileges. Membership (which, by law, requires a fee) entitles the traveler to use the private lounges at airports along their route, to refreshments served in these lounges, and to check-cashing privileges at most of their counters. Extras include special telephone numbers for individual reservations, embossed luggage tags, and a membership card for identification. Airlines serving Rome that offer membership in such clubs include the following:

> *British Airways:* The *Executive Club.* Single yearly membership £125 (about $200 at press time). Note that there is no discounted rate for a spouse.
> *Delta:* The *Crown Club.* Single yearly membership $150; spouse an additional $50 per year.

TWA: The *Ambassador Club.* Single yearly membership $150, spouse an additional $25; lifetime memberships also available.

Note that such companies do not have club facilities in all airports. Other airlines also offer a variety of special services in many airports.

CHARTER FLIGHTS: By booking a block of seats on a specially arranged flight, charter operators offer travelers air transportation for a substantial reduction over the full coach or economy fare. These operators may offer air-only charters (selling transportation alone) or charter packages (the flight plus a combination of land arrangements such as accommodations, meals, tours, or car rentals). Charters are especially attractive to people living in smaller cities or out-of-the-way places, because they frequently leave from nearby airports, saving travelers the inconvenience and expense of getting to a major gateway.

From the consumer's standpoint, charters differ from scheduled airlines in two main respects: You generally need to book and pay in advance, and you can't change the itinerary or the departure and return dates once you've booked the flight. In practice, however, these restrictions don't always apply. Today, although most charter flights still require advance reservations, some permit last-minute bookings (when there are unsold seats available), and some even offer seats on a standby basis.

Though charters almost always are round-trip, and it is unlikely that you would be sold a one-way seat on a round-trip flight, on rare occasions one-way tickets on charters are offered. Although it may be possible to book a one-way charter in the US, giving you more flexibility in scheduling your return, note that US regulations pertaining to charters may be more permissive than the charter laws of other countries. For example, if you want to book a one-way foreign charter back to the US, you may find advance booking rules in force.

Some things to keep in mind about charter travel:

1. It cannot be repeated often enough that if you are forced to cancel your trip, you can lose much (and possibly all) of your money unless you have cancellation insurance, which is a *must* (see *Insurance,* in this section). Frequently, if the cancellation occurs far enough in advance (often 6 weeks or more), you may forfeit only a $25 or $50 penalty. If you cancel only 2 or 3 weeks before the flight, there may be no refund at all unless you or the operator can provide a substitute passenger.

2. Charter flights may be canceled by the operator up to 10 days before departure for any reason, usually underbooking. Your money is returned in this event, but there may be too little time for you to make new arrangements.

3. Most charters have little of the flexibility of regularly scheduled flights regarding refunds and the changing of flight dates; if you book a return flight, you must be on it or lose your money.

4. Charter operators are permitted to assess a surcharge, if fuel or other costs warrant it, of up to 10% of the airfare up to 10 days before departure.

5. Because of the economics of charter flights, your plane almost always will be full, so you will be crowded, though not necessarily uncomfortable. (There is, however, a new movement among charter airlines to provide flight accommodations that are more comfort-oriented, so this situation may change in the near future.)

To avoid problems, *always* choose charter flights with care. When you consider a charter, ask your travel agent who runs it and carefully check the company. The Better Business Bureau in the company's home city can report on how many complaints, if any, have been lodged against it in the past. Protect yourself with trip cancellation and interruption insurance, which can help safeguard your investment if you or a traveling companion is unable to make the trip and must cancel too late to receive a full refund from the company providing your travel services. (This is advisable whether you're buying a charter flight alone or a tour package for which the airfare is provided by charter or scheduled flight.)

Bookings – If you do take a charter, read the contract's fine print carefully and pay particular attention to the following:

Instructions concerning the payment of the deposit and its balance and to whom the check is to be made payable. Ordinarily, checks are made out to an escrow account, which means the charter company can't spend your money until your flight has safely returned. This provides some protection for you. To ensure the safe handling of your money, make out your check to the escrow account, the number of which must appear by law on the brochure, though all too often it is on the back in fine print. Write the details of the charter, including the destination and dates, on the face of the check; on the back, print "For Deposit Only." Your travel agent may prefer that you make out your check to the agency, saying that it will then pay the tour operator the fee minus commission. It is perfectly legal to write the check as we suggest, however, and if your agent objects too vociferously (he or she should trust the tour operator to send the proper commission), consider taking your business elsewhere. If you don't make your check out to the escrow account, you lose the protection of that escrow should the trip be canceled. Furthermore, recent bankruptcies in the travel industry have served to point out that even the protection of escrow may not be enough to safeguard a traveler's investment. More and more, insurance is becoming a necessity. The charter company should be bonded (usually by an insurance company), and if you want to file a claim against it, the claim should be sent to the bonding agent. The contract will set a time limit within which a claim must be filed.

Specific stipulations and penalties for cancellations. Most charters allow you to cancel up to 45 days in advance without major penalty, but some cancellation dates are 50 to 60 days before departure.

Stipulations regarding cancellation and major changes made by the charterer. US rules say that charter flights may not be canceled within 10 days of departure except when circumstances — such as natural disasters or political upheavals — make it impossible to fly. Charterers may make "major changes," however, such as in the date or place of departure or return, but you are entitled to cancel and receive a full refund if you don't wish to accept these changes. A price increase of more than 10% at any time up to 10 days before departure is considered a major change; no price increase at all is allowed during the last 10 days immediately before departure.

At press time, only one charter company, *Tower Air,* regularly offered charter service to Italy. During high season, there are two flights weekly leaving for Rome and Milan from New York's Kennedy Airport. For reservations, call *Fantasy Holidays* (400 Jericho Turnpike, Suite 301, Jericho, NY 11563; phone: 800-645-2555 or 516-935-8500).

For the full range of possibilities at the time you plan to travel, you may want to subscribe to the travel newsletter *Jax Fax,* which regularly features a list of charter companies and packagers offering seats on charter flights and may be a source for other possible charter flights to Rome. For a year's subscription, send a check or money order for $12 to *Jax Fax* (397 Post Rd., Darien, CT 06820; phone: 203-655-8746).

DISCOUNTS ON SCHEDULED FLIGHTS: Promotional fares often are called discount fares because they cost less than what used to be the standard airline fare — full-fare economy. Nevertheless, they cost the traveler the same whether they are bought through a travel agent or directly from the airline. Tickets that cost less if bought from some outlet other than the airline do exist, however. While it is likely that the vast majority of travelers flying to Rome in the near future will be doing so on a promotional fare or charter rather than on a "discount" air ticket of this sort, it still is a good idea for cost-conscious consumers to be aware of the latest developments in the budget airfare scene. Note that the following discussion makes clear-cut distinctions among the types of discounts available based on how they reach the consumer; in actual practice, the distinctions are not nearly so precise.

Net Fare Sources – The newest notion for reducing the costs of travel services comes from travel agents who offer individual travelers "net" fares. Defined simply, a net fare is the bare minimum amount at which an airline or tour operator will carry a prospective traveler. It doesn't include the amount that normally would be paid to the travel agent as a commission. Traditionally, such commissions amount to about 10% on domestic fares and from 10% to 20% on international fares — not counting significant additions to these commission levels that are paid retroactively when agents sell more than a specific volume of tickets or trips for a single supplier. At press time, at least one travel agency in the US was offering travelers the opportunity to purchase tickets and/or tours for a net price. Instead of making its income from individual commissions, this agency assesses a fixed fee that may or may not provide a bargain for travelers; it requires a little arithmetic to determine whether to use the services of a net travel agent or those of one who accepts conventional commissions. One of the potential drawbacks of buying from agencies selling travel services at net fares is that some airlines refuse to do business with them, thus possibly limiting your flight options.

Travel Avenue is a fee-based agency that rebates its ordinary agency commission to the customer. For domestic flights, they will find the lowest retail fare, then rebate 7% to 10% (depending on the airline selected) of that price minus a $10 ticket-writing charge. The rebate percentage for international flights varies from 5% to 16% (again depending on the airline), and the ticket-writing fee is $25. The ticket-writing charge is imposed per ticket; if the ticket includes more than eight separate flights, an additional $10 or $25 fee is charged. Customers using free flight coupons pay the ticket-writing charge, plus an additional $5 coupon processing fee.

Travel Avenue will rebate its commissions on all tickets, including heavily discounted fares and senior citizen passes. Available 7 days a week, reservations should be made far enough in advance to allow the tickets to be sent by first class mail, since extra charges accrue for special handling. It's possible to economize further by making your own airline reservation, then asking *Travel Avenue* only to write/issue your ticket. For travelers outside the Chicago area, business may be transacted by phone and purchases charged to a credit card. For further information, contact *Travel Avenue* at 641 W. Lake St., Suite 201, Chicago, IL 60606-1012 (phone: 312-876-1116 in Illinois; 800-333-3335 elsewhere in the US).

Consolidators and Bucket Shops – Other vendors of travel services can afford to sell tickets to their customers at an even greater discount because the airline has sold the tickets to them at a substantial discount (usually accomplished by sharply increasing commissions to that vendor), a practice in which many airlines indulge, albeit discreetly, preferring that the general public not know they are undercutting their own "list" prices. Airlines anticipating a slow period on a particular route sometimes sell off a certain portion of their capacity to a wholesaler or consolidator. The wholesaler sometimes is a charter operator who resells the seats to the public as though they were charter seats, which is why prospective travelers perusing the brochures of charter operators with large programs frequently see a number of flights designated as "scheduled service." As often as not, however, the consolidator, in turn, sells the seats to a travel agency specializing in discounting. Airlines also can sell seats directly to such an agency, which thus acts as its own consolidator. The airline offers the seats either at a net wholesale price, but without the volume-purchase requirement that would be difficult for a modest retail travel agency to fulfill, or at the standard price, but with a commission override large enough (as high as 50%) to allow both a profit and a price reduction to the public.

Travel agencies specializing in discounting sometimes are called "bucket shops," a term fraught with connotations of unreliability in this country. But in today's highly competitive travel marketplace, more and more conventional travel agencies are selling consolidator-supplied tickets, and the old bucket shops' image is becoming respectable. Agencies that specialize in discounted tickets exist in most large cities, and usually can be found by studying the smaller ads in the travel sections of Sunday newspapers.

Before buying a discounted ticket, whether from a bucket shop or a conventional, full-service travel agency, keep the following considerations in mind: To be in a position to judge how much you'll be saving, first find out the "list" prices of tickets to your destination. Then, do some comparison shopping among agencies. Also bear in mind that a ticket that may not differ much in price from one available directly from the airline may, however, allow the circumvention of such things as the advance purchase requirement. If your plans are less than final, be sure to find out about any other restrictions, such as penalties for canceling a flight or changing a reservation. Most discount tickets are non-endorsable, meaning that they can be used only on the airline that issued them, and they usually are marked "nonrefundable" to prevent their being cashed for a list price refund.

A great many bucket shops are small businesses operating on a thin margin, so it's a good idea to check the local Better Business Bureau for any complaints registered against the one with which you're dealing — before parting with any money. If you still do not feel reassured, consider buying discounted tickets only through a conventional travel agency, which can be expected to have found its own reliable source of consolidator tickets — some of the largest consolidators, in fact, sell only to travel agencies.

A few bucket shops require payment in cash or by certified check or money order, but if credit cards are accepted, use that option. Note, however, if buying from a charter operator selling seats for both scheduled and charter flights, that the scheduled seats are not protected by the regulations — including the use of escrow accounts — governing the charter seats. Well-established charter operators, nevertheless, may extend the same protections to their scheduled flights, and when this is the case, consumers should be sure that the payment option selected directs their money into the escrow account.

The following are among the numerous consolidators offering discount fares to Europe. Available flights and destinations vary from time to time. Check at the time you plan to travel whether they offer any flights to Rome.

Bargain Air (655 Deep Valley Dr., Suite 355, Rolling Hills, CA 90274; phone: 800-347-2345 or 213-377-2919).

Maharaja/Consumer Wholesale (393 Fifth Ave., 2nd Floor, New York, NY 10016; phone: 212-391-0122 in New York; 800-223-6862 elsewhere in the US).

TFI Tours International (34 W. 37th St., 12th Floor, New York, NY 10001; phone: 212-736-1140).

Travac Tours and Charters (989 Sixth Ave., New York, NY 10018; phone: 212-563-3303).

25 West Tours (2490 Coral Way, Miami, FL 33145; phone: 305-856-0810; 800-423-6954 in Florida; 800-252-5052 elsewhere in the US).

Unitravel 1177 N. Warson Rd., St. Louis, MO 63132; phone: 314-569-0900 in Missouri; 800-325-2222 elsewhere in the US).

The newsletter *Jax Fax* (see "Charter Flights," above) is also a good source of information on consolidators.

■ **Note:** Although rebating and discounting are becoming increasingly common, there is some legal ambiguity concerning them. Strictly speaking, it is legal to discount domestic tickets, but not international tickets. On the other hand, the law that prohibits discounting, the Federal Aviation Act of 1958, is ignored consistently these days, in part because consumers benefit from the practice and in part because many illegal arrangements are indistinguishable from legal ones. Since the line separating the two is so fine that even the authorities can't always tell the difference, it is unlikely that most consumers would be able to do so, and in fact it is not illegal to *buy* a discounted ticket. If the issue of legality bothers you, ask the agency whether any ticket you're about to buy would be permissible under the above-mentioned act.

OTHER DISCOUNT TRAVEL SOURCES: An excellent source of information on economical travel opportunities is the *Consumer Reports Travel Letter,* published monthly by Consumers Union. It keeps abreast of the scene on a wide variety of fronts, including package tours, rental cars, insurance, and more, but it is especially helpful for its comprehensive coverage of airfares, offering guidance on all the options from scheduled flights on major or low-fare airlines to charters and discount sources. For a year's subscription, send $37 ($57 for 2 years) to *Consumer Reports Travel Letter* (PO Box 53629, Boulder, CO 80322-3629; phone: 800-999-7959). For information on other travel newsletters, see *Sources and Resources,* in this section.

Last-Minute Travel Clubs – Still another way to take advantage of bargain airfares is open to those who have a flexible schedule. A number of organizations, usually set up as last-minute travel clubs and functioning on a membership basis, routinely keep in touch with travel suppliers to help them dispose of unsold inventory at discounts of between 15% and 60%. A great deal of the inventory consists of complete tour packages and cruises, but some clubs offer air-only charter seats and, occasionally, seats on scheduled flights.

Members generally pay an annual fee and receive a toll-free hotline number to call for information on imminent trips. In some cases, they also receive periodic mailings with information on bargain travel opportunities for which there is more advance notice. Despite the suggestive names of the clubs providing these services, last-minute travel does not necessarily mean that you cannot make plans until literally the last minute. Trips can be announced as little as a few days or as much as 2 months before departure, but the average is from 1 to 4 weeks' notice.

Among the organizations regularly offering such discounted travel opportunities to Rome are the following:

> *Discount Club of America* (61-33 Woodhaven Blvd., Rego Park, NY 11374; phone: 800-321-9587 or 718-335-9612). Annual fee: $39 per family.
> *Encore Short Notice* (4501 Forbes Blvd., Lanham, MD 20706; phone: 800-242-9913). Annual fee: $48 per family.
> *Moment's Notice* (425 Madison Ave., New York, NY 10017; phone: 212-486-0503). Annual fee: $19.95 per family.
> *Traveler's Advantage* (3033 S. Parker Rd., Suite 1000, Aurora, CO 80014; phone: 800-548-1116). Annual fee: $49 per family.
> *Worldwide Discount Travel Club* (1674 Meridian Ave., Miami Beach, FL 33139; phone: 305-534-2082). Annual fee: $40 per person; $50 per family.

Generic Air Travel – Organizations that apply the same flexible-schedule idea to air travel only and sell tickets at literally the last minute also exist. The service they provide sometimes is known as "generic" air travel, and it operates somewhat like an ordinary airline standby service, except that the organizations running it offer seats on not one but several scheduled and charter airlines.

One pioneer of generic flights is *Airhitch* (2790 Broadway, Suite 100, New York, NY 10025; phone: 212-864-2000), which arranges flights to Rome from various US gateways. Prospective travelers register by paying a fee (applicable toward the fare) and stipulate a range of acceptable departure dates and their desired destination, along with alternate choices. The week before the date range begins, they are notified of at least two flights that will be available during the time period, agree on one, and remit the balance of the fare to the company. If they do not accept any of the suggested flights, they lose their deposit; if, through no fault of their own, they do not ultimately get on any agreed-on flight, all of their money is refunded. Return flights are arranged the same way.

Bartered Travel Sources – Suppose a hotel buys advertising space in a newspaper. As payment, the hotel gives the publishing company the use of a number of hotel rooms in lieu of cash. This is barter, a common means of exchange among hotels, airlines, car rental companies, cruise lines, tour operators, restaurants, and other travel service companies. When a bartering company finds itself with empty airline seats (or excess hotel rooms, or cruise ship cabin space, and so on) and offers them to the public, considerable savings can be enjoyed.

Bartered-travel clubs often offer discounts of up to 50% to members who pay an annual fee (approximately $50 at press time) which entitles them to select from the flights, cruises, hotel rooms, or other travel services that the club obtained by barter. Members usually present a voucher, club credit card, or scrip (a dollar-denomination voucher negotiable only for the bartered product) to the hotel, which in turn subtracts the dollar amount from the bartering company's account.

Selling bartered travel is a perfectly legitimate means of retailing. One advantage to club members is that they don't have to wait until the last minute to obtain flight or room reservations.

Among the companies specializing in bartered travel, several that frequently offer members travel services to Rome include the following:

IGT (In Good Taste) Services (1111 Lincoln Rd., 4th Floor, Miami Beach, FL 33139; phone: 800-444-8872 or 305-534-7900). Annual fee: $48 per family.

Travel Guide (18210 Redmond Way, Redmond, WA 98052; phone: 206-885-1213). Annual fee: $48 per family.

Travel World Leisure Club (225 W. 34th St., Suite 2203, New York, NY 10122; phone: 800-444-TWLC or 212-239-4855). Annual fee: $50 per family.

On Arrival

FROM THE AIRPORT TO THE CITY: Rome's Leonardo da Vinci Airport in Fiumicino handles both domestic and international flights. It is located about 21 miles (33 km) from downtown Rome. Ciampino Airport handles mostly charter traffic.

Taxi – From the airport, it is about 1 hour from downtown Rome by taxi. It can cost up to $55, with extra charge for baggages and nighttime surcharge.

Public Transportation – The best way (and less expensive) is to take the newly completed train *(metropolitana)* service between Leonardo da Vinci Airport and Stazione Ostiense in Piazza Piramide, just south of the Colosseum. One-way fare is $5. From there, you can take a taxi (which sometimes may be hard to find) or transfer to other *metropolitana* lines (for more information, see *Sources and Resources* in THE CITY) to your destination. However, if you are traveling with many bags, it might be easier on yourself if you take the taxi from the airport straight to your destination.

CAR RENTAL: While cars are useful for day trips outside Rome, they are usually more trouble than they are worth for touring within the city. A visitor to Rome and the rest of Italy needs to know, however, how to drive in the country and how to rent a car; there are differences from what you are used to at home.

Renting a car in Rome is not inexpensive, but it is possible to economize by determining your own needs and then shopping around among the car rental companies until you find the best deal. It might be less expensive to rent a car in the center of Rome than at the airport. Ask about special rates or promotional deals, such as weekend or weekly rates, bonus coupons for airline tickets, or 24-hour rates that include gas and unlimited mileage.

Renting from the US – Travel agents can arrange foreign rentals for clients, but it is just as easy to call and rent a car yourself. Listed below are some of the major international rental companies that have representation in Rome and have information and reservations numbers that can be dialed toll-free in the US:

Avis (phone: 800-331-1084). Has representatives at Leonardo da Vinci and Ciampino airports, and 10 other city locations.

Budget (phone: 800-527-0700). Has representatives at Leonardo da Vinci and Ciampino Airports, and 2 other city locations.

Dollar Rent-a-Car (known in Europe as *Eurodollar;* phone: 800-800-4000). Has representatives at Leonardo da Vinci Airport and 2 other city locations.

Hertz (phone: 800-654-3001). Has representatives at Leonardo da Vinci and Ciampino Airports, and 8 other city locations.

National (known in Europe as *Europcar;* phone: 800-CAR-EUROPE). Has representatives at Leonardo da Vinci Airport and 9 other city locations.

It also is possible to rent a car before you go by contacting any number of smaller or less well known US companies that do not operate worldwide. These organizations specialize in European auto travel, including leasing and car purchase in addition to car rental, or actually are tour operators with well-established European car rental programs. These firms, whose names and addresses are listed below, act as agents for a variety of European suppliers, offer unlimited mileage almost exclusively, and frequently manage to undersell their larger competitors by a significant margin.

Auto Europe (PO Box 1097, Camden, ME 04843; phone: 207-236-8235; 800-223-5555 throughout the US; 800-458-9503 in Canada).

Europe by Car (One Rockefeller Plaza, New York, NY 10020; phone: 212-581-3040 in New York State; 800-223-1516 elsewhere in the US; and 9000 Sunset Blvd., Los Angeles, CA 90069; phone: 800-252-9401 or 213-272-0424).

European Car Reservations (349 W. Commercial St., Suite 2950, East Rochester, NY 14445; phone: 800-535-3303).

Foremost Euro-Car (5430 Van Nuys Blvd., Suite 306, Van Nuys, CA 91401; phone: 818-786-1960 or 800-272-3299 in California; 800-423-3111 elsewhere in the US).

Kemwel Group Inc. (106 Calvert St., Harrison, NY 10528; phone: 800-678-0678 or 914-835-5555).

Meier's World Travel, Inc. (6033 W. Century Blvd., Suite 1080, Los Angeles, CA 90045; phone: 800-937-0700). In conjunction with major car rental companies, arranges economical rentals throughout Europe, including Rome.

One of the ways to keep the cost of car rentals down is to deal with a car rental consolidator, such as *Connex International* (23 N. Division St., Peekskill, NY 10566; phone: 800-333-3949 or 914-739-0066). *Connex*'s main business is negotiating with virtually all of the major car rental agencies for the lowest possible prices for its customers. This company arranges rentals throughout Europe, including Rome.

Local Rentals – It long has been common wisdom that the least expensive way to rent a car is to make arrangements in Europe. This is less true today than it used to be. Many medium to large European car rental companies have become the overseas suppliers of stateside companies such as those mentioned previously, and often the stateside agency, by dint of sheer volume, has been able to negotiate more favorable rates for its US customers than the European firm offers its own. Still lower rates may be found by searching out small, strictly local rental companies overseas, whether at less than prime addresses in major cities or in more remote areas. But to find them you must be willing to invest a sufficient amount of vacation time comparing prices on the scene. You also must be prepared to return the car to the location that rented it; drop-off possibilities are likely to be limited.

There is not a wide choice of local car rental companies in Rome. *Auto Maggiore* is a nationwide company. The main office is located at 8/A Via Po (phone: 851620). You may also call their US representative at 800-527-0202. Their branches are located throughout the city including the airport and railway stations. Another local car rental company in Rome is *Tropea* (1 Piazza Barberini; phone: 488-4682). Also, the branches of the Italian Government Travel Office may be able to supply the names of Italian car rental companies. The local yellow pages is another good place to begin.

Requirements – Whether you decide to rent a car in advance from a large international rental company with European branches or wait to rent from a local company, you should know that renting a car is rarely as simple as signing on the dotted line and roaring off into the night. To drive in Italy, you need only a valid US driver's license; however, if you plan to rent from a local company, you will likely be asked for an International Driving Permit (see below), and will have to convince the renting agency that (1) you are personally creditworthy, and (2) you will bring the car back at the stated time. This will be easy if you have a major credit card; most rental companies accept credit cards in lieu of a cash deposit, as well as for payment of your final bill. If you prefer to pay in cash, leave your credit card imprint as a "deposit," then pay your bill in cash when you return the car.

If you are planning to rent a car once you're in Italy, *Avis, Budget, Hertz,* and other US rental companies usually *will* rent to travelers paying in cash and leaving either a credit card imprint or a substantial amount of cash as a deposit. This is not necessarily standard policy, however, as other international chains and a number of local and regional European companies will *not* rent to an individual who doesn't have a valid credit card. In this case, you may have to call around to find a company that accepts cash.

Also keep in mind that although the minimum age to drive a car in Italy is 18 years, the minimum age to rent a car is set by the rental company. (Restrictions vary from company to company, as well as at different locations.) Many firms have a minimum age requirement of 21 years, some raise that to 23 or 25 years, and for some models of cars it rises to 30 years. The upper age limit at many companies is between 69 and 75; others have no upper limit or may make drivers above a certain age subject to special conditions.

Don't forget that all car rentals are subject to value added tax. This tax rarely is included in the rental price that's advertised or quoted, but it always must be paid — whether you pay in advance in the US or pay it when you drop off the car. In Italy, the VAT rate on car rentals is 19%; there is a wide variation in this tax from country to country.

Driving documents – A valid driver's license from his or her own state of residence is required for a US citizen to drive in Italy. In addition, an International Driving Permit (IDP), which is a translation of the US license in 9 languages, will be required if you plan to rent a car from a local firm.

You can obtain your IDP, before you leave, from most branches of the *American Automobile Association (AAA)*. Applicants must be at least 18 years old, and the application must be accompanied by two passport-size photos (some *AAA* branches have a photo machine available), a valid US driver's license, and a fee of $10. The IDP is good for 1 year and must be accompanied by your US license to be valid.

Proof of liability insurance also is required and is a standard part of any car rental contract. (To be sure of having the appropriate coverage, let the rental staff know in advance about any national borders you plan to cross.) Car rental companies also make provisions for breakdowns, emergency service, and assistance; ask for a number to call when you pick up the vehicle.

Rules of the road – Contrary to first impressions, Italian drivers are generally careful and quite patient, and rules of the road do exist in Rome. Driving in Italy is on the right side of the road, as in most of Europe. Passing is on the left; the left turn signal must be flashing before and while passing, and the right indicator must be used when pulling back to the right. Also, don't be intimidated by tailgaters — everyone does it.

According to law, those coming from the right at intersections have the right of way, as in the US, and pedestrians, provided they are in marked crosswalks, have priority over all vehicles. In many areas, though, signposting is meager, and traffic at intersections converges from all directions, resulting in a proceed-at-your-own-risk flow.

In the city, speed limits usually are 50 kph (about 30 mph). Outside the city, the speed limit is 90 kph (about 55 mph) on main roads and 130 kph (about 80 mph) on major highways (autostrade). However, the speed limit on autostrade is reduced to 110 kph (about 68 mph) on weekends, public holidays, and from mid-July to early-September.

■**Note:** Finding a parking spot in Rome is a major hassle. Street parking is not allowed anywhere in the city except late in the evening. Public parking lots are very expensive, and there are only two major underground parking lots: One is located at Villa Borghese on Via Pinciano, the other one just south of Villa Borghese at Via Ludivisi and Via Veneto. Anyone who parks in a restricted parking area risks having the car towed and receiving a heavy fine.

Gasoline – In Italy, gasoline (*benzina*) is sold by the liter (which is slightly more than 1 quart; approximately 3.8 liters equal 1 US gallon). Regular or leaded gas (also called *benzina*) generally is sold in two grades — called *normale* and *super.* Diesel fuel is widely available (diesel fuel pumps normally carry a sign for *gasolio*). Unleaded fuel (*benzina verde* or *benzina senza piombo*) is available in some gas stations outside Rome. However, since unleaded gas is still a rarity in some parts of Europe, your safest bet if you're planning to drive outside the city is to rent a car that takes leaded gasoline.

Gas prices everywhere rise and fall depending on the world supply of oil, and an American traveling overseas is further affected by the prevailing rate of exchange, so it is difficult to say exactly how much fuel will cost when you travel. It is not difficult to predict, however, that gas prices will be substantially higher than you are accustomed to paying in the US. And note: Gas prices in Italy are among the highest in Europe.

Travelers driving in Italy have at least one advantage over native drivers regarding the price they pay for fuel: Tourists can purchase discount coupons that can be redeemed later at gas stations around Italy. These coupons are available upon entry at major airports — including Rome's Leonardo da Vinci Airport, in Fiumicino — as well as at the border; the total number of coupons purchasable may vary from place to place, but whatever the number of coupons offered for sale, the face amount can be used at gas stations throughout the country to pay for approximately 15% to 20% more gas. Coupons must be purchased in foreign currency, and may be used by foreigners driving either their own or rental cars. The savings on gas makes auto touring a bit less pricey.

Package Tours

 If the mere thought of buying a package for visiting Rome conjures up visions of a march through the city in lockstep with a horde of frazzled fellow travelers, remember that packages have come a long way. For one thing, not all packages necessarily are escorted tours, and the one you buy does not have to include any organized touring at all — nor will it necessarily include traveling companions. If it does, however, you'll find that people of all sorts — many just like yourself — are taking advantage of packages today because they are economical and convenient, save you an immense amount of planning time, and exist in such variety that it's virtually impossible not to find one that suits at least the majority of your travel preferences. Given the high cost of travel these days, packages have emerged as a particularly wise buy.

In essence, a package is just an amalgam of travel services that can be purchased in a single transaction. A Rome package (tour or otherwise) may include any or all of the following: round-trip transatlantic transportation, transfers between the airport and the hotel, local transportation (and/or car rentals), accommodations, some or all meals, sightseeing, entertainment, taxes, tips, escort service, and a variety of incidental features that might be offered as options at additional cost. Its principal advantage is that it saves money: The cost of the combined arrangements invariably is well below the price of all of the same elements if bought separately, and, particularly if transportation is provided by charter or discount flight, the whole package could cost less than just a round-trip economy airline ticket on a regularly scheduled flight. A package provides more than economy and convenience: It releases the traveler from having to make individual arrangements for each separate element of a trip.

Tour programs generally can be divided into two categories — "escorted" (or locally hosted) and "independent." An escorted tour means that a guide will accompany the group from the beginning of the tour through to the return flight; a locally hosted tour means that the group will be met upon arrival at each location by a different local host. On independent tours (which are the ones generally available for visiting cities, such as Rome), there usually is a choice of hotels, meal plans, and sightseeing trips in each city, as well as a variety of special excursions. The independent plan is for travelers who do not want a totally set itinerary, but who do prefer confirmed hotel reservations. Always bring along complete contact information for your tour operator in case a problem arises, although US tour operators often have European affiliates who can give additional assistance or make other arrangements on the spot.

To determine whether a package — or, more specifically, *which* package — fits your travel plans, start by evaluating your interests and needs, deciding how much and what you want to spend, see, and do. Gather whatever package tour information is available for your schedule. Be sure that you take the time to read the brochure *carefully* to determine precisely what is included. Keep in mind that travel brochures are written to entice you into signing up for a package tour. Often the language is deceptive and devious. For example, a brochure may quote the lowest prices for a package tour based on facilities that are unavailable during the off-season, undesirable at any season, or just plain nonexistent. Information such as "breakfast included" (as it often is in packages to Rome) or "plus tax" (which can add up) should be taken into account. Note, too, that the prices quoted in brochures almost always are based on double occupancy: The rate listed is for each of two people sharing a double room, and if you travel alone, the supplement for single accommodations can raise the price considerably (see *Hints for Single Travelers,* in this section).

In this age of erratic airfares, the brochure most often will *not* include the price of an airline ticket in the price of the package, though sample fares from various gateway cities usually will be listed separately, to be added to the price of the ground arrangements. Before figuring your actual cost, check the latest fares with the airlines, because the samples invariably are out of date by the time you read them. If the brochure gives more than one category of sample fares per gateway city — such as an individual tour-basing fare, a group fare, an excursion, APEX, or other discount ticket — your travel agent or airline tour desk will be able to tell you which one applies to the package you choose, depending on when you travel, how far in advance you book, and other factors. (An individual tour-basing fare is a fare computed as part of a package that includes land arrangements, thereby entitling a carrier to reduce the air portion almost to the absolute minimum. Though it always represents a savings over full-fare coach or economy, lately the individual tour-basing fare has not been as inexpensive as the excursion and other discount fares that also are available to individuals. The group fare usually is the least expensive fare, and it is the tour operator, not you, who makes up the group.) When the brochure does include round-trip transportation in the package price, don't forget to add the cost of round-trip transportation from your home to the departure city to come up with the total cost of the package.

Finally, read the general information regarding terms and conditions and the responsibility clause (usually in fine print at the end of the descriptive literature) to determine the precise elements for which the tour operator is — and is not — liable. Here the tour operator frequently expresses the right to change services or schedules as long as equivalent arrangements are offered. This clause also absolves the operator of responsibility for circumstances beyond human control, such as floods, or injury to you or your property. While reading, ask the following questions:

1. Does the tour include airfare or other transportation, sightseeing, meals, transfers, taxes, baggage handling, tips, or any other services? Do you want all these services?
2. If the brochure indicates that "some meals" are included, does this mean a welcoming and farewell dinner, two breakfasts, or every evening meal?
3. What classes of hotels are offered? If you will be traveling alone, what is the single supplement?
4. Does the tour itinerary or price vary according to the season?
5. Are the prices guaranteed; that is, if costs increase between the time you book and the time you depart, can surcharges unilaterally be added?
6. Do you get a full refund if you cancel? If not, be sure to obtain cancellation insurance.
7. Can the operator cancel if too few people join? At what point?

One of the consumer's biggest problems is finding enough information to judge the reliability of a tour packager, since individual travelers seldom have direct contact with the firm putting the package together. Usually, a retail travel agent is interposed between customer and tour operator, and much depends on his or her candor and cooperation. So ask a number of questions about the tour you are considering. For example:

- Has the travel agent ever used a package provided by this tour operator?
- How long has the tour operator been in business? Check the Better Business Bureau in the area where the tour operator is based to see if any complaints have been filed against it.
- Is the tour operator a member of the *United States Tour Operators Association* (*USTOA;* 211 E. 51st St., Suite 12B, New York, NY 10022; phone: 212-944-5727)? *USTOA* will provide a list of its members upon request; it also offers a useful brochure, *How to Select a Package Tour.*
- How many and which companies are involved in the package?
- If air travel is by charter flight, is there an escrow account in which deposits will be held; if so, what is the name of the bank?

This last question is very important. US law requires that tour operators place every charter passenger's deposit and subsequent payment in a proper escrow account (see "Charter Flights," above).

■ **A word of advice:** Purchasers of vacation packages who feel they're not getting their money's worth are more likely to get a refund if they complain in writing to the operator — and bail out of the whole package immediately. Alert the tour operator or resort manager to the fact that you are dissatisfied, that you will be leaving for home as soon as transportation can be arranged, and that you expect a refund. They may have forms to fill out detailing your complaint; otherwise, state your case in a letter. Even if difficulty in arranging immediate transportation home detains you, your dated, written complaint should help in procuring a refund from the operator.

SAMPLE PACKAGES: Generally speaking, escorted tours cover whole countries or sections of countries. For stays that feature Rome only, you would be looking at an independent city package, sometimes known at a "stay-put" program. Basically the city package includes round-trip transfer between airport and hotel, a choice of hotel accommodations (usually including breakfast) in several price ranges, plus any number of other features you may not need or want but would lose valuable time arranging if you did. Common package features are 1 or 2 half-day guided tours of the city; a boat cruise; passes for unlimited local travel by bus or train; discount cards for shops, museums, and restaurants; temporary membership in and admission to clubs, discotheques, or other nightspots; and car rental for some or all of your stay. Other features may include anything from a souvenir travel bag to a tasting of local wines, dinner, and a show. The packages usually are a week long — although 4-day and 14-day packages also are available, and most packages can be extended by extra days — and often are hosted; that is, a representative of the tour company may be available at a local office or even in the hotel to answer questions, handle problems, and assist in arranging activities and option excursions.

Among companies offering tour packages in Rome are the following:

Abercrombie and Kent International (1520 Kensington Rd., Suite 212, Oak Brook, IL 60521; phone: 708-954-2944 in Illinois; 800-323-7308 elsewhere in the US). This luxury tour operator offers an 11-day train tour in Italy, visiting Rome, Assisi, Florence, Siena, and Venice. There are also many European itineraries that cover an excursion in Rome. For those who like to venture on their own, this company provides an independent fly-drive option.

American Express Travel Related Services (offices throughout the US; phone: 800-241-1700 for information and local branch offices). Offers city packages, with a 2-day minimum, and an individual 14-day rail package that covers Rome, Florence, Milan, and Venice. There are also different itineraries to Italy ranging from 12 to 18 days, all including a 1- or 2-day excursion in Rome.

Bennett (270 Madison Ave., New York, NY 10016; phone: 800-221-2420 or 212-532-5060). Offers 3-night or longer city packages, including to Rome, Florence, and Venice.

Brendan Tours (15137 Califa St., Van Nuys, CA 91411; phone: 800-421-8446 or 818-785-9696). Offers 9-day city packages to Rome, as well as a variety of 8- to 16-day combination packages that include Rome.

Collette Tours (124 Broad St., Pawtucket, RI 02860; phone: 800-752-2655 in New England, New York, and New Jersey; 800-832-4656 elsewhere in the US). Offers 13-day escorted tour of the major cities in Italy, including Rome.

Contiki Holidays (1432 E. Katella Ave., Anaheim, CA 92805; phone: 714-937-0611). This agency specializes in travel for those 18 to 35 years old. It offers 17- to 55-day motorcoach tours in Europe that include excursions in Rome. There's also a 13-day tour in Italy that covers Rome, Assisi, Florence, Sorrento, and Venice.

Dailey-Thorp Travel (315 W. 57th St., New York, NY 10019; phone: 212-307-1555). This music and opera specialist's recent itineraries have included a 12-day tour in Italy, visiting and attending performances at the famous opera houses in Rome, Florence, Milan, and Venice. Another 11-day tour attends performances by world-famous prima donnas in Rome, Barcelona, and Vienna.

David B. Mitchell & Company (200 Madison Ave., New York, NY 10016; phone: 800-372-1323 or 212-889-4822). Offers luxurious self-drive or chauffeured tours. Among their offerings is a 14-day La Terra Cotta package that visits Rome, as well as Florence, Siena, and Venice. Also arranges customized tours for 7-days or longer.

DER Tours (11933 Wilshire Blvd., Los Angeles, CA 90025; phone: 800-937-1234 or 213-479-4411). Offers 3-night or longer city packages to Rome, as well as Florence and Venice.

Donna Franca Tours (470 Commonwealth Ave., Boston, MA 02215; phone: 617-227-3111 in Massachusetts; 800-225-6290 elsewhere in the US). Offers 4-night city packages.

Europe Express (588 Broadway, Suite 505, New York, NY 10012; phone: 800-927-3876 or 212-334-0836). Offers 3-night or longer city packages to Rome, as well as Florence, Milan, and Venice.

Globus-Gateway and Cosmos (95-25 Queens Blvd., Rego Park, NY 11374; phone: 800-221-0090; and 150 S. Los Robles Ave., Pasadena, CA 91101; phone: 818-449-2019 or 800-556-5454). These affiliated agencies offer 15- to 28-day escorted trips in Europe that include excursions in Rome. There are also 9-, 14-, and 16-day itineraries in Italy covering its major cities, including Rome. Note that bookings must be made through a travel agent.

Insight International Tours (745 Atlantic Ave., Suite 720, Boston, MA 02111; phone: 800-582-8380 or 617-426-6666). It offers 14- to 38-day escorted tours in Italy and other European countries, all of which include 1- or 2-day excursions in Rome. There's also a 16-day tour of Italy that includes Rome. It can also arrange independent programs.

Jet Vacations (1775 Broadway, New York, NY 10019; phone: 800-JET-0999 or 212-247-0999). Offers city packages, with no specified length-of-stay requirements.

Marsans International (19 W. 34th St., Suite 302, New York, NY 10001; phone: 212-239-3880 in New York State; 800-223-6114 elsewhere in the US). Offers independent 5-day city packages. Note that their specialty is arranging packages for Spanish-speaking clients.

Meier's World Travel, Inc. (6033 W. Century Blvd., Suite 1080, Los Angeles, CA 90045; phone: 800-937-0700). Arranges 3-night customized city packages.

Perillo Tours (577 Chestnut Ridge Rd., Woodcliff Lake, NJ 07675; phone: 800-431-1515). Offers five escorted motorcoach tours of Italy, including a 13-day tour that visits Rome, as well as Florence and Venice.

Petrabax Tours (97-45 Queens Blvd., Suite 505, Rego Park, NY 11374; phone: 718-897-7272 in New York State; 800-367-6611 elsewhere). Offers 4-day or longer city tours. Also caters to Spanish-speaking clientele.

SuperCities (7855 Haskell Ave., Van Nuys, CA 91406; phone: 818-988-7844 or 800-633-3000). Offers 2- and 3-night packages. This tour operator is a wholesaler, so use a travel agent.

Travcoa (PO Box 2630, Newport Beach, CA 92658; phone: 800-992-2004 or 714-476-2800 in California; 800-992-2003 elsewhere in the US). Offers a 16-day trip in Italy, visiting major cities in the country, including Rome, Florence, Naples, and Venice. A 22-day itinerary covers England, France, Switzerland, and Italy, including excursions to Rome and Venice.

Travel Bound (599 Broadway, Penthouse, New York, NY 10012; phone: 212-334-1350 or 800-456-8656). Offers flexible city packages, depending on arrangements desired. This tour operator is a wholesaler, so use a travel agent.

Since Italy is a land of pilgrimage, it is also the destination of tours geared to Roman Catholic travelers. One company specializing in such tours is *Catholic Travel* (10018

Cedar La., Kensington, MD 20895; phone: 301-564-1904). The company plans about 10 Italy tours each year in high season, led by a spiritual director and visiting about 10 cities on a 15-day itinerary. A papal audience at the Vatican is included. For Jewish travelers, the *American Jewish Congress* (15 E. 84th St., New York, NY 10028; phone: 212-879-4588 in New York State; 800-221-4694 elsewhere in the US) regularly arranges tours to Europe in addition to its tours to Israel. Recent itineraries included a 16-day Grand Tour trip with 8 days in Italy (Rome, Florence, and Venice), with an overnight train ride to Paris on the *Venice Simplon–Orient Express.*

For the golfer — there are a number of courses around the city — customized golf packages to Italy are offered by *Golfing Holidays* (231 E. Millbrae Ave., Millbrae, CA 94030; phone: 415-697-0230) and *ITC Golf Tours* (4439 Atlantic Ave., Suite 205, Long Beach, CA 90807; phone: 800-257-4981 or 213-595-6905). These companies can arrange a golf packages anywhere and any way you want it, including Rome.

And horseback riding holidays are the province of *Equitour* (P.O. Box 807, Dubois, WY; phone: 307-455-3363 in Wyoming; 800-545-0019 elsewhere in the US), which offers 8-day riding packages near Rome and Florence.

Many of the major air carriers maintain their own tour departments or subsidiaries to stimulate vacation travel to the cities they serve. In all cases, the arrangements may be booked through a travel agent or directly with the company.

Alitalia (Tour Department) (666 Fifth Ave., 6th Floor, New York, NY 10103; phone: 800-442-5860 or 212-582-8900).

British Airways (Tour Department) (530 Fifth Ave., New York, NY 10036; phone: 800-AIRWAYS).

TWA Getaway (10 E. Stow Rd., Marlton, NJ 08053; phone: 800-GETAWAY).

■ **Note:** Frequently, the best city packages are offered by the hotels, which are trying to attract guests during the weekends, when business travel drops off, and during other off periods. These packages are often advertised in the local newspapers and sometimes in the travel sections of big metropolitan papers, such as *The New York Times.* It's worth asking about packages, especially family and special-occasion offerings, when you call to make a hotel reservation. Calling several hotels can garner you a variety of options from which to choose.

Preparing

How to Use a Travel Agent

 A reliable travel agent remains the best source of service and information for planning a trip abroad, whether you have a specific itinerary and require an agent only to make reservations or you need extensive help in sorting through the maze of airfares, tour offerings, hotel packages, and the scores of other arrangements that may be involved in a trip to Rome.

Know what you want from a travel agent so that you can evaluate what you are getting. It is perfectly reasonable to expect your agent to be a thoroughly knowledgeable travel specialist, with information about your destination and, even more crucial, a command of current airfares, ground arrangements, and other wrinkles in the travel scene.

Most travel agents work through computer reservations systems (CRS). These are used to assess the availability and cost of flights, hotels, and car rentals, and through them they can book reservations. Despite reports of "computer bias," in which a computer may favor one airline over another, the CRS should provide agents with the entire spectrum of flights available to a given destination, as well as the complete range of fares, in considerably less time than it takes to telephone the airlines individually — and at no extra charge to the client.

Make the most intelligent use of a travel agent's time and expertise; understand the economics of the industry. As a client, traditionally you pay nothing for the agent's services; with few exceptions, it's all free, from hotel bookings to advice on package tours. Any money the travel agent makes on the time spent arranging your itinerary — booking hotels or flights, or suggesting activities — comes from commissions paid by the suppliers of these services — the airlines, hotels, and so on. These commissions generally run from 10% to 15% of the total cost of the service, although suppliers often reward agencies that sell their services in volume with an increased commission, called an override. In most instances, you'll find that travel agents make their time and experience available to you at no cost, and you do not pay more for an airline ticket, package tour, or other product bought from a travel agent than you would for the same product bought directly from the supplier.

Exceptions to the general rule of free service by a travel agent are the agencies beginning to practice net pricing. In essence, such agencies return their commissions and overrides to their customers and make their income by charging a flat fee per transaction instead (thus adding a charge after a reduction for the commissions has been made). Net fares and fees are a growing practice, though hardly widespread.

Even a conventional travel agent sometimes may charge a fee for special services. These chargeable items may include long-distance telephone or cable costs incurred in making a booking, for reserving a room in a place that does not pay a commission (such as a small, out-of-the-way hotel), or for special attention such as planning a highly personalized itinerary. A fee also may be assessed in instances of deeply discounted airfares.

Choose a travel agent with the same care with which you would choose a doctor or lawyer. You will be spending a good deal of money on the basis of the agent's judgment, so you have a right to expect that judgment to be mature, informed, and interested. At the moment, unfortunately, there aren't many standards within the travel agent industry to help you gauge competence, and the quality of individual agents varies enormously.

At present, only nine states have registration, licensing, or other forms of travel agent–related legislation on their books. Rhode Island licenses travel agents; Florida, Hawaii, Iowa, and Ohio register them; and California, Illinois, Oregon, and Washington have laws governing the sale of transportation or related services. While state licensing of agents cannot absolutely guarantee competence, it can at least ensure that an agent has met some minimum requirements.

Perhaps the best way to find a travel agent is by word of mouth. If the agent (or agency) has done a good job for your friends over a period of time, it probably indicates a certain level of commitment and competence. Always ask for the name of the company *and* for the name of the specific agent with whom your friends dealt, for it is that individual who will serve you, and quality can vary widely within a single agency. There are some superb travel agents in the business, and they can facilitate vacation or business arrangements.

Entry Requirements and Documents

A valid US passport is the only document a US citizen needs to enter Italy, and then to reenter the US. As a general rule, a US passport entitles the bearer to remain in Italy for up to 3 months as a tourist. A resident alien of the US should inquire at the nearest Italian consulate (see *The Italian Embassy and Consulates in the US,* in this section, for addresses) to find out what documents are needed to enter Italy; similarly, a US citizen intending to work, study, or reside in Italy should also get in touch with the consulate, because a visa will then be required.

Vaccination certificates are required only if the traveler is entering from an area of contagion — which the US is not — as defined by the World Health Organization.

DUTY AND CUSTOMS: As a general rule, the requirements for bringing the majority of items *into Italy* is that they must be in quantities small enough not to imply commercial import. Among the items that may be taken into the country duty-free are 400 cigarettes, 2 bottles of wine, and 1 bottle of liquor. Personal effects and sports equipment appropriate for a pleasure trip also are allowed.

If you are bringing along a computer, camera, or other electronic equipment for your own use that you will be taking back to the US, you should register the item with the US Customs Service in order to avoid paying duty both entering and returning from Italy. (Also see *Customs and Returning to the US,* in this section.) For information on this procedure, as well as for a variety of pamphlets on US customs regulations, contact the local office of the US Customs Service or the central office, PO Box 7407, Washington, DC 20044 (phone: 202-566-8195).

Additional information regarding Italian customs regulations is available from the Italian Government Travel Office and the Italian embassy and consulates. See *Tourist Information Offices* and *The Italian Embassy and Consulates in the US,* in this section, for addresses.

■ **One rule to follow:** When passing through customs, it is illegal not to declare dutiable items; penalties range from stiff fines and seizure of the goods to prison terms. So don't try to sneak anything through — it just isn't worth it.

Insurance

 It is unfortunate that most decisions to buy travel insurance are impulsive and usually are made without any real consideration of the traveler's existing policies. Therefore, the first person with whom you should discuss travel insurance is your own insurance broker, not a travel agent or the clerk behind the airport insurance counter.

TYPES OF INSURANCE: To make insurance decisions intelligently, however, you first should understand the basic categories of travel insurance and what they cover. There are seven basic categories of travel insurance:

1. Baggage and personal effects insurance
2. Personal accident and sickness insurance
3. Trip cancellation and interruption insurance
4. Default and/or bankruptcy insurance
5. Flight insurance (to cover injury or death)
6. Automobile insurance (for driving your own or a rented car)
7. Combination policies

Baggage and Personal Effects Insurance – Ask your insurance agent if baggage and personal effects are included in your current homeowner's policy, or if you will need a special floater to cover you for the duration of a trip. The object is to protect your bags and their contents in case of damage or theft anytime during your travels, not just while you're in flight and covered by the airline's policy. Furthermore, only limited protection is provided by the airline and baggage liability varies from carrier to carrier. For most international flights, including domestic portions of international flights, the airline's liability limit is approximately $9.07 per pound or $20 per kilo (which comes to about $360 per 40-pound suitcase) for checked baggage and up to $400 per passenger for unchecked baggage. These limits should be specified on your airline ticket, but to be awarded any amount, you'll have to provide an itemized list of lost property, and if you're including new and/or expensive items, be prepared for a request that you back up your claim with sales receipts or other proof of purchase.

If you are carrying goods worth more than the maximum protection offered by the airline, consider excess value insurance. Additional coverage is available from insurance companies at an average, currently, of $1 to $2 per $100 worth of coverage, up to a maximum of $5,000. This insurance can also be purchased at some airline counters when you check in, though you should arrive early enough to fill out the necessary forms and to avoid holding up other passengers.

Major credit card companies also provide coverage for lost or delayed baggage — and this coverage often is over and above what the airline will pay. The basic coverage usually is automatic for all cardholders who use the credit card to purchase tickets, but to qualify for additional coverage, cardholders generally must enroll.

Additional baggage and personal effects insurance also is included in certain of the combination travel insurance policies discussed below.

■ **A note of warning:** Be sure to read the fine print of any excess value insurance policy; there often are specific exclusions, such as cash, tickets, furs, gold and silver objects, art, and antiques. Insurance companies ordinarily will pay only the depreciated value of the goods rather than their replacement value. The best way to protect your property is to take photos of your valuables, and keep a record of the serial numbers of such items as cameras, typewriters, laptop computers, radios, and so on. If an airline loses your luggage, you will be asked to fill out a Property Irregularity Report before you leave the airport. Also report the loss to the police

36 GETTING READY / Insurance

(since the insurance company will check with the police when processing your claim).

Personal Accident and Sickness Insurance – This covers you in case of illness during your trip or death in an accident. Most policies insure you for hospital and doctor's expenses, lost income, and so on. In most cases, it is a standard part of existing health insurance policies, though you should check with your broker to be sure that your policy will pay for any medical expenses incurred abroad. If not, take out a separate vacation accident policy or an entire vacation insurance policy that includes health and life coverage.

Two examples of such comprehensive health and life insurance coverage are the travel insurance packages offered by *Wallach & Co:*

HealthCare Global: This insurance package, which can be purchased for periods of 10 to 180 days, is offered for two age groups: Men and women up to age 75 receive $25,000 medical insurance and $50,000 accidental injury or death benefit; those from ages 76 to 84 are eligible for $12,500 medical insurance and $25,000 injury or death benefit. For either policy, the cost for a 10-day period is $25.

HealthCare Abroad: This program is available to individuals up to age 75. For $3 per day (minimum 10 days, maximum 90 days), policy holders receive $100,000 medical insurance and $25,000 accidental injury or death benefit.

Both of these basic programs also may be bought in combination with trip cancellation and baggage insurance at extra cost. For further information, write to *Wallach & Co.,* 243 Church St. NW, Suite 100-D, Vienna, VA 22180 (phone: 703-281-9500 in Virginia; 800-237-6615 elsewhere in the US).

Trip Cancellation and Interruption Insurance – Most charter and package tour passengers pay for their travel well before departure. The disappointment of having to miss a vacation because of illness or any other reason pales before the awful prospect that not all (and sometimes none) of the money paid in advance might be returned. So cancellation insurance for any package tour is a must.

Although cancellation penalties vary (they are listed in the fine print of every tour brochure, and before you purchase a package tour you should know exactly what they are), rarely will a passenger get more than 50% of this money back if forced to cancel within a few weeks of scheduled departure. Therefore, if you book a package tour or charter flight, you should have trip cancellation insurance to guarantee full reimbursement or refund should you, a traveling companion, or a member of your immediate family get sick, forcing you to cancel your trip or *return home early.*

The key here is *not* to buy just enough insurance to guarantee full reimbursement for the cost of the package or charter in case of cancellation. The proper amount of coverage should be sufficient to reimburse you for the cost of having to catch up with a tour after its departure or having to travel home at the full economy airfare if you have to forgo the return flight of your charter. There usually is quite a discrepancy between a charter fare and the amount charged to travel the same distance on a regularly scheduled flight at full economy fare.

Trip cancellation insurance is available from travel agents and tour operators in two forms: as part of a short-term, all-purpose travel insurance package (sold by the travel agent); or as specific cancellation insurance designed by the tour operator for a specific charter tour. Generally, tour operators' policies are less expensive, but also less inclusive. Cancellation insurance also is available directly from insurance companies or their agents as part of a short-term, all-inclusive travel insurance policy.

Before you decide on a policy, read each one carefully. (Either type can be purchased from a travel agent when you book the charter or package tour.) Be certain that your policy includes enough coverage to pay your fare from the farthest destination on your itinerary should you have to miss the charter flight. Also, be sure to check the fine print for stipulations concerning "family members" and "pre-existing medical conditions," as well as allowances for living expenses if you must delay your return due to bodily injury or illness.

Default and/or Bankruptcy Insurance – Although trip cancellation insurance usually protects you if *you* are unable to complete — or begin — your trip, a fairly recent innovation is coverage in the event of default and/or bankruptcy on the part of the tour operator, airline, or other travel supplier. In some travel insurance packages, this contingency is included in the trip cancellation portion of the coverage; in others, it is a separate feature. Either way, it is becoming increasingly important. Whereas sophisticated travelers long have known to beware of the possibility of default or bankruptcy when buying a charter flight or tour package, in recent years more than a few respected airlines unexpectedly have revealed their shaky financial condition, sometimes leaving hordes of stranded ticket holders in their wake. Moreover, the value of escrow protection of a charter passenger's funds lately has been unreliable. While default/bankruptcy insurance will not ordinarily result in reimbursement in time to pay for new arrangements, it can ensure that you will get your money back, and even independent travelers buying no more than an airplane ticket may want to consider it.

Flight Insurance – Airlines have carefully established limits of liability for injury to or the death of passengers on international flights. For all international flights to, from, or with a stopover in the US, all carriers are liable for up to $75,000 per passenger. For all other international flights, the liability is based on where you purchase the ticket: If booked in advance in the US, the maximum liability is $75,000; if arrangements are made abroad, the liability is $10,000. But remember, these liabilities are not the same thing as insurance policies; every penny that an airline eventually pays in the case of injury or death may be subject to a legal battle.

But before you buy last-minute flight insurance from an airport vending machine, consider the purchase in light of your total existing insurance coverage. A careful review of your current policies may reveal that you already are amply covered for accidental death. Be aware that airport insurance, the kind typically bought at a counter or from a vending machine, is among the most expensive forms of life insurance coverage, and that even within a single airport, rates for approximately the same coverage vary widely.

If you buy your plane ticket with a major credit card, you generally receive automatic insurance coverage at no extra cost. Additional coverage usually can be obtained at extremely reasonable prices, but a cardholder must sign up for it in advance.

Automobile Insurance – Public liability and property damage (third-party) insurance is compulsory in Europe, and whether you drive your own or a rental car you must carry insurance. Car rentals in Italy usually include public liability, property damage, fire, and theft coverage and, sometimes (depending on the car rental company), collision damage coverage with a deductible.

In your car rental contract, you'll see that for about $11 to $13 a day, you may buy optional collision damage waiver (CDW) protection. (If partial coverage with a deductible is included in the rental contract, the CDW will cover the deductible in the event of an accident, and can cost as much as $25 per day.) If you do not accept the CDW coverage, you may be liable for as much as the full retail value of the rental car if it is damaged or stolen; by paying for the CDW, you are relieved of all responsibility for any damage to the car. Before agreeing to this coverage, however, check with your own broker about your existing personal auto insurance policy. It very well may cover your entire liability exposure without any additional cost, or you automatically may be covered by the credit card company to which you are charging the cost of your rental. To find out the amount of rental car insurance provided by major credit cards, contact the issuing institutions.

You also should know that an increasing number of the major international car rental companies automatically are including the cost of the CDW in their basic rates. Car rental prices have increased to include this coverage, although rental company ad campaigns may promote this as a new, improved rental package "benefit." The disadvantage of this inclusion is that you may not have the option to turn down the CDW — even if you already are adequately covered by your own insurance policy or through a credit card company.

Your rental contract (with the appropriate insurance box checked off), as well as proof of your personal insurance policy, if applicable, are required as proof of insurance. If you will be driving your own car in Italy, you must carry an International Insurance Certificate (called a Green Card), available through insurance brokers in the US.

Combination Policies – Short-term insurance policies, which may include a combination of any or all of the types of insurance discussed above, are available through retail insurance agencies, automobile clubs, and many travel agents. These combination policies are designed to cover you for the duration of a single trip.

Companies offering policies of this type include the following:

Access America International (600 Third Ave., PO Box 807, New York, NY 10163; phone: 800-284-8300 or 212-490-5345).

Carefree Travel Insurance (Arm Coverage, PO Box 310, Mineola, NY 11501; phone: 800-645-2424 or 516-294-0220).

NEAR Services (450 Prairie Ave., Suite 101, Calumet City, IL 60409; phone: 708-868-6700 in the Chicago area; 800-654-6700 elsewhere in the US and Canada).

Tele-Trip Co. (PO Box 31685, 3201 Farnam St., Omaha, NE 68131; phone: 402-345-2400 in Nebraska; 800-228-9792 elsewhere in the US).

Travel Assistance International (1333 15th St. NW, Suite 400, Washington, DC 20005; phone: 202-331-1609 in Washington, DC; 800-821-2828 elsewhere in the US).

Travel Guard International (1145 Clark St., Stevens Point, WI 54481; phone: 715-345-0505 in Wisconsin; 800-826-1300 elsewhere in the US).

Travel Insurance PAK c/o *The Travelers Companies* (One Tower Sq., Hartford, CT 06183-5040; phone: 203-277-2319 in Connecticut; 800-243-3174 elsewhere in the US).

WorldCare Travel Assistance Association (605 Market St., Suite 1300, San Francisco, CA 94105; phone: 800-666-4993 or 415-541-4991).

Hints for Handicapped Travelers

From 40 to 50 million people in the US have some sort of disability, and over half this number are physically handicapped. Like everyone else today, they — and the uncounted disabled millions around the world — are on the move. More than ever before, they are demanding facilities they can use comfortably, and they are being heard.

The city of Rome has been rather slow in the development of facilities for the handicapped. Some of the major hotels are accessible to wheelchairs, but few are equipped with special handles and bars in the rooms. You may be able to find some major churches and museums equipped with ramps for wheelchair visitors. There are designated seats on buses for the handicapped. However, buses in Rome are always so crowded it may be extremely difficult for them to get onto one. A handicapped visitor also has to negotiate many steps before he or she can reach the platform in a *metropolitana* station. Sometimes it can be downright dangerous for them to do so. Generally, in order to thoroughly enjoy Rome's varied delights, a disabled traveler must be accompanied by an able-bodied companion.

PLANNING: Collect as much information as you can about facilities for travelers with your sort of disability in Rome. Make your travel arrangements well in advance and specify to all services involved the exact nature of your condition or restricted mobility. The best way to find out is to write or call the local tourist authority or hotel and ask specific questions. If you require a corridor of a certain width to maneuver a wheelchair or if you need handles on the bathroom walls for support, ask the hotel manager. A travel agent or the local chapter or national office of the organization that deals with your particular disability will supply the most up-to-date information on the subject. The following organizations offer general information on access:

ACCENT on Living (PO Box 700, Bloomington, IL 61702; phone: 309-378-2961). This information service for persons with disabilities provides a free list of travel agencies specializing in arranging trips for the disabled; for a copy send a self-addressed, stamped envelope. It also offers a wide range of publications, including a quarterly magazine ($8 per year; $14 for 2 years) for persons with disabilities.

Associazione Italiana per l'Assistenza Spastics (Italian Spastics Association; Via Cipro 4H, Rome 00136; phone: 41-389604). This is a major handicapped organization, with branches all over Italy. It not only provides information about and for those with cerebral palsy, it can also help arrange transportation for people with any type of disability in Rome.

Mobility International USA (*MIUSA;* PO Box 3551, Eugene, OR 97403; phone: 503-343-1284; both voice and TDD). This US branch of *Mobility International,* a nonprofit British organization with affiliates worldwide, offers members advice and assistance — including information on accommodations and other travel services, and publications applicable to the traveler's disability. It also offers a quarterly newsletter and a comprehensive sourcebook, *A World of Options for the 90s: A Guide to International Education Exchange, Community Service and Travel for Persons with Disabilities* ($14 for members; $16 for non-members). Membership includes the newsletter and is $20 a year; subscription to the newsletter alone is $10 annually.

National Rehabilitation Information Center (8455 Colesville Rd., Suite 935, Silver Spring, MD 20910; phone: 301-588-9284). A general information, resource, research, and referral service.

Paralyzed Veterans of America (*PVA;* PVA/ATTS Program, 801 18th St. NW, Washington, DC 20006; phone: 202-416-7708 in Washington, DC; 800-424-8200 elsewhere in the US). The members of this national service organization all are veterans who have suffered spinal cord injuries, but it offers advocacy services and information to all persons with a disability. *PVA* also sponsors *Access to the Skies,* a program that coordinates the efforts of the national and international air travel industry in providing airport and airplane access for the disabled. Members receive several helpful publications, as well as regular notification of conferences on subjects of interest to the disabled traveler.

Royal Association for Disability and Rehabilitation (*RADAR;* 25 Mortimer St., London W1N 8AB, England; phone: 44-71-637-5400). Offers a number of publications for the handicapped. Their comprehensive guide, *Holidays and Travel Abroad 1991/92 — A Guide for Disabled People,* focuses on international travel.

This publication can be ordered by sending payment in British pounds to *RADAR.* As we went to press, it cost just over £6; call for current pricing before ordering.

Society for the Advancement of Travel for the Handicapped (*SATH;* 26 Court St., Penthouse, Brooklyn, NY 11242; phone: 718-858-5483). To keep abreast of developments in travel for the handicapped as they occur, you may want to join *SATH,* a nonprofit organization whose members include consumers, as well as travel service professionals who have experience (or an interest) in travel for the handicapped. For an annual fee of $45 ($25 for students and travelers who are 65 and older), members receive a quarterly newsletter and have access to extensive information and referral services. *SATH* also offers a useful publication, *Travel Tips for the Handicapped* (a series of informative fact sheets); to order, send a self-addressed, #10 envelope and $1.

Travel Information Service (Moss Rehabilitation Hospital, 1200 W. Tabor Rd., Philadelphia, PA 19141-3099; phone: 215-456-9600 for voice; 215-456-9602 for TDD). This service assists physically handicapped people in planning trips and supplies detailed information on accessibility for a nominal fee.

Blind travelers should contact the *American Foundation for the Blind* (15 W. 16th St., New York, NY 10011; phone: 212-620-2147 in New York State; 800-232-5463 elsewhere in the US) and *The Seeing Eye* (Box 375, Morristown, NJ 07963-0375; phone: 201-539-4425); both provide useful information on resources for the visually impaired. *Note:* In Italy, Seeing Eye dogs must be accompanied by a certificate of inoculation against rabies, issued within 1 year and a health certificate from an attending veterinarian. *The American Society for the Prevention of Cruelty to Animals* (*ASPCA,* Education Dept., 441 E. 92 St., New York, NY 10128; phone: 212-876-7700) offers a useful booklet, *Traveling With Your Pet,* which lists inoculation and other requirements by country. It is available for $5 (including postage and handling).

In addition, there are a number of publications — from travel guides to magazines — of interest to handicapped travelers. Among these are the following:

Access to the World, by Louise Weiss, offers sound tips for the disabled traveler. Published by Facts on File (460 Park Ave. S., New York, NY 10016; phone: 212-683-2244 in New York State; 800-322-8755 elsewhere in the US; 800-443-8323 in Canada), it costs $16.95. Check with your local bookstore; it also can be ordered by phone with a credit card.

The Diabetic Traveler (PO Box 8223 RW, Stamford, CT 06905; phone: 203-327-5832) is a useful quarterly newsletter. Each issue highlights a single destination or type of travel and includes information on general resources and hints for diabetics. A 1-year subscription costs $15. When subscribing, ask for the free fact sheet including an index of special articles; back issues are available for $4 each.

Guide to Traveling with Arthritis, a free brochure available by writing to the Upjohn Company (PO Box 307-B, Coventry, CT 06238), provides lots of good, commonsense tips on planning your trip and how to be as comfortable as possible when traveling by car, bus, train, cruise ship, or plane.

Handicapped Travel Newsletter is regarded as one of the best sources of information for the disabled traveler. It is edited by wheelchair-bound Vietnam veteran Michael Quigley, who has traveled to 93 countries around the world. Issued every 2 months (plus special issues), a subscription is $10 per year. Write to *Handicapped Travel Newsletter,* PO Box 269, Athens, TX 75751 (phone: 214-677-1260).

Handi-Travel: A Resource Book for Disabled and Elderly Travellers, by Cinnie Noble, is a comprehensive travel guide full of practical tips for those with disabilities affecting mobility, hearing, or sight. To order this book, send $12.95, plus shipping and handling, to the *Canadian Rehabilitation Council for the Disabled*, 45 Sheppard Ave. E., Suite 801, Toronto, Ontario M2N 5W9, Canada (phone: 416-250-7490; both voice and TDD).

The Itinerary (PO Box 2012, Bayonne, NJ 07002-2012; phone: 201-858-3400). This bimonthly travel magazine for people with disabilities includes information on accessibility, listings of tours, news of adaptive devices, travel aids, and special services, as well as numerous general travel hints. A subscription costs $10 a year.

The Physically Disabled Traveler's Guide, by Rod W. Durgin and Norene Lindsay, rates accessibility of a number of travel services and includes a list of organizations specializing in travel for the disabled. It is available for $9.95, plus shipping and handling, from Resource Directories, 3361 Executive Pkwy., Suite 302, Toledo, OH 43606 (phone: 419-536-5353 in the Toledo area; 800-274-8515 elsewhere in the US).

Ticket to Safe Travel offers useful information for travelers with diabetes. A reprint of this article is available free from local chapters of the *American Diabetes Association*. For the nearest branch, contact the central office at 505 Eighth Ave., 21st Floor, New York, NY 10018 (phone: 212-947-9707 in New York State; 800-232-3472 elsewhere in the US).

Travel for the Patient with Chronic Obstructive Pulmonary Disease, a publication of the George Washington University Medical Center, provides some sound practical suggestions for those with emphysema, chronic bronchitis, asthma, or other lung ailments. To order, send $2 to Dr. Harold Silver, 1601 18th St. NW, Washington, DC 20009 (phone: 202-667-0134).

Traveling Like Everybody Else: A Practical Guide for Disabled Travelers, by Jacqueline Freedman and Susan Gersten, offers the disabled tips on traveling by car, cruise ship, and plane, as well as lists of accessible accommodations, tour operators specializing in tours for disabled travelers, and other resources. It is available for $11.95, plus postage and handling, from Modan Publishing, PO Box 1202, Bellmore, NY 11710 (phone: 516-679-1380).

Travel Tips for Hearing-Impaired People, a free pamphlet for deaf and hearing-impaired travelers, is available from the *American Academy of Otolaryngology* (One Prince St., Alexandria, VA 22314; phone: 703-836-4444). For a copy, send a self-addressed, stamped, business-size envelope to the academy.

Travel Tips for People with Arthritis, a free 31-page booklet published by the *Arthritis Foundation,* provides helpful information regarding travel by car, bus, train, cruise ship, or plane, planning your trip, and medical considerations, and includes listings of helpful resources, such as associations and travel agencies that operate tours for disabled travelers. For a copy, contact your local *Arthritis Foundation* chapter, or write to the national office, PO Box 19000, Atlanta, GA 30326 (phone: 404-872-7100).

A few more basic resources to look for are *Travel for the Disabled,* by Helen Hecker ($9.95), and by the same author, *Directory of Travel Agencies for the Disabled* ($19.95). *Wheelchair Vagabond,* by John G. Nelson, is another useful guide for travelers confined to a wheelchair (hardcover, $14.95; paperback, $9.95). All three are published by Twin Peaks Press, PO Box 129, Vancouver, WA 98666 (phone: 800-637-CALM or 206-694-2462).

The Italian Government Travel Office may also provide some information for the handicapped. (For the addresses of this agency's US branches, see *Tourist Information Offices,* in this section.)

Two organizations based in Great Britain offer information for handicapped persons traveling throughout Europe, including Italy. *Tripscope* (63 Esmond Rd., London W4 1JE, UK; phone: 44-81-994-9294) is a telephone-based information and referral service (not a booking agent) that can help with transportation options for journeys throughout Europe. It may, for instance, be able to recommend outlets leasing small family vehicles adapted to accommodate wheelchairs. *Tripscope* also provides information on cassettes for blind or visually impaired travelers, and accepts written requests for information from those with speech impediments. And for general information, there's *Holiday Care Service* (2 Old Bank Chambers, Station Rd., Horley, Surrey RH6 9HW, UK; phone: 44-293-774535), a first-rate, free advisory service on accommodations, transportation, and holiday packages throughout Europe for disabled visitors.

Regularly revised hotel and restaurant guides use the symbol of access (a person in a wheelchair; see the symbol at the beginning of this section) to point out accommodations suitable for wheelchair-bound guests. The red *Michelin Guide to Italy* (Michelin; $19.95), found in general and travel bookstores, is one such publication.

PLANE: The US Department of Transportation (DOT) has ruled that US airlines must accept all passengers with disabilities. As a matter of course, US airlines were pretty good about accommodating handicapped passengers even before the ruling, although each airline has somewhat different procedures. Foreign airlines also generally are good about accommodating the disabled traveler, but again, policies vary from carrier to carrier. Ask for specifics when you book your flight.

Disabled passengers always should make reservations well in advance and should provide the airline with all relevant details of their conditions. These details include information on mobility and equipment that you will need the airline to supply — such as a wheelchair for boarding or portable oxygen for in-flight use. Be sure that the person to whom you speak fully understands the degree of your disability — the more details provided, the more effective help the airline can give you.

On the day before the flight, call back to make sure that all arrangements have been prepared, and arrive early on the day of the flight so that you can board before the rest of the passengers. It's a good idea to bring a medical certificate with you, stating your specific disability or the need to carry particular medicine.

Because most airports have jetways (corridors connecting the terminal with the door of the plane), a disabled passenger usually can be taken as far as the plane, and sometimes right onto it, in a wheelchair. If not, a narrow boarding chair may be used to take you to your seat. Your own wheelchair, which will be folded and put in the baggage compartment, should be tagged as escort luggage to assure that it's available at planeside upon landing rather than in the baggage claim area. Travel is not quite as simple if your wheelchair is battery-operated: Unless it has non-spillable batteries, it might not be accepted on board, and you will have to check with the airline ahead of time to find out how the batteries and the chair should be packaged for the flight. Usually people in wheelchairs are asked to wait until other passengers have disembarked. If you are making a tight connection, be sure to tell the attendant.

Passengers who use oxygen may not use their personal supply in the cabin, though it may be carried on the plane as cargo when properly packed and labeled. If you will need oxygen during the flight, the airline will supply it to you (there is a charge) provided you have given advance notice — 24 hours to a few days, depending on the carrier.

Useful information on every stage of air travel, from planning to arrival, is provided in the booklet *Incapacitated Passengers Air Travel Guide.* To receive a free copy, write to the *International Air Transport Association* (Publications Sales Department, 2000 Peel St., Montreal, Quebec H3A 2R4, Canada; phone: 514-844-6311). Another helpful publication is *Air Transportation of Handicapped Persons,* which explains the general guidelines that govern air carrier policies. For a copy of this free booklet, write to the US Department of Transportation (Distribution Unit, Publications Section, M-443-2,

Washington, DC 20590) and ask for "Free Advisory Circular #AC-120-32." *Access Travel: A Guide to the Accessibility of Airport Terminals,* a free publication of the *Airport Operators Council International,* provides information on more than 500 airports worldwide — including major airports in Italy — and offers ratings of 70 features, such as accessibility to bathrooms, corridor width, and parking spaces. For a copy, contact the Consumer Information Center (Dept. 563W, Pueblo, CO 81009; phone: 719-948-3334).

Among the major carriers serving Italy, the following airlines have TDD toll-free lines in the US for the hearing-impaired:

> *Delta:* 800-831-4488.
> *TWA:* 800-252-0622 in California; 800-421-8480 elsewhere in the US.

GROUND TRANSPORTATION: Perhaps the simplest solution to getting around is to travel with an able-bodied companion who can drive. Another alternative in Italy is to hire a driver/translator with a car. The organizations listed above may be able to help you make arrangements — another source is your hotel concierge.

If you are accustomed to driving your own hand-controlled car and are determined to rent one, you may have to do some extensive research, as in Italy it is very difficult to find rental cars fitted with hand controls. If agencies do provide hand-controlled cars, they are apt to be offered only on a limited basis in major metropolitan areas, such as Rome, and usually come only with an extra charge. The best course is to contact the major car rental agencies listed in *Traveling by Plane,* in this section, well before your departure (at least 7 days, much earlier preferably); but be forewarned, you still may be out of luck. Other sources for information on vehicles adapted for the handicapped are the organizations discussed above.

The *American Automobile Association (AAA)* publishes a useful booklet, *The Handicapped Driver's Mobility Guide.* Contact the central office of your local *AAA* club for availability and pricing, which may vary at different branch offices.

Although taxis and public transportation also are available in Italy, accessibility for the disabled varies and may be limited in rural areas, as well as in some cities. Check with a travel agent or the Italian Government Travel Office for information.

TOURS: Programs designed for the physically impaired are run by specialists, and the following travel agencies and tour operators specialize in making group and individual arrangements for travelers with physical or other disabilities:

> *Access: The Foundation for Accessibility by the Disabled* (PO Box 356, Malverne, NY 11565; phone: 516-887-5798). A travelers' referral service that acts as an intermediary with tour operators and agents worldwide, and provides information on accessibility at various locations.
>
> *Accessible Journeys* (412 S. 45th St., Philadelphia, PA 19104; phone: 215-747-0171). Arranges for medical professional traveling companions — registered or licensed practical nurses, therapists, or doctors (all are experienced travelers). Several prospective companions' profiles and photos are sent to the client for perusal, and if one is acceptable, the "match" is made. The client usually pays all travel expenses for the companion, plus a certain amount in "earnings" to replace wages the companion would be making at his or her usual job.
>
> *Accessible Tours/Directions Unlimited* (720 N. Bedford Rd., Bedford Hills, NY 10507; phone: 914-241-1700 in New York State; 800-533-5343 elsewhere in the continental US). Arranges group or individual tours for disabled persons traveling in the company of able-bodied friends or family members. Accepts the unaccompanied traveler if completely self-sufficient.
>
> *C.I.T.* (Marco Polo House, 325 Lansdowne Rd., Croydon, Surrey CR9 1LL, Great Britain; phone: 81-686-0677). This tour operator can arrange transportation

between airport and hotels for wheelchair-bound travelers anywhere in Italy. It can also recommend hotels with special facilities for the handicapped.

Evergreen Travel Service (4114 198th St. SW, Suite 13, Lynnwood, WA 98036-6742; phone: 206-776-1184 or 800-435-2288 throughout the continental US and Canada). It offers worldwide programs for the disabled (Wings on Wheels Tours) and the sight-impaired/blind (White Cane Tours).

Flying Wheels Travel (143 W. Bridge St., Box 382, Owatonna, MN 55060; phone: 507-451-5005 or 800-535-6790). Handles both tours and individual arrangements.

Guided Tour (613 W. Cheltenham Ave., Suite 200, Melrose Park, PA 19126-2414; phone: 215-782-1370). Arranges tours for people with developmental and learning disabilities and sponsors separate tours for members of the same population who also are physically disabled or who simply need a slower pace.

Handi-Travel (First National Travel Ltd., Thornhill Sq., 300 John St., Suite 405, Thornhill, Ontario L3T 5W4, Canada; phone: 416-731-4714). Handles individual arrangements.

USTS Travel (11 E. 44th St., New York, NY 10017; phone: 800-487-8787 or 212-687-5121). Travel agent and registered nurse Mary Ann Hamm designs trips for individual travelers requiring all types of kidney dialysis and handles arrangements for the dialysis.

Whole Person Tours (PO Box 1084, Bayonne, NJ 07002-1084; phone: 201-858-3400). Handicapped owner Bob Zywicki travels the world with his wheelchair and offers a lineup of escorted tours (many conducted by him) for the disabled. Call for current itinerary at the time you plan to travel. *Whole Person Tours* also publishes *The Itinerary,* a bimonthly newsletter for disabled travelers (see the publication source list above).

Travelers who would benefit from being accompanied by a nurse or physical therapist also can hire a companion through *Traveling Nurses' Network,* a service provided by Twin Peaks Press (PO Box 129, Vancouver, WA 98666; phone: 800-637-CALM or 206-694-2462). For a $10 fee, clients receive the names of three nurses, whom they can then contact directly; for a $125 fee, the agency will make all the hiring arrangements for the client. Travel arrangements also may be made in some cases — the fee for this further service is determined on an individual basis.

A similar service is offered by *MedEscort International* (ABE International Airport, PO Box 8766, Allentown, PA 18105; phone: 800-255-7182 in the continental US; elsewhere, call 215-791-3111). The service arranges for clients to be accompanied by a nurse, paramedic, respiratory therapist, or physician. The fees are based on the disabled traveler's needs. *MedEscort* also can assist in making travel arrangements.

Hints for Single Travelers

Just about the last trip in human history on which the participants were neatly paired was the voyage of Noah's Ark. Ever since, passenger lists and tour groups have reflected the same kind of asymmetry that occurs in real life, as countless individuals set forth to see the world unaccompanied (or unencumbered, depending on your outlook) by spouse, lover, friend, companion, or relative.

The truth is that the travel industry is not very fair to people who vacation by themselves. People traveling alone almost invariably end up paying more than individuals traveling in pairs. Most travel bargains, including package tours, accommodations, resort packages, and cruises, are based on *double-occupancy* rates. The single traveler will have to pay a surcharge, called a single supplement, for exactly the same package. In extreme cases, this can add as much as 30% to 55% to the basic per-person rate.

The obvious, most effective alternative is to find a traveling companion. Even special "singles' tours" that promise no supplements usually are based on people sharing double rooms. Perhaps the most recent innovation along these lines is the creation of organizations that "introduce" the single traveler to other single travelers. Some charge fees, while others are free, but the basic service offered is the same: to match an unattached person with a compatible travel mate, often as part of the company's own package tours. Among such organizations are the following:

Jane's International (2603 Bath Ave., Brooklyn, NY 11214; phone: 718-266-2045). This service puts potential traveling companions in touch with one another. No age limit, no fee.

Odyssey Network (118 Cedar St., Wellesley, MA 02181; phone: 617-237-2400). Originally founded to match single women travelers, this company now includes men in its enrollment. *Odyssey* offers a quarterly newsletter for members who are seeking a travel companion, and occasionally organizes small group tours. A newsletter subscription is $50.

Partners-in-Travel (PO Box 491145, Los Angeles, CA 90049; phone: 213-476-4869). Members receive a list of singles seeking traveling companions; prospective companions make contact through the agency. The membership fee is $40 per year and includes a chatty newsletter (6 issues per year).

Travel Companion Exchange (PO Box 833, Amityville, NY 11701; phone: 516-454-0880). This group publishes a newsletter for singles and a directory of individuals looking for travel companions. On joining, members fill out a lengthy questionnaire and write a small listing (much like an ad in a personal column). Based on these listings, members can request copies of profiles and contact prospective traveling companions. It is wise to join well in advance of your planned vacation so that there's enough time to determine compatibility and plan a joint trip. Membership fees, including the newsletter, are $36 for 6 months or $60 a year for a single-sex listing; $66 and $120, respectively, for a complete listing. Subscription to the newsletter alone costs $24 for 6 months or $36 per year.

In addition, a number of tour packagers cater to single travelers. These companies offer packages designed for individuals interested in vacationing with a group of single travelers or in being matched with a traveling companion. Among these agencies are the following:

Singles in Motion (545 W. 236th St., Suite 1D, Riverdale, NY 10463; phone: 212-884-4464). Recent itineraries include 12- and 17-day programs in Italy with stops in Rome, as well as Florence, Milan, and Venice.

Singleworld (401 Theodore Fremd Ave., Rye, NY 10580; phone: 914-967-3334 or 800-223-6490 in the continental US). It offers its own package tours and cruises for singles, with departures categorized by age group — 35 or younger — or for all ages. Recent offerings that visit Rome include a 13-day Mediterranean cruise and a 14-day escorted tour of England, France, Italy, and Switzerland.

Student Travel International (STI) (8619 Reseda Blvd., Suite 103, Northridge, CA 91324; phone: 800-525-0525). Specializes in travel for 18- to 35-year-olds. Itineraries include 14- to 63-day European escorted tours, with excursions in Rome.

A good book for single travelers is *Traveling On Your Own,* by Eleanor Berman, which offers tips on traveling solo and includes information on trips for singles, ranging from outdoor adventures to educational programs. Available in bookstores, it also can be ordered by sending $12.95, plus postage and handling, to Random House, Order Dept., 400 Hahn Rd., Westminster, MD 21157 (phone: 800-733-3000).

Single travelers also may want to subscribe to *Going Solo,* a newsletter that offers helpful information on going on your own. Issued eight times a year, a subscription costs $36. Contact Doerfer Communications, PO Box 1035, Cambridge, MA 02238 (phone: 617-876-2764).

WOMEN AND STUDENTS: Two specific groups of single travelers deserve special mention: women and students. Countless women travel by themselves in Italy, and such an adventure need not be feared. One lingering inhibition many female travelers still harbor is that of eating alone in public places. The trick here is to relax and enjoy your meal and surroundings; while you may run across the occasional unenlightened waiter, a woman dining solo is no longer uncommon.

Studying Abroad – A large number of single travelers are students. Travel *is* education. Travel broadens a person's knowledge and deepens his or her perception of the world in a way no media or "armchair" experience ever could. In addition, to study a country's language, art, culture, or history in one of its own schools is to enjoy the most productive method of learning.

By "student" we do not necessarily mean a person who wishes to matriculate at a foreign university to earn a degree. Nor do we necessarily mean a younger person. A student is anyone who wishes to include some sort of educational program in a trip to Italy.

There are many benefits for students abroad, and the way to begin to discover them is to consult the *Council on International Educational Exchange (CIEE),* the US sponsor of the International Student Identity Card (ISIC), which permits reductions on airfare, other transportation, and entry fees to most museums and other exhibitions. The organization also is the source of the Federation of International Youth Travel Organizations (FIYTO) card, which provides many of the same benefits. For further information and applications, write to *CIEE* at one of the following addresses: 205 E. 42nd St., New York, NY 10017 (phone: 212-661-1414); 312 Sutter St., Suite 407, San Francisco, CA 94108 (phone: 415-421-3473); and 919 Irving St., Suite 102, San Francisco, CA 94122 (phone: 415-566-6222). Mark the letter "Attn. Student ID."

CIEE also offers a free, informative, annual, 64-page *Student Travel Catalog,* which covers all aspects of youth travel abroad for vacation trips, jobs, or study programs, and also includes a list of other helpful publications. It also sells *Work, Study, Travel Abroad: The Whole World Handbook,* an informative, chatty guide on study programs, work opportunities, and travel hints, with a particularly good section on Italy. It is available for $10.95, plus shipping and handling. The publications are available from the Information and Student Services Department at the New York address given above.

CIEE also sponsors charter flights to Europe that are open to students and nonstudents of any age. For example, flights between New York and Rome (with budget-priced add-ons available from Chicago, Cleveland, Miami, Minneapolis, Phoenix, Portland, Salt Lake City, San Diego, Seattle, and Spokane) arrive and depart at least three times a week from Kennedy (JFK) Airport during the high season.

Students and singles in general should keep in mind that numerous youth hostels exist in Rome. They always are inexpensive, generally clean and well situated, and they are a sure place to meet other people traveling alone. Hostels are run by the hosteling associations of 68 countries that make up the *International Youth Hostel Federation (IYHF);* membership in one of the national associations affords access to the hostels of the rest. To join the American affiliate, *American Youth Hostels (AYH),* contact the national office (PO Box 37613, Washington, DC 20013-7613; phone: 202-783-6161), or the local *AYH* council nearest you.

Those who go abroad without an *AYH* card may purchase a youth hostel International Guest Card (for the equivalent of about $18), and obtain information on local youth hostels by contacting *Associazione Italiana Alberghi per la Gioventù (AIG;* Via Cavour 44, Rome 00184; phone: 6-462342). This association also provides information on hostels throughout Italy.

Opportunities for study range from summer or academic-year courses in the language and civilization of Italy, designed specifically for foreigners (including those whose school days are well behind them), to long-term university attendance by those intending to take a degree.

Complete details on more than 3,000 courses available abroad (including at Italian universities) and suggestions on how to apply are contained in two books published by the *Institute of International Education* (IIE Books, 809 UN Plaza, New York, NY 10017; phone 212-883-8200): *Vacation Study Abroad* ($24.95, plus shipping and handling) and *Academic Year Abroad* ($31.95, plus shipping and handling). IIE Books also offers a free pamphlet called *Basic Facts on Study Abroad.*

The *National Registration Center for Study Abroad (NRCSA;* PO Box 1393, Milwaukee, WI 53201; phone: 414-278-0631) also offers a publication called *Worldwide Classroom: Study Abroad and Learning Vacations in 40 Countries: 1991–1992,* available for $8, which includes information on over 160 schools and cultural centers that offer courses for Americans, with the primary focus on foreign language and culture. At press time, *NRCSA*'s programs in Rome include language (in 4 different levels of skill) and cultural courses ranging from gastronomy, art history, politics and economics to Italian business and trade.

Those who are interested in a "learning vacation" abroad also may be interested in *Travel and Learn* by Evelyn Kaye. This guide to educational travel discusses a wide range of opportunities — everything from archaeology to whale watching — and provides information on organizations that offer programs in these areas of interest. The book is available in bookstores for $23.95; or you can send $26 (which includes shipping charges) to Blue Penguin Publications (147 Sylvan Ave., Leonia, NJ 07605; phone: 800-800-8147 or 201-461-6918). *Learning Vacations* by Gerson G. Eisenberg also provides extensive information on seminars, workshops, courses, and so on — in a wide variety of subjects. Available in bookstores, it also can be ordered from Peterson's Guides (PO Box 2123, Princeton, NJ 08543-2123; phone: 609-243-9111) for $11.95, plus shipping and handling.

If you are interested in a home-stay travel program, in which you learn about European culture by living with a family, contact the *Experiment in International Living* (PO Box 676, Brattleboro, VT 05302-0676; phone: 802-257-7751 in Vermont; 800-345-2929 elsewhere in the continental US), which sponsors home-stay educational travel in more than 40 countries, including locations in Rome. The organization aims its programs at high school or college students.

Another organization specializing in travel as an educational experience is the *American Institute for Foreign Study (AIFS;* 102 Greenwich Ave., Greenwich, CT 06830; phone: 800-727-AIFS, 203-869-9090, or 203-863-6087). Although it does not specialize in travel to Italy, many of its participants choose to study in Italy. However, at press time, it offered only a college program in Florence, sponsored by Richmond College in London. *AIFS* also caters to bona fide high school students, but its non-credit international learning programs are open to independent travelers of all ages (approximately 20% of *AIFS* students are over 25).

Hints for Older Travelers

Special discounts and more free time are just two factors that have given Americans over age 65 a chance to see the world at affordable prices. Senior citizens make up an ever-growing segment of the travel population, and the trend among them is to travel more frequently and for longer periods of time.

PLANNING: When planning a vacation, prepare your itinerary with one eye on your own physical condition and the other on your interests. One important factor to keep in mind is not to overdo anything and to be aware of the effects that the weather may have on your capabilities.

Older travelers may find the following publications of interest:

Discount Guide for Travelers Over 55, by Caroline and Walter Weintz, is an excellent book for budget-conscious older travelers. It is available by sending $7.95, plus shipping and handling, to Penguin USA (Att. Cash Sales, 120 Woodbine St., Bergenfield, NJ 07621); when ordering, specify the ISBN number: 0-525-48358-6.

Going Abroad: 101 Tips for the Mature Traveler offers tips on preparing for your trip, commonsense precautions en route, and some basic travel terminology. This concise, free booklet is available from *Grand Circle Travel,* 347 Congress St., Boston, MA 02210 (phone: 800-221-2610 or 617-350-7500).

International Health Guide for Senior Citizen Travelers, by Dr. W. Robert Lange, covers such topics as trip preparations, food and water precautions, adjusting to weather and climate conditions, finding a doctor, motion sickness, jet lag, and so on. Also includes a list of resource organizations that provide medical assistance for travelers. It is available for $4.95 postpaid from Pilot Books, 103 Cooper St., Babylon, NY 11702 (phone: 516-422-2225).

Mature Traveler is a monthly newsletter that provides information on travel discounts, places of interest, useful tips, and other topics of interest for travelers 49 and up. To subscribe, send $21.95 to GEM Publishing Group, PO Box 50820, Reno, NV 89513 (phone: 702-786-7419).

Travel Easy: The Practical Guide for People Over 50, by Rosalind Massow, discusses a wide range of subjects — from trip planning, transportation options, and preparing for departure to avoiding and handling medical problems en route. It's available for $6.50 to members of the *American Association of Retired Persons (AARP),* and for $8.95 to non-members; call about current charges for postage and handling. Order from *AARP* Books, c/o Customer Service, Scott, Foresman & Company, 1900 E. Lake Ave., Glenview, IL 60025 (phone: 708-729-3000).

Travel Tips for Older Americans is a useful booklet that provides good, basic advice. This US State Department publication (stock number: 044-000-02270-2) can be ordered by sending a check or money order for $1 to the Superintendent of Documents (US Government Printing Office, Washington, DC 20402) or by calling 202-783-3238 and charging the order to a credit card.

Unbelievably Good Deals & Great Adventures That You Absolutely Can't Get Unless You're Over 50, by Joan Rattner Heilman, offers travel tips for older travelers, including discounts on accommodations and transportation, as well as a list of organizations for seniors. It is available for $7.95, plus shipping and handling, from Contemporary Books, 180 N. Michigan Ave., Chicago, IL 60601 (phone: 312-782-9181).

DISCOUNTS AND PACKAGES: Many hotel chains, airlines, cruise lines, bus companies, car rental companies, and other travel suppliers offer discounts to older travelers. For instance, *TWA* offers those age 62 and over (and one traveling companion per qualifying senior citizen) 10% discounts on flights from the US to Rome. Other airlines also offer discounts for passengers age 60 (or 62) and over, which also may apply to one traveling companion. For information on current prices and applicable restrictions, contact the individual carriers.

Some discounts, however, are extended only to bona fide members of certain senior citizens organizations. Because the same organizations frequently offer package tours to both domestic and international destinations, the benefits of membership are twofold: Those who join can take advantage of discounts as individual travelers and also reap the savings that group travel affords. In addition, because the age requirements for some of these organizations are quite low (or nonexistent), the benefits can begin to accrue early. In order to take advantage of these discounts, you should carry proof of your age (or eligibility). A driver's license, membership card in a recognized senior citizens organization, or a Medicare card should be adequate. Among the organizations dedicated to helping older travelers see the world are the following:

American Association of Retired Persons (*AARP;* 1909 K St. NW, Washington, DC 20049; phone: 202-872-4700). The largest and best known of these organizations. Membership is open to anyone 50 or over, whether retired or not; dues are $5 a year, $12.50 for 3 years, or $35 for 10 years, and include spouse. The *AARP* Travel Experience Worldwide program, available through *American Express Travel Related Services,* offers members travel programs worldwide designed exclusively for older travelers. Members can book these services by calling *American Express* at 800-927-0111 for land and air travel.

Mature Outlook (Customer Service Center, 6001 N. Clark St., Chicago, IL 60660; phone: 800-336-6330). Through its *TravelAlert,* vacation packages are available to members at special savings. Hotel and car rental discounts and travel accident insurance also are available. Membership is open to anyone 50 years of age or older, costs $9.95 a year, and includes a bimonthly newsletter and magazine, as well as information on package tours.

National Council of Senior Citizens (1331 F St., Washington, DC 20005; phone: 202-347-8800). Here, too, the emphasis is on keeping costs low. This nonprofit organization offers members a different roster of package tours each year, as well as individual arrangements through its affiliated travel agency *(Vantage Travel Service).* Although most members are over 50, membership is open to anyone (regardless of age) for an annual fee of $12 per person or couple. Lifetime membership costs $150.

Certain travel agencies and tour operators offer special trips geared to older travelers. Among them is *Sun Holidays* (26 Sixth St., Suite 603, Stamford, CT 06905; phone: 800-243-2057 or 203-323-1166), which specializes in year-round travel, including to Florence, Rome, and Venice, for senior citizens and offers extended-stay packages in winter.

Many travel agencies, particularly the larger ones, are delighted to make presentations to help a group of senior citizens select destinations. A local chamber of commerce should be able to provide the names of such agencies. Once a time and place are determined, an organization member or travel agent can obtain group quotations for transportation, accommodations, meal plans, and sightseeing. Larger groups usually get the best breaks.

Another choice open to older travelers is a trip that includes an educational element. *Elderhostel,* a nonprofit organization, offers programs at educational institutions worldwide, including Rome. The foreign programs generally last about 2 weeks, and include double occupancy accommodations in hotels or student residence halls and all meals. Travel to the programs usually is by designated scheduled flights, and participants can arrange to extend their stay at the end of the program. Elderhostelers must be at least

60 years old (younger if a spouse or companion qualifies), in good health, and not in need of a special diet. For a free catalogue describing the program and current offerings, write to *Elderhostel* (75 Federal St., Boston, MA 02110; phone: 617-426-7788). Those interested in the program also can borrow slides at no charge or purchase an informational videotape for $5.

Hints for Traveling with Children

 What better way to encounter the world's variety than in the company of the young, wide-eyed members of your family? Their presence does not have to be a burden or an excessive expense. The current generation of discounts for children and family package deals can make a trip together quite reasonable.

PLANNING: Here are several hints for making a trip with children easy and fun:

1. Children, like everyone else, will derive more pleasure from a trip if they know something about their destination before they arrive. Begin their education about a month before you leave. Using maps, travel magazines, and books, give children a clear idea of where you are going and how far away it is.
2. Children should help to plan the itinerary, and where you go and what you do should reflect some of their ideas. If they already know something about the sites they'll visit, they will have the excitement of recognition when they arrive.
3. Children also will enjoy learning some Italian phrases — a few basics like *"ciao!"* ("hello"), *"addio"* ("good-bye"), and *"grazie"* ("thank you").
4. Familiarize your children with lire. Give them an allowance for the trip, and be sure they understand just how far it will or won't go.
5. Give children specific responsibilities: The job of carrying their own flight bags and looking after their personal things, along with some other light chores, will give them a stake in the journey.
6. Give each child a diary or scrapbook to take along.

One resource that might be helpful to both your children and yourself is the Berlitz Italian 90-minute Cassette Pak, an instructional language tape together with a book specifically designed for travelers' use. The book/cassette package is available for $15.95, plus shipping and handling, from Macmillan Publishing Company, Front and Brown Sts., Riverside, NJ 08075 (phone: 800-257-5755).

And for parents, *Travel With Your Children* (*TWYCH;* 80 Eighth Ave., New York, NY 10011; phone: 212-206-0688) publishes a newsletter, *Family Travel Times,* that focuses on families with young travelers and offers helpful hints. An annual subscription (10 issues) is $35 and includes a copy of the "Airline Guide" issue (updated every other year), which focuses on the subject of flying with children. This special issue is available separately for $10.

Another newsletter devoted to family travel is *Getaways.* This quarterly publication provides reviews of family-oriented literature, activities, and useful travel tips. To subscribe, send $25 to *Getaways,* Att. Ms. Brooke Kane, PO Box 11511, Washington, DC 20008 (phone: 703-534-8747).

Also of interest to parents traveling with their children is *How to Take Great Trips With Your Kids,* by psychologist Sanford Portnoy and his wife, Joan Flynn Portnoy. The book includes helpful tips from fellow family travelers, tips on economical accommodations and touring by car, recreational vehicle, and train, as well as over 50 games to play with your children en route. It is available for $8.95, plus shipping and handling, from Harvard Common Press, 535 Albany St., Boston, MA 02118 (phone: 617-423-5803).

Another book on family travel, *Travel with Children* by Maureen Wheeler, offers a wide range of practical tips on traveling with children, and includes accounts of the author's family travel experiences. It is available for $10.95, plus shipping and handling, from Lonely Planet Publications, Embarcadero West, 112 Linden St., Oakland, CA 94607 (phone: 510-893-8555).

Finally, parents arranging a trip with their children may want to deal with an agency specializing in family travel such as *Let's Take the Kids* (1268 Devon Ave., Los Angeles, CA 90024; phone: 213-274-7088 or 800-726-4349). In addition to arranging and booking trips for individual families, this group occassionally organizes trips for single-parent families traveling together. They also offer a parent travel network, whereby parents who have been to a particular destination can evaluate it for others.

PLANE: Begin early to investigate all available family discounts and charter flights, as well as any package deals and special rates offered by the major airlines. When you make your reservations, tell the airline that you are traveling with a child. Children ages 2 through 11 generally travel at about a 20% to 30% discount off regular full-fare adult ticket prices on domestic flights. This children's fare, however, usually is much higher than the excursion fare, which may be used by any traveler, regardless of age. An infant under 2 years of age usually can travel free if it sits on an adult's lap. A second infant without a second adult would pay the fare applicable to children ages 2 through 11.

Although some airlines will, on request, supply bassinets for infants, most carriers encourage parents to bring their own safety seat on board, which then is strapped into the airline seat with a regular seat belt. This is much safer — and certainly more comfortable — than holding the child in your lap. If you do not purchase a seat for your baby, you have the option of bringing the infant restraint along on the off-chance that there might be an empty seat next to yours — in which case some airlines will let you use that seat at no charge for your baby and infant seat. However, if there is no empty seat available, the infant seat no doubt will have to be checked as baggage (and you may have to pay an additional charge), since it generally does not fit under the seat or in the overhead racks.

The safest bet is to pay for a seat — this usually will be the same as fares applicable to children ages 2 through 11. It usually is less expensive to pay for an adult excursion rate than the discounted children's fare.

Be forewarned: Some safety seats designed primarily for use in cars do not fit into plane seats properly. Although nearly all seats manufactured since 1985 carry labels indicating whether they meet federal standards for use aboard planes, actual seat sizes may vary from carrier to carrier. At the time of this writing, the FAA was in the process of reviewing and revising the federal regulations regarding infant travel and safety devices — it was still to be determined if children should be *required* to sit in safety seats and whether the airlines will have to provide them.

If using one of these infant restraints, you should try to get bulkhead seats, which will provide extra room to care for your child during the flight. You also should request a bulkhead seat when using a bassinet — again, this is not as safe as strapping the child in. On some planes bassinets hook into a bulkhead wall; on others it is placed on the floor in front of you. (Note that bulkhead seats often are reserved for families traveling with small children.) As a general rule, babies should be held during takeoff and landing.

Request seats on the aisle if you have a toddler or if you think you will need to use the bathroom frequently. Carry onto the plane all you will need to care for and occupy your children during the flight — formula, diapers, a sweater, books, favorite stuffed animals, and so on. Dress your baby simply, with a minimum of buttons and snaps, because the only place you may have to change a diaper is at your seat or in a small lavatory.

On US carriers, you also can ask for a hot dog or hamburger instead of the airline's regular dinner if you give at least 24 hours' notice. Some, but not all, airlines have baby food aboard, and the flight attendant can warm a bottle for you. While you should bring along toys from home, also ask about children's diversions. Some carriers have terrific free packages of games, coloring books, and puzzles.

When the plane takes off and lands, make sure your baby is nursing or has a bottle, pacifier, or thumb in its mouth. This sucking will make the child swallow and help to clear stopped ears. A piece of hard candy will do the same thing for an older child.

Parents traveling by plane with toddlers, children, or teenagers may want to consult *When Kids Fly,* a free booklet published by Massport (Public Affairs Department, 10 Park Plaza, Boston, MA 02116-3971; phone: 617-973-5600), which includes helpful information on airfares for children, infant seats, what to do in the event of overbooked or canceled flights, and so on.

■**Note:** Newborn babies, whose lungs may not be able to adjust to the altitude, should not be taken aboard an airplane. And some airlines may refuse to allow a pregnant woman in her 8th or 9th month to fly. Check with the airline ahead of time, and carry a letter from your doctor stating that you are fit to travel — and indicating the estimated date of birth.

ACCOMMODATIONS AND MEALS: Often a cot for a child will be placed in a hotel room at little or no extra charge. If you wish to sleep in separate rooms, special rates sometimes are available for families; some places do not charge for children under a certain age. In many of the larger chain hotels, the staffs are more used to children. These hotels also are likely to have swimming pools or gamerooms — both popular with most youngsters. Apartments, condominiums, and other rental options offer families privacy, flexibility, some kitchen facilities, and often lower costs.

Most better hotels will try to arrange for a sitter for the times you will want to be without the children — for an evening's entertainment or a particularly rigorous stint of sightseeing. Whether the sitter is hired directly or through an agency, ask for and check references.

At mealtime, don't deny yourself or your children the delights of a new style of cooking. Children like to know what kind of food to expect, so the family can have the pleasure of looking up Italian dishes before leaving. Encourage your children to try new things, although sometimes you can find American-style food in Rome.

Things to Remember
1. Pace the days with children in mind. Break the touring time into half-day segments, with running around or "doing" time built in.
2. Don't forget that a child's attention span is far shorter than an adult's. Children don't have to see every sight or all of any sight to learn something from their trip; watching, playing with, and talking to other children can be equally enlightening.
3. Let your children lead the way sometimes; their perspective is different from yours, and they may lead you to things you would never have noticed on your own.
4. Remember the places that children love to visit: aquariums, zoos, amusement parks, beaches, and so on. Among the activities that may pique their interest are bicycling, snorkeling, boat trips, horseback riding, visiting children's museums, and viewing natural habitat exhibits. Children's favorites in Rome include the Castel Sant'Angelo — the historical fortresses, bastions, and cannons can be interesting sights to the young ones, and at the same time they might be able to learn a little about the history of Italy; the zoo at Villa Borghese, which covers a large

area of the expansive park, and is a reproduction of the natural habitats of many animals; and a trip down the Tiber, which can prove to be an enjoyable family experience.

Staying Healthy

The surest way to return home in good health is to be prepared for medical problems that might occur while on vacation. Below, we've outlined some things about which you need to think before you go.

Older travelers or anyone suffering from a chronic medical condition, such as diabetes, high blood pressure, cardiopulmonary disease, asthma, or ear, eye, or sinus trouble, should consult a physician before leaving home. Those with conditions requiring special consideration when traveling should think about seeing, in addition to their regular physician, a specialist in travel medicine. For a referral in a particular community, contact the nearest medical school or ask a local doctor to recommend such a specialist. Dr. Leonard Marcus, a member of the *American Committee on Clinical Tropical Medicine and Travelers' Health,* provides a directory of more than 100 travel doctors across the country. For a copy, send a 9-by-12-inch self-addressed, stamped envelope to Dr. Marcus at 148 Highland Ave., Newton, MA 02165 (phone: 617-527-4003).

FIRST AID: Put together a compact, personal medical kit including Band-Aids, first-aid cream, antiseptic, nose drops, insect repellent, aspirin, an extra pair of prescription glasses or contact lenses (and a copy of your prescription for glasses or contact lenses), sunglasses, over-the-counter remedies for diarrhea, indigestion, and motion sickness, a thermometer, and a supply of those prescription medicines you take regularly.

In a corner of your kit, keep a list of all the drugs you have brought and their purpose, as well as duplicate copies of your doctor's prescriptions (or a note from your doctor). As brand names may vary in different countries, it's a good idea to ask your doctor for the generic name of any drugs you use so that you can ask for their equivalent should you need a refill.

It also is a good idea to ask your doctor to prepare a medical identification card that includes such information as your blood type, your social security number, any allergies or chronic health problems you have, and your medical insurance information. Considering the essential contents of your medical kit, keep it with you, rather than in your checked luggage.

HELPFUL PUBLICATIONS: Practically every phase of health care — before, during, and after a trip — is covered in *The New Traveler's Health Guide,* by Drs. Patrick J. Doyle and James E. Banta. It is available for $4.95, plus postage and handling, from Acropolis Books Ltd., 13950 Park Center Rd., Herndon, VA 22071 (phone: 800-451-7771 or 703-709-0006).

The *Traveling Healthy Newsletter,* which is published six times a year, also is brimming with health-related travel tips. For a year's subscription, which costs $24, contact Dr. Karl Neumann (108-48 70th Rd., Forest Hills, NY 11375; phone: 718-268-7290). Dr. Neumann also is the editor of the useful free booklet *Traveling Healthy,* which is available by writing to the *Travel Healthy Program* (PO Box 10208, New Brunswick, NJ 08906-9910; phone: 215-732-4100).

For more information regarding preventive health care for travelers, contact the *International Association for Medical Assistance to Travelers* (*IAMAT;* 417 Center St., Lewiston, NY 14092; phone: 716-754-4883). The Centers for Disease Control also publishes an interesting booklet, *Health Information for International Travel.* To order send a check or money order for $5 to the Superintendent of Documents (US Government Printing Office, Washington, DC 20402), or charge it to your credit card by calling 202-783-3238. For information on vaccination requirements, disease outbreaks, and other health information pertaining to traveling abroad, you also can call the Centers for Disease Control's 24-hour International Health Requirements and Recommendations Information Hotline: 404-332-4559.

On the Road

Credit and Currency

 It may seem hard to believe, but one of the greatest (and least understood) costs of travel is money itself. So your one single objective in relation to the care and retention of travel funds is to make them stretch as far as possible. Herewith, a primer on making money go as far as possible overseas.

CURRENCY: The basic unit of Italian currency is the *lire*. This is distributed in coin denominations of 50, 100, 200, and 500 lire. Paper money is issued in bills of 1,000, 2,000, 5,000, 10,000, 50,000, and 100,000 lire. The value of Italian currency in relation to the US dollar fluctuates daily, affected by a wide variety of phenomena.

To avoid problems anywhere along the line, it's advisable to fill out any customs forms provided when leaving the US on which you can declare all money you are taking with you — cash, traveler's checks, and so on. US law requires that anyone taking more than $10,000 into or out of the US must report this fact on customs form No. 4790, which is available from US Customs. If taking over $10,000 out of the US, you must report this *before* leaving the US; if returning with such an amount, you should include this information on your customs declaration. Although travelers usually are not questioned by customs officials about currency when entering or leaving, the sensible course is to observe all regulations just to be on the safe side.

In Rome, as in the rest of Italy, you will find the official rate of exchange posted in banks, airports, money exchange houses, and some shops. As a general rule, expect to get more local currency for your US dollar at banks than at any other commercial establishment. Exchange rates do change from day to day, and most banks offer the same (or very similar) exchange rates. (In a pinch, the convenience of cashing money in your hotel — sometimes on a 24-hour basis — *may* make up for the difference in the exchange rate.) Don't try to bargain in banks or hotels — no one will alter the rates for you.

A money exchange house *(ufficio di cambio)* is a financial institution that charges a fee for the service of exchanging dollars into local currency. When considering alternatives, be aware that although the rate varies among these establishments, the rates of exchange offered are bound to be slightly less favorable than the terms offered at nearby banks — again, don't be surprised if you get fewer lire for your dollar than the rate published in the papers.

That said, however, the following rules of thumb are worth remembering:

Rule number one: Never (repeat: *never*) exchange dollars for foreign currency at hotels, restaurants, or retail shops. If you do, you are sure to lose a significant amount of your US dollar's buying power. If you do come across a storefront exchange counter offering what appears to be an incredible bargain, there's too much counterfeit specie in circulation to take the chance. (see Rule number three, below.)

Rule number two: Estimate your needs carefully; if you overbuy you lose twice — buying and selling back. Every time you exchange money, someone is making a profit, and rest assured it isn't you. Use up foreign notes before leaving, saving just enough for last-minute incidentals, and tips.

Rule number three: Don't buy money on the black market. The exchange rate may be better, but it is a common practice to pass off counterfeit bills to unsuspecting foreigners who aren't familiar with the local currency. It's usually a sucker's game, and you almost always are the sucker; it also can land you in jail.

Rule number four: Learn the local currency quickly and keep abreast of daily fluctuations in the exchange rate. These are listed in the English-language *International Herald Tribune* daily for the preceding day, as well as in every major newspaper in Europe. Rates change to some degree every day. For rough calculations, it is quick and safe to use round figures, but for purchases and actual currency exchanges, carry a small pocket calculator to help you compute the exact rate. Inexpensive calculators specifically designed to convert currency amounts quickly for travelers are widely available.

When changing money, don't be afraid to ask how much commission you're being charged, and the exact amount of the prevailing exchange rate. In fact, in any exchange of money for goods or services, you should work out the rate before making any payment.

TRAVELER'S CHECKS: It's wise to carry traveler's checks instead of (or in addition to) cash, since it's possible to replace them if they are stolen or lost. Issued in various denominations and available in both US dollars and Italian lire, with adequate proof of identification (credit cards, driver's license, passport), traveler's checks are as good as cash in most hotels, restaurants, stores, and banks. Don't assume, however, that restaurants, small shops, and other establishments are going to be able to change checks of large denominations.

Although traveler's checks are available in foreign currencies such as Italian lire, the exchange rates offered by the issuing companies in the US generally are far less favorable than those available from banks both in the US and abroad. Therefore, it usually is better to carry the bulk of your travel funds abroad in US dollar–denomination traveler's checks.

Every type of traveler's check is legal tender in banks around the world, and each company guarantees full replacement if checks are lost or stolen. After that the similarity ends. Some charge a fee for purchase, while others are free; you can buy traveler's checks at almost any bank, and some are available by mail. Most important, each traveler's check issuer differs slightly in its refund policy — the amount refunded immediately, the accessibility of refund locations, the availability of a 24-hour refund service, and the time it will take for you to receive replacement checks. For instance, *American Express* guarantees replacement of lost or stolen traveler's checks in under 3 hours at any *American Express* office — other companies may not be as prompt. In Rome, the *American Express* office is located at 38 Piazza di Spagna (phone: 67641). Travelers should keep in mind that *American Express*'s 3-hour policy is based on the traveler being able to provide the serial numbers of the lost checks. Without these numbers, refunds can take much longer.

We cannot overemphasize the importance of knowing how to replace lost or stolen checks. All of the traveler's check companies have agents around the world, both in their own name and at associated agencies (usually, but not necessarily, banks), where refunds can be obtained during business hours. Most of them also have 24-hour toll-free telephone lines, and some will even provide emergency funds to tide you over on a Sunday.

Be sure to make a photocopy of the refund instructions that will be given you at the time of purchase. To avoid complications should you need to replace lost checks (and to speed up the process), keep the purchase receipt and an accurate list, by serial number, of the checks that have been spent or cashed. Always keep these records separate from the checks and the original records themselves (you may want to give them to a traveling companion to hold).

Following is a list of the major companies issuing traveler's checks and the numbers to call in the event that loss or theft makes replacement necessary:

American Express: The company advises travelers in Europe to call 44-273-571600 (in Brighton, England), collect. Another (slower) option is to call 801-968-8300 (in the US), collect or contact the nearest *American Express* office (see above for the Rome address).

Bank of America: In Rome and elsewhere worldwide, call 415-624-5400 or 415-622-3800, collect.

Citicorp: In Rome and elsewhere worldwide, call 813-623-1709 or 813-626-4444, collect.

MasterCard: In Rome, call the New York office at 212-974-5696, collect.

Thomas Cook MasterCard: In Rome, call 609-987-7300 (in the US) or 44-733-502995 (in England), collect, and they will direct you to the nearest branch of *Thomas Cook* or *Wagons-Lits,* their European agent.

Visa: In Rome, call 415-574-7111, collect. In Europe, you also can call this London number collect: 44-71-937-8091.

CREDIT CARDS: Some establishments you encounter during the course of your travels may not honor any credit cards and some may not honor all cards, so there is a practical reason to carry more than one. Most US credit cards, including the principal bank cards, are honored in Rome; however, keep in mind that some cards may be issued under different names in Europe. For example, *MasterCard* may go under the name *Access* or *Eurocard,* and *Visa* often is called *Carte Bleue* — wherever these equivalents are accepted, *MasterCard* and *Visa* may be used. The following is a list of credit cards that enjoy wide international acceptance:

American Express: For information call 800-528-4800 in the US; to report a lost or stolen *American Express* card in Rome, contact the local *American Express* office (see address above) or call 212-477-5700, collect.

Carte Blanche: For medical, legal, and travel assistance in Rome, call 214-680-6480, collect. For information call 800-525-9135 in the US; to report a lost or stolen *Carte Blanche* card in Spain, call 303-790-2433, collect.

Diners Club: For medical, legal, and travel assistance in Rome, call 214-680-6480, collect. For information call 800-525-9135 in the US; to report a lost or stolen *Diners Club* card in Rome, call 303-790-2433, collect.

Discover Card: For information call 800-DISCOVER in the US; to report a lost or stolen *Discover* card, in Rome call 302-323-7652, collect.

MasterCard: For 24-hour emergency lost card service, call 314-275-6690, collect, from abroad.

Visa: For 24-hour emergency lost card service in Rome, call 415-574-7700, collect.

SENDING MONEY ABROAD: If you have used up your traveler's checks, cashed as many emergency personal checks as your credit card allows, drawn on your cash advance line to the fullest extent, and still need money, have it sent to you via one of the following services:

American Express (phone: 800-543-4080). Offers a service called "Moneygram," completing money transfers in anywhere from 15 minutes to 5 days. The sender can go to any *American Express* office in the US and transfer money by presenting cash, a personal check, money order, or credit card — *Discover, MasterCard, Visa,* or *American Express Optima Card* (no other *American Express* or other credit cards are accepted). *American Express Optima* cardholders also can arrange for this transfer over the phone. To collect at the other end, the receiver must show identification (passport, driver's license, or other picture ID) at the *American Express* office in Rome and present a passport as identification. For further information on this service, call 800-543-4080.

Western Union Telegraph Company (phone: 800-325-4176 throughout the US). A friend or relative can go, cash in hand, to any *Western Union* office in the US, where, for a *minimum* charge of $13 (it rises with the amount of the transaction), the funds will be transferred to a representative of *Western Union* in Rome. (There are 2 in Rome.) When the money arrives, you will not be notified — you must go to the bank to inquire. Transfers generally take only about 15 minutes. The funds will be turned over in local currency, based on the rate of exchange in effect on the day of receipt. For a higher fee, the US party to this transaction may call *Western Union* with a *MasterCard* or *Visa* number to send up to $2,000.

If you are literally down to your last lira, the nearest US consulate (see *Medical and Legal Aid and Consular Services,* in this section) will let you call home to set these matters in motion.

CASH MACHINES: Automatic teller machines (ATMs) are increasingly common worldwide. If your bank participates in one of the international ATM networks (most do), the bank will issue you a "cash card" along with a personal identification code or number (also called a PIC or PIN). You can use this card at any ATM in the same electronic network to check your account balances, transfer monies between checking and savings accounts, and — most important for a traveler — withdraw cash instantly. Network ATMs generally are located in banks, commercial and transportation centers, and near major tourist attractions.

Some financial institutions offer exclusive automatic teller machines for their own customers only at bank branches. At the time of this writing, ATMs that *are* connected generally belong to one of the following two international networks: *Cirrus,* which has over 55,000 ATMs in more than 22 countries, and the *Plus System,* which has over 30,000 automatic teller machines worldwide. However, at the time of this writing, neither one of them had installed ATMs in Rome.

Accommodations

Those watching their wallets will be pleased to find that compared with most of the rest of Europe, hotel prices in Rome tend to be quite reasonable. Although it is still relatively affordable, Italy has experienced inflation, and the recent decline in the strength of the US dollar has not helped. At the lower end of the price scale, you will not necessarily have to forgo charm. While a fair number of inexpensive establishments are simply no-frills, "generic" places to spend the night, even the sparest room may have the cachet of once having been the nightly retreat of a monk or nun. And some of the most delightful places to stay are the smaller, less expensive, often family-run small inns. For more information, see *Best in Town* in THE CITY.

Time Zones, Business Hours, and Public Holidays

TIME ZONES: The countries of Europe fall into three time zones. Greenwich Mean Time — the time in Greenwich, England, at longitude 0°0′ — is the base from which all other time zones are measured. Areas in zones west of Greenwich have earlier times and are called Greenwich Minus; those to the east have later times and are called Greenwich Plus. For example, New York City — which falls into the Greenwich Minus 5 time zone — is 5 hours earlier than Greenwich, England.

Italy is in the Greenwich Plus 1 time zone — which means that the time is 1 hour later than it is in Greenwich, England, and when it is noon in Rome, it is 6 AM in New York.

As do most Western European nations, Italy moves its clocks ahead an hour in late spring and an hour back in the fall, although the date of the change tends to be about a week earlier (in spring) and a week later (in fall) than the dates we have adopted in the US. For about 2 weeks a year, then, the time difference between the US and Italy is 1 hour more or less than usual.

Italian and other European timetables use a 24-hour clock to denote arrival and departure times, which means that hours are expressed sequentially from 1 AM. By this method, 9 AM is recorded as 0900, noon as 1200, 1 PM as 1300, 6 PM as 1800, midnight as 2400, and so on. For example, the departure of a train at 7 AM will be announced as "0700"; one leaving at 7 PM will be noted as "1900."

BUSINESS HOURS: In Rome, as throughout Italy, most businesses and shops are open Mondays through Fridays from 9 AM to 1 PM, then from 3:30 or 4 PM until 7 or 8 PM, although more and more businesses now are open through midday and close at 5 PM. Many shops also are open on Saturday mornings. Some major department stores and shopping centers stay open through midday and are open Mondays through Saturdays from 9:30 AM to 6:30 PM.

Weekday banking hours in Rome are from 8:30 AM to 1:30 PM and from 3 to 4 PM.(-SOUTH-)e closed on Saturdays and Sundays.

Restaurant hours are similar to those in the US. Most restaurants are open all week during the high season and close 1 day each week during the off-season — the day varies from restaurant to restaurant.

PUBLIC HOLIDAYS: In Rome, as in the rest of Italy, the public holidays (and their dates this year) are as follows:

New Year's Day (January 1)
Epiphany (January 6)
Good Friday (April 17)
Easter Monday (April 20)
Liberation Day (April 25)
Labor Day (May 1)
Feast of Saints Peter and Paul (June 29)
Assumption of the Virgin (August 15)
All Saints' Day (November 1)
Day of Immaculate Conception (December 8)
Christmas Day (December 25)
Santo Stefano (December 26)

Mail and Electricity

MAIL: The main post office, located at 19 Piazza San Silvestro (phone: 6771), is open from 8:30 AM to 8 PM weekdays (until noon on Saturdays). Rome's most efficient post office for mail going out of Italy is the Vatican Post Office (Piazza San Pietro), open from 8:30 AM to 7 PM weekdays (until 6 PM Saturdays). Postal rates change frequently; stamps *(francobolli)* can be bought at the post office, at authorized tobacconists *(tobaccheria),* and at some hotels.

Be advised that delivery from Rome can be erratic (postcards often are given lowest priority, so don't use them for important messages). Air mail letters from Italy to the US usually take at least 4 to 7 days.

If your correspondence is important, you may want to send it via a special courier service; *DHL International* has an office at 1 Via S. Eulalia, Cagliari 09100, Sardegna (phone: 6-72421). *Federal Express* also has an offfice at Via Appia, Km. 16,800, Ciampino 00040 (phone: 783-3060). The cost is considerably higher than sending something via the postal services — but the assurance of its timely arrival may be worth it.

If you're mailing to an address within Italy, a good way to ensure or speed delivery is to use the postal code. And since small towns in Italy may have similar names, the postal code always should be specified — delivery of a letter may depend on it. If you do not know the correct postal code, call the Italian Government Travel Office (see *Tourist Information Offices,* in this section, for telephone numbers) — they should be able to look it up for you.

There are several places that will receive and hold mail for travelers in Italy. Mail sent to you at a hotel and clearly marked *fermo in posta* (literally, "hold mail") is one safe approach. Italian post offices, including the main Rome office, also will extend this service to you if the mail is addressed to the equivalent of US general delivery — called *fermo posta* or *Posta Restante.* Address the mail to Ferma Posta, 19 Piazza San Silvestro, Rome 00187. Call 6771 to inquire about mail. Also, don't forget to take your passport with you when you go to collect it. Most Italian post offices require formal identification before they will release anything; there also may be a small charge for picking up your mail.

If you are an *American Express* customer (a cardholder, a carrier of *American Express* traveler's checks, or traveling on an *American Express Travel Service* tour) you can have mail sent to its office in Rome. Letters are held free of charge — registered mail and packages are not accepted. You must be able to show an *American Express* card, traveler's checks, or a voucher proving you are on one of the company's tours to avoid paying for mail privileges. Those who aren't clients must pay a nominal charge each time they inquire if they have received mail, whether or not they actually have a letter. Mail should be addressed to you, care of *American Express,* and should be marked "Client Mail Service."

While US embassies and consulates abroad will not under ordinary circumstances accept mail for tourists, they *may* hold mail for US citizens in an emergency situation, especially if the papers sent are important. It is best to inform them either by separate letter or cable, or by phone (particularly if you are in the country already), that you will be using their address for this purpose.

ELECTRICITY: The US runs on 110-volt, 60-cycle alternating current; Rome (and the rest of Italy) runs on 220-volt, 50-cycle alternating current. (Some large tourist hotels also offer 110-volt currency for your convenience; if not, they usually have convertors available.) The difference between US and Italian voltage means that, without a converter, at 220 volts the motor of a US appliance used overseas would run at twice the speed at which it's meant to operate and would quickly burn out.

Medical and Legal Aid
and Consular Services

MEDICAL AID ABROAD: Nothing ruins a vacation or business trip more effectively than sudden injury or illness. Medical institutes in Italy, especially in the larger cities, generally provide the same basic specialties and services that are available in the US.

Before you go, be sure to check with your insurance company about the applicability of your hospitalization and major medical policies while you're abroad; many policies do not apply, and others are not accepted in Rome. Older travelers should know that Medicare does not make payments outside the US.

There are two types of hospitals in Italy — public and private. The non-public ones are called *case di cura* (houses of care or cure), villas, or clinics — to distinguish them from public hospitals. There also are some private clinics *(cliniche),* which are like small hospitals and can provide medial aid for less serious cases. Foreign travelers will have to pay full fees for medical service, which, depending on your coverage, may or may not be reimbursed by your insurance compay.

Italian law specifies that seriously injured, ill, or unconscious persons be taken directly to one of the public hospitals. (After treatment in the emergency room, *pronto soccorso,* a patient in stable condition may transfer to the hospital of his or her choice.) The efficiency and speed of the service will be variable. If you require an ambulance, be aware that, in some cases, it may provide only transportation to the nearest public hospital. At the time of this writing, advanced EMS technology (similar to that provided in the US) was only just being added in Italy.

If a bona fide emergency occurs, the fastest way to get attention may be to take a taxi to the emergency room of the nearest hospital. In Rome go to the *Salvador Mundi International Hospital* (67-77 Viale della Mura Gianicolensi; phone: 839-3154). It is a major hospital with advanced equipment and technology to deal with acute medical situations, and most of the staff speak English. Another choice is *Policlinico* (1 Umberto, Viale Policlinico; phone: 492341). A good emergency room in downtown Rome is *Ospedale San Giacomo* (off Via del Corso, near Piazza del Popolo; phone: 67261). An alternative is to dial the free national "emergency" number used to summon the police, fire trucks, and ambulances — 113 in Italy; you may also dial 112 for the police. Many of the operators can answer in simple English.

If a doctor is needed for something less than an emergency, there are several ways to find one. If you are staying in a hotel or at a resort, ask for help in reaching a doctor or other emergency services, or for the house physician, who may visit you in your room or ask you to visit an office. Travelers staying at a hotel of any size probably will find that the doctor on call speaks at least a modicum of English — if not, request one who does.

Dialing the nationwide emergency number (113) also may be of help in locating a physician. It also usually is possible to obtain a referral through a US consulate (see addresses and phone numbers below) or directly through a hospital, especially if it is an emergency.

If you have a minor medical problem, a pharmacist might offer some help. Drugstores *(farmacie)* in Italy take turns for 24-hour service; check the newspapers for their listings of *farmacie di turno,* or call 110. Two major pharmacies in Rome are *Internazionale* (49 Piazza Barberini; phone: 462996) and *Cola di Rienzo* (213 Via Cola di Rienzo; phone: 351816). Both are open nights.

Bring along a copy of any prescription you may have from your doctor in case you should need a refill. In the case of minor complaints, Italian pharmacists may do some prescribing and *may* fill a foreign prescription; however, do not count on this. In most cases, you will need a local doctor to rewrite the prescription. Even in an emergency, a traveler will more than likely be given only enough of a drug to last until a local prescription can be obtained.

Emergency assistance also is available from the various medical programs designed for travelers who have chronic ailments or whose illness requires them to return home:

International Association for Medical Assistance to Travelers (*IAMAT;* 417 Center St., Lewiston, NY 14092; phone: 716-754-4883). Entitles members to the services of participating doctors around the world, as well as clinics and hospitals in various locations. Participating physicians agree to adhere to a basic charge of around $40 to see a patient referred by *IAMAT.* To join, simply write to *IAMAT;* in about 3 weeks you will receive a membership card, the booklet of members, and an inoculation chart. A nonprofit organization, *IAMAT* appreciates donations; with a donation of $25 or more, you will receive a set of worldwide climate charts detailing weather and sanitary conditions. (Delivery can take up to 5 weeks, so plan ahead.)

International SOS Assistance (PO Box 11568, Philadelphia, PA 19116; phone: 800-523-8930 or 215-244-1500). Subscribers are provided with telephone access — 24 hours a day, 365 days a year — to a worldwide, monitored, multilingual network of medical centers. A phone call brings assistance ranging from a telephone consultation to transportation home by ambulance or aircraft, or, in some cases, transportation of a family member to wherever you are hospitalized. Individual rates are $35 for 2 weeks of coverage ($3.50 for each additional day), $70 for 1 month, or $240 for 1 year; couple and family rates also are available.

Medic Alert Foundation (2323 N. Colorado, Turlock, CA 95380; phone: 800-ID-ALERT or 209-668-3333). If you have a health condition that may not be readily perceptible to the casual observer — one that might result in a tragic error in an emergency situation — this organization offers identification emblems specifying such conditions. The foundation also maintains a computerized central file from which your complete medical history is available 24 hours a day by phone (the telephone number is clearly inscribed on the emblem). The onetime membership fee (between $25 and $45) is based on the type of metal from which the emblem is made — the choices range from stainless steel to 10K gold-filled.

TravMed (PO Box 10623, Baltimore, MD 21204; phone: 800-732-5309 or 301-296-5225). For $3 per day, subscribers receive comprehensive medical assistance while abroad. Major medical expenses are covered up to $100,000, and special transportation home or of a family member to wherever you are hospitalized is provided at no additional cost.

■ **Note:** Those who are unable to take a reserved flight due to personal illness or who must fly home unexpectedly due to a family emergency should be aware that airlines may offer a discounted airfare (or arrange a partial refund) if the traveler can demonstrate that his or her situation is indeed a legitimate emergency. Your inability to fly or the illness or death of an immediate family member usually must be substantiated by a doctor's note or the name, relationship, and funeral home from which the deceased will be buried. In such cases, airlines often will waive certain advance purchase restrictions or you may receive a refund check or voucher for future travel at a later date. Be aware, however, that this bereavement fare may not necessarily be the least expensive fare available and, if possible, it is best to have a travel agent check all possible flights through a computer reservations system (CRS).

 LEGAL AID AND CONSULAR SERVICES: There is one crucial place to keep in mind when outside the US, namely, the US Embassy and Consulate, which are located at 119/A and 121 Via Vittorio Veneto, respectively (phone: 46741).

If you are injured or become seriously ill, or if you encounter legal difficulties, the consulate is the first place to turn, although its powers and capabilities are limited. It will direct you to medical assistance and notify your relatives if you are ill; it can advise you of your rights and provide a list of lawyers if you are arrested, but it cannot interfere with the local legal process.

For questions about US citizens arrested abroad, how to get money to them, and other useful information, call the *Citizens' Emergency Center* of the Office of Special

Consular Services in Washington, DC, at 202-647-5225. (For further information about this invaluable hotline, see below.)

A consulate exists to aid US citizens in serious matters, such as illness, destitution, and the above legal difficulties. It is not there to aid in trivial situations, such as canceled reservations or lost baggage, no matter how important these matters may seem to the victimized tourist. If you should get sick, the US consul can provide names of doctors, dentists, local hospitals, and clinics; the consul also will contact family members in the US and help arrange special ambulance service for a flight home. In a situation involving "legitimate and proven poverty" of an US citizen stranded abroad without funds, the consul will contact sources of money (such as family or friends in the US), apply for aid to agencies in foreign countries, and in the last resort — which is *rarely* — arrange for repatriation at government expense, although this is a loan that must be repaid. And in case of natural disasters or civil unrest, consulates around the world handle the evacuation of US citizens if it becomes necessary.

As mentioned above, the US State Department operates a *Citizens' Emergency Center,* which offers a number of services to US citizens abroad and their families at home. In addition to giving callers up-to-date information on trouble spots, the center will contact authorities abroad in an attempt to locate a traveler or deliver an urgent message. In case of illness, death, arrest, destitution, or repatriation of an US citizen on foreign soil, it will relay information to relatives at home if the consulate is unable to do so. Travel advisory information is available 24 hours a day to people with touch-tone phones (phone: 202-647-5225). Callers with rotary phones can get information at this number from 8:15 AM to 10 PM (eastern standard time) on weekdays, 9 AM to 3 PM Saturdays. In the event of an emergency, this number also may be called during these hours. For emergency calls only, at all other times, call 202-634-3600 and ask for the duty officer.

Drinking and Drugs

 DRINKING: It is more than likely that some of the warmest memories of a trip to Rome will be moments of conviviality shared over a drink in a neighborhood bar or sunlit café. Visitors will find that liquor, wine, and brandies in Italy are distilled to the same proof and often are the same labels as those found at home.

Italian bars and cafés open at about 7 AM or earlier to serve coffee and breakfast, and most remain open until midnight. In Italy, there is no legal drinking age and eateries do not need a license to serve liquor. You may find it strange to see both bars and cafés serving up anything from coffee to cocktails, ice cream, and light meals.

As in the US, national taxes on alcohol affect the prices of liquor in Italy, and as a general rule, mixed drinks — especially imported liquors such as whiskey and gin — are more expensive than at home. If you like a drop before dinner, a good way to save money is to buy a bottle of your favorite brand at the airport before leaving the US and enjoy it in your hotel before setting forth.

Visitors to Italy may bring in 2 bottles of wine and 1 bottle of liquor per person duty-free. If you are buying any quantity of alcohol (such as a case of wine) in Italy and traveling through other European countries on your route back to the US, you will have to pass through customs and pay duty at each border crossing, so you might want to arrange to have it shipped home. Whether bringing it with you or shipping, you will have to pay US import duties on any quantity over the allowed 1 liter (see *Customs and Returning to the US,* in this section).

DRUGS: Illegal narcotics are as prevalent in Italy as in the US, but the moderate legal penalties and vague social acceptance that marijuana has gained in the US have no equivalents in Italy. Due to the international war on drugs, enforcement of drug laws is becoming increasingly strict throughout the world. Local European narcotics officers and customs officials are renowned for their absence of understanding and lack of a sense of humor — especially where foreigners are involved.

Opiates and barbiturates, and other increasingly popular drugs — "'white powder" substances like heroin, cocaine, and "crack" (the cocaine derivative) — continue to be of major concern to narcotics officials. Most European countries — including Italy — have toughened laws regarding illegal drugs and narcotics, and it is important to bear in mind that the type or quantity of drugs involved is of minor importance. Particularly for foreigners, the maximum penalties may be imposed for possessing even *traces* of illegal drugs. There is a high conviction rate in these cases, and bail for foreigners is rare. Persons arrested are subject to the laws of the country they are visiting, and there isn't much that the US consulate can do for drug offenders beyond providing a list of lawyers. The best advice we can offer is this: Don't carry, use, buy, or sell illegal drugs.

Those who carry medicines that contain a controlled drug should be sure to have a current doctor's prescription with them. Ironically, travelers can get into almost as much trouble coming through US customs with over-the-counter drugs picked up abroad that contain substances that are controlled in the US. Cold medicines, pain relievers, and the like often have codeine or codeine derivatives that are illegal, except by prescription, in the US. Throw them out before leaving for home.

■ **Be forewarned:** US narcotics agents warn travelers of the increasingly common ploy of drug dealers asking travelers to transport a "gift" or other package back to the US. Don't be fooled into thinking that the protection of US law applies abroad — accused of illegal drug trafficking, you will be considered guilty until you prove your innocence. In other words, do not, under any circumstances, agree to take anything across the border for a stranger.

Tipping

In Rome, as throughout Italy and most of the rest of Europe, you will find the custom of including some kind of service charge on the bill for a meal more common than in North America. This can confuse Americans unfamiliar with the custom. On the one hand, many a traveler, unaware of this policy, has left many a superfluous tip. On the other hand, travelers aware of this policy may make the mistake of assuming that it takes care of everything. It doesn't. While "service included" in theory eliminates any question about how much and whom to tip, in practice there still are occasions when on-the-spot tips are appropriate. Among these are tips to show appreciation for special services, as well as tips meant to say "thank you" for services rendered. So keep a pocketful of 1,000 lire bills (or coins) ready, and hand these out like dollar bills.

In Italian restaurants, the service charge *(servizio compreso)* is usually calculated in the prices listed; if not, it will be added to the final bill. For the most part, if you see a notation at the bottom of the menu (such as compreso or incluso), the charge should be included in the prices; otherwise, the service charge has not yet been added. To further confuse the issue, not every restaurant notes what its policy is. If you are at all unsure, ask a waiter.

This service charge generally ranges from 10% to 15%. In the rare instance where it isn't added, a 15% tip to the waiter — just as in the US — usually is a safe figure, although one should never hesitate to penalize poor service or reward excellent and efficient attention by leaving less or more. In Italy, the service charge usually goes to the restaurant, and it is a common practice to leave 5% to 10% (less if you're in a moderate restaurant, more in an expensive one).

Although it's not necessary to tip the maître d' of most restaurants — unless he has been especially helpful in arranging a special party or providing a table (slipping him something in a crowded restaurant *may* get you seated sooner or procure a preferred table) — when tipping is desirable or appropriate, the least amount should be the local equivalent of $5. In the finest restaurants, where a multiplicity of servers are present, plan to tip 5% to the captain. The sommelier (wine waiter) is entitled to a gratuity of approximately 10% of the price of the bottle.

As in restaurants, visitors usually will find a service charge of 10% to 15% included in their final bill at most Rome hotels (again, the service charge is usually included in their listed room rates). No additional gratuities are required — or expected — beyond this billed service charge. It is unlikely, however, that a service charge will be added to bills in small family-run guesthouses or other modest establishments. In these cases, guests should let their instincts be their guide; no tipping is expected by members of the family who own the establishment, but it is a nice gesture to leave something for others — such as a dining room waiter or a maid — who may have been helpful. A gratuity of around $1 per night is adequate in most cases.

If a hotel does not automatically add a service charge, it is perfectly proper for guests to ask to have an extra 10% to 15% added to their bill, to be distributed among those who served them. This may be an especially convenient solution in a large hotel, where it's difficult to determine just who out of a horde of attendants actually performed particular services.

For those who prefer to distribute tips themselves, a chambermaid generally is tipped at the rate of approximately $1 per day. Tip the concierge or hall porter for specific services only, with the amount of such gratuities dependent on the level of service provided. For any special service you receive in a hotel, a tip is expected — the current equivalent of $1 being the minimum for a small service.

Bellhops, doormen, and porters at hotels and transportation centers generally are tipped at the rate of $1 per piece of luggage, along with a small additional amount if a doorman helps with a cab or car. Once upon a time, taxi drivers in Europe would give you a rather odd look if presented with a tip for a fare, but times have changed, and 10% to 15% of the amount on the meter is now a standard gratuity.

Miscellaneous tips: Tipping ushers in a movie house, theater, or concert hall used to be the rule, but is becoming less common — the best policy is to check what other patrons are doing and follow suit. Most of the time, the program is not free, and in lieu of a tip it is common practice to purchase a program from the person who seats you. Sightseeing tour guides also should be tipped. If you are traveling in a group, decide together what you want to give the guide and present it from the group at the end of the tour. If you have been individually escorted, the amount paid should depend on the degree of your satisfaction, but it should not be less than 10% of the total tour price. Museum and monument guides also usually are tipped, and it is a nice touch to tip a caretaker who unlocks a small church or turns on the lights in a chapel.

In barbershops and beauty salons, tip as you would at home, keeping in mind that the percentages vary according to the type of establishment — 10% in the most expensive salons; 15% to 20% in less expensive establishments. (As a general rule, the person who washes your hair should get an additional small tip.) The washroom attendants in these places, or wherever you see one, should get a small tip — they usually set out a little plate with a coin already on it indicating the suggested denomination. Don't forget service station attendants, for whom a tip of around 50¢ for cleaning the windshield or other attention is not unusual.

Tipping always is a matter of personal preference. In the situations covered above, as well as in any others that arise where you feel a tip is expected or due, feel free to express your pleasure or displeasure. Again, never hesitate to reward excellent and efficient attention and to penalize poor service. Give an extra gratuity and a word of thanks when someone has gone out of his or her way for you. Either way, the more personal the act of tipping, the more appropriate it seems. And if you didn't like the service — or the attitude — don't tip.

Duty-Free Shopping and Value Added Tax

DUTY-FREE SHOPS: Note that at the time of this writing, because of the newly integrated European economy, there was some question as to the fate and number of duty-free shops that would be maintained at international airports in member countries of the European Economic Community (EEC). It appears, however, that those traveling between EEC countries and any country *not* a member of the Common Market will still be entitled to buy duty-free items. Since the United States is not a Common Market member, duty-free purchases by US travelers will, presumably, remain as they have been even after the end of 1992.

If common sense says that it always is less expensive to buy goods in an airport duty-free shop than to buy them at home or in the streets of a foreign city, travelers should be aware of some basic facts. Duty-free, first of all, does not mean that the goods travelers buy will be free of duty when they return to the US. Rather, it means that the shop has paid no import tax in acquiring goods of foreign make, because the goods are not to be used in the country where the shop is located. This is why duty-free goods are available only in the restricted, passengers-only area of international airports or are delivered to departing passengers on the plane. In a duty-free store, travelers save money only on goods of foreign make because they are the only items on which an import tax would be charged in any other store. There usually is no saving on locally made items, although in countries such as Italy that impose value added taxes (see below) that are refundable to foreigners, the prices in airport duty-free shops are minus this tax, sparing travelers the often cumbersome procedures they otherwise have to follow to obtain a VAT refund.

Beyond this, there is little reason to delay buying locally made merchandise and/or souvenirs until reaching the airport. In fact, because airport duty-free shops usually pay high rents, the locally made goods they sell may well be more expensive than they would be in downtown stores. The real bargains are foreign goods, but — let the buyer beware — not all foreign goods automatically are less expensive in an airport duty-free shop. You can get a good deal on even small amounts of perfume, costing less than the usually required minimum purchase, tax-free. Other fairly standard bargains include spirits, smoking materials, cameras, clothing, watches, chocolates, and other food and luxury items — but first be sure to know what these items cost elsewhere. Terrific savings do exist (they are the reason for such shops, after all), but so do overpriced items that an unwary shopper might find equally tempting. In addition, if you wait to do your shopping at airport duty-free shops, you will be taking the chance that the desired item is out of stock or unavailable.

Duty-free shops are located in most major international airports throughout Europe, including Rome.

VALUE ADDED TAX: Commonly abbreviated as VAT, this is a tax levied by various European countries, including Italy, and added to the purchase price of most goods and services. The standard VAT (known as IVA in Italy) is 19% on most purchases, but it can be as much as 30% on luxury items. However, the rate will likely be changed in 1992 when the Economic Community comes into effect. At press time, discussions were still being held to decide on one uniform VAT for all EC members.

The tax is intended for residents (and already is included in the price tag), but visitors are also required to pay it unless they have purchases shipped by the store directly to an address abroad. If visitors pay the tax and take purchases with them, however, they generally are entitled to a refund.

In order to qualify for a refund, you must make a single purchase of a minimum value of 625,000 lire (about $480 US at press time) — numerous purchases in one store or from several stores cannot be combined. In most cases, you must ask the store to provide a receipt and describe in full details the purchased item. This receipt must be stamped by the customs officer when you leave the country. Visitors leaving Italy must have all of their receipts for purchases and refund vouchers stamped by customs; as customs officials may well ask to see the merchandise, it's a good idea not to pack it in the bottom of your suitcase. Within 90 days from the date of original issue, a copy of that stamped receipt must be sent back to the store, which can then start the procedure for requesting a refund. Also, you can arrange with the store owner whether you wish to have the refund credited to your credit card or have a check sent to you.

Also note that at Malpensa Airport in Milan and Leonardo da Vinci Airport (better known as Fiumicino) in Rome you may be able to receive an on-the-spot cash VAT refund at desks near customs and passport control (an Italian customs official can direct you). There will be a small charge for this service, deducted from the refund.

A VAT refund by dollar check or by credit to a credit card account is relatively hassle-free. If it arrives in the form of a foreign currency check and if the refund is less than a significant amount, charges imposed by US banks for converting foreign currency refund checks — which can run as high as $15 or more — could make the whole exercise hardly worth your while.

Far less costly is sending your foreign currency check (after endorsing it) to *Ruesch International,* which will covert it to a check in US dollars for a $2 fee (deducted from the dollar check). Other services include commission-free traveler's checks and foreign currency, which can be ordered by mail. Contact *Ruesch International* at one of the following address: 191 Peachtree St., Atlanta, GA 30303 (phone: 404-222-9300); 3 First National Plaza, Suite 2020, Chicago, IL 60602 (phone: 312-332-5900); 1925 Century Park E., Suite 240, Los Angeles, CA 90067 (phone: 213-277-7800); 608 Fifth Ave., "Swiss Center," New York, NY 10020 (phone: 212-977-2700); and 1350 Eye St. NW, 10th Floor and street level, Washington, DC 20005 (phone: 800-424-2923 or 202-408-1200).

■ **Buyer Beware:** You may come across shops *not* at airports that call themselves duty-free shops. These require shoppers to show a foreign passport but are subject to the same rules as other stores, including paying import duty on foreign items. What "tax-free" means in the case of these establishments is something of an advertising strategy: They are announcing loud and clear that they do, indeed, offer the VAT refund service — sometimes on the spot (minus a fee for higher overhead). Prices may be no better at these stores, and could be even higher due to this service.

Customs and Returning to the US

Whether you return to the United States by air or sea, you must declare to the US Customs official at the point of entry everything you have bought or acquired while in Europe. The customs check can go smoothly, lasting only a few minutes, or can take hours, depending on the officer's instinct. To speed up the process, keep all your receipts handy and try to pack your purchases together in an accessible part of your suitcase. It might save you from unpacking all your belongings.

DUTY-FREE ARTICLES: In general, the duty-free allowance for US citizens returning from abroad is $400. This duty-free limit covers purchases that accompany you and are for personal use. This limit includes items used or worn while abroad, souvenirs for friends, and gifts received during the trip. A flat 10% duty based on the "fair retail value in country of acquisition" is assessed on the next $1,000 worth of merchandise brought in for personal use or gifts. Amounts above those two levels are dutiable at a variety of rates. The average rate for typical tourist purchases is about 12%, but you can find out about specific items by consulting *Tariff Schedules of the United States* in a library or at any US Customs Service office.

Families traveling together may make a joint declaration to customs, which permits one member to exceed his or her duty-free exemption to the extent that another falls short. Families also may pool purchases dutiable under the flat rate. A family of three, for example, would be eligible for up to a total of $3,000 at the 10% flat duty rate (after each member had used up his or her $400 duty-free exemption) rather than three separate $1,000 allowances. This grouping of purchases is extremely useful when considering the duty on a high-tariff item, such as jewelry or a fur coat.

Personal exemptions can be used once every 30 days; in order to be eligible, an individual must have been out of the country for more than 48 hours. If any portion of the exemption has been used once within any 30-day period or if your trip is less than 48 hours long, the duty-free allowance is cut to $25.

There are certain articles, however, that are duty-free only up to certain limits. The $25 allowance includes the following: 10 cigars (not Cuban), 60 cigarettes, and 4 ounces of perfume. Individuals eligible for the full $400 duty-free limit are allowed 1 carton of cigarettes (200), 100 cigars, and 1 liter of liquor or wine if the traveler is over 21. Alcohol above this allowance is liable for both duty and an Internal Revenue tax. Antiques, if they are 100 or more years old and you have proof from the seller of that fact, are duty-free, as are paintings and drawings if done entirely by hand.

To avoid paying duty twice, register the serial numbers of foreign-made watches and electronic equipment with the nearest US Customs bureau before departure; receipts of insurance policies also should be carried for other foreign-made items. (Also see the note at the end of *Entry Requirements and Documents,* in this section.)

Gold, gold medals, bullion, and up to $10,000 in currency or negotiable instruments may be brought into the US without being declared. Sums over $10,000 must be declared in writing.

The allotment for individual "unsolicited" gifts mailed from abroad (no more than one per day per recipient) is $50 retail value per gift. These gifts do not have to be declared and are not included in your duty-free exemption (see below). Although you should include a receipt for the purchases with each package, the examiner is empowered to impose a duty based on his or her assessment of the value of the goods. The duty owed is collected by the US Postal Service when the package is delivered (also see below). More information on mailing packages home from abroad is contained in the US Customs Service pamphlet *Buyer Beware, International Mail Imports* (see below for where to write for this and other useful brochures).

CLEARING CUSTOMS: This is a simple procedure. Forms are distributed by airline or ship personnel before arrival. (Note that a $5-per-person service charge — called a user fee — is collected by airlines to help cover the cost of customs checks, but this is included in the ticket price.) If your purchases total no more than the $400 duty-free limit, you need only fill out the identification part of the form and make an oral declaration to the customs inspector. If entering with more than $400 worth of goods, you must submit a written declaration.

Customs agents are businesslike, efficient, and not unkind. During the peak season, clearance can take time, generally because of the strain imposed by a number of jumbo jets simultaneously discharging their passengers, not because of unwarranted zealousness on the part of the customs people.

Efforts to streamline procedures used to include the so-called Citizens' Bypass Program, which allowed US citizens whose purchases were within their duty-free allowance to go to the "green line," where they simply showed their passports to the customs inspector. Although at the time of this writing this procedure still is being followed at some international airports in the US, most airports have returned to an earlier system. US citizens arriving from overseas now have to go through a passport check by the Immigration & Naturalization Service (INS) before recovering their baggage and proceeding to customs. (This additional wait will delay clearance on re-entry into the US, although citizens will not be on the same line as foreign visitors.) Although all passengers have to go through this passport inspection, those entering with purchases within the duty-free limit may be spared a thorough customs inspection. Inspectors still retain the right to search any luggage they choose, however, so don't do anything foolish.

It is illegal not to declare dutiable items; not to do so, in fact, constitutes smuggling, and the penalty can be anything from stiff fines and seizure of the goods to prison sentences. It simply isn't worth doing. Nor should you go along with the suggestions of foreign merchants who offer to help you secure a bargain by deceiving customs officials in any way. Such transactions frequently are a setup, using the foreign merchant as an agent of US customs. Another agent of US customs is TECS, the Treasury Enforcement Communications System, a computer that stores all kinds of pertinent information on returning citizens. There is a basic rule to buying goods abroad, and it should never be broken: *If you can't afford the duty on something, don't buy it.* Your list or verbal declaration should include all items purchased abroad, as well as gifts received abroad, purchases made at the behest of others, the value of repairs, and anything brought in for resale in the US.

Do not include in the list items that do not accompany you, i.e., purchases that you have mailed or had shipped home. These are dutiable in any case, even if for your own use and even if the items that accompany your return from the same trip do not exhaust your duty-free exemption. It is a good idea, if you have accumulated too much while abroad, to mail home any personal effects (made and bought in the US) that you no longer need rather than your foreign purchases. These personal effects pass through US Customs as "American goods returned" and are not subject to duty.

If you cannot avoid shipping home your foreign purchases, however, the US Customs Service suggests that the package be clearly marked "Not for Sale," and that a copy of the bill of sale be included. The US Customs examiner usually will accept this as indicative of the article's fair retail value, but if he or she believes it to be falsified or feels the goods have been seriously undervalued, a higher retail value may be assigned.

FORBIDDEN ITEMS: Narcotics, plants, and many types of food are not allowed into the US. Drugs are totally illegal, with the exception of medication prescribed by a physician. It's a good idea not to travel with too large a quantity of any given prescription drug (although, in the event that a pharmacy is not open when you need it, bring along several extra doses) and to have the prescription on hand in case any question arises either abroad or when re-entering the US.

Any sculpture that is part of an architectural structure, any authentic archaeological find, or other artifacts may not be exported from Italy without the permission of Beni Culturali e Ambientali (Ministry of Culture; 27 Via del Collegio Romano, Rome 00187; phone: 6-6723) or call Leonardo da Vinci Airport (phone: 601212) and ask for customs information. If you do not obtain prior permission of the proper regulatory agencies, such items will be confiscated at the border, and you will run the risk of being fined or imprisoned.

Tourists have long been forbidden to bring into the US foreign-made, US-trade-marked articles purchased abroad (if the trademark is recorded with customs) without written permission. It's now permissible to enter with one such item in your possession as long as it's for personal use.

The US Customs Service implements the rigorous Department of Agriculture regulations concerning the importation of vegetable matter, seeds, bulbs, and the like. Living vegetable matter may not be imported without a permit, and everything must be inspected, permit or not. Approved items (which do not require a permit) include dried bamboo and woven items made of straw; beads made of most seeds (but not jequirity beans — the poisonous scarlet and black seed of the rosary pea); cones of pine and other trees; roasted coffee beans; most flower bulbs; flowers (without roots); dried or canned fruits, jellies, or jams; polished rice, dried beans and teas; herb plants (not witchweed); nuts (but not acorns, chestnuts, or nuts with outer husks); dried lichens, mushrooms, truffles, shamrocks, and seaweed; and most dried spices.

Other processed foods and baked goods usually are okay. Regulations on meat products generally depend on the country of origin and manner of processing. As a rule, commercially canned meat, hermetically sealed and cooked in the can so that it can be stored without refrigeration, is permitted, but not all canned meat fulfills this requirement. Be careful when buying European-made pâté, for instance. Goose liver pâté in itself is acceptable, but the pork fat that often is part of it, either as an ingredient or a rind, may not be. Even canned pâtés may not be admitted for this reason. (The imported ones you see in US stores have been prepared and packaged according to US regulations.) So before stocking up on a newfound favorite, it pays to check in advance — otherwise you might have to leave it behind.

The US Customs Service also enforces federal laws that prohibit the entry of articles made from the furs or hides of animals on the endangered species list. Beware of shoes, bags, and belts made of crocodile and certain kinds of lizard, and anything made from tortoiseshell; this also applies to preserved crocodiles, lizards, and turtles sometimes sold in gift shops. And if you're shopping for big-ticket items, beware of fur coats made from the skins of spotted cats. They are sold in Europe, but they will be confiscated upon your return to the US, and there will be no refund. For information about other animals on the endangered species list, contact the Department of the Interior, US Fish and Wildlife Service (Publications Unit, 4401 N. Fairfax Dr., Room 130, Arlington, VA 22203; phone: 703-358-1711), and ask for the free publication *Facts About Federal Wildlife Laws.*

Also note that some foreign governments prohibit the export of items made from certain species of wildlife, and the US honors any such restrictions. Before you go shopping in any foreign country, check with the US Department of Agriculture (G110 Federal Bldg., Hyattsville, MD 20782; phone: 301-436-8413) and find out what items are prohibited by the country you will be visiting.

The US Customs Service publishes a series of free pamphlets with customs information. It includes *Know Before You Go,* a basic discussion of customs requirements pertaining to all travelers; *Buyer Beware, International Mail Imports; Travelers' Tips on Bringing Food, Plant, and Animal Products into the United States; Importing a Car; GSP and the Traveler; Pocket Hints; Currency Reporting; Pets, Wildlife, US Customs; Customs Hints for Visitors (Nonresidents);* and *Trademark Information for Travelers.* For the entire series or individual pamphlets, write to the US Customs Service (PO Box 7407, Washington, DC 20044) or contact any of the seven regional offices — in Boston, Chicago, Houston, Long Beach (California), Miami, New Orleans, and New York. The US Customs Service has a tape-recorded message whereby callers using Touch-Tone phones can get more information on various topics; the number is 202-566-8195. These pamphlets provide great briefing material, but if you still have questions when you're in Europe, contact the nearest US consulate.

Sources and Resources

Tourist Information Offices

North American branches of the Italian Government Travel Office generally are the best sources of travel information, and most of their many, varied publications are free for the asking. For the best results, request general information on specific provinces or cities, as well as publications relating to your particular areas of interest: accommodations, restaurants, special events, sports, guided tours, and facilities for specific sports. There is no need to send a self-addressed, stamped envelope with your request, unless specified. Following are the tourist information offices located in the US and Canada:

Chicago: 500 N. Michigan Ave., Chicago, IL 60611 (phone: 312-644-0990).
New York: 630 Fifth Ave., Suite 1565, New York, NY 10111 (phone: 212-245-4822).
San Francisco: 360 Post St., Suite 801, San Francisco, CA 94108 (phone: 415-392-6206).

The Italian Embassy and Consulates in the US

The Italian government maintains an embassy and a number of consulates in the US. One of their primary functions is to provide visas for certain resident aliens (depending on their country of origin) and for Americans planning to visit for longer than 6 months, or to study, reside, or work in Italy. Consulates also are empowered to sign official documents and to notarize copies or translations of US documents, which may be necessary for those papers to be considered legal in Italy.

The Italian Embassy is located at 1601 Fuller St. NW, Washington, DC 20009 (phone: 202-328-5500). Listed below are the Italian consulates in the US. In general, these offices are open 9 AM to 1 PM, Mondays through Fridays — call ahead to be sure.

Italian Consulates in the US
Boston: Italian Consulate-General, 100 Boylston St., Suite 900, Boston, MA 02116 (phone: 617-542-0483).
Chicago: Italian Consulate-General, 500 N. Michigan Ave., Chicago, IL 60611 (phone: 312-467-1550).
Detroit: Italian Consulate, Buhl Bldg., 535 Griswold, Suite 1840, Detroit, MI 48226 (phone: 313-963-8560).
Houston: Italian Consulate, 1300 Post Oak Rd., Suite 660, Houston, TX 77056 (phone: 713-850-7520).

Los Angeles: Italian Consulate-General, 12400 Wilshire Blvd., Suite 300, Los Angeles, CA 90025 (phone: 213-820-0622).

New Orleans: Italian Consulate, 630 Camp St., New Orleans, LA 70130 (phone: 504-524-2271).

New York: Italian Consulate, 690 Park Ave., New York, NY 10021 (phone: 212-737-9100).

Philadelphia: Italian Consulate-General, 421 Chestnut St., Philadelphia, PA 19106 (phone: 215-592-7329).

San Francisco: Italian Consulate-General, 2590 Webster St., San Francisco, CA 94115 (phone: 415-931-4924).

The Italian Cultural Institute (Istituto Italiano di Cultura) is the Italian Embassy's cultural arm abroad. It serves as a liaison between the American and Italian people and is an especially good source of information. There are five branches in the US:

Chicago: 500 N. Michigan Ave., Suite 530, Chicago, IL 60611 (phone: 312-822-9545).

Los Angeles: 12400 Wilshire Blvd., Suite 310, Los Angeles, CA 90025 (phone: 213-207-4737).

New York City: 686 Park Ave., New York, NY 10021 (phone: 212-879-4242).

San Francisco: 425 Bush St., Suite 305, San Francisco, CA 94108 (phone: 415-788-7142).

Washington, DC: 1601 Fuller St. NW, Washington, DC 20009 (phone: 202-328-5526).

The New York branch maintains a library of books, periodicals, and newspapers that is open to the public; San Francisco, too, has a small library, open to the public by appointment. A free booklet published three times a year lists cultural events in Italy — theater, folklore, cinema, and exhibitions. Copies are available on request from any of the offices listed above.

Theater and Special Event Tickets

 As you read this book, you will learn about events that spark your interest — everything from music festivals and special theater seasons to sporting championships — along with telephone numbers and addresses to which to write for descriptive brochures, reservations, or tickets. The Italian Government Travel Office can supply information on these and other special events and festivals that take place in Rome and the rest of Italy, though they cannot in all cases provide the actual program or detailed information on ticket prices.

Since many of these occasions often are fully booked well in advance, think about having your reservation in hand before you go. In some cases, tickets may be reserved over the phone and charged to a credit card, or you can send an international money order or foreign draft. If you do write, remember that any request from the US should be accompanied by an International Reply Coupon to ensure a response (send two of them for an airmail response). These international coupons, money orders, and drafts are available at US post offices.

For further information, write for the *European Travel Commission*'s extensive list of events scheduled for the entire year for its 24 member countries (including Italy). For a free copy, send a self-addressed, stamped, business-size (4 x 9½) envelope to "European Events," *European Travel Commission,* PO Box 1754, New York, NY 10185.

Books, Newspapers, Magazines, and Newsletters

BOOKS: Throughout GETTING READY TO GO, numerous books and brochures have been recommended as good sources of further information on a variety of topics.

Suggested Reading – The list below is made up of books we have seen and think worthwhile; it is by no means complete — but meant merely to start you on your way. These titles include some informative guides to special interests, solid fictional tales, and books that call your attention to things you might not notice otherwise.

Travel

Italian Days, by Barbara Grizutti Harrison (Houghton-Mifflin; $12.95).

Italian Gardens, by Alex Ramsey and Helena Attlee (Seven Hills Books; $19.95).

Italy: The Places in Between, by Kate Simon (HarperCollins; $12.95, paperback).

Playing Away, by Michael Mewshaw (Holt; $9.95).

When in Rome: The Humanists' Guide to Italy, by S.J. Perelman (Catbird Press; $9.95).

History, Biography, and Culture

The Agony and the Ecstasy, by Irving Stone (Doubleday hardcover, $19.95; NAL paperback, $5.95).

The Architecture of the Italian Renaissance, by Peter Murray (Schocken; $10.95).

The Art of the Renaissance, by Linda and Peter Murray (World of Art Series, Thames and Hudson; $11.95).

Autobiography, by Benvenuto Cellini (Penguin Classics; $5.95).

Christopher Columbus, by Gianni Granzotto (University of Oklahoma Press; $11.95).

The Civilization of the Renaissance in Italy, by Jacob Burckhardt (HarperCollins; Vol. 1: $6.95; Vol. 2: $7.95).

A Concise Encyclopedia of the Italian Renaissance, edited by J. R. Hale (World of Art Series, Thames and Hudson; $11.95).

The Decline and Fall of the Roman Empire, by Edward Gibbon (Penguin; $6.95).

The Diary of the First Voyage of Christopher Columbus, edited by Oliver Dunn and James E. Kelly, Jr. (University of Oklahoma Press; $65 hardcover, $24.95 paperback).

Four Voyages of Christopher Columbus, by Cecil Jane (Dover Publications; $12.-95).

The High Renaissance and Mannerism, by Linda Murray (World of Art Series, Thames and Hudson; $11.95).

History of Italian Renaissance Art: Painting, Sculpture, Architecture, by Frederick Hartt (Abrams; $55).

The Italians, by Luigi Barzini (Atheneum; $9.95).

The Last Italian Portrait of a People, by William Murray (Prentice Hall Press; $21.95).

The Prince, by Niccolò Machiavelli (Prometheus Books; $3.95).

The Romans, by R. H. Barrow (Penguin; $5.95).

Roman Art and Architecture, by Mortimer Wheeler (World of Art Series, Thames and Hudson; $11.95).

The Story of Art, by E. H. Gombrich (Prentice Hall; $36.67).

Literature

Crown of Columbus, by Michael Dorris and Louise Erdrich (HarperCollins; $22).

The Evening of the Holiday, by Shirley Hazzard (Penguin; $6.95).

The Marshall and the Madwomen, by Magdalen Nabb (Penguin; $3.95).

The Name of the Rose, by Umberto Eco (Warner Books; $5.95).

Summer's Lease, by John Mortimer (Penguin; $7.95).

Food, Wine, and Shopping

Celebrating Italy, by Carol Field (William Morrow; $24.95).

The Classic Italian Cook Book and More Classic Italian Cooking, by Marcella Hazan (Knopf hardcover, $25; Ballantine paperback; $5.95).

Eating In Italy: A Traveler's Guide to the Gastronomic Pleasures of Northern Italy, by Faith Heller Willinger (Morrow; $12.45).

The Food of Italy, by Waverley Root (Vintage; $10.95).

Honey from a Weed, by Patience Gray (North Point Press; $15.95).

Italian Wine, by Victor Hazan (Knopf; $18.95).

Italy the Beautiful Cookbook, by Lorenza de Medici (Knapp Press; $39.95).

Made in Italy: A Shopper's Guide to Rome, Florence, Venice, and Milan, by Annie Brody and Patricia Schultz (Workman Publishers; $14.95).

Marling Menu-Master for Italy, by Clare F. and William E. Marling (Altarinda Books; $5.95).

Pasta Classica, by Julia Della Croce (Penguin; $25).

Simon & Schuster's Guide to Italian Wines (Simon & Schuster; $8.95, paperback).

The Wine Atlas of Italy, by Burton Anderson (Simon & Schuster; $40).

Wines of Italy, by David Gleave (Price Stearn; $12.95).

In addition, *Culturgrams* is a handy series of pamphlets that provide a good sampling of information on the people, cultures, sights, and bargains to be found in over 90 countries around the world. Each four-page, newsletter-size leaflet covers one country, and Italy is included in the series. The topics included range from customs and courtesies to lifestyles and demographics. These fact-filled pamphlets are published by the David M. Kennedy Center for International Studies at Brigham Young University; for an order form contact the group c/o Publication Services (280 HRCB, Provo, UT 84602; phone: 801-378-6528). When ordering from 1 to 5 *Culturgrams,* the price is $1 each; 6 to 49 pamphlets cost 50¢ each; and for larger quantities, the price per copy goes down proportionally.

Another source of cultural information is *Do's and Taboos Around the World,* compiled by the Parker Pen Company and edited by Roger E. Axtell. It focuses on protocol, customs, etiquette, hand gestures and body language, gift giving, the dangers of using US jargon, and so on, and can be fun to read even if you're not going anyplace. It's available for $10.95 in bookstores or through John Wiley & Sons, 1 Wiley Dr., Somerset, NJ 08875 (phone: 212-850-6418).

NEWSPAPERS AND MAGAZINES: A subscription to the *International Herald Tribune* is a good idea for dedicated travelers. This English-language newspaper is written and edited mostly in Paris and is *the* newspaper read most regularly and avidly by Americans abroad to keep up with world news, US news, sports, the stock market (US and foreign), fluctuations in the exchange rate, and an assortment of help-wanted ads, real estate listings, and personals, global in scope. Published 6 days a week (no Sunday paper), it is available at newsstands throughout the US and in cities worldwide. It can be found on most newsstands in Rome, and larger hotels usually have copies in the lobby for guests — if you don't see a copy, ask the hotel concierge if it is available. A 1-year subscription in the US costs $349. To subscribe, write or call the Subscription Manager, *International Herald Tribune,* 850 Third Ave., 10th Floor, New York, NY 10022 (phone: 800-882-2884 or 212-752-3890).

Among the major US publications that can be bought (generally a day or two after distribution in the US) in many of the larger cities, such as Rome, at hotels, airports, and newsstands, are the *The New York Times, USA Today,* the *Wall Street Journal,* and the *Washington Post.* As with other imports, expect these and other US publications to cost considerably more in Italy than in the US.

Before or after your trip, you may want to subscribe to *Italy Italy.* Issued 6 times a year, this magazine is full of beautifully illustrated travel articles. Subscriptions are available for $30 a year from *Speedimpex,* 45-45 39th St., Long Island City, NY 11104 (phone: 718-392-7477).

NEWSLETTERS: Throughout GETTING READY TO GO we have mentioned specific newsletters that our readers may be interested in consulting for further information. One of the very best sources of detailed travel information is *Consumer Reports Travel Letter.* Published monthly by Consumers Union (PO Box 53629, Boulder, CO 80322-3629; phone: 800-999-7959), it offers comprehensive coverage of the travel scene on a wide variety of fronts. A year's subscription costs $37; 2 years, $57.

In addition, the following travel newsletters provide useful up-to-date information on travel services and bargains:

Entree (PO Box 5148, Santa Barbara, CA 93150; phone: 805-969-5848). This newsletter caters to a sophisticated, discriminating traveler with the means to explore the places mentioned. Subscribers have access to a 24-hour hotline providing information on restaurants and accommodations around the world. Monthly; a year's subscription costs $59.

Travel Smart (Communications House, 40 Beechdale Rd., Dobbs Ferry, NY 10522; phone: 914-693-8300 in New York; 800-327-3633 elsewhere in the US). This monthly covers a wide variety of trips and travel discounts. A year's subscription costs $44.

■ **Computer Services:** Anyone who owns a personal computer and a modem can subscribe to a database service providing everything from airline schedules and fares to restaurant listings. Two such services of particular use to travelers are *CompuServe* (5000 Arlington Center Blvd., Columbus, OH 43220; phone: 800-848-8199 or 614-457-8600; $39.95 to join, plus usage fees of $6 to $12.50 per hour) and *Prodigy Services* (445 Hamilton Ave., White Plains, NY 10601; phone: 800-822-6922 or 914-993-8000; $12.95 per month's subscription, plus variable usage fees). Before using any computer bulletin-board services, be sure to take precautions to prevent downloading of a computer "virus." First install one of the programs designed to screen out such nuisances.

Weights and Measures

 When traveling in Italy, you'll find that just about every quantity, whether it is length, weight, or capacity, will be expressed in unfamiliar terms. In fact, this is true for travel almost everywhere in the world, since the US is one of the last countries to make its way to the metric system. Your trip to Rome may serve to familiarize you with what one day may be the weights and measures at your grocery store.

There are some specific things to keep in mind during your trip. Fruits and vegetables at a market are recorded in kilos (kilograms), as is your luggage at the airport and your body weight. (This latter is particularly pleasing to people of significant size, who instead of weighing 220 pounds hit the scales at a mere 100 kilos.) A kilo equals 2.2

pounds and 1 pound is .45 kilo. Body temperature is measured in degrees centigrade or Celsius rather than on the Fahrenheit scale, so that a normal body temperature is 37C, not 98.6F, and freezing is 0 degrees C rather than 32F.

Gasoline is sold by the liter (approximately 3.8 liters to 1 gallon). Tire pressure gauges and other equipment measure in kilograms per square centimeter rather than pounds per square inch. Highway signs are written in kilometers rather than miles (1 mile equals 1.6 kilometers; 1 kilometer equals .62 mile). And speed limits are in kilometers per hour, so think twice before hitting the gas when you see a speed limit of 100. That means 62 miles per hour.

The tables and conversion factors listed below should give you all the information you will need to understand any transaction, road sign, or map you encounter during your travels.

CONVERSION TABLES
METRIC TO US MEASUREMENTS

Multiply:	by:	to convert to:
LENGTH		
millimeters	.04	inches
meters	3.3	feet
meters	1.1	yards
kilometers	.6	miles
CAPACITY		
liters	2.11	pints (liquid)
liters	1.06	quarts (liquid)
liters	.26	gallons (liquid)
WEIGHT		
grams	.04	ounces (avoir.)
kilograms	2.2	pounds (avoir.)

US TO METRIC MEASUREMENTS

LENGTH		
inches	25.0	millimeters
feet	.3	meters
yards	.9	meters
miles	1.6	kilometers
CAPACITY		
pints	.47	liters
quarts	.95	liters
gallons	3.8	liters
WEIGHT		
ounces	28.0	grams
pounds	.45	kilograms

TEMPERATURE

$$°F = (°C \times 9/5) + 32 \qquad °C = (°F - 32) \times 5/9$$

APPROXIMATE EQUIVALENTS		
Metric Unit	**Abbreviation**	**US Equivalent**
LENGTH		
meter	m	39.37 inches
kilometer	km	.62 mile
millimeter	mm	.04 inch
CAPACITY		
liter	l	1.057 quarts
WEIGHT		
gram	g	.035 ounce
kilogram	kg	2.2 pounds
metric ton	MT	1.1 tons
ENERGY		
kilowatt	kw	1.34 horsepower

USEFUL WORDS AND PHRASES

Useful Words and Phrases

Unlike the French, who have a reputation for being snobbish and brusque if you don't speak their language perfectly, the Italians do not expect you to speak Italian — but are very flattered when you try. In many circumstances, you won't have to, because staffs at most hotels and tourist attractions, as well as at a fair number of restaurants, speak serviceable English, or at least a modicum of it, which they usually are eager to improve — and that means practicing on you. If you find yourself in a situation where your limited Italian is the only means of communication, take the plunge. Don't be afraid of misplaced accents or misconjugated verbs. (Italians themselves often lapse into the all-purpose infinitive form of the verb when speaking with a novice.) In most cases you will be understood and then will be advised on the menu, or pointed in the right direction. The list on the following pages is a selection of commonly used words and phrases to speed you on your way.

Note that in Italian, nouns are either masculine or feminine, as well as singular or plural, and the adjectives that modify them must correspond. Most nouns ending in *o* are masculine; the *o* becomes an *i* in the plural. The masculine articles are *un* (indefinite), *il* (definite singular), and *i* (definite plural), except before words beginning with the *s* sound (however spelled) and with *i* + vowel, where they are *uno, lo,* and *gli.* Most nouns ending in *a* are feminine; the *a* becomes *e* in the plural. The feminine articles are *una* (indefinite), *la* (definite singular), and *le* (definite plural). Final vowels or articles usually are contracted to an apostrophe (') before words beginning with vowels, as in *l'acqua* (the water). Singular nouns ending in *e* can be either masculine or feminine; *e* becomes *i* in the plural. Adjectives follow the nouns they modify.

Italy has several markedly different regional dialects, each with its own vocabulary and pronunciation rules. There is, however, a relatively generally accepted standard used on national radio and television and understood, if not used, by almost everybody. Traditional spelling reflects standard pronunciation fairly well. These suggestions should help you pronounce most words intelligibly.

> *i* is pronounced as in *machine.*
>
> *e* is pronounced with a sound somewhere between the vowels of *let* and *late.* It is never diphthongized, as in *lay.* Final *e* is never silent.
>
> *a* is pronounced as in *father.*
>
> *o* is pronounced with a sound somewhere between the vowels of *ought* and *boat.* It is never diphthongized, as in *know.*
>
> *u* is pronounced as in *rude.*

In vowel letter sequences, both vowels are pronounced; *i* and *u* before vowels usually are pronounced *y* and *w,* respectively.

Italian consonants are pronounced as in English with these exceptions:

> Consonants spelled double are pronounced double. Compare the *k* sounds of blacker (single consonant) and black cur (double consonant), and the *d* sounds of the Italian *cade* (he falls) and *cadde* (he fell).

p and *t* are unaspirated; that is, they are pronounced as in *spit* and *stop*, not as in *pit* and *top*.

t and *d* are dental; the tongue tip touches the upper teeth, not the gums.

s before a vowel or between a vowel and a voiced consonant *(b, d, g, v, m, n, l, r)* is pronounced *z*.

ci stands for *ch* (as in English *chip*), as does *c* before *e* or *i*: *ciao!* is pronounced *chow*.

gh always stands for *g*, as in English *ghost*.

gi stands for *j*, as does *g* before *e* or *i*: *buon giorno* is pronounced *bwon jorno*.

gn stands for the medial consonant of English *canyon*: *bagno* (bath) is pronounced *banyo*.

gl stands for the medial consonant of English *billion*: *gli* (pronoun and article) is pronounced *lyee*.

h is never pronounced.

q is pronounced as *k*; *qu* is pronounced *kw*: *cinque* (five) is pronounced *chinkweh*.

r is "rolled," as it is in Spanish or Scots.

z is pronounced *dz* word initially; within words it is pronounced either *dz* or *ts*, depending on the word.

More often than not, the vowel preceding the last consonant in the word is accented. Final vowels marked with an accent are stressed.

These are only the most basic rules, and even they may seem daunting at first, but they shouldn't remain so for long. Nevertheless, if you can't get your mouth to speak Italian, try your hands at it: With a little observation, you'll pick it up quickly and be surprised at how often your message will get across.

Greetings and Everyday Expressions

Good morning!

(also, Good day!)	*Buon giorno!*
Good evening!	*Buona sera!*
Hello!	
(familiar)	*Ciao!*
(on the telephone)	*Pronto!*
How are you?	*Come sta?*
Pleased to meet you!	*Piacere!* or *Molto lieto/a!*
Good-bye!	*Arrivederci!*
(final)	*Addio!*
So long! (familiar)	*Ciao!*
Good night!	*Buona notte!*
Yes!	*Sì!*
No!	*No!*
Please!	*Per favore* or *per piacere!*
Thank you!	*Grazie!*
You're welcome!	*Prego!*
Excuse me!	
(I beg your pardon.)	*Mi scusi!*
(May I get by?; on a bus or in a crowd)	*Permesso!*
I don't speak Italian.	*Non parlo italiano.*
Do you speak English?	*Parla inglese?*

Is there someone there who speaks English?	*C'è qualcuno che parla inglese?*
I don't understand.	*Non capisco.*
Do you understand?	*Capisce?*

My name is . . .	*Mi chiamo . . .*
What is your name?	*Come si chiama?*
miss	*signorina*
madame	*signora*
mister	*signor(e)*

open	*aperto*
closed	*chiuso*
. . .for annual vacation	*chiuso per ferie*
. . .for weekly day of rest	*chiuso per riposo settimanale*
. . .for restoration	*chiuso per restauro*
Is there a strike?	*C'è uno sciopero?*
Until when?	*Fino a quando?*

entrance	*entrata*
exit	*uscita*
push	*spingere*
pull	*tirare*

today	*oggi*
tomorrow	*domani*
yesterday	*ieri*

Checking In

I would like. . .	*Vorrei. . .*
I have reserved. . .	*Ho prenotato. . .*
a single room	*una camera singola*
a double room	*una camera doppia*
a quiet room	*una camera tranquilla*
with private bath	*con bagno privato*
with private shower	*con doccia privata*
with air conditioning	*con aria condizionata*
with balcony	*con balcone/terrazza*
for one night	*per una notte*
for a few days	*per qualche giorno*
for a week	*per una settimana*
with full board	*con pensione completa*
with half board	*con mezza pensione*

Does the price include. . .	*Il prezzo comprende. . .*
breakfast	*la prima colazione*
service charge	*servizio*
taxes	*tasse*

What time is breakfast served?	*A che ora si serve la prima colazione?*
It doesn't work.	*Non funziona.*

May I pay with traveler's
checks?   *Posso pagare con traveler's checks?*

Do you accept this credit
card?   *Accettate questa carta di credito?*

Shopping

bakery	*il panificio*
bookstore	*la libreria*
butcher shop	*la macelleria*
camera shop	*il negozio d'apparecchi fotografici*
delicatessen	*la salumeria/la pizzicheria*
department store	*il grande magazzino*
drugstore (for medicine)	*la farmacia*
grocery	*la drogheria/la pizzicheria*
jewelry store	*la gioielleria*
newsstand	*l'edicola/il giornalaio*
pastry shop	*la pasticceria*
perfume (and cosmetics) store	*la profumeria*
shoestore	*il negozio di scarpe*
supermarket	*il supermercato*
tobacconist	*il tabaccaio*

cheap	*a buon mercato*
expensive	*caro/a*
large	*grande*
larger	*più grande*
too large	*troppo grande*
small	*piccolo/a*
smaller	*più piccolo*
too small	*troppo piccolo*
long	*lungo/a*
short	*corto/a*
antique	*antico/a*
old	*vecchio/a*
new	*nuovo/a*
used	*usato/a*
handmade	*fatto/a a mano*
washable	*lavabile*

How much does it cost?	*Quanto costa?*
What is it made of?	*Di che cosa è fatto/a?*
camel's hair	*pelo di cammello*
cotton	*cotone*
corduroy	*velluto a coste*
lace	*pizzo*
leather	*pelle/cuoio*
linen	*lino*
silk	*seta*
suede	*pelle scamosciata*
synthetic material	*materiale sintetico*
wool	*lana*

brass	*ottone*
bronze	*bronzo*

copper	*rame*
gold	*oro*
gold plate	*placcato d'oro*
silver	*argento*
silver plate	*placcato d'argento*
stainless steel	*acciaio inossidabile*
wood	*legno*

Colors

beige	*beige*
black	*nero/a*
blue	*celeste* or *azzurro/a*
(navy)	*blu*
brown	*marrone*
gray	*grigio/a*
green	*verde*
orange	*arancio*
pink	*rosa*
purple	*viola*
red	*rosso/a*
white	*bianco/a*
yellow	*giallo/a*
dark	*scuro/a*
light	*chiaro/a*

Getting Around

north	*nord*
south	*sud*
east	*est*
west	*ovest*
right	*destra*
left	*sinistra*
straight ahead	*sempre diritto*
far	*lontano/a*
near	*vicino/a*
gas station	*la stazione di rifornimento/stazione per benzina*
train station	*la stazione ferroviaria*
bus stop	*la fermata dell'autobus*
subway	*la metropolitana*
airport	*l'aeroporto*
travel agency	*l'agenzia di viaggio*
map	*una carta geografica*
one-way ticket	*un biglietto di sola andata*
round-trip ticket	*un biglietto di andata e ritorno*
track	*il binario*
first class	*prima classe*
second class	*seconda classe*
no smoking	*non fumare/divieto di fumare*
tires	*le gomme/i pneumatici*
oil	*l'olio*

gasoline
  generic reference or
    regular (leaded) gas   *la benzina*
  unleaded gas   *benzina verde* or *benzina senza piombo*
  diesel gas   *diesel* or *gasolio*
Fill it up, please.   *Faccia il pieno, per favore.*

Where is . . . ?   *Dov'è . . . ?*
Where are . . . ?   *Dove sono . . . ?*
How many kilometers are
  we from . . . ?   *Quanti chilometri siamo da . . . ?*
Does this bus go to . . . ?   *Quest'autobus va a . . . ?*
What time does it leave?   *A che ora parte?*

Danger	*Pericolo*
Dead End	*Strada Senza Uscita*
Detour	*Deviazione*
Do Not Enter	*Vietato l'Accesso*
Falling Rocks	*Caduta Massi*
Men Working	*Lavori in Corso*
No Parking	*Divieto di Sosta*
No Passing	*Divieto di Sorpasso*
One Way	*Senso Unico*
Pay Toll	*Pagamento Pedaggio*
Pedestrian Zone	*Zona Pedonale*
Reduce Speed	*Rallentare*
Ring Road	*Raccordo Anulare*
Stop	*Alt*
Use Headlights in Tunnel	*Accendere i Fari in Galleria*
Yield	*Dare la Precedenza*

Personal Items and Services

aspirin	*l'aspirina*
Band-Aids	*i cerotti*
barbershop	*il barbiere*
beauty shop	*l'istituto di bellezza*
condom	*il profilattico/il preservativo*
dry cleaner	*la tintoria*
hairdresser	*il parucchiere per donna*
laundromat	*la lavanderia automatica*
laundry	*la lavanderia*
post office	*l'ufficio postale*
sanitary napkins	*gli assorbenti igienici*
shampoo	*lo shampoo*
shaving cream	*la crema da barba*
shoemaker	*il calzolaio*
soap	*il sapone*
soap powder	*il sapone in polvere*
stamps	*i francobolli*
tampons	*i tamponi*
tissues	*i fazzoletti di carta*
toilet	*il gabinetto/la toletta/il bagno*

toilet paper	*la carta igienica*
toothbrush	*lo spazzolino da denti*
toothpaste	*il dentifricio*

Where is the men's/ladies' room?	*Dov'è la toletta?*
The door will say:	
for men	*Uomini* or *Signori*
for women	*Donne* or *Signore*
Is it occupied/free?	*E occupato/libero?*

Days of the Week

Monday	*lunedì*
Tuesday	*martedì*
Wednesday	*mercoledì*
Thursday	*giovedì*
Friday	*venerdì*
Saturday	*sabato*
Sunday	*domenica*

Months

January	*gennaio*
February	*febbraio*
March	*marzo*
April	*aprile*
May	*maggio*
June	*giugno*
July	*luglio*
August	*agosto*
September	*settembre*
October	*ottobre*
November	*novembre*
December	*dicembre*

Numbers

zero	*zero*
one	*uno*
two	*due*
three	*tre*
four	*quattro*
five	*cinque*
six	*sei*
seven	*sette*
eight	*otto*
nine	*nove*
ten	*dieci*
eleven	*undici*
twelve	*dodici*
thirteen	*tredici*
fourteen	*quattordici*
fifteen	*quindici*
sixteen	*sedici*
seventeen	*diciassette*

eighteen	*diciotto*
nineteen	*diciannove*
twenty	*venti*
thirty	*trenta*
forty	*quaranta*
fifty	*cinquanta*
sixty	*sessanta*
seventy	*settanta*
eighty	*ottanta*
ninety	*novanta*
one hundred	*cento*

Eating Out

ashtray	*un portacenere*
bottle	*una bottiglia*
chair	*una sedia*
cup	*una tazza*
fork	*una forchetta*
knife	*un coltello*
napkin	*un tovagliolo*
plate	*un piatto*
spoon	*un cucchiaio*
table	*una tavola*
beer	*una birra*
cocoa	*una cioccolata*
coffee	*un caffè* or *un espresso*
coffee with milk (served in a bar with steamed milk)	*un cappuccino*
(usually served at breakfast or at a bar, with warm milk — more than is in a cappuccino)	*un caffè latte*
fruit juice	*un succo di frutta*
lemonade	*una limonata*
mineral water	*acqua minerale*
carbonated	*gassata*
not carbonated	*non gassata*
orangeade	*un'aranciata*
tea	*un tè*
water	*acqua*
red wine	*vino rosso*
rosé wine	*vino rosato*
white wine	*vino bianco*
cold	*freddo/a*
hot	*caldo/a*
sweet	*dolce*
(very) dry	*(molto) secco*
bacon	*la pancetta*
bread/rolls	*il pane/i panini*

butter	*il burro*
eggs	*le uova*
hard-boiled	* un uovo sodo*
poached	* uova affogate/in camicia*
soft-boiled	* uova à la coque*
scrambled	* uova strapazzate*
sunny-side up	* uova fritte all'occhio di bue*
honey	*il miele*
jam/marmalade	*la confettura/la marmellata*
omelette	*la frittata*
orange juice	*la spremuta d'arancia*
pepper	*il pepe*
salt	*il sale*
sugar	*lo zucchero*
Waiter!	*Cameriere!*
I would like. . .	*Vorrei. . .*
a glass of	* un bicchiere di*
a bottle of	* una bottiglia di*
a half bottle of	* una mezza bottiglia di*
a carafe of	* una caraffa di*
a liter of	* un litro di*
a half liter of	* un mezzo litro di*
a quarter liter of	* un quarto di*
The check, please.	*Il conto, per favore.*
Is the service charge included?	*Il servizio è incluso?*

Pasta Shapes

round or semicircular ravioli	*agnolotti*
small rings used in soup	*anellini*
small pockets, usually stuffed	*anolini*
large stuffed tubes	*cannelloni*
angel's hair — extra-thin spaghetti	*capelli d'angelo*
little hats	*cappelletti*
short curly noodles	*cavatelli*
ridged shells	*conchiglie*
crêpes	*crespelle*
bows	*farfalle*
flat, straight noodles	*fettuccine*
spirals	*fusilli*
potato dumplings	*gnocchi*
very wide, flat pasta, used in layers	*lasagna*
narrow, flat spaghetti	*linguine*
general term for hollow pasta	*maccheroni*
little ears	*orecchiette*
barley shape; looks like rice	*orzo*
broad noodles	*pappardelle*
green pasta made with spinach	*pasta verde*
quills	*penne*

stuffed squares	*ravioli*
large grooved tubes	*rigatoni*
corkscrews	*rotini*
stars	*stelline*
flat noodles	*tagliatelle*
stuffed rings	*tortellini*
large stuffed rings	*tortelloni*
little tubes	*tubetti*
squiggly thin spaghetti	*vermicelli*
large grooved macaroni	*ziti*

THE CITY

ROME

If you're traveling from the north, you'll quickly understand why *Italia meridionale,* or southern Italy, begins in Rome: ancient stone ruins basking in the southern sun, baroque swirls teasing the senses at every turn, religious art exploding with color and Catholic sensuality — celebrating life with the conspicuous joie de vivre (here known as *gioia di vivere*) of southern Europe. Rome reaches out to your senses, blinding you with colors, beckoning you to stay. Its appeal is gripping and obviously romantic, inspiring throughout history many an illustrious northern visitor — such as Goethe, Keats, Byron, and Shelley — though today these romantic souls might be repelled by the insufferable noise, the screaming traffic, the exasperating strikes, political demonstrations, and general chaos of modern Rome. Yet despite the familiar symptoms of contemporary blight, Rome remains the Eternal City, ancient capital of the Western world, and center of Christianity for nearly 2,000 years.

Rome lies roughly in the center of the region of Lazio (Latium), just below the knee of boot-shaped Italy, between the Tyrrhenian Sea to the west and the Apennine Mountains to the east. The Tiber River gently curves through the city, with ancient Rome on its east bank, Vatican City and Trastevere (*tras* means across; *tevere,* Tiber) on its west. The original seven hills of Rome are all on the left bank, as is its modern center — the shopping areas that surround Piazza di Spagna (the so-called Spanish Steps), Piazza del Popolo, Via del Corso, Via del Tritone, and the legendary Via Veneto, celebrated in Fellini's film *La Dolce Vita.*

The 3rd-century Aurelian Walls still surround ancient Rome as well as most of papal and modern Rome. The city is unique because its fine buildings span so many centuries of history. There are Etruscan and ancient Roman remains, the most famous of which are the Colosseum and the Forum; buildings from the early Christian period such as the Castel Sant'Angelo; and a wealth of dazzling Renaissance and baroque architecture — from St. Peter's itself to Piazza del Campidoglio, the square designed by Michelangelo. The city abounds in churches, palaces, parks, piazze, statues, and fountains — all of which sparkle in the golden light and clear blue sky of the region.

Rome's beginnings are shrouded in a romantic legend that attributes the city's birth to Romulus and Remus, twin sons of the war god Mars and Rhea, a Vestal Virgin, who encountered Mars in a forest one day. The babies, left to die on the shore of the Tiber River at the foot of the Palatine Hill, were rescued and suckled through infancy by an old she-wolf and grew up to lead a band of adventurers and outlaws. Romulus, the stronger leader of the two, is said to have founded Rome in 753 BC, killing his brother to become its first king.

But earlier traces of habitation have been found on the Palatine Hill — one of the original seven hills — the site of Roma Quadrata, a primitive Rome squared off by a surrounding rectangular wall. Below were the shallows of the Tiber River, where flocks of animals crossed, and trading took place in earlier times. The traditional founding date perhaps refers to when the first settlements of shepherds and farmers on the Palatine took on the shape of a city and the Latins, Sabines, and Etruscans who peopled the area had fused under one system of laws. The name *Roma* was probably a derivation of *Ruma,* an Etruscan noble name.

Following a succession of seven legendary kings, a republic was declared in 509 BC, and a period of expansion began. By 270 BC or so, the entire Italian peninsula was under the protection of Rome, and the resulting political unification brought about a cultural unity as well, a new Roman style in art and literature. Hannibal's defeat at Zama in 201 BC, an event that brought the Second Punic War to an end, prepared the way for further expansion: Rome's dominion over the Mediterranean and its eventual supremacy over Alexander the Great's empire in the East and over Spain and Gaul in the West.

A long period of civil war ended with Julius Caesar's defeat of Pompey in 48 BC, but the brilliant conqueror of Gaul was assassinated in the Senate 4 years later. His great-nephew and heir, Octavian, continued in the victorious vein, becoming, with the honorific name of Augustus, Rome's first emperor and one of its best administrators. Augustus is said to have found Rome a city of brick and to have left it a city of marble; the Theater of Marcellus and the Mausoleum of Augustus are among his many fine constructions that survive today.

The reign of Augustus (27 BC–AD 14) saw Roman civilization at its peak, and it ushered in 2 centuries of peace known as the Pax Romana. Wherever they went, the Romans introduced brilliant feats of engineering and architecture, as well as their own culture, government, and law. Persecution of the Christians, which had begun as early as Nero's reign — he blamed the burning of Rome on the new sect and executed large numbers of them in AD 64 — came to an end in the early 4th century, when Constantine the Great issued the Edict of Milan, guaranteeing freedom of worship for all religions. But Rome by now had become top-heavy with its own administration; the empire was divided in 395, with an eastern section in Byzantium (with its capital at Constantinople, now Istanbul). This was the beginning of the end.

Rome's grandeur had long passed by the 5th century, when a series of economic crises, internal decadence and corruption, and repeated barbarian invasions led to the final fall of the empire with the deposition of her last emperor, Romulus Augustulus, in 476.

Thus began the Dark Ages, fraught with struggles between the empire and the church, which was centered in the papacy at Rome. Struggles between empire and papacy ensued. The Holy See, under Pope Clement V, actually fled Rome in the 14th century, taking up residence in Avignon, France, for 70 years. During that period, the city of Rome declined, and its population, which had been as many as a million at the time of Augustus, shrank to less than 50,000. The Capitoline Hill and once-bustling Roman Forum became pastures for goats and cows. Sheep grazed in St. Peter's.

The popes returned in 1377, and Rome again became the capital of the

Catholic world. Under papal patronage it was soon reborn artistically and culturally. During the 15th century, restoration of St. Peter's began, prior to its complete reconstruction; the Vatican complex was built; and new palaces, churches, and well-planned streets changed the face of the city. Powerful popes commissioned artists and architects to beautify Rome, and their genius created sumptuous palaces, splendid villas, and squares adorned with fountains and obelisks, until a second city grew out of the ruins of ancient Rome to match its former splendor. The 17th century brought the birth of baroque Rome, with its dominating figure, the architect, sculptor, and painter Gian Lorenzo Bernini, whose masterpieces perhaps still best symbolize the spirit of this magnificent and undeniably theatrical city.

The comfortable security of the popes was shaken by the arrival of Napoleon Bonaparte in 1798. He soon set up a republic of Rome, deporting Pope Pius VI briefly to France, and in 1805 he was crowned King of Italy, proclaiming Rome a sort of second capital of the French Empire. In 1809, Napoleon declared the papal territories a part of France and in return was excommunicated by Pope Pius VII, who was deported to Fontainebleau. By 1815, the Napoleonic regime had collapsed, the papal kingdom was reconciled with France, and the pope was back in Rome, but the sparks of nationalistic passion had already been ignited in Italian hearts.

Friction between papal neutralism and patriotic fervor drove Pope Pius IX out of Rome to Gaeta in 1848. In 1849, Rome was again proclaimed a republic, under the leadership of patriot Giuseppe Mazzini. Twice the French tried to restore the temporal power of the pope in Rome, meeting strong resistance from Republican forces led by Garibaldi. Finally, in 1870, the Italians entered Rome through a breach in the Aurelian Walls at Porta Pia and incorporated the city into the kingdom of Italy. That act dissolved the pontifical state and made Italian unity complete. A year later, Rome became the capital of the kingdom.

Mussolini's march on Rome in 1922 began the infamous Fascist regime that lasted until his downfall some 20 years later. The city was then occupied by the Germans until its liberation in 1944 by the Allies. In 1946, a referendum was held and Italy was declared a republic — just as it had been nearly 2½ millennia earlier.

Today, Rome is still the capital of Italy and of the Catholic church, as well as the home of some 3.5 million people (up from 260,000 inhabitants in 1870). Many Romans are employed in tourism-related industries and in government — in a city often strangled by bureaucratic problems. Besides filmmaking (in its cinematic heyday, Rome was called "Hollywood on the Tiber") and a certain amount of printing, there is some small-scale production of foodstuffs, pharmaceuticals, building materials, armaments, plastics, glass, clothing, religious articles, and handmade crafts. Thousands of artisans work in *botteghe* (shops) that open onto the streets in the area around Piazza Navona and in Trastevere.

For a society with significant problems — insufficient housing, impossible traffic, a soaring cost of living, and worrisome pollution — today's Romans still enjoy a relaxed way of life, as they have done for centuries. Perhaps nowhere north of Naples is the *arte di arrangiarsi* — the art of making do, or surviving with style — learned with such skill and practiced with such a timeless sense of resignation.

The *dolce vita* nightlife, more a figment of Fellini's imagination than a reality for any more than a handful of rich and/or famous Romans, has become subdued, but an unmistakable air of conviviality still prevails.

Not even soaring prices have limited the traditional Roman pastime of lingering lunches and late-night dinners at the city's 5,000 or so restaurants and trattorie. A sunny day at any time of the year still fills the cobblestone squares with diners at open-air eateries. They usually are engaged in animated conversation over their robust Roman food and inexpensive carafe wine from the Castelli (the surrounding hill towns such as Frascati). Most visitors are pleased to "do as the Romans do." No sense worrying about high prices and pollution if the inhabitants don't.

Roma, Non Basta Una Vita (Rome, A Lifetime Is Not Enough), by the late Italian author and journalist Silvio Negro, hints, with justification, at the impossibility of ever knowing everything about this city. For visitors who harbor the illusion of having seen all the ruins, churches, and monuments of Rome's glorious past, it may be time to begin discovering her countless hidden treasures, best done by walking the back streets and alleyways of the historic center (cars have limited access to many of them). Returning visitors will notice a spruced-up look — there are newly renovated palazzi everywhere, painted in the pale pastels popular in the early years of this century. And the *1990 World Cup* soccer games spurred on some transportation improvements as well — a new tram line and an efficient train service from Fiumicino Airport to downtown Rome.

If you feel suffocated by city life, try a day or two in the neighboring countryside. The surrounding Lazio region, sandwiched between the Tyrrhenian Sea and the Apennines, offers seaside resorts, rolling hills topped by medieval towns, picturesque lakes, rivers, and green meadows studded with umbrella pines, cypress trees, and wildflowers. Take an organized excursion to the Villa d'Este and Hadrian's Villa in Tivoli; to the Castelli Romani, or Roman hill towns, where the pope has his summer home; or to the excavations of Ostia Antica, the ancient port of Rome.

But take time to sit back and enjoy Rome. Visit the Forum and the Colosseum by day, and return at night when the ruins are bathed in gentler light to meditate over the rise and fall of ancient Rome. Watch the play of water in the Trevi Fountain or any of Rome's nearly 1,000 other fountains of every size and shape. See the ancient Roman Theater of Marcellus, which has been a Roman amphitheater, a medieval fort, a Renaissance palace, and which now contains apartments. Enjoy the savory cooking of the Lazio region. Ride a rented bicycle or jog in the Villa Borghese. Sip an *aperitivo* on the famed Via Veneto or at one of the many *caffès* that suddenly appear in unexpected corners of the historic city center.

Locally it is believed that on the last day of the world, while all the rest of humankind broods and repents, the Romans will throw a great farewell party, a gastronomic feast to end them all, with wine flowing from the city's many fountains. With the apocalypse not yet at hand, and despite the agonies besetting the country at large, the Eternal City remains eternally inviting.

ROME AT-A-GLANCE

SEEING THE CITY: Enjoy the magnificent view of all of Rome and the surrounding hill towns from Piazzale Garibaldi at the top of the Gianicolo (Janiculum hill). It's best at sunset. Another panorama is visible from the top of St. Peter's dome. For a view of Rome dominated by St. Peter's, go to the terrace of the Pincio, next to the Villa Borghese, above Piazza del Popolo. And the most unusual view is of the dome of St. Peter's as seen in miniature through the keyhole of the gate to the priory of the Knights of Malta, on Piazza dei Cavalieri di Malta at the end of Via di Santa Sabina, on the Aventine hill. The picturesque piazza was designed by engraver Piranesi, a surrealist in spirit though he lived in the 18th century. For a real treat, a bird's-eye view of Rome is available via helicopter. Leaving from the Centro Sperimentale d'Aviazione at Urbe Airport (825 Via Salaria; phone: 812-3017), the $125 per-person fee yields 15 minutes of breathtaking spectacle. (Minimum of five passengers; reserve 1 week in advance.)

SPECIAL PLACES: Rome cannot be seen in a day, 3 days, a week, or even a year. If your time is limited to a few days, an organized bus tour is your best bet. (A quick and interesting one covers some 45 major sights in 3 hours. Although there is no guide, a short brochure gives the highlights. It leaves Piazza dei Cinquecento at 3:30 PM, in winter at 2:30 PM, and costs about $6. Check the *ATAC* booth in the square for bus No. 110; it operates daily in season, only on weekends out of season.) The Dutch Roman Catholic sisters of Foyer Unitas (30 Via Santa Maria dell'Anima; phone: 686-5951) lead free (though an offering is appreciated) tours to many sites around the city and the Vatican, and give slide presentations on various subjects (not always religious in nature). In addition, they offer information about Rome to anyone who drops in. Walking tours (usually in English) generally take place on Tuesdays, Thursdays, and some Saturdays. Then, when you've seen where your interests lie, grab your most comfortable walking shoes and a map. Most of historic Rome, which also is the city's center today, is within the 3rd-century Aurelian Walls and is delightfully walkable. For more information on walking tours see DIRECTIONS.

For practical purposes, the "must sees" below are divided into ancient, papal, and modern Rome, but elements of two or all three categories often are found in one site — such as a sleek modern furniture shop in a Renaissance palace built with stones from the Colosseum. A further heading focuses on the palaces, fountains, splendid piazzas, and streets of Rome. The ancient center of the city is very close to Piazza Venezia, the heart of the modern city, and most of the sights of ancient Rome are around the Capitoline, Palatine, and Aventine hills. They can be seen on foot — though they were not built — in 1 day. Much of papal Rome is centered in the Vatican, but since all of Rome is a religious center, some of its many fascinating and beautiful churches are included under this heading. (For other churches, and for museums not mentioned below, see "Museums" in *Sources and Resources*.) Two bits of trivia worth noting: Throughout Rome, you will come across the initials *SPQR,* which stand for *Senatus Populusque Romanus* (the senate and the people of Rome). Ancient Romans used these letters to distinguish public works from private holdings, and as part of the city's inheritance they are still to be seen today — on everything from a magnificent monument to a mundane manhole cover. What's more, there really are seven hills of ancient Rome, and for the record they are called the Palatine, Capitoline, Quirinal, Viminal, Esquiline, Caelian, and the Aventine.

Virtually all the museums, monuments, and archaeological sites run by the state or city are closed on Sunday afternoons, and many on Mondays. Opening and closing hours change often (some are closed indefinitely because of strikes, personnel shortages, or restorations — it is estimated that only a third of Italy's artworks are exhibited), so check with your hotel, the tourist office, or the daily newspapers before starting out. Where possible, we have listed hours that seem relatively reliable.

Warning: Pickpockets work all around the city, but are especially numerous on such bus lines as the No. 56 to Via Veneto, and the Nos. 62 and 64 to the Vatican, and at the most popular tourist spots, even though plainclothes police scour these areas. Watch out especially for gangs of Gypsy children who will surround you and make straight for your wallet or purse. They haunt the Tiber bridges and the quayside walk to Porta Portese. Carry your shoulder bag on the arm *away* from passing vehicular traffic to avoid bag snatchers on motor scooters. Do not hang purses on café or restaurant chairs. Avoid carrying your passport and any significant amount of money around with you, and be sure to store valuables in a hotel safe-deposit box.

ANCIENT ROME

Colosseo (Colosseum) – It's said that when the Colosseum falls, Rome will fall — and the world will follow. This symbol of the eternity of Rome, the grandest and most celebrated of all its monuments, was completed in AD 80, and it is a logical starting point for a visitor to ancient Rome. See it in daylight, and return to see it by moonlight. The enormous arena, one-third of a mile in circumference and 137 feet high, once accommodated 50,000 spectators. To provide shade in the summer, a special detachment of sailors stretched a great awning over the top. There were 80 entrances (progressively numbered, except for the four main ones), allowing the crowds to quickly claim their marble seats. Underneath were subterranean passages where animals and apparatus were hidden from view. In the arena itself, Christians were thrown to lions, wild beasts destroyed one another, and gladiators fought to the death. Gladiatorial combats lasted until 404, when Honorius put an end to them (possibly after a monk had thrown himself into the arena in protest and was killed by the angry crowd); animal combats were stopped toward the middle of the 6th century.

The Colosseum was abused by later generations. It was a fort in the Middle Ages; something of a quarry during the Renaissance, when its marble and travertine were used in the construction of St. Peter's and other buildings; and in the 18th century it even became a manure depot for the production of saltpeter. Yet it remains a symbol of the grandeur of Rome. Open daily. Admission charge for the upper level. Piazzale del Colosseo. For more information about the Colosseum and its surrounding sites, see *Walk 4: Memorable Monuments — From the Colosseum to a Keyhole* in DIRECTIONS.

Palatino (Palatine Hill) – Adjacent to the Colosseum and the Roman Forum, the Palatine is where Rome began. Its Latin name is the source of the word "palace." In fact, great men — Cicero, Crassus, Marc Antony — lived on this regal hill, and the Emperors of Rome — Augustus, Tiberius, Caligula, Nero, Domitian, Septimius Severus — built their palaces here, turning the hill into an imperial preserve. A 12th-century author called the spot the "palace of the Monarchy of the Earth, wherein is the capital seat of the whole world." In ruins by the Middle Ages, the ancient structures were incorporated into the sumptuous Villa Farnese in the 16th century, and the Farnese Gardens were laid out, the first botanical gardens in the world.

The Palatine is a lovely spot for a walk or a picnic. See especially the so-called House of Livia (actually of her husband, Augustus), with its remarkable frescoes; Domitian's Palace of the Flavians, built by his favorite architect, Rabirius; the impressive stadium; the view from the terrace of the Palace of Septimius Severus; and the remains of the Farnese Gardens at the top, with another superb panorama of the nearby Forums. Closed Tuesdays; admission charge includes the Roman Forum. Enter at Via di San Gregorio or by way of the Roman Forum on Via dei Fori Imperiali.

Foro Romano (Roman Forum) – Adjoining the Palatine Hill is the Roman Forum, a mass of ruins overgrown with weeds and trees that was the commercial, civil, and religious center of ancient Rome. Its large ceremonial buildings included three triumphal arches, two public halls, half a dozen temples, and numerous monuments and statues. Set in what was once a marshy valley at the foot of the Capitoline Hill, the Forum was abandoned after the barbarian invasions and had become a cattle pasture by the Renaissance. When excavations began during the last century, it was under 20 feet of dirt.

Highlights of the Forum include the triumphal Arch of Septimius Severus, built by that emperor in AD 203; the Arch of Titus (AD 81), adorned with scenes depicting the victories of Titus, especially his conquest of Jerusalem and the spoils of Solomon's Temple; the ten magnificent marble columns — with a 16th-century baroque façade — of the Temple of Antoninus and Faustina; the eight columns of the Temple of Saturn (497 BC), site of the *Saturnalia,* the precursor of our *Mardi Gras;* three splendid Corinthian columns of the Temple of Castor and Pollux (484 BC); the Temple of Vesta and the nearby House of the Vestal Virgins, where highly esteemed virgins guarded the sacred flame of Vesta and their virginity — under the threat of being buried alive if they lost the latter. The once imposing Basilica of Maxentius (Basilica di Massenzio), otherwise known as the Basilica of Constantine, because it was begun by one and finished by the other, still has imposing proportions: 328 by 249 feet. Only the north aisle and three huge arches remain of this former law court and exchange.

As this is one of the most bewildering archaeological sites, a guide is extremely useful, especially for short-term visitors. A detailed plan and portable sound guide are available (in English) at the entrance. Open from 9 AM to one hour before sunset. Closed Mondays. Admission charge includes the Palatine Hill. Entrance on Via dei Fori Imperiali, opposite Via Cavour.

Fori Imperiali (Imperial Forums) – Next to the Roman Forum and now divided in two by Via dei Fori Imperiali is the civic center begun by Caesar to meet the demands of the expanding city when the Roman Forum became too congested. It was completed by Augustus, with further additions by later emperors. Abandoned in the Middle Ages, the Imperial Forums were revived by Mussolini, who constructed Via dei Fori Imperiali in 1932.

Two of the major sights are Trajan's Forum and Trajan's Market. Trajan's Forum, although not open to visitors, can be seen from the sidewalk surrounding it. It is memorable for the formidable 138-foot-high Trajan's Column, composed of 19 blocks of marble, now beautifully restored. The column is decorated with a spiral frieze depicting the Roman army under Trajan during the campaign against the Dacians — some 2,500 figures climbing toward the top where, since 1588, a statue of St. Peter has stood instead of the original one of Trajan. The Market (entered at 94 Via IV Novembre) is a 3-story construction with about 150 shops and commercial exchanges, some newly restored. Admission charge for Trajan's Market (closed Sunday afternoons and Mondays). Via dei Fori Imperiali.

Carcere Mamertino (Mamertine Prison) – Just off Via dei Fori Imperiali between the Roman Forum and the Campidoglio is the prison where the Gallic rebel leader Vercingetorix died and where, according to legend, St. Peter was imprisoned by Nero and used a miraculous spring to baptize his fellow inmates. From 509 to 27 BC it was a state prison where many were tortured and slaughtered. Much later, the prison became a chapel consecrated to St. Peter (called San Pietro in Carcere). To Charles Dickens it was a "ponderous, obdurate old prison . . . hideous and fearsome to behold." The gloomy dungeons below, made of enormous blocks of stone, are among the oldest structures in Rome. Via San Pietro in Carcere off Via dei Fori Imperiali.

Circo Massimo (Circus Maximus) – A few ruins dot the open grassy valley that once was the site of the great 4th-century BC arena. Originally one-third of a mile long and big enough to accommodate 250,000 spectators, the horseshoe shape of this racetrack served as a pattern for the other circuses that later arose in the Roman world. Today, the obelisks that decorated a long central shelf can be seen in Rome's Piazza del Laterano and Piazza del Popolo. The medieval tower that still stands is one of the few remains of the great fortresses built by the Frangipane family. Behind the Palatine Hill. For more information, see *Walk 4: Memorable Monuments — From the Colosseum to a Keyhole* in DIRECTIONS.

Pantheon – This, the best preserved of Roman buildings, was founded in 27 BC by Agrippa, who probably dedicated it to the seven planetary divinities, and rebuilt by Hadrian in AD 125. It became a Christian church in 606 and contains the tombs of Raphael and the first two Kings of Italy. The building is remarkable for its round plan combined with a Greek-style rectangular porch of 16 Corinthian columns (three were replaced in the Renaissance), for the ingenuity evident in the construction of the dome, and for its balanced proportions (the diameter of the interior and the height of the dome are the same). Closed Mondays. No admission charge. Piazza della Rotonda. For more information, see *Walk 1: From Kings to Countesses — Pantheon and Piazza Navona* in DIRECTIONS.

Terme di Caracalla (Baths of Caracalla) – These ruins are in the southern part of the city, near the beginning of the Appia Antica. Built in the 3rd century, they accommodated 1,600 bathers, but all that's left are sun-baked walls and some wall paintings. The vast scale makes a picturesque ruin, however, and Shelley composed "Prometheus Unbound" here. Operas are staged here in the summer. Baths are open from 9 AM to one hour before sunset. Admission charge. Enter on Viale delle Terme di Caracalla, just short of Piazzale Numa Pompilio. For more information, see *Quintessential Rome* in DIVERSIONS and *Walk 10: The Appian Way* in DIRECTIONS.

Porta San Sebastiano (St. Sebastian Gate) – This majestic opening in the 3rd-century Aurelian Walls (which encircle the city of Rome for 12 miles, with 383 defense towers) marks the beginning of the Appia Antica. It was, in fact, originally called the Porta Appia, and was rebuilt in the 5th century and restored again in the 6th century. Every Sunday morning, guided tours walk along the walls from Porta San Sebastiano to Porta Latina, affording good views of the Baths of Caracalla, the Appia Antica, and the Alban hills in the distance. The *Museo delle Mura* (Museum of the Walls), incorporated into the two medieval towers of the gate, contains local archaeological finds. Open Tuesdays through Saturdays from 9 AM to 1:30 PM; Tuesdays, Thursdays, and Saturdays from 4 to 7 PM; and Sundays from 9 AM to 1 PM. Admission charge. 18 Porta San Sebastiano (phone: 788-7035).

Via Appia Antica (Appian Way) – Portions of this famous 2,300-year-old road are still paved with the well-laid stones of the Romans. By 190 BC the Appian Way extended all the way from Rome to Capua, Benevento, and Brindisi on Italy's southeastern coast. Although its most famous sights are the Catacombs (see below), many other interesting ruins are scattered along the first 10 miles (16 km) of the route, which were used as a graveyard by patrician families because Roman law forbade burial (but not cremation) within the walls. Among the sights worth seeing is the Domine Quo Vadis chapel, about a half mile beyond Porta San Sebastiano. It was built in the mid-9th century on the site where St. Peter, fleeing from Nero, had a vision of Christ. St. Peter said, "Domine quo vadis?" ("Lord, whither goest thou?"). Christ replied that he was going back to Rome to be crucified again because Peter had abandoned the Christians in a moment of danger. Peter then returned to Rome to face his own martyrdom. Also see the Tomb of Cecilia Metella, daughter of a Roman general, a very picturesque ruin not quite 2 miles (3 km) from Porta San Sebastiano. Open daily from 9 AM to 1:30 PM. Admission charge. For more information, see *Walk 10: The Appian Way* in DIRECTIONS.

Catacombe di San Callisto (Catacombs of St. Calixtus) – Of all the catacombs in Rome, these are the most famous. Catacombs are burial places in the form of galleries, or tunnels — miles of them, arranged in as many as 5 tiers — carved under-

ground. Marble or terra cotta slabs mark the openings where th
rest. Early Christians hid, prayed, and were buried in them fro
4th centuries. After Christianity became the official religion
longer necessary, but they remained places of pilgrimage l
remains of so many early martyrs. St. Cecilia, St. Eusebius, .
are buried here. Take a guided bus tour or a public bus. At the ca.
are often priests, conduct regular tours in several languages. Close
Admission charge. 110 Via Appia Antica.

Terme di Diocleziano (Baths of Diocletian) – West of the center of Rome, .
far from the train station, are the largest baths in the empire, built in AD 305 to hold
3,000 people. The site now houses both the Church of Santa Maria degli Angeli,
adapted by Michelangelo from the hall of the tepidarium of the baths, and the *Museo
Nazionale Romano delle Terme* (National Museum of Rome of the Baths). One of the
great archaeological museums of the world, it contains numerous objects from ancient
Rome — paintings, statuary, stuccowork, bronzes, objets d'art, and even a mummy of
a young girl. Admission charge to the museum, which is open Tuesdays through
Saturdays from 9 AM to 1:45 PM and Sundays from 9 AM to 1 PM. The church is on
Piazza della Repubblica; the museum entrance is on Piazza dei Cinquecento (phone:
460530).

Castel Sant'Angelo – Dramatically facing the 2nd-century Ponte Sant'Angelo (St.
Angelo Bridge — lined with statues of angels, including two originals by Bernini), this
imposing monument was built by Hadrian in AD 139 as a burial place for himself and
his family, but it has undergone many alterations, including the addition of the square
wall with bastions at each corner named after the four evangelists. Later, as a fortress
and prison, it saw a lot of history, especially in the 16th century. Some of the victims
of the Borgias met their end here, popes took refuge here from antipapal forces (an
underground passage connects it to the Vatican), and Benvenuto Cellini spent time as
a prisoner on the premises. The last act of Puccini's opera *Tosca* takes place here. It
is now a museum containing relics, works of art, ancient weapons, a prison cell, and
a recently restored, 300-year-old papal bathtub. Open Mondays from 2 to 7:30 PM,
Tuesdays through Saturdays from 9 AM to 7:30 PM, Sundays and holidays from 9 AM
to 1 PM. Admission charge. Lungotevere Castello.

Teatro di Marcello (Theater of Marcellus) – Begun by Caesar, completed by
Augustus, and named after the latter's nephew, this was the first stone theater in
Rome and was said to have been the model for the Colosseum. It seated from 10,000
to 14,000 spectators and was in use for over 300 years. During the Middle Ages,
what remained of the edifice became a fortress, and during the 16th century, the
Savelli family transformed it into a palace, which later passed to the powerful Orsini
family. The sumptuous apartments at the top still are inhabited by the Orsinis, whose
emblem of a bear (*orso*) appears on the gateway in Via di Monte Savello, where the
theater's stage once stood. Via del Teatro di Marcello. The palace can be visited only
with a permit from City Hall: *Comune di Roma,* Ripartizione X, 29 Via del Portico
d'Ottavia. For more information, see *Walk 7: Medieval Rome — Pilgrims and Perils*
in DIRECTIONS.

Largo Argentina – Just west of Piazza Venezia are the remains of four Roman
temples, which, still unidentified, are among the oldest relics in Rome. It was at this
site that Julius Caesar actually was assassinated (the Senate was meeting here temporar-
ily because of fire damage to the Forum). The area, also the home of Rome's largest
stray cat colony, is slated for much-needed archaeological excavation and restoration.
Corso Vittorio Emanuele II.

Piramide di Caio Cestio (Pyramid of Gaius Cestius) – In the southern part of
the city, near the Protestant cemetery, is Rome's only pyramid. Completely covered
with white marble, 121 feet high, it has a burial chamber inside decorated with frescoes
and inscriptions. (*Note:* The interior can be visited only with special permission from

intendenza Comunale ai Musei, Monumenti, 3 Piazza Caffarelli.) Piazzale
.se.

PAPAL ROME

Città del Vaticano (Vatican City) – The Vatican City State, the world's second-smallest country (the smallest is also in Rome, the Sovereign Military Order of Malta, on Via Condotti), fits into a land area of less than 1 square mile within the city of Rome. Headquarters of the Roman Catholic church, the Vatican has been an independent state under the sovereignty of the pope since the Lateran Treaties were concluded in 1929. The Vatican has its own printing press and newspaper (*Osservatore Romano*), its own currency, railway, and radio station, as well as its own post office and postage stamps (thriving right now, with the surrounding Italian post offices functioning so badly, so do all your mailing from here! Vatican stamps may be used in Rome but not elsewhere in Italy, while Italian stamps may *not* be used in Vatican mailboxes). Souvenir packets of stamps can be purchased at the Philatelic Service in the office building on the left side of St. Peter's Church, entered under the Arch of the Bells. The Vatican's extraterritorial rights cover the other major basilicas (Santa Maria Maggiore, San Giovanni in Laterano, and San Paolo Fuori le Mura), the pope's summer home at Castel Gandolfo, and a few other buildings. It is governed politically by the pope and protected by an army of Swiss Guards (since 1506, when the corps was formed by Pope Julius II) whose uniforms were designed by Raphael. The changing of the guards takes place daily — at 9:30 and 11 AM, and 12:30, 2, 3:30, 4:30, and 5:30 PM.

General audiences are held by the pope every Wednesday on St. Peter's Square (at 10 AM during the summer; 11 AM in winter); in bad weather they are held in the Sala Udienza Paolo VI. Special audiences can be arranged for groups of 25 to 50 persons. Given John Paul II's propensity for travel, however, it is a good idea to check on his whereabouts before trekking off to the Vatican to see him. To arrange for free tickets to papal audiences, write to Bishop Dino Monduzzi (Prefettura della Casa Pontificia, Vatican City 00120, Italy). Be sure to include your address in Rome. Reservations will be confirmed by mail before the audience, but tickets will be delivered by messenger the day before. Last-minute bookings can be made in person from 9 AM to noon, up to 24 hours in advance, space permitting. They are available at the Prefettura office, located at the bronze doors of the right wing of the colonnade of St. Peter's Square.

Guided tours in English are offered year-round of Vatican City, including the underground excavations, the gardens, the Sistine Chapel, and the radio station. Sign up at the Ufficio Scavi (Excavations Office; near the Arch of the Bells; phone: 698-5318) for a 90-minute tour of the pre-Constantine necropolis in the Vatican, where it is believed that St. Peter is buried (closed Sundays; admission charge). Book a tour of the gardens at the *Vatican Tourist Information Office* (on the left side of St. Peter's Square, facing the church; phone: 698-4866). They are offered daily except Wednesdays and Sundays, from 10 AM to noon; in English on Thursdays. Admission charge. Also ask at the information office about tours of the Sistine Chapel (or make prior arrangements for a group visit through a travel agency). Weekdays from 8:30 AM to 1 PM, there is a free 1-hour tour of Vatican Radio (3 Piazza Pia; phone: 698-34643), which broadcasts in 33 languages to 100 countries. Tickets also are available through Foyer Unitas (30 Via Santa Maria dell'Anima; phone: 686-5951) and Santa Susanna Catholic Church (14 Via XX Settembre; phone: 482-7510). Visits to the famous *Vatican Mosaic Workshop,* a school where students have been making miniature and full-size mosaic pictures for centuries, can be arranged by writing to Mons. Virgilio Noe (*Studio del Mosaico Vaticano,* Vatican City 00120, Italy; phone: 698-4466).

Piazza San Pietro (St. Peter's Square) – This 17th-century architectural masterpiece was created by Gian Lorenzo Bernini, the originator of the baroque style in Rome. The vast, open area is elliptical, with two semicircular colonnades, each four deep in

Doric columns, framing the façade of St. Peter's Basilica. The colonnades are surmounted with statues of saints. An 83½-foot obelisk, shipped in a specially made boat from Heliopolis to Rome by Caligula, marks the center of the square and is flanked by two fountains that are still fed by the nearly 4-century-old Acqua Paola aqueduct, which brings water from just north of Rome. Find the circular paving stone between the obelisk and one of the fountains and turn toward a colonnade: From that vantage point it will appear to be only a single row of columns.

Basilica di San Pietro (St. Peter's Basilica) – The first church here was built by Constantine on the site where St. Peter was martyred and subsequently buried. Some 11 centuries later it was the worse for wear, so renovation and then total reconstruction were undertaken. Michelangelo deserves a great deal of the credit for the existing church, but not all of it: Bramante began the plans in the early 16th century, with the dome of the Pantheon in mind; Michelangelo finished them in mid-century, thinking of Brunelleschi's dome in Florence. Giacomo della Porta took over the project at Michelangelo's death, actually raising the dome by the end of the century. In the early 17th century, Carlo Maderno made some modifications to the structure and completed the façade, and by the middle of the century Bernini was working on his colonnades. Open daily in summer from 7 AM to 7 PM, in winter from 7 AM to 6 PM. The vast dome of St. Peter's is visible from nearly everywhere in the city, just as the entire city is visible from the summit of the dome. For a fee, a visitor may go up into the dome by elevator, then take a staircase to the top for a panoramic view of Rome or a bird's-eye view of the pope's backyard. Also inside the basilica is the *Museo Storico* (Historical Museum; phone: 698-3410), which houses part of the Vatican's treasures. The dome and museum are open daily in summer from 8:30 AM to 5:30 PM, in winter from 8:30 AM to 4:30 PM. No admission charge.

The door farthest to the right of the portico is the Holy Door, opened and closed by the pope at the beginning and end of each *Jubilee Year,* usually only four times a century. The door farthest to the left is by the modern Italian sculptor Giacomo Manzù and dates from the 1960s. Among the treasures and masterpieces inside the basilica are the famous *Pietà* by Michelangelo (now encased in bulletproof glass since its mutilation and restoration in 1972); the *Baldacchino* by Bernini, a colossal baroque amalgam of architecture and decorative sculpture weighing 46 tons; and the 13th-century statue of St. Peter by Arnolfo di Cambio, his toes kissed smooth by the faithful. The interior of St. Peter's is gigantic and so overloaded with decoration that it takes some time to get a sense of the whole. Piazza San Pietro.

Musei Vaticani (Vatican Museums) – The Vatican's museum complex houses one of the most impressive collections in the world, embracing works of art of every epoch. It also contains some masterpieces created on the spot, foremost of which is the extraordinary Sistine Chapel, with Michelangelo's frescoes of the *Creation* on the ceiling (painted from 1508 to 1512) and his *Last Judgment* on the altar wall (1534 to 1541). The highly controversial restoration of the ceiling (sponsored by Japan's largest TV network) — only the first phase of the project — was completed 2 years ago after 10 years of work, and the removal of centuries of soot revealed unexpected vibrancy in Michelangelo's colors. A new lighting system also was installed in the chapel, and footnotes are being added to art histories. The second phase — restoration of the *Last Judgment* — is expected to take at least another year. The chapel is open in summer from 9 AM to 4 PM, the rest of the year from 9 AM to 1 PM.

While Michelangelo was painting the Sistine Chapel ceiling for Pope Julius II, the 25-year-old Raphael was working on the Stanza della Segnatura, one of the magnificent Raphael Rooms commissioned by the same pope, which would occupy the painter until his death at the age of 37. Also part of the Vatican museum complex are the *Pio-Clementino Museum of Greco-Roman Antiquities,* which houses such marvelous statues as *Laocoön and His Sons* and the *Apollo Belvedere;* the *Gregorian Etruscan Museum;*

the *Pinacoteca* (Picture Gallery); the Library; and the Gregorian Profane, Pio-Cristiano, and Missionary-Ethnological sectors. Open 8:45 AM to 1:45 PM (longer in summer); closed Sundays except the last Sunday of the month, when the complex is open at no charge; other times there is an admission charge. Entrance on Viale Vaticano (phone: 698-3333).

San Giovanni in Laterano (Church of St. John Lateran) – Founded by Pope Melchiades in the 4th century, this is the cathedral of Rome, the pope's parish church, in effect. It suffered barbarian vandalism, an earthquake, and several fires across the centuries; its interior was largely rebuilt in the 17th century by Borromini, who maintained the 16th-century wooden ceiling (the principal façade belongs to the 18th century). Older sections are the lovely cloisters, dating from the 13th century, and the baptistry, from the time of Constantine. The adjoining Lateran Palace was built in the 15th century on the site of an earlier one that had been the home of the popes from Constantine's day to the Avignon Captivity and that had been destroyed by fire. In front of the palace and church are the Scala Santa (Holy Stairs), traditionally believed to have come from the palace of Pontius Pilate in Jerusalem and to have been climbed by Christ at the time of the Passion. The 28 marble steps, climbed by worshipers on their knees, lead to the Sancta Sanctorum, once the popes' private chapel (not open to the public, but visible through the grating). Both the chapel and the stairs were part of the earlier Lateran Palace but survived the fire. Also in the piazza is the oldest obelisk in Rome. Piazza di San Giovanni in Laterano.

Santa Maria Maggiore (Church of St. Mary Major) – A 5th-century church, rebuilt in the 13th century, with an 18th-century façade and the tallest campanile in Rome. It has particularly interesting 5th-century mosaics and a ceiling that was, according to tradition, gilded with the first gold to arrive from the New World. Piazza di Santa Maria Maggiore.

PIAZZAS, PALACES, AND OTHER SIGHTS

Piazza del Campidoglio – The Capitoline was the smallest of the original seven hills, but since it was the political and religious center of ancient Rome, it was also the most important. When the need arose in the 16th century for some modern city planning, the task was given to someone worthy of the setting. Thus, the harmonious square seen today, with its delicate, elliptical, star-patterned pavement centered on a magnificent 2nd-century bronze equestrian statue of Marcus Aurelius (removed for restoration), is the design of none other than Michelangelo. The piazza is flanked by palaces on three sides: Palazzo Nuovo and Palazzo dei Conservatori, facing each other and together making up the *Musei Capitolini* (Capitoline Museums), and the Palazzo Senatorio, between the two, which houses officials of the municipal government. The *Capitoline Museums* are famous for an especially valuable collection of antique sculptures, including the *Capitoline Venus,* the *Dying Gaul,* a bronze statue (known as the *Spinario*) of a boy removing a thorn from his foot, and the *Capitoline Wolf,* an Etruscan bronze to which Romulus and Remus were added during the Renaissance. Open Tuesdays through Saturdays from 9 AM to 1:30 PM, and Sundays from 9 AM to 1 PM. Admission charge. For more information, see *Walk 9: Masterworks of Architecture Through the Ages* in DIRECTIONS.

Piazza di Spagna (Spanish Steps) – One of the most picturesque settings of 18th-century Rome was named after a palace that housed the Spanish Embassy to the Holy See. The famous Spanish Steps actually were built by the French to connect the French quarter above with the Spanish area below. One of Rome's fine French churches, Trinità dei Monti, hovers over the 138 steps at the top, as does an ancient obelisk placed there by Pius VI in 1789. At the bottom of the steps — which in the spring are covered with hundreds of pots of azaleas — is the Barcaccia Fountain, depicting a sinking barge, inspired by the Tiber's flooding in 1589. Modern art historians disagree on whether this fountain, the oldest architectural feature of the square, was designed by Pietro Bernini or his son, the famous Gian Lorenzo Bernini.

Over the years, the steps have become a haunt of large crowds of young visitors, and all manner of crafts sales, caricature sketchers, and musicians contribute to the throng. The house where John Keats spent the last 3 months of his life and died, in February 1821, is next to the Spanish Steps at No. 26. It is now the *Keats-Shelley Memorial House* (phone: 678-4235), a museum dedicated to the English Romantic poets, especially Keats, Shelley, Byron, and Leigh Hunt, with a library of more than 9,000 volumes of their works. Open weekdays from 9 AM to 1 PM and 2:30 to 5:30 PM. Admission charge. 26 Piazza di Spagna (phone: 678-4235).

Via Condotti – A sort of Fifth Avenue of Rome, lined with the city's most exclusive shops, including *Gucci, Bulgari,* and *Ferragamo.* Only a few blocks long, it begins at the foot of the Spanish Steps, ends at Via del Corso, and is a favorite street for window shopping and the ritual evening *passeggiata,* or promenade, since it is — like much of the area — closed to traffic. Via Condotti's name derives from the water conduits built under it by Gregory XIII in the 16th century.

One of Via Condotti's landmarks is the famous *Caffè Greco,* at No. 86, long a hangout for Romans and foreigners. Among its habitués were Goethe, Byron, Liszt, Buffalo Bill, Mark Twain, Oscar Wilde, and the Italian painter Giorgio de Chirico. The place is full of busts, statues, and varied mementos of its clientele, and the somber waiters still dress in tails. Another landmark, at No. 68, is the smallest sovereign state in the world, consisting of one historic palazzo. If you peek into its charming courtyard, you'll see cars with number plates bearing the letters SMOM (the Sovereign Military Order of Malta). Besides its own licenses, the order, founded during the Crusades, also issues a few passports and has its own diplomatic service and small merchant fleet.

Piazza del Popolo – This semicircular square at the foot of the Pincio was designed in neo-classical style by Valadier between 1816 and 1820. At its center is the second-oldest obelisk in Rome, dating from the 13th century BC. Twin-domed churches (Santa Maria di Montesanto and Santa Maria dei Miracoli) face a ceremonial gate where the Via Flaminia enters Rome. Next to the gate is the remarkable early Renaissance Church of Santa Maria del Popolo, an artistic treasure containing two paintings by Caravaggio, sculptures by Bernini, and frescoes by Pinturicchio, among others. The piazza's two open-air cafés, *Rosati* and *Canova,* are favorite meeting places.

Piazza Navona – This harmonious ensemble of Roman baroque is today a favorite haunt of Romans and tourists alike. It is also one of Rome's most historic squares, built on the site of Domitian's stadium. In the center is Bernini's fine Fontana dei Fiumi (Fountain of the Rivers), the huge figures representing the Nile, Ganges, Danube, and Plata. On the west side of the square is the Church of Sant'Agnese in Agone, much of it the work of a Bernini assistant, Borromini. There was little love lost between the two men, and according to a popular local legend, the hand of the Plata figure is raised in self-defense, just in case the façade of the church falls down, while the Nile figure hides under a veil to avoid seeing Borromini's mistakes. However, since the fountain was completed a year before the church was begun, the story doesn't hold water. From the 17th to the mid-19th century, the square would be flooded on August weekends, and the aristocrats of the city would cool off by splashing through the water in their carriages. Nowadays, during the *Christmas* season, until *Epiphany,* it is lined with booths selling sweets, toys, and nativity figures. For more information, see *Walk 1: From Kings to Countesses — Pantheon and Piazza Navona* in DIRECTIONS.

Piazza Farnese – This square is dominated by Palazzo Farnese, the most beautiful 16th-century palace in Rome. Commissioned by Cardinal Alessandro Farnese (later Pope Paul III), it was begun in 1514 by Sangallo the Younger, continued by Michelangelo, and completed by Della Porta in 1589. Opera fans will know it as the location of Scarpia's apartment in the second act of Puccini's *Tosca.* Today it is occupied by the French Embassy and can be visited only with special permission. The two fountains on the square incorporate bathtubs of Egyptian granite brought from the Baths of Caracalla. For more information, see *Walk 3: The Campo* in DIRECTIONS.

Piazza Campo dei Fiori – Very near Piazza Farnese, one of Rome's most colorful squares is the scene of a general market every morning. In the center — surrounded by delicious cheeses, salamis, ripe fruit and vegetables, and *fiori* (flowers) of every kind — is a statue of the philosopher Giordano Bruno, who was burned at the stake here for heresy in 1600. Watch your wallet — this is a favorite hangout for thieves. For more information, see *Quintessential Rome* in DIVERSIONS and *Walk 3: The Campo* in DIRECTIONS.

Piazza Mattei – A delightful clearing on the edge of the ancient Jewish ghetto, this small square's famous Fontana delle Tartarughe (Fountain of the Tortoises), sculpted in 1585 by Taddeo Landini, is one of Rome's most delightful. Four naked boys lean against the base and toss life-size bronze tortoises into a marble bowl above. The water moves in several directions, creating a magical effect in the tiny square.

Piazza del Quirinale – The Quirinal Palace was built by the popes in the late 16th to early 17th century as a summer residence, became the royal palace after the unification of Italy, and is now the official residence of the president of Italy. The so-called Monte Cavallo (Horse Tamers') Fountain is composed of two groups of statues depicting Castor and Pollux with their horses and a granite basin from the Forum once used as a cattle trough. The obelisk in the center is from the Mausoleum of Augustus. The square affords a marvelous view of Rome and St. Peter's. A band plays daily during the changing of the guard at 4 PM in winter, 4:30 PM in summer.

Fontana di Trevi (Trevi Fountain) – Designed by Nicola Salvi and completed in 1762, the Trevi Fountain (newly renovated after more than 2 years of work) took 30 years to build and is the last important monumental baroque work in Rome. Incongruously situated in a tiny square tucked away amidst narrow, cobblestone streets, the magnificent fountain is quite striking when you suddenly come upon it at the turn of a corner. The colossal Oceanus in stone rides a chariot drawn by sea horses and is surrounded by a fantasy of gods, tritons, and horses. A low-voltage electronic field has been installed to discourage (but not injure) pigeons from perching on the fountain. According to legend, you will return to Rome if you stand with your back to the fountain and throw a coin over your left shoulder into the fountain. Young Roman men like to congregate in the small square on summer evenings, trying to pick up foreign women. Some prefer to pick your pocket — so be careful. Piazza di Trevi. For more information, see *Quintessential Rome* in DIVERSIONS and *Walk 9: Masterworks of Architecture Through the Ages* in DIRECTIONS.

Piazza Barberini – At the foot of Via Veneto, this square in northern Rome has two of Bernini's famous fountains: the Triton Fountain in travertine, representing a triton sitting upon a scallop shell supported by four dolphins and blowing a conch shell; and the Fountain of the Bees on the corner of the Veneto, with three Barberini bees (of that family's crest) on the edge of a pool spurting thin jets of water into the basin below.

Villa Borghese (Borghese Gardens) – In the northern section of the city, this is Rome's most magnificent park, with hills, lakes, villas, and vistas. It is the former estate of Cardinal Scipione Borghese, designed for him in the 17th century and enlarged in the 18th century. Two museums are here: the *Galleria Borghese,* housed in the cardinal's small palace and noted for its Caravaggios, its Bernini sculptures, and Antonio Canova's statue of the reclining *Pauline Borghese;* and the *Galleria Nazionale d'Arte Moderna,* with its Italian modern works. Open Tuesdays through Saturdays from 9 AM to 2 PM, Sundays from 9 AM to 1 PM. No admission charge. The Villa Borghese is a wonderful place to sit and picnic in the shade of an umbrella pine on a hot summer day. Enter through the Porta Pinciana, at the top of Via Veneto, or walk up to the

Pincio from Piazza del Popolo. The main entrance is at Piazzale Flaminio, just outside the Porta del Popolo.

Cimitero Protestante (Protestant Cemetery) – In the southern part of the city, behind the pyramid of Gaius Cestius, the Protestant cemetery is principally a foreign enclave that harbors the remains of many adopted non-Catholics who chose to live and die in Rome: Keats, Shelley, Trelawny, Goethe's illegitimate son, and the Italian Communist leader Gramsci. There is nothing sad here — no pathos, no morbid sense of death — and few gardens are as delightful on a spring morning. 6 Via Caio Cestio.

Jewish Ghetto and Synagogue – On the banks of the Tiber River, near the Garibaldi Bridge, is this vibrant section of town, once a walled area, that is rich with restaurants offering Roman-Jewish specialties and tiny shops. The synagogue, located on the Lungotevere Cenci by the Tiber, houses a permanent exhibition of ritual objects from the 16th to the 19th century, plus documents of recent history. Open daily except Saturdays and on Jewish holidays. For more information, see *Walk 7: Medieval Rome — Pilgrims and Perils* in DIRECTIONS.

Tiber Island – In the oldest part of the city, between Trastevere and the Jewish ghetto, is this small, 900-foot-long island in the Tiber River. Roman legend has it that the island grew from a seed of grain tossed in after the Etruscan kings were forced out. Noteworthy is the Chiesa di San Bartolomeo (Church of St. Bartholomew) — set into its steps is a medieval marble font carved from an ancient column said to mark a sacred spring and early temple to Asclepius, the Greek god of healing. Victims of the city's 3rd-century plague were sent here, and today a hospital here still cares for sick Romans. A small historical museum devoted to the island (*Museo Storico dell'Isola Tiberina*) was set to open as we went to press. There also is a tiny park on the marble-paved point of the island, a good spot to read or enjoy a picnic. The *Antico Caffè dell'Isola* has 2 rooms inside with tables for snacks. Next door is the popular trattoria *Sora Lella.* For more information, see *Walk 2: The Bridges* in DIRECTIONS.

MODERN ROME

Monumento a Vittorio Emanuele II (Monument to Victor Emmanuel II) – Sometimes called the Vittoriano, this most conspicuous landmark of questionable taste was completed in 1911 to celebrate the unification of Italy. Built of white Brescian marble and overwhelming the Capitoline Hill, it is often derided by Romans as the "wedding cake" or the "typewriter." It contains Italy's Tomb of the Unknown Soldier from World War I, and from the top you can see the network of modern boulevards built by Mussolini to open out the site of ancient Rome: Via dei Fori Imperiali, Via di San Gregorio, Via del Teatro di Marcello, and Via Nazionale — a busy and somewhat chaotic shopping street leading to the railroad station. Turn your back to the monument and note the 15th-century Palazzo Venezia to your left. It was from the small balcony of this building, his official residence, that Mussolini made his speeches. Piazza Venezia.

Via Vittorio Veneto – Popularly known as Via Veneto, this wide, café-lined street winds from a gate in the ancient Roman wall, the Porta Pinciana, down past the American Embassy to Piazza Barberini. The portion around Via Boncompagni is elegant, but the street also attracts a mixed crowd — from down-and-out actors and decadent Roman nobility to seedy gigolos and male prostitutes. Well-to-do Americans still stay in the fine hotels. The entire area, including the adjacent Via Bissolati with its many foreign airline offices, is well patrolled by police.

Porta Portese – Rome's flea market takes place on the edge of Trastevere on Sundays from dawn to about 1 or 2 PM. It's a colorful, crowded, and chaotic happening. Genuine antiques are few and far between, quickly scooped up before most people are out of bed. Still, you'll find some interesting junk, new and secondhand clothes, shoes, jeans, items brought by Eastern European immigrants, pop records, used tires and car parts, black market cigarettes — everything from Sicilian puppets to old postcards, sheet music, and broken bidets. Some say that if your wallet is stolen at the entrance, you'll find it for sale near the exit. Via Portuense.

OUT OF TOWN

Esposizione Universale di Roma (EUR) – Mussolini's ultramodern quarter was designed southwest of the center for an international exhibition that was supposed to take place in 1942 but never did. It's now a fashionable garden suburb and the site of international congresses and trade shows as well as of some remarkable sports installations built for the *1960 Olympic Games,* including the *Palazzo dello Sport,* with a dome by Pier Luigi Nervi. The *Museo della Civiltà Romana* (Museum of Roman Civilization) is worth seeing for its thorough reconstruction of ancient Rome at the time of Constantine. Open Tuesdays, Wednesdays, Fridays, and Saturdays from 9 AM to 1:30 PM, Thursdays from 4 to 7 PM, and Sundays from 9 AM to 1 PM. Admission charge. 10 Piazza Giovanni Agnelli (phone: 592-6135).

Ostia Antica – This immense excavation site about 15 miles (24 km) southwest of Rome was once the great trading port of ancient Rome, much closer to the mouth of the Tiber than it is today. The ruins — picturesquely set among pines and cypresses — first were uncovered in 1914, and new treasures are being discovered constantly. They have not had much chance to crumble, and they reveal a great deal about the building methods of the Romans and the management of a far-flung empire.

A visit takes at least half a day. Among the chief sites are the Piazzale delle Corporazioni (Corporations' Square), once 70 commercial offices, with mottoes and emblems in mosaics revealing that the merchants were shipwrights, caulkers, rope makers, furriers, and shipowners from all over the ancient world; the Capitolium (a temple) and Forum, baths, apartment blocks, and several private houses, especially the House of Cupid and Psyche; and the restored theater. Recent excavations have brought evidence of the town's Jewish community. Take the Decumanus Maximus to the end, turn left, and a few hundred yards away, on what was once the seashore, a synagogue stands, a moving testimonial to the Jewish presence in Rome in earliest times. Open daily except Mondays from 9 AM to 1 hour before sunset. A local museum (phone: 565-0022) traces the development of Ostia Antica and displays some outstanding statues, busts, and frescoes. Open daily except Mondays from 9 AM to 5 PM. Admission charge. To reach Ostia Antica, take the *metropolitana* from Stazione Termini, a train from Stazione Ostiense (the best choice), an *ACOTRAL* bus from Via Giolitti, or the *Tiber II* boat, daily from March through September (see *Getting Around*).

Lido di Ostia (also known as Lido di Roma) – Located 2½ miles (4 km) southwest of Ostia, it's a popular, polluted, and crowded seaside resort. Here and at other pleasant beaches both north and south of Rome, pollution has been so bad in recent years that swimming has been banned at many of them, but the view and the restaurants are pleasant, especially on summer evenings.

Castelli Romani – Rome's "castles" are actually 13 hill towns set in the lovely Alban Hills region southeast of Rome, an area where popes and powerful families of the past built fortresses, palaces, and other retreats. The mountains, the volcanic lakes of Nemi and Albano, chestnut groves, olive trees, and vines producing the famous Castelli wine continue to make the area a favorite destination of Romans who want to get away from the city on a fine day. Particularly charming are Frascati, known for its villas and its wines; Grottaferrata, famous for its fortified monastery, which can be visited; beautiful Lake Nemi, with its vivid blue waters and wooded surroundings, where Diana was worshiped; and Monte Cavo, a mountain whose summit can be reached by a toll road and which offers a panorama of the Castelli from a height of 3,124 feet. The Castelli Romani are best seen on an organized tour or by car — but beware of Sunday traffic.

■ **EXTRA SPECIAL:** Fountain fans should not miss Tivoli, a charming town perched on a hill and on a tributary of the Tiber (the Aniene) about 20 miles (32 km) east of Rome. It's famous for its villas, gardens, and, above all, cascading waters — all immortalized by Fragonard's 18th-century landscapes. Called *Tibur* by the ancient Romans, it was even then a resort for wealthy citizens, who bathed in its thermal waters, which remain therapeutic to this day.

The Villa d'Este, built for a cardinal in the 16th century, is the prime attraction — or, rather, its terraced gardens are. They contain some 500 fountains, large and small, including the jets of water lining the famous Avenue of the Hundred Fountains and the huge Organ Fountain, so named because it once worked a hydraulic organ. The villa and gardens are open to the public daily; admission charge. The fountains are gushing once again after being turned off because of fears that the water was polluted, but you'll have to look at them from behind a railing. On summer nights the fountains are beautifully illuminated, and there's a sound-and-light show. Nearby, the Villa Gregoriana, built by Pope Gregory XVI in the 19th century, has sloping gardens and lovely cascades (which are best on Sundays, since most of the water is used for industrial purposes on other days), but it is definitely to be seen only after you have seen the Villa d'Este. It, too, is open daily; admission charge.

Only 4 miles (6 km) southwest of Tivoli is Villa Adriana (Hadrian's Villa), the most sumptuous of the villas left from ancient Roman times. It was built from AD 125 to 134 by the Emperor Hadrian, whose pleasure was to strew the grounds with replicas of famous buildings he had seen elsewhere in his empire. Extensively excavated and surrounded by greenery, the ruins of the villa include the Maritime Theater, built on an island and surrounded by a canal; the Golden Square in front of the remains of the palace; and the Terrace of Tempe, with a view of the valley of the same name. There are statues, fountains, cypress-lined avenues, pools, lakes, and canals. Closed Mondays; admission charge. You can see Tivoli with a guided tour or take an *ACOTRAL* bus from Via Gaeta or a train from Stazione Termini. Villa Adriana also can be reached by bus from Via Gaeta, but note that while one bus, leaving every hour, stops first at Villa Adriana and then at Tivoli, the other, leaving every half hour, goes directly to Tivoli and entails getting off at a cross-roads and walking about a half mile to Villa Adriana. If you rent a car (a wise choice), take the "autostrada per l'Aquila" to the Tivoli exit, then follow the signs.

SOURCES AND RESOURCES

 TOURIST INFORMATION: The Ente Provinciale per il Turismo (EPT) for Rome and Lazio (headquartered at 11 Via Parigi; phone: 488-1851) has a main information office (5 Via Parigi; phone: 488-3748), with branches at Stazione Termini and in the customs area at Leonardo da Vinci Airport at Fiumicino. There also are branches at the Feronia "Punto Blu" and Frascati Est service areas of the A1 and A2 highways, respectively, for those arriving by car. All branches stock various booklets, maps, and hotel listings, all free. Ask for the English language monthly listing of events, *Carnet.*

The US Embassy and Consulate are at 119/A and 121 Via Vittorio Veneto respectively (phone: 46741).

For some good background material about Rome, see Georgina Masson's *Companion Guide to Rome* and Eleanor Clark's *Rome and a Villa,* both useful and amusing. A locally published book on the city's hidden treasures, *In Rome They Say,* by Margherita Naval, is also good reading; 30 walks through the city are described and mapped in *The Heart of Rome.* There are several English-language bookstores in the Spanish Steps area: the *Lion Bookshop* (181 Via del Babuino), *Anglo-American Book Company* (57 Via della Vite), and the *Bookshelf* (in the *Tritone Gallery,* 23 Via Due Macelli). The *Economy Book Center* (136 Via Torino) is particularly good for paperbacks.

For those especially interested in art history and archaeology, a team of professionals in both fields is available to take individuals or groups on private English-language tours of Rome, as well as 1- and 2-day trips outside the city. For information, contact Peter Zalewski (6 Via Cristoforo Colombo, Marcellina di Roma; phone: 774-425451; fax: 774-425122). An English-speaking German, Ruben Popper (12 Via dei Levii; phone: 761-0901), who has lived in Rome for 30 years, also leads tours (mostly walking) of the city.

Local Coverage – The *International Herald Tribune,* now also printed in Rome, is available at most newsstands each morning; it often lists major events in Italy in its Saturday "Weekend" section. *A Guest in Rome* is published by the Golden Key Association of Concierges. *La Repubblica, Corriere della Sera,* and *Il Messaggero* are daily newspapers that list local events on weekends; *La Repubblica* has an interesting Thursday supplement called "TrovaRoma" that lists the week's events, shows, theater, new movies, and more. *Wanted in Rome* is a useful handout found in American shops and schools.

Food – *La Guida d'Italia* — updated annually — is a comprehensive guide to restaurants and wine shops in Rome and throughout Italy. In Italian, it is published by *L'Espresso* and is available at newsstands. Another popular book — and with a fresher and zestier approach (but also in Italian) — is *Roma,* a restaurant guide published by Gambero Rosso.

 TELEPHONE: The city code for Rome is 6. When calling from within Italy, dial 06 before the local number.

The procedure for calling the US from Italy is as follows: dial 00 (the international access code) + 1 (the US country code) + the area code + the local number. For instance, to call New York from Rome, dial 00 + 1 + 212 + the local number. For calling from one Italian city to another, simply dial 0 + the city code + the local number; and for calls within the same city code coverage area, simply dial the local number.

Italcable, Italy's major international phone company, introduced a new feature, Country Direct Service, in 1989. By dialing 172-1011 from any telephone in Rome, Florence, Naples, or Milan, you can phone the US direct, either by calling collect or by using your credit card. An American operator will answer. (Note that as we went to press, *Italcable* was in the process of extending this service to include other cities throughout Italy.)

Pay telephones in Rome can be found in cafés and restaurants (look for the sign outside — a yellow disk with the outline of a telephone or a receiver in black) and, less commonly, in booths on the street. (All too often, however, these are out of order — if you're lucky, a *guasto* sign will warn you.) There are two kinds of pay phones: The old-fashioned kind works with a *gettone* (token) only, which can be bought for 200 lire from a bar or restaurant cashier and at newsstands; newer phones function with *gettoni,* 200-lire, or two 100-lire coins. To use a *gettone,* place it in the slot at the top of the phone. When your party answers — and *not* before — push the button at the top of the phone, causing the token to drop (otherwise the answering party will not be able to hear you). If your party doesn't answer, hang up and simply lift the unused *gettone* out of the slot. In newer phones using either *gettoni* or coins, the coins or *gettoni* drop automatically when you put them in, as in US phones; if your party doesn't answer, you have to press the return button (sometimes repeatedly) to get them back.

Although the majority of Italian pay phones still take tokens or coins, phones that take specially designated phone cards are increasingly common, particularly in metropolitan areas and at major tourist destinations. These telephone cards have been instigated to cut down on vandalism, as well as to free callers from the necessity of carrying around a pocketful of change, and are sold in various lire denominations. The units per card, like message units in US phone parlance, are a combination of time and distance. To use such a card, insert it into a slot in the phone and dial the number you wish to reach. A display gradually will count down the value that remains on your card. When you run out of units on the card, you can insert another. In Italy, these phone cards are available from any SIP telephone center.

Although you can use a telephone company credit card number on any phone, pay phones that take major credit cards are increasingly common worldwide, particularly in transportation and tourism centers. Also now available is the "affinity card," a combined telephone calling card/bank credit card that can be used for domestic and international calls. Cards of this type include the following:

AT&T/Universal (phone: 800-662-7759). Cardholders can charge calls to the US from overseas.

Executive Telecard International (phone: 800-950-3800). Cardholders can charge calls to the US from overseas, as well as between most European countries.

Sprint Visa (phone: 800-446-7625). Cardholders can charge calls to the US from overseas.

Similarly, *MCI VisaPhone* (phone: 800-866-0099) can add phone card privileges to the services available through your existing *Visa* card. This service allows you to use your *Visa* account number, plus an additional code, to charge calls on any touch-tone phone in the US and Europe.

 GETTING AROUND: Bicycle and Moped – Pollution and insufferable traffic jams have made bicycling a popular, if sometimes dangerous, alternative to driving for many Romans. *Collati* (82 Via del Pellegrino; phone: 654-1084) rents bikes. Others can be found at Piazza San Silvestro, Piazza del Popolo, Piazza di Spagna, Piazza Augusto Imperatore, Lungotevere Marzio, and at Viale della Pineta and Viale dei Bambini in the Villa Borghese Gardens. To rent a moped, scooter, or motorbike, try *Scoot-a-long* (304 Via Cavour; phone: 678-0206); *Scooters for Rent* (66 Via della Purificazione, near Piazza Barberini; phone: 488-5485), which also rents bikes; and *St. Peter Moto* (43 Via Porta Castello, near St. Peter's; phone: 687-5714). By law, helmets must be worn while riding scooters or motorbikes.

Boat – From March through September, weather and water level permitting, the *Tiber II* carries 300 passengers on half-day cruises along the river to Ostia Antica and back. It departs at 9:30 AM daily — though the trip is subject to change due to water levels and demand, so check first. For information and reservations, call *Tourvisa* at 445-3224 or the *Associazione Amici del Tevere* (Friends of the Tiber Society) at 637-0268. From May to September, the *Acquabus* plies the river daily, except Mondays, beating the road traffic, from Tiber Island to Duca d'Aosta Bridge near the *Olympic Stadium*. The trip takes 45 minutes each way and runs every 25 minutes. Pay the 1,000-lire (about 75¢) fare on board. Contact *Tourvisa* for information. For boat charters, contact *Aquarius* (32 Corso Vittorio Emanuele; phone: 687-1437).

Bus – *ATAC* (*Azienda Tramvie e Autobus Comune di Roma*), the city bus company, is the rather weak backbone of Rome's public transportation system. During August the number of buses in use is greatly reduced while drivers are on vacation. Most central routes are extremely crowded, getting off where you'd like is sometimes impossible, pickpockets are rampant, and some lines discontinue service after 9 PM, midnight, or 1 AM. Tickets, which currently cost about 75¢, must be purchased before boarding and are available at certain newsstands, tobacco shops, and bars. (Be aware that these outlets frequently exhaust their ticket supply, and the fine for riding without a ticket is about $40.) Remember to get on the bus via the back doors, stamp your ticket in the machine, and exit via the middle doors (the front doors are used only by *abbonati,* season ticket holders). There are no transfer tickets, but visitors can save money by buying 90-minute or full-day tickets, called "Big," at the *ATAC* information booth in Piazza dei Cinquecento or at principal bus stations, such as those at Piazza San Silvestro and Piazza Risorgimento. Tourists will appreciate the tiny, electric-powered No. 119, which loops through downtown Rome between Piazza del Popolo and close to Piazza Navona, passing the Spanish Steps. A weekly bus pass also is available, and route maps — *Roma in Metrobus* — are sold at the *ATAC* information booth and at the Ufficio Abbonamenti of *ATAC* at Largo Giovanni Montemartini, as well as at some newsstands. For information, call 46951. Bus service to points out of town is run by *ACOTRAL* (including buses to Leonardo da Vinci Airport at Fiumicino). For information, call 593-5551. The Rome telephone directory's *TuttoCittà* supplement lists every street in the city and contains detailed maps of each zone as well as postal codes, bus routes, and taxi stands.

Car Rental – Major car rental firms such as *Avis* (38/A Via Sardegna; phone: 470-1229 in Rome, 167-863063 toll-free in Italy), *Budget* (24 Via Sistina; phone: 461905), *Europcar* (7 Via Lombardia; phone: 465802), and *Hertz* (156 Via Veneto; phone: 321-6831 or 321-6834), as well as several reliable Italian companies such as *Maggiore* (8/A Via Po; phone: 851620), have offices in the city and at the airport and railway stations. *Tropea* (1 Piazza Barberini; phone: 488-4682; fax: 482-8336) has rental and chauffeur-driven cars.

Leonardo da Vinci Airport (outside Rome) has desks at which tourists may buy coupons that can be redeemed at gas stations around Italy. Coupons must be purchased in foreign currency. Note that gas stations close for 2 hours at lunch and at 7 PM in winter, 7:30 PM in summer. Most are closed Sundays. Self-service stations operate with 10,000-lire ($8) notes. An efficient — and often economic — way to tour is by limousine. Hotels can suggest some, but a few to contact are *Capitol* (33 Via del Galoppatoio; phone: 360-5866); *Coop. UARA* (261 Via Panisperna; phone: 679-2320); and *Italo Mazzei Roma* (123 Via Trionfale; phone: 310963). Generally, it's not a good idea to hire free-lance taxis; drivers usually are unlicensed, and charge up to double the price of the regular taxi fare. For more information on car rental, see *Traveling by Plane* in GETTING READY TO GO.

Horse-Drawn Carriages – Rome's *carrozzelle* accommodate up to five passengers and are available at major city squares (Piazza San Pietro, di Spagna, Venezia, and Navona), in front of the Colosseum, near the Trevi Fountain, on Via Veneto, and in the Villa Borghese. They can be hired by the half hour, hour, half day, or full day. Arrange the price with the driver before boarding — 1 hour currently costs about $50 minimum.

Subway – The *metropolitana,* Rome's subway, consists of two lines. *Linea A* runs roughly east–west, from an area close to the Vatican, across the Tiber, through the historic center (Piazza di Spagna, Piazza Barberini, Stazione Termini), and over to the eastern edge of the city past Cinecittà, the filmmaking center; a branch goes to the Tiburtina train station, where numerous long-distance trains stop. *Linea B,* which is partly an underground and partly a surface railroad, runs north–south, from Stazione Termini to the Colosseum and, with a stop at the Ostiense station at Piazza Piramide to connect with the train to Leonardo da Vinci Airport, down to the southern suburb of EUR. The fare is about 80¢, and tickets are sold at certain newsstands, tobacco shops, and bars, as well as at most stations. Only a few stations are staffed with ticket sellers; there also are ticket-dispensing machines, but they only accept coins, so be prepared. Subway entrances are marked by a large red "M."

Taxi – Cabs can be hailed or found at numerous stands, which are listed in the yellow pages with their phone numbers. The *Radio Taxi* telephone numbers are 3570, 3875, 4994, and 8433. Taxi rates are increasing regularly, and drivers are obliged to show you, if asked, the current list of added charges. The current minimum fare is about $5 for the first 2 miles (3 km) or (if stalled in traffic) the first 9 minutes. After 10 PM, a night charge is added, and there are surcharges for holidays and for suitcases.

Train – Rome's main train station is Stazione Termini (phone: 4775 for information). There are several suburban stations, but the visitor is unlikely to use them except for Stazione Ostiense, from which trains depart for Ostia Antica and the Lido di Ostia (phone: 575-0732).

LOCAL SERVICES: Dentist (English-Speaking) – Dr. Peter Althoff (280 Via Salaria; phone: 844-3317); Dr. Charles Kennedy (29 Via della Fonte di Fauno; phone: 578-3639).

Dry Cleaner – *Tintoria Maddalena* (40 Piazza Maddalena; phone: 654-3348); *Minerva* (71/A Via del Gesù; phone: 679-2310); and *Mosca* (23 Via Belisario; phone: 482-7255).

Limousine Service – *Biancocavallo* (126 Via Tiburtina; phone: 520-2957); *Nazionale* (32/B Via Milano; phone: 481-8587; fax: 481-4530); *International* (60 Via Ludovisi; phone: 474-6078 or 475-0872); *Traiano* (19 Via Sant'Agata dei Goti; phone: 679-1518; fax: 678-7996).

Medical Emergency – *Policlinico* (1 Umberto, Viale Policlinico; phone: 492341); *Red Cross Ambulances* (phone: 5100). English-speaking physicians: Dr. Ettore Lollini (Salvador Mundi International Hospital, 67-77 Viale della Mura Gianicolensi; phone: 586041 or 839-3154); Dr. Frank Silvestri (36 Via Ludovisi; phone: 485706 or 332-2017); Dr. Susan Levenstein (Via Tritone; phone: 654-5708 or 475-8429); Dr. Vincenzo Baci (43 Via Cesare Balbo; phone: 474-1021). For an emergency house visit, around the clock, call 482-6741. In downtown Rome, the *San Giacomo Hospital* (off Via del Corso; phone: 67261) has an efficient first-aid service. The *Croce Rossa* (Red Cross; phone: 5100) provides ambulances.

Messenger Service – *Romana Recapiti* (two locations: 38 Via Vicenza; phone: 559-0917 or 559-0993; and 68 Via Palestro; phone: 495-6990); *Pony Express* (phone: 3309).

National/International Courier – National: *Carlo Ciucci* (18-20 Viale del Vignola; phone: 360-7803 or 360-5622). International: *DHL International* (two locations: 1 Via S. Eulalio and at Ciampino Airport; phone: 72421 for both); *Stelci & Tavani* (103 Via Alessandro Severo; phone: 541-4460; fax: 541-1334); *Federal Express* will pick up at your hotel (phone: 675-2673; fax: 791-5831); *Fast Cargo* (141 Via dell'Omo; phone: 228-8305; fax: 228-8340); *XP-Express Parcel Systems Italy* (Ciampino Airport; phone: 796-0382); *Rinaldi* (34 Via Smerillo; phone: 410911; fax: 411-1565); *UPS/Alimondo* (329 Via della Magliana; phone: 527-3371; fax: 528-4859).

Office Equipment Rental – *Centro Macchina Ufficio* (48/B-52 Via Tagliamento; phone: 867465 or 869233); *Executive Service* (68 Via Savoia; phone: 853241); *International Services Agency* (35 Piazza di Spagna; phone: 684-0287 or 684-0288).

Pharmacy – *Internazionale* (49 Piazza Barberini; phone: 462996); *Cola di Rienzo* (213 Via Cola di Rienzo; phone: 351816). Both are open nights. To find out about drugstores open on Saturday afternoons and holidays, call 1921, or check the newspapers for their listings of *farmacie di turno.*

Photocopies – *Sandy* (58-59 Via San Basilio; phone: 475-8533 or 461346); *Centro Eliografico Prati* (7 Piazza dei Quiriti, near the Lepanto subway stop; phone: 389657 or 316643); *Centro Rank Xerox* (28 Largo delle Stimmate; phone: 654-1898; fax: 686-7542).

Post Office – The main post office (19 Piazza San Silvestro; phone: 6771) is open from 8:30 AM to 8 PM weekdays (until noon Saturdays). An express service called CAI (Corriere Accelerato Italiano) Post is now available at major post offices. Otherwise, Rome's most efficient post office for mail going out of Italy is the Vatican Post Office (Piazza San Pietro), open from 8:30 AM to 7 PM weekdays (until 6 PM Saturdays).

Secretary/Stenographer (English-Speaking) – *Rome At Your Service* (75 Via Orlando; phone: 484583 or 484429); *Executive Service* (78 Via Savoia; phone: 853241). Both can provide translation services. *Copisteria al Tritone* (17 Via Crispi; phone: 679-7190) has word processing facilities, a fax machine, and secretarial services in English.

Tailor – *Cifonelli* (68 Via Sella; phone: 488-1827); *Caraceni* (two locations: 61/B Via Campania, phone: 488-2594; and 50 Via Sardegna, phone: 474-4023); *Coccurello,* for smaller budgets (7 Via Manfredi; phone: 802360 or 534-7038).

Telex/Facsimile Transmissions – Telexes and telegrams can be sent 24 hours daily from 18 Piazza San Silvestro (phone: 679-5530), next to the main post office. Fax service also is available there weekdays from 8:30 AM to 8 PM, and Saturdays from 8:30 AM to noon.

Translator – *World Translation Centre* (181 Via di Santa Maria Maggiore; phone: 475-5986, 461039, or 485922); *Agenzia Barberini* (5 Piazza Barberini; phone: 474-1738 or 488-1497; fax: 488-5491); *Alfa International* (29 Via Lucrezio Caro; phone: 323-0077; fax: 322-2038); *Rome at Your Service* (75 Via Orlando; phone: 484583); *Outer Relations Office* (123 Via Sistina; phone: 463951); *Executive Service* (78 Via Savoia; phone: 854-3241; fax: 844-0738). For simultaneous translations, contact *Centro Congressi* (23 Via Sallustiana; phone: 485990 or 465392); or *STOC* (two locations: 44 Via G. de Ruggiero, phone: 540-5621; and 203 Via Laurentina, phone: 540-3741).

Tuxedo Rental – *Misano,* 88 Via Nazionale (phone: 488-2005).

Other – *Convention Centers: Palazzo dei Congressi* has 30 meeting rooms for up to 4,000 (Piazzale Kennedy in EUR; phone: 591-2735; fax: 592-4044); *Centro Internazionale Roma* (*CIR*) has 8 meeting rooms for up to 8,000 (619 Via Aurelia; phone: 6644; fax: 663-2689); *Palazzo dello Sport* has meeting rooms for up to 5,000 (Piazzale dello Sport; phone: 592-5107); *Palazzo Brancaccio* is available for conferences and is centrally located (7 Via Monte Oppio; phone: 487-3177). Also centrally located is the Renaissance *Palazzo Taverna* (37 Via di Monte Giordano; phone: 683-3785), which is available for receptions and business lunches. The Orsini-Odescalchi Castle (25 miles from Rome, in Bracciano) is a 15th-century castle, richly furnished and decorated with frescoes, that can be rented for receptions of up to 500. *Office Space Rental (fully equipped): Amministrazione Principe Livio Odescalchi* (80 Piazza SS. Apostoli; phone: 679-2154); *Executive Service* (68 Via Savoia; phone: 853241; fax: 844-0738); *International Business Centre* (121 Piazzale di Porta Pia; phone: 886-3051); *Tiempo* (50 Via Barberini; phone: 482-5151 or 482-1456); and *Center Office* (132 Via del Tritone; phone: 488-1995 or 474-7641). *Desktop Publishing: Scribe Desktop Publishing* (45 Via Paola Falconieri; phone: 531-5050).

 SPECIAL EVENTS: The events of the church calendar — too numerous to mention here — are extra special in Rome. For *Natale* (*Christmas*), relatively modest decorations go up around the city, almost all churches display their sometimes movable, elaborate *presepi* (nativity scenes), and a colorful toy and candy fair begins in Piazza Navona. The season, including the fair, lasts until January 6, *Epiphany,* when children receive gifts from a witch known as the Befana to add to those Babbo Natale (Father Christmas) or the Bambìn Gesù (Baby Jesus) brought them at *Christmas.* The intervening *Capodanno* or *New Year* is celebrated with a bang here as in much of the rest of Italy — firecrackers snap, crackle, and pop from early evening, and (though less than in the past) at midnight all manner of old, discarded objects come flying out of open windows. (Don't be on the street!) During the *Settimana Santa* (Holy Week), the city swarms with visitors. Religious ceremonies abound, particularly on *Good Friday,* when pilgrims, on their knees, climb the Scala Santa at St. John Lateran and the pope conducts the famous *Via Crucis* (Way of the Cross) procession between the Colosseum and the Palatine Hill. At noon on *Easter Sunday,* he pronounces the *Urbi et Orbi* blessing in St. Peter's Square. The day after *Easter* is *Pasquetta* (Little Easter), when Romans usually go out to the country for a picnic or an extended lunch in a rustic trattoria.

The arrival of spring is celebrated in April with a colorful display of potted azaleas covering the Spanish Steps, and in May a picturesque street nearby, Via Margutta, is filled with an exhibition of paintings by artists of varied talents. (The Via Margutta art fair is repeated in the fall.) In May, too, Villa Borghese's lush Piazza di Siena becomes the site of the *International Horse Show,* and soon after that is the *Italian Open* tennis tournament at *Foro Italico.* An antiques show also takes place in spring and fall along the charming Via dei Coronari (near Piazza Navona), and there's an *International Rose Show* in late spring at the delightful Roseto di Valle Murcia on the Aventine Hill. In late May or June the vast *Fiera di Roma,* a national industrial exhibition, takes place at the fairgrounds along Via Cristoforo Colombo. In mid-July the *Festa di Noiantri* is celebrated in one of Rome's oldest quarters, Trastevere. This is a great pagan feast, involving plenty of eating, music, and fireworks — as filmed by Fellini in his surrealistic/realistic *Roma.*

There are also innumerable characteristic *feste* or *sagre* (festivals, usually celebrating some local food or beverage at the height of its season) in the many hill towns surrounding Rome. The *Sagra dell'Uva* (Grape Festival), at Marino on the first Sunday in October, celebrates the new vintage with grapes sold from stalls set up in the quaint old streets and wine instead of water gushing out of the fountain in the main square! Also worth seeing is the *Infiorata* at Genzano di Roma. On a Sunday in mid-June, a brightly colored carpet of beautifully arranged flowers is laid along the entire Via Livia. Both towns are about 15 miles (24 km) south of Rome in the Castelli Romani (see "Out of Town" in *Special Places*).

 MUSEUMS: Many museums are described in *Special Places.* Included in the following list of additional museums are churches that should be seen because of their artistic value. Many museums are closed on Mondays, and some charge no admission on Sundays. Always check the hours before setting out (although most open at 9 AM and close for lunch).

Galleria Colonna – The Colonna family collection (in their home) of mainly 17th-century Italian paintings. Open Saturdays only, from 9 AM to 1 PM. Palazzo Colonna, 17 Via della Pilotta (phone: 679-4362).

Galleria Doria Pamphili – The private collection of the Doria family, housed in a sculpture hall and apartments, of Italian and foreign paintings from the 15th to the 17th century, including a portrait of Christopher Columbus. Open Tuesdays, Fridays, Saturdays, and Sundays, 10 AM to 1 PM. Palazzo Doria, 1/A Piazza del Collegio Romano (phone: 679-4365). For more information, see *Walk 5: The Streets of the Shadow Boxes* in DIRECTIONS.

Galleria Nazionale d'Arte Antica (National Gallery of Ancient Art) – Recently renovated, this museum exhibits paintings by Italian artists from the 13th to the 18th century, plus some Dutch and Flemish works. Open Mondays through Saturdays from 9 AM to 2 PM, Sundays from 9 AM to 12:30 PM. Palazzo Barberini, 13 Via delle Quattro Fontane (phone: 481-4591).

Galleria Nazionale d'Arte Moderna (National Gallery of Modern Art) – Particularly noteworthy are the pre–World War I Italian painters and the futurists. Open daily from 9 AM to 1:30 PM; on Thursdays and Fridays, it also is open from 3 to 7 PM. 131 Viale Belle Arti (phone: 802751).

Galleria Spada – Renaissance art and Roman marble work from the 2nd and 3rd centuries; also two huge, rare antique globes that were used on Dutch ships in the 16th century. Open Mondays and Tuesdays from 9 AM to 2 PM, Wednesdays and Saturdays from 9 AM to 2 PM and 3 to 7 PM, and Sundays and holidays from 9 AM to 1 PM. Palazzo Spada, 13 Piazza Capo di Ferro (phone: 686-1158).

Museo Napoleonico (Napoleonic Museum) – Memorabilia of the emperor's family during their rule in Rome. 1 Via Umberto I (phone: 654-0286).

Museo Nazionale d'Arte Orientale (National Museum of Oriental Art) – Pottery, bronzes, stone, and wooden sculpture from the Middle and Far East. Open Mondays through Saturdays from 9 AM to 2 PM, Sundays and holidays from 9 AM to 1 PM. 248 Via Merulana (phone: 737948).

Museo Nazionale Etrusco di Valle Giulia (National Etruscan Museum of the Giulia Valley) – The country's most important Etruscan collection, in a 16th-century villa by Vignola. Open Tuesdays through Saturdays from 9 AM to 7 PM, Sundays from 9 AM to 1 PM. 9 Piazzale di Valle Giulia (phone: 360-1951).

Museo di Palazzo Venezia (Palazzo Venezia Museum) – Tapestries, paintings, sculpture, and varied objects, as well as important temporary exhibits. Open Mondays from 9 AM to 2 PM, Tuesdays through Saturdays from 9 AM to 7 PM, and Sundays from 9 AM to 1 PM. 118 Via del Plebiscito (phone: 679-8865).

Museo Preistorico ed Etnografico Luigi Pigorini (Luigi Pigorini Prehistoric and Ethnographic Museum) – A unique collection of objects from Italy's early history. Open Mondays from 2 to 7 PM, Wednesdays through Saturdays from 9 AM to 7 PM, and Sundays from 9 AM to 1 PM. 1 Via Lincoln (phone: 591-0702).

Museo di Roma (Museum of Rome) – Paintings, sculptures, and other objects illustrating the history of Rome from the Middle Ages to the present. Open daily from 9 AM to 1:30 PM. 10 Piazza San Pantaleo (phone: 687-5880).

Museo della Sinagoga (Synagogue Permanent Collection) – Adjacent to the synagogue is this small museum with exhibits on the arts and history of Rome's Jewish community through the centuries. Open Mondays through Thursdays from 9:30 AM to 2 PM and 3 to 5 PM, Fridays from 9:30 AM to 2:30 PM, and Sundays from 9:30 AM to 12:30 PM. Lungotevere Cenci (phone: 686-4193).

San Carlo alle Quattro Fontane (St. Charles at the Four Fountains) – A small baroque church by Borromini, it was designed to fit into one of the pilasters of St. Peter's. Via del Quirinale, corner Via delle Quattro Fontane.

San Clemente – An early Christian basilica with frescoes and a remarkable mosaic. Piazza di San Clemente.

San Luigi dei Francesi (St. Louis of the French) – The French national church, built in the 16th century and containing three Caravaggios. Piazza San Luigi dei Francesi.

Sant'Agostino (St. Augustine) – A 15th-century church containing the *Madonna of the Pilgrims* by Caravaggio and the *Prophet Isaiah* by Raphael. Piazza di Sant'Agostino.

Sant'Andrea al Quirinale (St. Andrew at the Quirinale) – A baroque church by Bernini, to be compared with Borromini's church on the same street. Via del Quirinale. For more information, see *Walk 9: Masterpieces of Architecture Through the Ages* in DIRECTIONS.

Santa Maria d'Aracoeli (St. Mary of the Altar of Heaven) – A Romanesque-Gothic church with frescoes by Pinturicchio and a 14th-century staircase built in thanksgiving for the lifting of a plague. Piazza d'Aracoeli.

Santa Maria in Cosmedin – A Romanesque church known for the *Bocca della Verità* (Mouth of Truth) in its portico — a Roman drain cover in the shape of a face whose mouth, according to legend, will bite off the hand of anyone who has told a lie. Piazza della Bocca della Verità. For more information, see *Walk 2: The Bridges* in DIRECTIONS.

Santa Maria sopra Minerva (St. Mary over Minerva) – Built over a Roman temple, with (unusual for Rome) a Gothic interior, frescoes by Filippino Lippi, and Michelangelo's statue of St. John the Baptist. Piazza della Minerva. For more information, see *Walk 1: From Kings to Countesses — Pantheon and Piazza Navona* in DIRECTIONS.

Santa Maria in Trastevere – An ancient church, the first in Rome dedicated to the Virgin, with 12th- and 13th-century mosaics. Piazza Santa Maria in Trastevere.

Santa Maria della Vittoria (St. Mary of the Victory) – Baroque to the core, especially in Bernini's Cornaro Chapel. Via XX Settembre.

San Pietro in Vincoli (St. Peter in Chains) – Erected in the 5th century to preserve St. Peter's chains, this church contains Michelangelo's magnificent statue of Moses. Piazza di San Pietro in Vincoli.

Santa Sabina – A simple 5th-century basilica, with its original cypress doors, a 13th-century cloister and bell tower, and stunning views of the city. Piazza Pietro d'Illiria.

SHOPPING: Rome is a wonderful place to shop. You'll find the great couturiers, many of whom have boutiques as well, and most important Italian firms have branches here. While elegant clothing by top Italian designers will cost less here than back home, don't expect any bargain-basement finds. The best buys are in quality, hand-finished leather goods, jewelry, fabrics, shoes, and sweaters.

The chicest shopping area is around the bottom of the Spanish Steps, beginning with the elegant Via Condotti, which runs east to west and is lined with Rome's most exclusive shops, such as *Gucci* and *Ferragamo* for leather goods, and *Bulgari, Beltrami, Cartier, Di Consiglio, Massoni, Merli, Rapi,* and *Van Cleef* for exquisite jewelry. Via del Babuino, which connects the Spanish Steps to Piazza del Popolo, has traditionally been better known for its antiques shops, but is coming into its own as a high-fashion street, as is nearby Via Bocca di Leone, where there are such designers' boutiques as *Valentino, Ungaro, Versace, Trussardi,* and *Yves Saint Laurent.* Running parallel to Via Condotti are several more streets, most closed to traffic, with fashionable boutiques, such as Via Borgognona (*Fendi, Versace, Missoni, Laura Biagiotti,* and *Testa*), Via delle Carrozze, Via Frattina (for men's fashions at *Testa,* women's at *Max Mara,* as well as costume jewelry, lingerie, and some ceramics), Via Vittoria, and Via della Croce (known particularly for its delicious but pricey delicatessens such as *Ercoli,* or *Fior Fiore* for cheese, bread, and cookies). All of these streets end at Via del Corso, the main street of Rome, which runs north to south and is lined with shops tending to resemble each other more and more with their offerings of the latest fashions in shoes, handbags, and sportswear, particularly along the stretch between Piazza del Popolo and Largo Chigi, where Via del Tritone begins. There are some fine shops along Via del Tritone, Via Sistina, and in the Via Veneto area.

On the other side of the river toward the Vatican are two popular shopping streets that are slightly less expensive, Via Cola di Rienzo and Via Ottaviano. Also somewhat less expensive is Via Nazionale, near the railroad station. For inexpensive new and secondhand clothes, visit the daily market on Via Sannio, near San Giovanni, and the flea market on Sunday mornings at Porta Portese. For old prints and odds and ends, try the market at Piazza della Fontanella Borghese every morning except Sunday; antiques can be found along Via del Babuino, Via dei Coronari, Via del Boverno Vecchio, Via del Governo Vecchio, Via Margutta, and Via Giulia.

Fairly new on the Roman shopping scene is *Cinecittà Due,* an air conditioned shopping mall that has over 100 shops. Easily accessible by subway, it is open daily except Sundays from 9 AM to 8:30 PM.

Store hours are capricious. Shops usually are open in winter from 10 AM to 1 PM and 4 to 7:30 PM; closed Monday mornings. Summer morning hours are the same, but in the afternoon, stores are open from 4:30 to 8 PM; closed Saturday afternoons. A few, such as the popular department store *UPIM* on Via del Tritone, are open all day.

The following are a few recommended shops in Rome:

Arte – Household and hope-chest linen, such as tablecloths, and hand-embroidered curtains at this shop near the Campo de' Fiori. 39 Via dei Giubbonari.

Balloon – Chinese silk is used to make Italian-style women's shirts in this store, which is so popular that there are six in Rome and one in Paris. 35 Piazza di Spagna, 495 Via Flaminia Vecchia, and other locations.

Battistoni – Men's conservative clothing. The Duke of Windsor had his shirts made here — secretly, so as not to offend Britain's shirtmakers. 61A Via Condotti.

Bertè – Old and new toys. 108 Piazza Navona.

Bises – A place for fine fabrics. 93 Via del Gesù. *Bises' Boutique Uomo,* for men, is at 1-3-5 Corso Vittorio Emanuele.

Bomba e De Clercq – Exclusive sweaters and blouses with hand-crafted details. 39 Via dell'Oca, behind Piazza del Popolo.

Borsalino – World-renowned hats. 157/B Via IV Novembre.

Bruno Magli – Top-quality shoes and boots of classical elegance. 70 Via Veneto, 1 Via del Gambero, and 237 Via Cola di Rienzo.

Buccellati – For connoisseurs: A fine jeweler with a unique way of working with gold. 31 Via Condotti.

Bulgari – One of the world's most famous high-style jewelers, offering fabulous creations in gold, silver, platinum, and precious stones. 10 Via Condotti.

Capodarte – The latest styles in shoes and boots — many with matching bags — and some stylish fashions for women. 14/A Via Sistina.

Carlo Palazzi – Creative, high-quality fashions for men. 7/C Via Borgognona.

Carlo Pasquali – Old prints, engravings, original lithographs, and drawings. Near the Trevi Fountain. 25 Largo di Brazzà.

Cartoleria al Pantheon – Marbled paper, some handmade and suitable for framing. Ask to see the one-of-a-kind paper mosaic-covered diaries and notebooks. Ideal for small gifts. 15 Via della Rotonda.

Cascianelli – Old maps of Rome, as well as prints and rare books. 14 Largo Febo.

Cerruti 1881 – Favorite fashions for Italian yuppies of all ages. Their jackets last a lifetime. 20 Piazza San Lorenzo in Lucina.

Cesari – Two locations, with fine household linen, including tablecloths and place-mats, lingerie and beachwear at 195 Via Barberini; exquisite upholstery fabrics by the meter at 96 Via Frattina.

Cicogna – The ultimate (or nearly) in children's clothing. 138 Via Frattina and 268 Via Cola di Rienzo.

Croff Centro Casa – Inexpensive household items and gifts, some of Italian design. 197 Via Cola di Rienzo, 137 Via Tomacelli, and 52 Via XX Settembre.

Davide Cenci – Classic elegance for men and women. Italian diplomats buy their pin-striped suits and trenchcoats here. 4-7 Via Campo Marzio.

Discount dell'Alta Moda – Last season's *alta moda* at discount prices. 16/A Via Gesù.

Discount System – A high-fashion discount store, featuring clothing, shoes, and leather goods up to 50% off retail. 35 Via Viminale.

Essences – Natural fragrances and the house's own blends of toilet water and perfume. 88 Piazza della Cancelleria.

Ex Libris – Antique books, prints, and rare maps are found in this charming shop. 77/A Via dell'Umiltà.

Fendi – Canvas and leather bags, furs and faux furs, luggage, and clothing. 39 Via Borgognona. Shoes and purse accessories. 4/E Via Borgognona and 55/A Largo Goldoni.

Ferragamo – For high-style women's shoes. 66 Via Condotti.

Filippo – An avant-garde boutique for men and women. 7 *bis* Via Borgognona and 6 Via Condotti.

Fiorucci – Famed, funky sportswear and shoes. 12 Via Genova, 19 Via della Farnesina, 236 Via Nazionale, 27 Via della Maddalena, and elsewhere.

Fornari – Fine silver and other gifts. 71-72 Via Frattina.

Franco Maria Ricci – Sumptuously printed books by a discriminating publisher, sold in an elegant setting. 4/D Via Borgognona.

Funke – Top-quality shoes for men and women plus cordial service. Near the Pantheon. 52 Piazza della Maddalena.

Gabbiano – Modern artworks by Italians and others (there's also a branch in New York City). 51 Via della Frezza.

Galtrucco – All kinds of fabrics, especially pure silk. 23 Via del Tritone.

Genny – Ever-popular boutique for women. 27 Piazza di Spagna.

Gianfranco Ferré – High fashion for women. 6 Via Borgognona.

Gianni Versace – The Milanese designer's Rome outlets. 41 Via Borgognona and 29 Via Bocca di Leone.

Giorgio Armani – High fashion for men and women. 102 and 139 Via del Babuino.

Gucci – Be ready to wait in line for men's and women's shoes, luggage, handbags, and other leather goods. 8 Via Condotti.

Krizia – Elegant women's boutique. 11/B Piazza di Spagna.

Laura Biagiotti – Elegant women's wear. 43 Via Borgognona, corner of Via Belsiana.

Laurent – Good buys in leatherwear. 3 Via Frattina.

Libreria Archeologica – For the bookworm whose passion is the past. The specialty is Rome and Italy, but a few of the books on archaeology and ancient history have a broader reach. 2 Via Palermo.

Libreria Editrice Vaticana – A vast selection of art and archaeological books as well as books on religion and theology at the Vatican's own publisher's outlet. Next to the Vatican's post office in Piazza San Pietro.

Lio Bazaar – Amusing women's shoes. 35 Via Borgognona.

Lion Bookshop – The city's oldest English-language bookstore, chock-full of volumes on Rome's history, travel, and food. 181 Via del Babuino.

Luna di Carta – All types of crafts made from paper — handmade papier-mâché fruit, small sculptures, and hand-colored prints. Il Vicolo dell'Atleta.

Maccalè – Yet another fine boutique for women. 69 Via della Croce.

Mail – English and western saddlery and other riding gear. 154 Via Germanico.

Mario Lucchese – Everything for the golfer, including handmade spike-soled shoes and other tee-time apparel. 162 Via del Babuino.

Mario Valentino – Fine shoes and leather goods. 58 and 84 Via Frattina.

Marisa Pignataro – Outstanding knit dresses and tops in pure wool with interesting color combinations. 20 Via dei Greci.

Maud Frizon – Highly original shoes for women, with corresponding prices. 38 Via Borgognona.

Miranda – Colorful women's woven shawls and jackets. 220 Via delle Carrozze.

Missoni – High-fashion knitwear in unique weaves of often costly blended yarns, such as linen with wool and silk. 38/B Via Borgognona. *Missoni Uomo,* for men, is at 78 Piazza di Spagna.

Ai Monasteri – Products ranging from bath oils to honey and liqueurs from more than 20 monasteries. 72 Corso del Rinascimento.

Moriondo & Gariglio – Delicious hand-dipped chocolates and violets crystallized in sugar. 2 Via della Pilotta.

Myricae – Hand-painted ceramics and such, made by Italian craftsmen from Sardinia to Deruta. 36 Via Frattina.

Naj Oleari – Famed cotton fabrics and accessories from bags to lampshades. 25/A Via di San Giacomo and 32 Via dei Greci.

Nazareno Gabrielli – Excellent leather goods. 3-5 Via Sant'Andrea delle Fratte and 29 Via Borgognona.

Dell'Orologio – Decorative and figurative 20th-century art, including Art Deco, Futurist, and right now. 8 Piazza dell'Orologio.

Ottica Scientifica – Eyeglasses and contact lenses, fitted by one of Rome's best and most scrupulous optometrists; camera supplies and electronic equipment, too. 19 Via delle Convertite, near Piazza San Silvestro.

Ottocento Italiano – The 19th-century look in Italian furniture made from antique wood. They also make bookcases to order. 26 Via Nizza (near Piazza Fiume).

Perla – Avant-garde looks for young women. 88 Piazza di Spagna.

Perrone – Gloves — leather and other. 92 Piazza di Spagna.

Petochi – A treasure trove of fine jewelry and old and new tea services. 23 Piazza di Spagna.

Pineider – Italy's famed stationer. 68-69 Via Due Macelli and Piazza Cardelli.

Polidori – Exclusive menswear and tailoring at 84 Via Condotti and 4/C Via Borgognona; finest pure silks and other fabrics at 4/A Via Borgognona.

Le Quattro Stagioni – A delightful array of handmade ceramics by artisans from all over Italy. US shipping can be arranged. 30/B Via dell'Umiltà.

Ramírez – Latest shoe fashions at reasonable prices. 73 Via del Corso and 85 Via Frattina.

Raphael Salato – For famous-maker Italian men's and women's shoes. 104 and 149 Via Veneto; 34 Piazza di Spagna.

Rinascente – One of the few department stores, offering good buys on gloves, scarves, and clothing for all ages. Piazza Colonna and Piazza Fiume.

Roland's – The specialty here is luxury coats for men and women. Piazza di Spagna.

Salotto – Made-to-order shirts for both sexes. 18 Via di Parione.

Sansone – Large selection of Italian and imported luggage, trunks, and travel bags, as well as wallets, purses, knapsacks, and so on. Repairs and custom designs. 4 Via XX Settembre.

Schostal – Since 1870, traditional supplier of stockings (in silk, linen, cotton, and so on) and other undergarments for men and women. Moderate prices. 158 Via del Corso.

Soggetti – A 2-story showroom of Italy's famed high-style home furnishings and decorating objects — not easy to find in Rome. Near the Piazza Venezia on Via IV Novembre.

Al Sogno Giocattoli – Toys, including huge stuffed animals in amusing window displays. 53 Piazza Navona.

Spazio Sette – Two stories of Italian and imported fine design — everything from pot holders to teapots, placemats, lamps, notebooks, quilts, and furniture. Just off Largo Argentina. 7 Via dei Barbieri.

Stefanel – Lively, youthful sportswear at a dozen branches, the most central of which are 148 Via del Corso, 31-32 Via Frattina, 41 Via del Tritone, 227 Via Nazionale, and 191-193 Via Cola di Rienzo.

Testa – For offbeat, resort, and casual clothes for men. 13 Via Borgognona, and 42 and 104-106 Via Frattina.

Trevi Moda – Best buy for moderately priced, high-quality leather shoes and handbags, located in a favorite tourist area. 33 Via Lavatore.

Trimani – Founded in 1821, this is Rome's oldest wine shop. Its marble decorations are a national monument. 20 Via Goito.

L'Ulivo – Ceramics, handmade by the owner as well as by artisans from Puglia. 61 Via del Monte della Farina.

Valentino – Bold, high-fashion clothes for men and women. 12 Via Condotti and 15-18 Via Bocca di Leone for women; 61 Via del Babuino for men, women, and children; haute couture salon at 24 Via Gregoriana.

Vertecchi – Rome's most important stationer and artists' supplier; also gifts and design products. 38 and 70 Via della Croce, 18 Via Pietro da Cortona, and 12/F Via Attilio Regolo.

SPORTS AND FITNESS: Auto Racing – The *Autodromo di Roma* (*Valle Lunga* racetrack, Campagnano di Roma, Via Cassia, Km 34; phone: 904-1027). Take a bus from Via Lepanto.

Fitness Centers – Rome has relatively few fitness centers and gyms, and those that exist tend to be cramped. An exception is the roomy, well-equipped, and (unusual for Rome) air conditioned *Roman Sport Center* (in the underground passage to the *metropolitana* stop at the top of Via Veneto in the Villa Borghese, 33 Via del Galoppatoio; phone: 320-1667). Although it is a private club, its American owner makes special arrangements for visitors to use the pool, squash court, aerosol room, sauna, Jacuzzi, and two workout gyms, as well as aerobics classes. Another private club, the *Navona Health Center* (39 Via dei Banchi Vecchi; phone: 689-6104), also will open its 3-room gym in an ancient historical palazzo to non-members. Fitness centers accessible to the public include *Aldrovandi Health Center* (11 Via Michele Mercati; phone: 322-1435); *American Workout Studio* (5 Via Giovanni Amendola; phone: 474-6299), run by a former Jane Fonda Workshop instructor; and *Barbara Bouchet Bodyshop* (162 Viale Parioli; phone: 807-5049). Most others are by membership only.

Golf – Both the *Circolo del Golf Roma* (716/A Via Appia Nuova; phone: 788-6159), about 8 miles (12 km) from the center, and the *Olgiata Golf Club* (15 Largo Olgiata; phone: 378-9141), about 12 miles (19 km), have 18-hole courses and extend guest privileges to members of foreign clubs. The former is open to guests Tuesdays through Saturdays; the latter, Tuesdays to Fridays. There also is the 9-hole *Golf Club Fioranello* (Via Appia Nuova, Santa Maria delle Mole; phone: 608058). At *Acquasanta* (Via Appia Nuova; phone: 780-4307), visitors can play Tuesdays through Fridays (if they show a home club membership card) on an 18-hole course. Tee off with spectacular views of ancient ruins in the background; the club also has a lovely swimming pool and an excellent restaurant.

Horseback Riding – For lessons at various levels of proficiency, rentals by the hour (sometimes a subscription for several hours is required), or guided rides in the country, contact the *Circolo Ippico Appia Antica* (Via Appia Nuova, Km 16.5; phone: 724-0197); *Società Ippica Romana* (30 Via dei Monti della Farnesina; phone: 396-6386 or 396-5404); *Scuola d'Equitazione Le Piane* (Campagnano; phone: 904-2478 or 904-1925), or *Circolo Buttero Fontana Nuova* (near Sacrofano, outside Rome; phone: 903-6040). For weekend or week-long riding vacations, contact *Agriturist* (phone: 651-2342) or *Turismo Verde* (phone: 396-9931).

Horse Racing – Trotting races take place at the *Ippodromo Tor di Valle* (Via del Mare, Km 13; phone: 592-6786). Flat races take place at the *Ippodromo delle Capannelle* (1255 Via Appia, Km 12; phone: 799-3143) in the spring and fall.

Jogging – There are two tracks at the *Galoppatoio* in the Villa Borghese; enter at the top of Via Veneto or from Piazza del Popolo. Villa Glori has a 1,180-meter track, which is illuminated at night; the large Villa Pamphili has three tracks, as does Villa Ada, and Villa Torlonia has one pretty track flanked by palm and acacia trees; at *Acqua Acetosa* there is also a dressing room open until 5 PM; and the Baths of Caracalla provide another good running spot (between the road and the Terme).

Soccer – Two highly competitive teams, *Roma* and *Lazio,* play on Sundays from September to May at the *Olympic Stadium* (site of the final game of the *1990 World Cup*), *Foro Italico* (phone: 36851).

Swimming – The pools at the *Cavalieri Hilton* (101 Via Cadlolo; phone: 31511) and the *Aldrovandi Palace* hotel (15 Via Ulisse Aldrovandi; phone: 322-3993) are open to non-guests for a fee. Public pools include the *Piscina Olimpica* (*Foro Italico;* phone: 360-8591 or 360-1498) and the *Piscina delle Rose* (EUR; phone: 592-6717). Swimming in the sea near Rome has become dangerous due to very high levels of pollution; signs prohibiting swimming speckle many nearby beaches. The beach nearest Rome is at Ostia, and it's among the most polluted, very crowded, and strung from end to end with bathing establishments charging admission for entry and use of changing rooms. There are stretches of free beach at Castel Fusano and Castel Porziano, southeast of Ostia; the first is reachable by subway from Stazione Termini. Fregene, farther north along the coast, is very popular with fashionable (and mostly topless) Romans. There's also swimming at Lake Bracciano, about 20 miles (32 km) north of Rome, but no changing facilities. Avoid Sunday crowds.

Tennis – Most courts belong to private clubs. Those at the *Cavalieri Hilton* (101 Via Cadlolo; phone: 31511) and at the *Sheraton Roma* (Viale del Pattinaggio; phone: 5453) are open to non-guests for a fee. There are public courts occasionally available at the *Foro Italico* (phone: 361-9021). Also open to the public is the *Società Ginnastica Roma* (5 Via del Moro Torto; phone: 488-5566), which has 5 courts, open from 9 AM to 9 PM; and in the Appia Antica area, the 4-court *Oasi di Pace* (2 Via degli Eugenii; phone: 718-4550), which also has a swimming pool.

Windsurfing – Windsurf boards and lessons are available at *Castel Porziano* (*primo cancello,* or first gate); in Fregene at the *Stabilimento La Baia* (phone: 646-1647) and the *Miraggio Sporting Club* (phone: 646-1802); and at the *Centro Surf Bracciano* (Lake Bracciano; no phone).

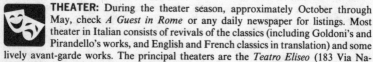 **THEATER:** During the theater season, approximately October through May, check *A Guest in Rome* or any daily newspaper for listings. Most theater in Italian consists of revivals of the classics (including Goldoni's and Pirandello's works, and English and French classics in translation) and some lively avant-garde works. The principal theaters are the *Teatro Eliseo* (183 Via Nazionale; phone: 488-2114), the *Teatro Argentina* (Largo Argentina; phone: 654-4601), the *Teatro Valle* (23 Via Teatro Valle; phone: 654-3794), and the *Teatro Quirino* (1 Via Minghetti; phone: 679-4585). A season of classical drama (in Italian, and sometimes in Greek) is held in July each year in the open-air *Teatro Romano di Ostia Antica* (phone: 565-1913). The *Teatro Sistina* (129 Via Sistina; phone: 482-6841) is Rome's best music hall, offering top class, often imported, musical entertainment on Monday nights, when the regular rep is resting (in the fall, they usually run top-name Brazilian entertainment Monday nights). The charming, turn-of-the-century cabaret theater *Salone Margarita* (75 Via Due Macelli; phone: 679-8269) offers late-night shows and Sunday afternoon concerts. For films in English, check the newspapers for *Cinema Pasquino* (in Trastevere, Vicolo del Piede; phone: 580-3622) and the *Cinema Alcazar* (14 Via Merry del Val; phone: 588-0099), which often has English-language movies on Mondays and Thursdays.

 MUSIC: Again, for current schedules, check *A Guest in Rome* or the daily newspapers. The regular opera season at the *Teatro dell'Opera* (1 Piazza Beniamino Gigli, corner Via Firenze; phone: 461755 or 463641) runs from December through May. The best way to get tickets for good seats is through your hotel concierge or major travel agencies. If you choose to buy them yourself, go to the box office at 10 AM, no more than 3 days prior to the performance. Be prepared to wait — the line moves slowly. During July and August there is a summer opera season at the Baths of Caracalla. (Tickets are on sale at the *Teatro dell'Opera* box office or, on the day of performance, at Caracalla.) The *Rome Ballet* Company also performs at the *Teatro dell'Opera*. Rome's *RAI* symphony orchestra, one of four orchestras run by Radiotelevisione Italiana, the state television network, holds its concert season at the *Auditorio del Foro Italico* (1 Piazza Lauro de Bosis; phone: 365625), from October to June. At roughly the same time, the venerable *Accademia Nazionale di Santa Cecilia* gives first class concerts with international guest artists, either at the *Auditorio Santa Cecilia* (4 Via della Conciliazione; phone: 654-1044) or at the smaller *Sala Concerti* (Concert Hall; 18 Via dei Greci; box office, 6 Via Vittoria; phone: 679-0389). Between October and May, the *Accademia Filarmonica Romana* sponsors a series of concerts at the *Teatro Olimpico* (17 Piazza Gentile da Fabriano; phone: 396-2635 or 393304) — its summer season is held in the garden at the academy headquarters (118 Via Flaminia; phone: 360-1752) — and the *Istituzione Universitaria dei Concerti* holds concerts at the *Auditorium San Leone Magno* (38 Via Bolzano; phone: 853216), and at the university's *Aula Magna* (1 Piazzale Aldo Moro; phone: 361-0051). Other concerts occasionally are held at the *Auditorio del Gonfalone* (32 Via del Gonfalone; phone: 687-5952), and around Rome by the *Coro Polifonico Romano*. Still other musical groups use the *Teatro Ghione* (37 Via delle Fornaci; phone: 637-2294). Finally, there are concerts in many, many churches throughout the year, especially around *Christmas,* and music festivals — classical, jazz, pop, and folk — outdoors in the parks and picturesque piazze during the summer.

NIGHTCLUBS AND NIGHTLIFE: Nightspots are born and die so quickly, slip into and out of fashion so easily, so that visitors would do well to check with Thursday's "TrovaRoma" supplement to the daily *La Repubblica* for an up-to-date idea of what's going on. Since the 1950s, the few nightclubs are clustered around the big hotel/tourist office area of Via Veneto (although obviously there are exceptions). By US standards, their prices are high. In most, the drink minimum is about $25, and a bottle of champagne will cost at least $125. For the younger set on the lookout for disco, jazz, and general hanging-out spots with a few extras — sometimes as much as a piano bar or as little as a dart board — a walk through Trastevere or the Testaccio area around Rome's old general markets and slaughterhouse (the newer bohemian area now that Trastevere has become gentrified) will turn up a host of intriguing places.

Among the nightclubs, small, swanky, expensive *Tartarughino* (near Piazza Navona, 1 Via della Scrofa; phone: 678-6037) is popular with the political set. Everyone seems to know each other, so it seems like a private club. A slightly younger crowd gathers at *Gilda* (near the Spanish Steps, 97 Via Mario de' Fiore; phone: 678-4838), known for its live music and pricey restaurant. *Cica Cica Bum* (pronounced *Chee*-ka *Chee*-ka *Boom* (38 Via Liguria; phone: 464745), with 1940s decor and both easy listening and disco music. Also fashionable is *Open Gate* (22 Via San Nicola da Tolentino; phone: 475-0464), which also has a restaurant and is not far from the Via Veneto. Also fashionable are *Open Gate* (22 Via San Nicola da Tolento; phone: 474-6301), not far from the Via Veneto; and *Jackie O'* (11 Via Boncompagni; phone: 461401). Both are restaurants, but prepare to spend.

The disco *Piper '90* (9 Via Tagliamento; phone: 841-4459) has been packing people in literally for generations. It changes its show every night, so be sure to call ahead to find out if there's a fashion show or break dance demonstration. *La Makumba* (19 Via degli Olimpionici; phone: 396-4392) plays African, Caribbean, and Latin music. The *Kripton* (52 Via Luciani; phone: 870504) is very in with the gilded younger set. It has a bar and restaurant. *La Tentazione* (Km 17.2 on Via Domentana; no phone) goes in for disco happenings, while *Vicolo delle Stelle* (22 Via Cesare Beccaria; phone: 361-

1240) plays disco, rap, soul, and funk music until dawn. *Bulli e Pupi* (on the Aventine Hill, 11/A Via San Saba; phone: 578-2022) is not for executives, but for their offspring. The posh *Hosteria dell'Orso* (33 Via dell'Orso; phone: 656-4904) is a surefire and dignified solution to everyone's musical tastes — the dimly lit, comfortable *Blue Bar* on the main floor offers laid-back piano or guitar music, and *La Cabala* upstairs is a disco scene for titled young Romans. It's in one of Rome's loveliest, centuries-old buildings, not far from the Piazza Navona (closed Sundays). There also is a restaurant (see *Eating Out*). *Hysteria* (3 Via Giovanelli; phone: 864-4587) is the newest "in" spot for dancing and drinking; it has the same owner as the swanky *Jackie O'*, Beatrice Jannozzi. There is live music some weekends and a VIP corner where only celebrities are seated. The locals love it. *Veleno* (27 Via Sardegna, off Via Veneto; phone: 493583) packs in the motor scooter crowd rather than the jet set. For live music and disco dancing in downtown historical Rome, there is the very special *Casanova* (36 Piazza Rondanini; phone: 654-7314). *Notorious* (22 Via San Nicola da Tolentino; phone: 474-6888) mingles disco with dining. *L'Incontro* (near Piazza del Popolo; phone: 361-0934) has a piano bar and disco.

Especially good jazz can be heard (despite the noise of diners in its restaurant) at *Saint Louis Music City* (13/A Via del Cardello; phone: 474-5076) and *Alexanderplatz* (9 Via Ostia; phone: 372-9398). Also try the well-regarded *Café Caruso* (36 Via Monte Testaccio; phone: 574-7720). *Yes Brazil* (in Trastavere, Via San Francesco a Ripa; phone: 581-6267) has live music from 7 to 9 PM and Latin disco after until 1 AM. Two other favorites for live music are *Caffè Latino* (96 Via di Monte Testaccio; phone: 574-4020) and *Grigio Notte* (30/B Via dei Fenaroli; phone: 686-8340) for jazz, salsa, and drinks.

If you're just an amiable barfly who might like to strike up a pleasant conversation in English, the place to go is the bar at the *D'Inghilterra* hotel (14 Via Bocca di Leone; phone: 672161); there is no music except for the tinkling of ice cubes, but the bartender is the nicest in town. Also drop by another occasional American haunt, *Little Bar* (54/A Via Gregoriana — the street where the big fashion houses are located; no phone).

For those with a *funiculi funicula* idea of Italy as peasant exuberance expressed through music, you can spend an evening joining in with the singing waiters and waitresses at the twin restaurants (opened in the 1960s in Trastevere by two American brothers) *Da Meo Patacca* (30 Piazza dei Mercanti; phone: 581-6198) and *Da Ciceraucchio* (1 Via del Porto; phone: 580-6046). You might think that you won't be able to stand all the noise, but the wine flows freely and fun is on the house; so take the kids along and enjoy.

BEST IN TOWN

CHECKING IN: The *Italian Government Travel Office* (*ENIT*) offers lists of hotels in Rome, giving the class of each, its address, and a few other details (such as the existence of a restaurant, air conditioning, parking facilities, and so on), but no telephone numbers. One-star, or fourth class, hotels are not listed, and price ranges for individual hotels are not given, but a general range of prices for each of the four hotel categories is included.

The rates posted in Italian hotel rooms include service charges and value added tax (VAT — 19% in five-star hotels, 9% in others), so receiving the bill at the end of a stay rarely is a cause for shock. If the locality imposes a visitor's tax (a minimal amount, called the *imposta di soggiorno*), that, too, usually is included in the posted price. No surcharge may be made for central heating, but a surcharge (often per person) for air conditioning is allowed.

In Italy, a single room is a *camera singola;* a double room is a *camera doppia.* If you request a single and are given a double, it may not cost more than the maximum price for a single room. If you specify a double, you may be asked whether you prefer a *camera a due letti* (twin-bedded room) or a *camera matrimoniale* (with a double bed). A single room to which an extra bed has been added may not cost more than a double room, and a double room to which an extra bed has been added may not increase in price by more than 35%. And the price of a double usually holds whether it's occupied by one or two people.

If you are traveling on a shoestring, you will be interested to know that a great many rooms that do not have a private bath or shower (*bagno privato* or *doccia privata*) do have a sink with hot and cold running water (occasionally cold water only) and often a bidet. Sometimes there even is a toilet. Thus you can save money by denying yourself the luxury of a private bathroom and still not be totally without convenience. Some places have showers or baths down the hall that guests may use — often for free or for a nominal fee.

Rentals – An attractive alternative for the visitor planning to stay in Rome for a week or more is to rent an apartment or villa. These offer a wide range of luxury and convenience, depending on the price you want to pay. One of the advantages of staying in a house, apartment (usually called a "flat" overseas), or other rented vacation home is that you will feel much more like a visitor than a tourist.

Known to Europeans as a "holiday let" or a "self-catering holiday," a vacation in a furnished rental has both the advantages and disadvantages of living "at home" abroad. It can be less expensive than staying in a first class hotel, although very luxurious and expensive rentals are available, too. It has the comforts of home, including a kitchen, which means potential savings on food. Furthermore, it gives a sense of the country that a large hotel often cannot. On the other hand, a certain amount of housework is involved because if you don't eat out, you have to cook, and though some rentals (especially the luxury ones) include a cleaning person, most don't. (If the rental doesn't include daily cleaning, arrangements often can be made with a maid service.)

For a family, two or more couples, or a group of friends, the per-person cost — even for a luxurious rental — can be quite reasonable. Weekly and monthly rates are available to reduce costs still more. But best of all is the amount of space that no conventional hotel room can equal. As with hotels, the rates for properties in Rome are seasonal, rising during the peak travel season, while for others they remain the same year-round. To have your pick of the properties available, you should begin to make arrangements for a rental at least 6 months in advance.

There are several ways of finding a suitable rental property. Most provincial and local tourist boards in Italy have information on companies arranging rentals in their areas. US branches of the Italian Government Travel Office have lists of agents who specialize in villa and apartment rentals, and the Rome board issues a guide to villas and flats for rent that meet some range of minimum standards.

Many tour operators regularly include a few rental packages among their offerings; these generally are available through a travel agent. In addition, a number of companies specialize in rental vacations. Their plans typically include rental of the property (or several properties, but usually for a minimum stay per location), a rental car, and airfare.

The companies listed below rent properties in Rome. They handle the booking and confirmation paperwork and can be expected to provide more information about the properties than that which might ordinarily be gleaned from a short listing in an accommodations guide.

Castles, Cottages and Flats (7 Faneuil Hall Marketplace, Boston, MA 02109; phone: 617-742-6030). Handles apartments in the city; some villas outside the city. Small charge ($5) for receipt of main catalogue, refundable upon booking.

Eastone Overseas Accommodations (198 Southampton Dr., Jupiter, FL 33458; phone: 407-575-6991). Handles apartments, cottages, and villas.

Europa-Let (PO Box 3537, Ashland, OR 97520; phone: 800-462-4486 or 503-482-5806). Offers apartments and villas.

Grandluxe International (165 Chestnut St., Allendale, NJ 07401; phone: 201-327-2333). Rents farmhouses on the outskirts of the city.

International Lodging Corp. (300 1st Ave., Suite 7C, New York, NY 10009; phone: 212-228-5900). Rents flats.

Rent a Vacation Everywhere (*RAVE;* 328 Main St. E., Suite 526, Rochester, NY 14604; phone: 716-454-6440). Rentals include moderate to luxurious apartments in Rome.

Vacanze in Italia (PO Box 297, Falls Village, CT 06031; phone: 800-533-5405). This organization has some small apartments in Rome.

VHR Worldwide (235 Kensington Ave., Norwood, NJ 07648; phone: 201-767-9393, locally; 800-NEED-A-VILLA). Rents apartments.

Villas International Ltd. (605 Market St. Suite 510, San Francisco, CA 94105; phone: 800-221-2260). Rents apartments.

And for further information, including a general discussion of all forms of vacation rentals, evaluating costs, and information on rental opportunities in Rome, see *A Traveler's Guide to Vacation Rentals in Europe.* Available in general bookstores, it also can be ordered from Penguin USA (120 Woodbine St., Bergenfield, NJ 07621; phone: 800-526-0275 and ask for cash sales) for $11.95, plus postage and handling.

In addition, a useful publication, the *Worldwide Home Rental Guide,* lists properties throughout Europe, as well as the managing agencies. Issued twice annually, single copies may be available at larger newsstands for $10 an issue. For a year's subscription, send $18 to *Worldwide Home Rental Guide,* PO Box 2842, Sante Fe, NM 87504 (phone: 505-988-5188).

When considering a particular vacation rental property, look for answers to the following questions:

- How do you get from the airport to the property?
- What size and number of beds are provided?
- How far is the property from whatever else is important to you, such as a golf course or nightlife?
- How far is the nearest market?
- Are baby-sitters, cribs, bicycles, or anything else you may need for your children available?
- Is maid service provided daily?
- Is air conditioning and/or a phone provided?
- Is a car rental part of the package? Is a car necessary?

Home Exchanges – Still another alternative for travelers who are content to stay in one place during their vacation is a home exchange: The Smith family from Chicago moves into the home of the Rossi family in Rome, while the Rossis enjoy a stay in the Smiths' home. The home exchange is an exceptionally inexpensive way to ensure comfortable, reasonable living quarters with amenities that no hotel possibly could offer; often the trade includes a car. Moreover, it allows you to live in a new community in a way that few tourists ever do: For a little while, at least, you will become something of a resident.

Several companies publish directories of individuals and families willing to trade homes with others for a specific period of time. In some cases, you must be willing to list your own home in the directory; in others, you can subscribe without appearing in it. Most listings are for straight exchanges only, but each directory also has a number of listings placed by people interested in either exchanging or renting (for instance, if they own a second home). Other arrangements include exchanges of hospitality while owners are in residence or youth exchanges, where your teenager is put up as a guest in return for your putting up their teenager at a later date. A few house-sitting opportunities also are available. In most cases, arrangements for the actual exchange take place directly between you and the foreign host. There is no guarantee that you will find a listing in the area in which you are interested, but each of the organizations given below includes Italian homes among its hundreds or even thousands of foreign listings.

Home Base Holidays (7 Park Ave., London N13 5PG, England; phone: 81-886-8752). For $48 a year, subscribers receive four listings, with an option to list in all four.

Intervac US/International Home Exchange Service (Box 190070, San Francisco, CA 94119; phone: 415-435-3497). Some 8,000 listings. For $45 (plus postage), subscribers receive copies of the three directories published yearly, and are entitled to list their home in one of them; a black-and-white photo may be included with the listing for an additional $11. A $5 discount is given to travelers over age 62.

Loan-A-Home (2 Park La., Apt. 6E, Mt. Vernon, NY 10552; phone: 914-664-7640). Specializes in long-term (4 months or more — excluding July and August) housing arrangements worldwide for students, professors, businesspeople, and retirees, although its two annual directories (with supplements) carry a small list of short-term rentals and/or exchanges. $35 for a copy of one directory and one supplement; $45 for two directories and two supplements.

Vacation Exchange Club (PO Box 820, Haleiwa, HI 96712; phone: 800-638-3841). Some 10,000 listings. For $50, the subscriber receives two directories — one in late winter, one in the spring — and is listed in one.

World Wide Exchange (1344 Pacific Ave., Suite 103, Santa Cruz, CA 95060; phone: 408-476-4206). The $45 annual membership fee includes one listing (for house, yacht, or motorhome) and three guides.

Worldwide Home Exchange Club (13 Knightsbridge Green, London SW1X 7QL, England; phone: 71-589-6055; or 806 Brantford Ave., Silver Spring, MD 20904; no phone). Handles over 1,500 listings a year worldwide. For $25 a year, you will receive two listings, as well as supplements.

Better Homes and Travel (formerly *Home Exchange International*), with an office in New York, and representatives in Los Angeles, London, Paris, and Milan, functions differently in that it publishes no directory and shepherds the exchange process most of the way. Interested parties supply the firm with photographs of themselves and their homes, information on the type of home they want and where, and a registration fee of $50. The company then works with its other offices to propose a few possibilities, and only when a match is made do the parties exchange names, addresses, and phone numbers. For this service, *Better Homes and Travel* charges a closing fee, which ranges from $150 to $500 for switches from 2 weeks to 3 months in duration, and from $300 to $600 for longer switches. Contact *Better Homes and Travel* at 30 E. 33rd St., New York, NY 10016 (phone: 212-689-6608).

Home Stays – If the idea of actually staying in a private home as the guest of an Italian family appeals to you, check with the *United States Servas Committee,* which maintains a list of hosts throughout the world (at present, there are about 750 listings in Italy) willing to throw open their doors to foreigners, entirely free of charge.

The aim of this nonprofit cultural program is to promote international understanding and peace, and every effort is made to discourage freeloaders. *Servas* will send you an application form and the name of the nearest of some 200 interviewers around the US for you to contact. After the interview, if you're approved, you'll receive documentation certifying you as a *Servas* traveler. There is a membership fee of $45 per person, as well as a deposit of $15 to receive the host list, refunded on its return. The list gives the name, address, age, occupation, and other particulars of each host, including languages spoken. From then on, it is up to you to write to prospective hosts directly, and *Servas* makes no guarantee that you will be accommodated.

Servas stresses that you should choose only people you really want to meet, and that during your stay (which normally lasts between 2 nights and 2 weeks) you should be interested mainly in your hosts, not in sightseeing. It also suggests that one way to show your appreciation once you've returned home is to become a host yourself. The minimum age of a *Servas* traveler is 18 (however, children under 18 may accompany their parents), and though quite a few are young people who've just finished college, there are travelers (and hosts) in all age ranges and occupations. Contact *Servas* at 11 John St., Room 407, New York, NY 10038 (phone: 212-267-0252).

You also might be interested in a publication called the *International Meet-the-People Directory,* published by the *International Visitor Information Service.* It lists several agencies in a number of foreign countries (37 worldwide, 18 in Europe, including Italy) that arrange home visits for Americans, either for dinner or overnight stays. To order a copy, send $5.95 to the *International Visitor Information Service* (733 15th St. NW, Suite 300, Washington, DC 20005; phone: 202-783-6540). For other local organizations and services offering home exchanges, contact the local tourist authority.

■ **A warning about telephone surcharges in hotels:** A lot of digits may be involved once a caller starts dialing beyond national borders, but avoiding operator-assisted calls can cut costs considerably and bring rates into a somewhat more reasonable range — except for calls made through hotel switchboards. One of the most unpleasant surprises travelers encounter in many foreign countries is the amount they find tacked on to their hotel bill for telephone calls, because foreign hotels routinely add on astronomical surcharges. (It's not at all uncommon to find 300% or 400% added to the actual telephone charges.)

Until recently, the only recourse against this unconscionable overcharging was to call collect when phoning from abroad or to use a telephone credit card — available through a simple procedure from any local US phone company. (Note, however, that even if you use a telephone credit card, some hotels still may charge a fee for line usage.) Now *American Telephone and Telegraph (AT&T)* offers *USA Direct,* a service that connects users, via a toll-free number, with an *AT&T* operator in the US, who will then put the call through at the standard international rate. Another new feature of this service is that travelers abroad can reach US toll-free (800) numbers by calling a *USA Direct* operator, who will connect them. Charges for all calls made through *USA Direct* appear on the caller's regular US phone bill. To reach this service in Italy, dial 172-1011. For a brochure and wallet card listing the toll-free number for other European countries, contact International Information Service, *AT&T Communications,* 635 Grant St., Pittsburgh, PA 15219 (phone: 800-874-4000).

AT&T also has put together *Teleplan,* an agreement among certain hoteliers that sets a limit on surcharges for calls made by guests from their rooms. As we went to press, *Teleplan* was in effect only in selected hotels in Rome. *Teleplan* agreements stipulate a flat, low rate for credit card or collect calls, and a flat percentage on calls paid for at the hotel. For further information, contact *AT&T*'s International Information Service (address above).

Until these services become universal, it's wise to ask for the surcharge rate *before* calling from a hotel. If the rate is high, it's best to use a telephone credit card, make a collect call, or place the call and ask the party to call right back. If none of these choices is possible, to avoid surcharges make international calls from the local post office or one of the special telephone centers located throughout Italy.

Hotels – Of the more than 500 hotels in Rome, the following are recommended either for some special charm, location, or bargain price in their category. Those without restaurants are noted, although all serve breakfast if desired, and all have heating and telephones in the rooms unless otherwise stated. In high season prices can be staggering; expect to pay from $550 up to $700 for a double room with bath in the hotels listed as very expensive, from $350 to $550 for hotels in the expensive price range, from $150 to $350 in the moderate category, and under $150 (to as low as $90) in the inexpensive category. Off-season rates are about 10% lower.

Cavalieri Hilton International – Far from the historic center of Rome at the top of a lovely hill (Monte Mario) overlooking much of the city, with shuttle buses to Via Veneto and Piazza di Spagna running hourly during shopping hours only. But the swimming pool is especially desirable in summer, and the rooftop restaurant, *La Pergola,* wins high praise from food critics. A resort property with year-round swimming, tennis, a sauna, and other diversions, it has 387 rooms. Business facilities include meeting rooms for up to 2,100, English-speaking concierge, foreign currency exchange, secretarial services in English, audiovisual equipment, photocopiers, cable television news, translation services, and express checkout. 101 Via Cadlolo (phone: 31511; fax: 315-12241; telex: 625337HILTRO I). Very expensive.

Eden – Among the most elegant in Rome, this hotel has excellent service, the intimate *Charles Roof Garden* restaurant (see *Eating Out*), and a panoramic bar. There are 116 air conditioned rooms with TV sets. Business facilities include meeting rooms for up to 214, English-speaking concierge, foreign currency exchange, secretarial services in English, audiovisual equipment, photocopiers, cable television news, translation services, and express checkout. 49 Via Ludovisi (phone: 474-3551; fax: 482-1584; telex: 610567EDENRM I). Very expensive.

Excelsior – Big, bustling, but efficient, it dominates the Via Veneto, next to the US Embassy. It's a favorite with Americans, and the bar is a popular meeting place. There are 383 rooms in this member of the CIGA chain. Business facilities include 24-hour room service, meeting rooms for up to 400, English-speaking concierge, foreign currency exchange, secretarial services in English, audiovisual equipment, photocopiers, computers, cable television news, translation services, and express checkout. 125 Via Veneto (phone: 4708; fax: 482-6205; telex: 610232EXCEROI). Very expensive.

Grand – The pride of the CIGA chain in Rome, and traditionally the capital's most dignified hotel. It is truly grand — formal, well run, and elegant in style and service. It has 175 rooms and a central (if not exactly prime) location between the railroad station and Via Veneto areas. Its *Le Restaurant* is pretty near perfect (see *Eating Out*) and the two bars are cozy and chic — indeed, perfect, according to a recent industry poll on Roman watering holes. Afternoon tea also is served, with harp music. Business facilities include 24-hour room service, meeting rooms for up to 400, English-speaking concierge, foreign currency exchange, secretarial services in English, audiovisual equipment, photocopiers, computers, cable television news, translation services, and express checkout. 3 Via Vittorio Emanuele Orlando (phone: 4709; fax: 474-7307; telex: 610210GRANDRO I). Very expensive.

Hassler–Villa Medici – At the top of the Spanish Steps and within easy striking distance of the best shopping in Rome, favored by a loyal clientele. Guestrooms could stand some refurbishing, and the public rooms have seen better days. Each of the 108 rooms is individually decorated, and manager Albert Wirth is an attentive host. The roof garden restaurant has only so-so food, but splendid views, and offers Sunday brunch. Business facilities include meeting rooms for up to 180, English-speaking concierge, foreign currency exchange, secretarial services in English, audiovisual equipment, photocopiers, cable television news, translation services, and express checkout. 6 Piazza Trinità dei Monti (phone: 679-0770; fax: 678-9991; telex: 61028 HASLER I). Very expensive.

Aldrovandi Palace – Quiet, with 139 rooms in a fashionable residential area next to the Villa Borghese, and not far from Via Veneto, it has a delightful park with a swimming pool and a full-facility health club. Its restaurant, *Relais le Piscine,* is next door at 6 Via Mangili. Business facilities include 24-hour room service, meeting rooms for up to 400, English-speaking concierge, foreign currency exchange, secretarial services in English, audiovisual equipment, photocopiers, computers, cable television news, translation services, and express checkout. The hotel is at 15 Via Ulisse Aldrovandi (phone: 322-3993; fax: 322-1435; telex: 616141ALDROV I). Expensive.

Ambasciatori Palace – Across the street from the US Embassy, it has 145 generally spacious rooms, old-fashioned amenities, and a very convenient location. Business facilities include 24-hour room service, meeting rooms for up to 200, English-speaking concierge, foreign currency exchange, secretarial services in English, audiovisual equipment, photocopiers, cable television news, translation services, and express checkout. 70 Via Veneto (phone: 47493; fax: 474-3601; telex: 610241HOTAMB I). Expensive.

Atlante Star – Near the Vatican, this large, modern hotel boasts a roof garden with a splendid view of St. Peter's dome, an excellent restaurant, and an efficiently equipped business center. Parking is available, as is the rental of a private plane for island-hopping. Business facilities include 24-hour room service, meeting rooms for up to 83, English-speaking concierge, foreign currency exchange, secretarial services in English, audiovisual equipment, photocopiers, computers, cable television news, translation services, and express checkout. 34 Via Vitelleschi (phone: 687-9558; fax: 687-2300; telex: 622355). Expensive.

Holiday Inn Crowne Plaza Minerva – The reopening of this 134-room, well-located hotel, where Stendhal used to stay, was something of an event for downtown Rome. Its pricey restoration preserved the old baroque adornment. *La Cesta,* its restaurant (see *Eating Out*), has not yet won over all the food experts, but is quite good. Near the Pantheon. Business facilities include meeting rooms for up to 250, English-speaking concierge, foreign currency exchange, secretarial services in English, audiovisual equipment, photocopiers, cable television news, translation services, and express checkout. Piazza della Minerva (phone: 684-1888; fax: 679-4165; telex: 620091). Expensive.

Lord Byron – A small (47 rooms) first-rate place in the fashionable Parioli residential district, this once was a private villa, and it maintains the atmosphere of a private club. It has a celebrated restaurant, *Relais Le Jardin* (see *Eating Out*). Business facilities include 24-hour room service, meeting rooms for up to 100, English-speaking concierge, foreign currency exchange, secretarial services in English, audiovisual equipment, photocopiers, cable television news, translation services, and express checkout. 5 Via Giuseppe de Notaris (phone: 322-49541; fax: 322-0405; telex: 611216HBYRON I). Expensive.

Majestic – Completely restored with 100 rooms and suites, this air conditioned, century-old hostelry (the oldest on Via Veneto) is across the street from the American Embassy. Its opulently decorated reception room has a handsome fresco ceiling. There is a restaurant and the terrace bar offers a fine view of the Roman skyline. Business facilities include 24-hour room service, meeting rooms for up to 150, English-speaking concierge, secretarial services in English, audiovisual equipment, photocopiers, computers, cable television news, translation services, and express checkout. 50 Via Veneto (phone: 486841; fax: 488-0984; telex: 622262). Expensive.

Nazionale – Another old favorite (of Sartre and de Beauvoir, among others), the 86 renovated rooms here are very central, next to the Chamber of Deputies, between Via del Corso and the Pantheon. Business facilities include meeting rooms for up to 900, English-speaking concierge, foreign currency exchange, secretarial services in English, audiovisual equipment, photocopiers, and express checkout. 131 Piazza Montecitorio (phone: 678-9251; fax: 678-6677; telex: 6211427NATEL I). Expensive.

Parco dei Principi – This modern hotel is on the edge of Villa Borghese in the Parioli residential district, not far from Via Veneto. It has 203 rooms, and a small swimming pool in a lovely garden. Business facilities include meeting rooms for up to 500, English-speaking concierge, foreign currency exchange, secretarial services in English, audiovisual equipment, photocopiers, computers, translation services, and express checkout. 5 Via Gerolamo Frescobaldi (phone: 855-1758; fax: 884-5104; telex: 610517PRISOM I). Expensive.

Raphael – Behind Piazza Navona, it's a favorite of Italian politicians (it's near the Senate and the Chamber of Deputies), with 83 rooms. Some are small, some could use a bit of refurbishing, but loyal patrons love the antiques in the lobby, the cozy bar, and the location. The roof terrace has one of Rome's finest views. Business facilities include 2 English-speaking concierges, foreign currency exchange, secretarial services in English, photocopiers, cable television news, translation services, and express checkout. 2 Largo Febo (phone: 650881; fax: 687-8993; telex: 622396RHOTEL). Expensive.

Sheraton Roma – With 631 rooms and 25 suites, air conditioning, and a conference center that can handle up to 1,200 people, this modern, efficient hotel is also the one with the most sports facilities. Located in the suburb of EUR about 25 minutes south of central Rome, it has ample parking and regular shuttle-bus service to downtown and to the nearby Leonardo da Vinci Airport. There are 2 restaurants and a piano bar. Pluses include a health club, squash and tennis courts, outdoor pool, jogging circuit, sauna, and masseur. Business facilities include 24-hour room service, English-speaking concierge, foreign currency exchange, secretarial services in English, audiovisual equipment, photocopiers, computers, cable television news, translation services, and express checkout. Viale del Pattinaggio (phone: 5453; fax: 594-3281; telex: 626077SHEROM I). Expensive.

Sole al Pantheon – For those without a car, this 400-year-old, 25-room hostelry is in a perfect location. Lavishly renovated from the days when the poet Ariosto stayed here, today's conveniences include air conditioning and some spacious rooms (a few of the guestrooms have Jacuzzis). Shut your eyes to the garish decor in the lobby, and focus instead on the fine views from the upper rooms. Business facilities include an English-speaking concierge, foreign currency exchange, photocopiers, translation services, and express checkout. 73 Piazza della Rotonda (phone: 678-0441; fax: 684-0689). Expensive.

Cicerone – In the residential and commercial area of Prati on the Vatican side of the river, but convenient nevertheless because it's just across from Piazza del Popolo and the Spanish Steps. It has modern and spacious public areas, 237 well-appointed rooms, friendly, attentive service, and a large garage. Business facilities include meeting rooms for up to 200, English-speaking concierge, foreign currency exchange, secretarial services in English, audiovisual equipment, photocopiers, cable television news, translation services, and express checkout. 55/C Via

Cicerone (phone: 3576; fax: 654-1383; telex: 622498CICER I). Expensive to moderate.

Columbus – In a restored 15th-century palace right in front of St. Peter's, this 107-room hotel offers antique furniture, paintings, and a garden — a lot of atmosphere for the price. 33 Via della Conciliazione (phone: 686-4874). Expensive to moderate.

Eliseo – Just off Via Veneto, this has traditional furnishings (with a slightly French air) in the public rooms and in some of the 50 guestrooms; others are supermodern. A roof restaurant looks out over the tops of the umbrella pines in the Villa Borghese. 30 Via di Porta Pinciana (phone: 460556). Expensive to moderate.

Flora – At the top of Via Veneto, right next to the Villa Borghese, the 174 rooms are traditional, reliable, and not without charm. Business facilities include meeting rooms for up to 200, English-speaking concierge, foreign currency exchange, secretarial services in English, audiovisual equipment, photocopiers, computers, translation services, and express checkout. 191 Via Veneto (phone: 497281). Expensive to moderate.

Forum – Built around a medieval tower in the middle of the Imperial Forums, this charming 79-room hotel is a bit out of the way but worth any inconvenience for the spectacular view of ancient Rome from its roof garden. The food here is less spectacular. 25 Via Tor dei Conti (phone: 679-2446). Expensive to moderate.

D'Inghilterra – Extremely popular with knowledgeable travelers, its 102 rooms have numbered Anatole France, Mark Twain, and Ernest Hemingway among many illustrious guests. Particularly attractive are the top-floor suites, some with flowered terraces. Be sure to ask for a spacious room; some are small, inevitable in older, downtown hotels. There is a small and simpatico restaurant (the *Roman Garden*), and the ever-crowded bar is a cozy haven for Roman patricians. Business facilities include meeting rooms for up to 50, English-speaking concierge, audiovisual equipment, photocopiers, computers, cable television news, and express checkout. Near the Spanish Steps, in the middle of the central shopping area. 14 Via Bocca di Leone (phone: 672161; fax: 684-0828; telex: 614552). Expensive to moderate.

Anglo-Americano – Just off Piazza Barberini, it has 115 rooms, and the back ones look out on the garden of Palazzo Barberini. Business facilities include English-speaking concierge, and photocopiers. 12 Via delle Quattro Fontane (phone: 472941; fax: 474-6428; telex: 626147ANCAM I). Moderate.

Degli Aranci – Small and quiet, it's in the Parioli residential district and has 48 rooms, a bar, and a lovely garden restaurant. Business facilities include 24-hour room service, meeting rooms for up to 40, English-speaking concierge, secretarial services in English, audiovisual equipment, photocopiers, translation services, and express checkout. 11 Via Barnaba Oriani (phone: 879774; fax: 879774; telex: 621071). Moderate.

Atlas – With 45 rooms and a flowered roof garden, this place has a central location. 3 Via Rasella (phone: 488-2140). Moderate.

Campo dei Fiori – Near the Campo dei Fiori square — a market area since the 1500s — the Renaissance palaces, the giant Palazzo Cancelleria, and the Palazzo Farnese (French Embassy), which was partly designed by Michelangelo, it is one of the coziest (and narrowest) in the area. The rustic rooms are small and sparsely decorated, but the exposed brick walls, hand-painted bathroom ceilings, and detailed architecture make up for the lack of space. For guests willing to climb 6 flights, there's a wonderful view of the city from the roof garden. No restaurant or bar. Business facilities include meeting rooms for up to 40, translation services, and express checkout. 6 Via del Biscione (phone: 687-4886). Moderate.

Cardinal – On Renaissance Rome's stateliest street, this restored 66-room palace (attributed to Bramante) is convenient for exploring some of the city's hidden treasures, but less so for shopping in the city center. No restaurant. 62 Via Giulia (phone: 654-2719). Moderate.

Fontana – A restored, air conditioned 13th-century monastery next to the Trevi Fountain, with cell-like rooms — though 10 of the 30 rooms have great views of the fabulous fountain — and a lovely rooftop bar. A bargain in every way. Business facilities include meeting rooms for up to 35, English-speaking concierge, and secretarial services in English. 96 Piazza di Trevi (phone: 678-6113). Moderate.

Pullman Boston – The roof garden is just one of the selling points of this carefully renovated 120-room hostelry, well located between Via Veneto and the Spanish Steps. Business travelers will appreciate the services. Business facilities include meeting rooms for up to 90, English-speaking concierge, secretarial services in English, audiovisual equipment, cable television news, translation services, and express checkout. The breakfast buffet is a serendipitous plus. Good value. 47 Via Lombardia (phone: 473951; in the US, 800-223-9862; fax: 482-1019; telex: 622247ETAPRM I). Moderate.

La Residenza – An exceptional bargain on a quiet street just behind Via Veneto. Old-fashioned and well-maintained, it has 27 rooms and feels much more like a private villa than a hotel. Book well in advance. Full American breakfast, but no restaurant per se. Business facilities include meeting rooms for up to 25, English-speaking concierge, foreign currency exchange, secretarial services in English, photocopiers, cable television news, and translation services. No credit cards accepted. 22 Via Emilia (phone: 488-0789; fax: 485721; telex: 410423). Moderate.

Santa Chiara – Beautifully renovated last year, this centrally located, 94-room hostelry has been in the Corteggiani family since 1834. No dining room, but close to many restaurants. Business facilities include meeting rooms for up to 40, English-speaking concierge, audiovisual equipment, photocopiers, cable television news, and express checkout. 21 Via Santa Chiara (phone: 683-3763; fax: 687-3144). Moderate.

Scalinata di Spagna – Tiny, but spectacularly placed overlooking the Spanish Steps, it's opposite the pricey *Hassler*. There are 14 rooms, no restaurant. 17 Piazza Trinità dei Monti (phone: 684-0598). Moderate.

Senato – Newly renovated, this 50-room hotel with delightful views of the Pantheon from the front rooms has air conditioning. A good value. Business facilities include English-speaking concierge, foreign currency exchange, photocopiers, and express checkout. 73 Piazza della Rotonda (phone: 679-3231; fax: 684-0297). Moderate.

Sitea – Gianni de Luca and his Scottish wife, Shirley, have bestowed the coziness of a private home on their 40-room, 5-floor hotel opposite the *Grand*. Rooms have high ceilings, crystal chandeliers, and hand-painted Florentine dressers. Other amenities: sitting rooms and a sun-drenched penthouse bar. 90 Via Vittorio Emanuele Orlando (phone: 482-7560). Moderate.

Trevi – Located in a recently renovated palazzo only a few steps from the fabled fountain. Tiny (20 rooms, all with private baths), this 4-story hotel offers many amenities, including air conditioning. 20 Vicolo del Babuccio (phone: 684-1406). Moderate.

Villa Florence – A charming 19th-century patrician villa in a residential area a few minutes' drive from the Via Veneto. The comfortable, modern rooms have TV sets, radio, and mini-bar, and are complemented by touches of ancient Rome in the public areas. Parking facilities and nice gardens. 28 Via Nomentana (phone: 440-3036). Moderate.

Aberdeen – Small and unpretentious, this completely renovated 26-room inn stars for its prime location near Parliament. Some rooms are air conditioned, and there's a buffet breakfast. 48 Via Firenze (phone: 481-9340; fax: 482-1092). Moderate to inexpensive.

Canova – All 15 comfortable rooms in this quiet hostelry are air conditioned. There is a small café on the roof and an inexpensive restaurant next door. Well located between the Roman Forum and Santa Maria Maggiore. 10/A Via Urbana (phone: 481-9123; fax: 481-9123). Moderate to inexpensive.

Clodio – A modern 61-room hotel on the Prati side of the river, close to RAI's headquarters and to the *Foro Italico,* where the *International Tennis Championship* is held every May. 10 Via Santa Lucia (phone: 317541; telex: 625050). Moderate to inexpensive.

Coronet – Guests won't find luxurious accommodations at this pensione, but it is in a central area just a few blocks from the Piazza Venezia. Inside the Palazza Doria, a palace which still is the home of the family who built it, some of its rooms have private baths. No restaurant. Business facilities include English-speaking concierge and foreign currency exchange. 5 Piazza Grazioli (phone: 679-2341). Inexpensive.

Dinesen – Off Via Veneto and next to the Villa Borghese, the 20 rooms in this charming place with a 19th-century air are a real bargain. Breakfast is included. No restaurant. 18 Via di Porta Pinciana (phone: 460932). Inexpensive.

Fabrello White – For basic, affordable accommodations, this pensione is a good bet. Not all of the 33 rooms have baths, but some have terrace views of the river. On the right bank of the Tiber, it's a 10-minute walk to the Spanish Steps. 11 Via Vittoria Colonna (phone: 360-4446/7). Inexpensive.

Gregoriana – On the street of the same name — high fashion's headquarters in Rome — this tiny (19 air conditioned rooms) gem attracts the fashionable. Its decor is reminiscent of Art Deco, with room letters (rather than numbers) by the late fashion illustrator Erté. No restaurant, though a continental breakfast is included. No credit cards accepted. 18 Via Gregoriana (phone: 679-4269 or 679-7988). Inexpensive.

King – The 61 rooms in this well-positioned, immaculate hotel are reasonably priced. No restaurant, though breakfast is served. Business facilities include English-speaking concierge, foreign currency exchange, secretarial services in English, photocopiers, cable television news, translation services, and express checkout. 131 Via Sistina (phone: 474-1515; fax: 487-1813; telex: 626236KINGHO I). Inexpensive.

Locarno – Near the Piazza del Popolo and the Spanish Steps, this Belle Epoque hotel often attracts artists, writers, and intellectuals. The 35 rooms have Victorian furniture, and many are large enough to include couches and desks. A clever touch here — guest bikes for getting around. During winter, a fire burns in the lounge, and in the summer drinks and breakfast are served on the terrace. Business facilities include meeting rooms for up to 15, English-speaking concierge, secretarial services in English, photocopiers, and express checkout. 22 Via della Penna (phone: 361-0841; fax: 321-5249; telex: 622251HOTLOC I). Inexpensive.

Margutta – Try for the two rooms on the roof (Nos. 50 and 51), complete with fireplaces and surrounded by a terrace. This 21-room hotel is near Piazza del Popolo and has an English-speaking concierge. No restaurant. 34 Via Laurina (phone: 679-8440). Inexpensive.

Sant'Anselmo – In a small villa on the Aventine Hill, this beflowered bargain has 26 rooms, a family atmosphere, but no restaurant. (Nearby are 4 other villas — with this one, totaling about 120 rooms — each with similar accommodations and prices, and all run by the same management.) Reservations necessary well in advance. Business facilities include meeting rooms for up to 50, English-speaking concierge, foreign currency exchange, secretarial services in English, and photo-copiers. 2 Piazza di Sant'Anselmo (phone: 574-5174; fax: 578-3604; telex: 622812). Inexpensive.

Teatro di Pompeo – History, literally, is at the root of this hotel, as its foundation was originally laid in 55 BC and is said to have supported the Pompey's Theater, where Julius Caesar met his untimely end. On a quiet street, its 12 charming rooms have hand-painted tiles and beamed ceilings. No restaurant. Business facilities include meeting rooms for up to 20, English-speaking concierge, foreign currency exchange, audiovisual equipment, and photocopiers. 8 Largo del Pallaro (phone: 687-2566; fax: 687-2566). Inexpensive.

 EATING OUT: The ancient Romans were the originators of the first fully developed cuisine of the Western world. Drawing on an abundance of fine, natural ingredients from the fertile Roman countryside and influenced by Greece and Asia Minor, they evolved a gastronomic tradition still felt in kitchens the world over.

While the lavish and exotic banquets of exaggerated proportions described in detail by Roman writers such as Petronius and Pliny no doubt existed, they were relatively infrequent and probably more a vulgar show of *nouveaux riches* than typical examples of local custom. The old nobility, then as now, must have found such conspicuous consumption in poor taste, and in fact, the beginnings of genuine Roman gastronomic traditions were more likely among the humble masses, who dined on such staples as lentils and chick-peas, still regularly offered in Roman trattorie. Even the ancient Romans' beloved sauce of rotted fish, *garum,* is echoed in the olive oil, crushed anchovy bits, and garlic sauce that anoints the quintessential Roman salad green, crisp and curly *puntarelle.*

Unfortunately, today's authentically Roman kitchens are dwindling in number. One by one, the old-fashioned, inexpensive mamma-papa trattorie are becoming Chinese restaurants, of which Rome now boasts 140 — none of them too terrific. In addition, fast-food joints have arrived with a vengeance and with the *1990 World Cup* soccer games, every restaurateur renovated his or her locale — and the price list as well. So don't be surprised if an old favorite trattoria now is all tarted up and pricey.

Rome's traditional fare is further threatened by the standardized fad menus, which include such vogues as *rughetta* (rugola), tucked everywhere and often cooked to little effect. Watch out, too, for the new handy way to deal with leftover carpaccio (raw slivers of beef), sautéed *stracci* ("rags"). The trendy dessert continues to be *tiramisù,* a Tyrolean calorie bomb of mascarpone cheese, liqueur, and coffee. The very ease of its preparation, with no cooking involved, is elbowing out better and more interesting desserts.

The bright side is that a new generation of well-trained cooks is bringing back forgotten regional dishes and devising new versions of old standbys. These relative youngsters call their fare "creative cuisine," the fruit of their labors, and are well worth seeking out. The decreasing number of authentic Roman kitchens makes the survivors all the more precious, and it means that while a careful diner will test the new, he or she also will seek out and cherish the authentic old.

Real Roman cooking is quite like the real Roman people — robust and hearty, imbued with a total disregard for tomorrow. There's no room in the popular Roman philosophy of *carpe diem* for thoughts of cholesterol or calories or preoccupations with heartburn, hangovers, or garlic-laden breath. These considerations disappear before a steaming dish of fragrant *spaghetti alla matriciana* (tomato, special bacon, and tangy *pecorino* — ewe's milk cheese), deep-fried *filetti di baccalà* (salt cod fillet), or *coda alla vaccinara* (oxtail stewed in tomato, onion and celery) — all accompanied by the abundant wines of the surrounding hill towns, the Castelli Romani.

Since Rome is close to the sea, its restaurants offer abundant fresh fish — particularly on Tuesdays and Fridays — but it is costly. All restaurants are required to identify frozen fish as well as other frozen ingredients. Don't hesitate to try the *antipasta marinara* (a mixture of seafoods in a light sauce of olive oil, lemon, parsley, and garlic), the *spaghetti alle vongole* (spaghetti with clam sauce — the clamshells come as well), and as a main course, trout from the nearby lakes or rockfish from the Mediterranean.

Veal is typically Roman, served as *saltimbocca alla romana* (literally, "hop-into-the-mouth," flavored with ham, sage, and marsala wine) or roasted with the fresh rosemary that grows in every garden. *Abbacchio al forno* is milk-fed baby lamb roasted with garlic and rosemary, and *abbacchio brodettato,* ever harder to find, is cooked in a sauce of egg yolks and lemon juice. *Abbacchio scottadito* ("finger burning") are tiny grilled lamb chops. On festive occasions, *maialetto* (suckling pig) appears on the menu; it is stuffed with herbs, roasted, and thickly sliced. Its street-stand version is eaten betweeen thick slabs of country bread. Watch, too, for such Roman specialties as *tripa* (tripe flavored with mint, parmesan cheese, and tomato sauce), *coniglio* (rabbit), *capretto* (kid), *coratella* (lamb's heart), *animelle* (sweetbreads), and, in season, *cinghiale* (wild boar). Wild boar dried sausages are popular as an antipasto course, along with salamis; the local Roman salami is prepared with tasty fennel seeds.

Pasta dishes include the incredibly simple *spaghetti alla carbonara* (with egg, salt pork, and *pecorino* cheese). *Penne all'arrabbiata* are short pasta in a tomato and garlic sauce "rabid" with hot peppers. The familiar *fettuccine all'Alfredo* depends upon the quality of the homemade strips of egg pasta in a rich sauce of cream, butter, and parmesan.

Fresh, seasonal vegetables, which often are treated as a separate course, provide the base for many a savory antipasto, accompany the main dish, and are even munched raw — for instance, *finocchio al pinzimonio* (fennel dipped into the purest of olive oil seasoned with salt and pepper) — after a particularly heavy meal to "clean the palate." Several local greens are unknown to visitors, such as *agretti, bieta, cicoria,* and *broccolo romano* — the last two often boiled briefly, then sautéed with olive oil, garlic, and hot red peppers. Salad ingredients include red radicchio, wild aromatic herbs, and the juicy tomatoes so cherished during the sultry summer months when they are served with ultra-aromatic basil — the sun's special gift to Mediterranean terraces and gardens. Tomatoes are also stuffed with rice and roasted; yellow, red, and green sweet peppers, eggplant, mushrooms, green and broad beans, and zucchini are favorite vegetables for antipasto; while asparagus and artichokes are especially prized in season. The latter is stuffed with mint and garlic and is stewed with olive oil seasoning *alla romana,* or opened out like a flower and deep-fried *alla giudia* (Jewish-style).

After such a meal, Romans normally have fresh fruit for dessert, although there is no shortage of sweet desserts (such as *montebianco, zuppa inglese,* and, of course, *gelato* (ice cream). For a final *digestivo,* bottles brought to the table may include *Sambuca Romana* (it has an aniseed base), *grappa* (made from the third and fourth grape pressings and normally over 60 proof!), and some sort of *amaro* (which means bitter, but is more often quite sweet).

A full meal, including house wine, may cost between $50 and $60 for two in a modest restaurant, while the same fare may cost twice that amount if the restaurant is even marginally fashionable. Most dining is à la carte, although a *menù turistico* is offered at some unpretentious trattorie for very reasonable prices, and a few tony establishments now serve sampler menus (*menù degustazione*) at a slightly lower price. Less expensive are the quick-service, often cafeteria-style, *rosticcerie* and *tavole calde* (literally "hot tables"). A delightful novelty is the spate of small wine tasting establishments that offer light snacks at lunch with a glass of fine wine; some also provide pasta or a mixed vegetable platter. Most café-bars serve sandwiches as well as that delicious and filling health snack, *frullato di frutta* (a mixture of frothy blended fruit and milk). Be careful when ordering fresh fish or Florentine steaks *al chilo* — by weight — as this may swell a bill way out of proportion, even at average-priced restaurants. When in Rome, start your day as the Romans do with a tiny, but terrific cup of coffee at one of the many coffee-bars like *Antico Caffè Greco* (86 Via Condotti); *Rosati* (4-5 Piazza del Popolo); *Sant' Eustachio Il Caffè* (82 Piazza Sant' Eustachio); or *Tazzo a'Oro* (6 Via degli Orfani). Also, always ask prices when ordering wine. Good Italian wines can cost as much as $30 and up per bottle. Dinner for two (with wine) costs from $175 to $250 in restaurants listed below as very expensive; $100 to $175 in restaurants classed as expensive; $60 to $100 is moderate; and below $60 is inexpensive.

Alberto Ciarla – Alberto, long an impassioned diver and spearfisherman, is a restaurateur who knows where to find fresh oysters (which he sometimes serves raw), lobster, and fish. Ciarla is rated one of Rome's finest chefs; *L'Espresso* guide gives him its highest marks, three chef's toques. His herbed pasta sauces are a welcome change from the more usual ways of preparing Italy's favorite food. For meat lovers, the "Alter Ego" menu offers a pâté of wild pigeon, baby lamb, and game — including venison — in season. The ever-large, noisy crowd brightens up the black decor (even down to the tablecloths). In good weather, there's alfresco dining on a little piece of a Trastevere street. Dinner only; closed Sundays. Reservations advised. Major credit cards accepted. 40 Piazza San Cosimato (phone: 581-8668). Very expensive.

Il Pianeta Terra – This Planet Earth comes close to paradise. A young couple, half Tuscan and half Sicilian, has created an elegant, traditional, yet adventurous dining place in the heart of Rome. Starters such as ravioli stuffed with sea bass in a pistachio sauce or pasta with clams and broccoli lead to exciting main courses, such as the squab stuffed with artichokes or with oysters and clams, and to delicate desserts. The wine list is intelligently chosen. Note: the *menù degustazione* can cost more than an à la carte meal. Dinner only; closed Mondays and from mid-July through August. Reservations necessary. Major credit cards accepted. 94-95 Via Arco del Monte (phone: 686-9893 or 679-9828). Very expensive.

Relais Le Jardin – The sumptuous dining room of the *Lord Byron* hotel is still Rome's foremost restaurant. Chef Antonio Sciullo's creations blend the unlikely into the surprising and sometime sublime. The menu follows the seasons — you will find zucchini blossoms stuffed with bean purée, ravioli with a delicate pigeon ragout, and scallops lurking in a watercress flan. The dessert soufflé has a crunchy hazelnut topping. Service is appropriately sophisticated, as are the wines. Closed Sundays and August. Reservations necessary. Major credit cards accepted. *Lord Byron Hotel,* 5 Via Giuseppe de Notaris (phone: 322-4541). Very expensive.

La Rosetta – One of Rome's most famed fish restaurants, it is small, jam-packed, and chic. The chef grills, fries, boils, or bakes to perfection any — or a mixture of all — of the fish and seafood flown in from his native Sicily. A favorite specialty is *pappardelle al pescatore* (wide noodles in a piquant tomato sauce with mussels, clams, and parsley) or Sicilian-style *pasta con le sarde,* flavored with wild fennel. Closed Sundays, Mondays at lunchtime, and August. Reservations necessary. Major credit cards accepted. 9 Via della Rosetta (phone: 686-1002). Very expensive.

El Toulà – The well-heeled, well-traveled, and aristocratic assemble here for Cortina- and Venice-inspired fare; in winter that means hearty game dishes such as venison and, year-round, fish, such as the poppyseed-daubed salmon in oyster sauce. A favorite dessert is a large shortbread biscuit. There's an impressive wine list, but you might have to put up with hearing the man at the next table negotiating a major deal, as the tables are quite close together. Closed Saturday lunch, Sundays, and August. Reservations necessary. Major credit cards accepted. 29/B Via della Lupa (phone: 687-3750). Very expensive.

Andrea – Tops for the Via Veneto area. In season, fettuccine with artichoke sauce; always on the menu, ricotta-stuffed fresh ravioli. Pleasant service, a serviceable house wine, and sweeties to sweeten the bill. Closed Sundays and 3 weeks in August. Reservations necessary. Major credit cards accepted. 26 Via Sardegna (phone: 446-3707). Expensive.

Le Cabanon – French and Tunisian food are served in an intimate ambience accompanied by Mediterranean melodies sung by the well-traveled owner, Enzo Rallo. South American or French singers ably fill in the gaps. The usual onion soup and escargots, as well as a delicious Tunisian *brik à l'oeuf* (a pastry concealing a challengingly dripping egg within), couscous, and *merguez* sausages are among the choices. Open evenings only, and until late. Closed Sundays and August. Reservations necessary. No credit cards accepted. 4 Vicolo della Luce (phone: 581-8106). Expensive.

La Cesta – Centrally located in the *Holiday Inn Crowne Plaza Minerva* is this delightfully restored 19th-century restaurant. You can enjoy quiet dining for business as well as pleasure under splendid Venetian glass chandeliers. Besides a somewhat standard menu, there is a daily list of Roman and international specialties. The fare is excellent, if not brilliant. Open daily. Reservations advised. Major credit cards accepted. 69 Piazza della Minerva (phone: 684-1888). Expensive.

Charles Roof Garden – A breathtaking view and creative Italian fare is offered at this restaurant on top of the *Eden* hotel. Regional specialties include homemade *tonnarelli* (thick noodles) with lemon sauce, while the café on the terrace offers a snacks menu. Open daily. Reservations necessary. Major credit cards accepted. 49 Via Ludovisi (phone: 474-3551). Expensive.

Il Convivio – A welcome addition on a street of artisans and antiques dealers, chef Angelo Trioiani and his brother Massimo have just 10 tables on which to lavish their version of "creative cuisine." A special menu (with lower prices) is available at lunchtime. A fine wine list. Closed Sundays. Reservations advised. Major credit cards accepted. 44 Via dell'Orso (phone: 686-9432). Expensive.

Girarrosto Toscano – Old fashioned and serious, it's a fine eatery for lovers of classic Tuscan fare. The sizzling Florentine steaks and fresh fish are grilled to perfection. The rest is perfect, too, but this is not always a restful place. Closed Wednesdays. Reservations necessary. Major credit cards accepted. 29 Via Campania (phone: 482-1899). Expensive.

Hosteria dell'Orso – Although this is widely known as a tourist place, the traditional Italian fare offered in an elegant 13th-century building is quite good. Upstairs is a disco (see *Nightclubs and Nightlife*), and downstairs is a piano bar. Closed Sundays. Reservations necessary. Major credit cards accepted. 33 Via dell'Orso (phone: 656-4904). Expensive.

La Lampada – This is the only Roman restaurant that specializes in truffles and wild mushrooms, but don't anticipate bargains, and don't expect the truffles to be fresh beyond the autumn/winter season. The risotto is made with white truffles, and the carpaccio with a grating of both black and white truffles (from Norcia and Alba, respectively). Closed Sundays. Reservations necessary. Major credit cards accepted. 25 Via Quintino Sella (phone: 474-4323). Expensive.

Papà Giovanni – It's small and intimate, with paintings and wine bottles lining the walls, and the bar is very well stocked — sip a kir as an *aperitivo* while choosing from over 700 wines. The highly praised fare is basically refined Roman, with truffles a seasonal specialty. Try *panzerotti al tartufo* (small ravioli with truffles). The interesting menu varies, so ask your waiter for current specialties. Closed Sundays. Reservations necessary. Major credit cards accepted. 4 Via dei Sediari (phone: 686-5308). Expensive.

Passetto – For classical Roman cooking, this Belle Epoque restaurant is a beloved local institution. In addition to the excellent antipasto, try the *filetto con carciofi* (steak with artichokes) and *porcini* mushrooms with asparagus, if they're in season. Closed Sundays and Monday afternoons. Reservations advised. Major credit cards accepted. 13-14 Via Zanardelli (phone: 654-0569 or 687-9937). Expensive.

Il Peristilio – The decor is sumptuous, with fine objets d'art, tasteful cutlery and china, and a refined aura. Air conditioning, a piano bar, and polite waiters complete the picture; the quality of the food may blur it. Closed Mondays. Reservations necessary. Major credit cards accepted. 6/B Via Col di Lana (phone: 322-3623). Expensive.

Pino e Dino – Although the founders have gone, current management continues their menu of interesting regional dishes. The restaurant is on one of Rome's more picturesque squares, but a cozy winter meal indoors, surrounded by wine bottles and artisan products from all over Italy, is just as enticing. Closed Mondays and most of August. Reservations necessary. Major credit cards accepted. 22 Piazza di Montevecchio (phone: 656-1319). Expensive.

Quinzi e Gabrieli – Seafood is a very serious subject here. It is prepared as naturally as possible for a maximum of 22 diners. In season, the oyster bar is popular. Closed Sundays and August. Reservations necessary. Major credit cards accepted. Near the Pantheon, at 5 Via delle Coppelle (phone: 687-9389). Expensive.

Le Restaurant – This elegant dining room at the *Grand* hotel serves continental cuisine and has a menu that changes with the season. Decor, flowers, and waiters in tails all reflect the *Grand* approach to luxury. Open daily. Reservations necessary. Major credit cards accepted. 3 Via Vittorio Emanuele Orlando (phone: 4709). Expensive.

Ai Tre Scalini – Not to be confused with the renowned *gelateria* and café *Tre Scalini,* the food and wines here are special. Owners Roanna Dupre and Matteo Cicala change the menu frequently, but you'll be lucky if you find the fish soup or the fish-stuffed ravioli. A sampler menu is offered. The decor is simple; there are only seven tables, 30 diners in all, so reservations are necessary. Closed Mondays. Major credit cards accepted. 16 Via dei Santi Quattro (phone: 732695). Expensive.

Alvaro al Circo Massimo – Let Alvaro suggest what's best that day and you'll not go wrong, whether it's fresh fish, game such as *fagiano* (pheasant) or *faraona* (guinea hen), or mushrooms (try grilled *porcini*). The ambience is rustic indoors, and there are tables outdoors during the summer. Closed Mondays. Reservations generally are not necessary. Major credit cards accepted. 53 Via dei Cerchi (phone: 678-6112). Expensive to moderate.

Dal Bolognese – Strategically set next to the popular *Caffè Rosati* on Piazza del Popolo and with a menu nearly as long as the list of celebrities who frequent this fashionable eatery, it's run by two brothers from Bologna. Stargazers will still enjoy such specialties as homemade *tortelloni* (pasta twists stuffed with ricotta cheese) and the *bollito misto* (boiled beef, tongue, chicken, pig's trotter). There are tables outdoors in good weather. Closed Sunday evenings, Mondays, and most of August. Reservations necessary. Major credit cards accepted. 1 Piazza del Popolo (phone: 361-1426). Expensive to moderate.

Il Canto del Riso – There are two, actually — summer and winter. In warmer days it's a gussied-up river barge lurking under the Ponte Cavour, while in winter the restaurant makes its home in a historic building in old Rome. The name means "the Rice Song," and a northern connection (Veneto/Friuli) explains the preponderance of rice dishes: *risotto ai capasanti* (rice with scallops) is only one of more than a dozen rice starters. There is live music in the evening. Closed Sunday nights, Mondays, and in bad weather. Reservations advised in summer. Major credit cards accepted. Summer: Walk down to the river from Lungotevere Mellini, on the Vatican side (phone: 361-0430); winter: 21 Cordonata (phone: 678-6227). Expensive to moderate.

Cesarina – Year in, year out, here's the place to enjoy a well-prepared *bollito misto* from the rich cart of meats and sausage, with the green sauce *comme il faut.* In summer, the fresh fish may appeal more, as will the air conditioning. Year-round, the pasta Bolognese-style is a traditional favorite. Closed Sundays. Reservations necessary. Major credit cards accepted. 109 Via Piemonte (phone: 488-0828). Expensive to moderate.

Checchino dal 1887 – Among the most traditional of all dining places, it's renowned for its light touch with such Roman staples as oxtail, tripe, brains with artichokes, and *spaghetti con pajatta* (spaghetti in a tomato sauce with lamb's intestines). Try the *bucatini all'amatriciana* (a hearty pasta dish with bacon). Closed Sunday evenings and Mondays. Reservations advised. Major credit cards accepted. 30 Via Monte Testaccio (phone: 574-6318 or 574-3816). Expensive to moderate.

Comparone – Roomy and cheery, with plenty of tables outside in the piazza, this is an old favorite of *trasteverini* and visitors alike. The menu is traditional Roman. Closed Mondays. Reservations necessary. Major credit cards accepted. 47 Piazza in Piscinula (phone: 581-6249). Expensive to moderate.

Cornucopia – At this eatery in Trastevere, the few tables outdoors in this lovely piazza offer a view of medieval buildings. Inside, it is air conditioned, small, and inviting. The fare is seafood only, except in winter, when game also is on the menu. At lunchtime, a special limited menu (a choice of seven dishes with a glass of sparkling white wine, mineral water, and coffee) is available at an especially low price. Closed Mondays. Reservations necessary. Major credit cards accepted. 18 Piazza in Piscinula (phone: 580-0380). Expensive to moderate.

Cul de Sac 2 – On a tiny street in Trastevere, the owners of the wine shop *Cul de Sac 1* have created an elegant and attractive restaurant offering *cucina creativa.* Dishes such as lobster with creamed broccoli are carefully prepared, as is the wine list. Closed Sunday evenings, Mondays, and August. Reservations advised. Major credit cards accepted. 21 Vicolo dell'Atleta (phone: 581-3324). Expensive to moderate.

Fortunato al Pantheon – Barely a block from the Pantheon, this eatery is a favorite among politicos and writers. Fish in all ways — grilled, in risotto or pasta — is the specialty, and it is usually as fine as this eatery's long-standing reputation. Tables outside in summer. Closed Sundays and August 15–30. Reservations necessary. American Express accepted. 55 Via del Pantheon (phone: 679-2788). Expensive to moderate.

Al Gladiatore – This old-fashioned, cozy trattoria overlooking the Colosseum is known for its fresh fish. Closed Wednesdays. No reservations. Major credit cards accepted. 5 Piazza Colosseo (phone: 700-0533). Expensive to moderate.

La Maiella – On a delightful square colorfully illuminated in the summer for outdoor dining, this efficient organization with delicious food owes its fame and popularity to owner/manager Signor Antonio. The pope (while still a cardinal) was among his clientele, and the Roman-Abruzzian menu is nearly as long as the Bible. Fresh seafood, truffles, and the alfresco dining are the major attractions. Closed Sundays and a week in August. Reservations advised in the evenings. Major credit cards accepted. 45 Piazza Sant'Apollinare (phone: 686-4174). Expensive to moderate.

Nino – A reliable place, frequented by artists, actors, and aristocrats, and near the Spanish Steps, it is truly Tuscan. The cuisine is composed of the best ingredients, ably yet simply prepared, and the service is serious. Specialties: *zuppa di fagioli alla Francovich* (thick Tuscan white bean soup with garlic), *bistecca alla fiorentina* (thick succulent T-bone steak), and for dessert *castagnaccio* (semisweet chestnut cake). Excellent wine list. Closed Sundays. Reservations advised. Major credit cards accepted. 11 Via Borgognona (phone: 679-5676). Expensive to moderate.

Orient Express – Italians in the know dine here. Antique railway fixtures and menu items that track the famous route from Istanbul (shish kebab) to Paris (delicious onion soup) are what gives this small, pleasant eatery its name. The owners are a former Italian diplomat and his ex-schoolteacher wife. In Trastevere. Closed Sundays. Reservations necessary. American Express accepted. 80 Via Ponte Sisto (phone: 580-9868). Expensive to moderate.

Osteria dell'Antiquario – This small dining spot on a picturesque little square along the antiques shop–lined Via dei Coronari prides itself on genuine Roman fare, well prepared with the finest seasonal ingredients. Alfresco dining in fine weather. Closed Sundays. Reservations advised. Major credit cards accepted. 27 Piazza San Simeone (phone: 687-9694). Expensive to moderate.

Paris – The Cappellanti family of chefs add a creative zing to traditional Roman-Jewish and strictly Roman dishes such as *pasta e ceci* (pasta with chick-peas). Closed Sunday evenings, Mondays, and August. Reservations necessary. Major credit cards acepted. 7/A Piazza San Calisto (phone: 581-5378). Expensive to moderate.

Piccolo Mondo – Not exactly a "find," this cheerful and busy restaurant behind Via Veneto has been popular with Italians and foreigners alike for decades. Among the many varied antipasti displayed at the entrance are exquisite *mozzarellini alla panna* (small balls of fresh buffalo's milk cheese swimming in cream), as well as eggplant and peppers prepared in several tempting ways. There are sidewalk tables in good weather. Closed Sundays and the first 3 weeks of August. Reservations advised. Major credit cards accepted. 39 Via Aurora (phone: 481-4595). Expensive to moderate.

Piperno – A summer dinner outdoors on this quiet Renaissance *piazzetta,* next to the Palazzo Cenci — which still reeks "of ancient evil and nameless crimes" — is sheer magic. Indoors it is modern and less magical, and the classic Roman-Jewish cooking can be a bit heavy. The great specialty is *fritto vegetariano* (zucchini flowers, mozzarella cheese, salt cod, rice and potato balls, and artichokes — the latter *alla giudia,* or "Jewish-style"). Closed Sunday nights, Mondays, and August. Reservations necessary. Major credit cards accepted. 9 Monte de' Cenci (phone: 654-2772). Expensive to moderate.

Romolo – Summer dining is alfresco, in the dappled sunlight of a 450-year-old arbor, but eating is a delight year-round in this famed tavern in Trastevere where the painter Raphael courted the baker's daughter, la Fornarina. A favorite of Romans and tourists alike is the tasty *spaghetti alla bocaiola* (with a sauce of tomatoes, mushrooms, and tuna) and the grilled, herbed scampi kebabs. Another specialty is *mozzarella alla Fornarina* (melted cheese wrapped in prosciutto and accompanied by a fried artichoke). The wine list is excellent. Closed Mondays and August. Reservations necessary in summer. Major credit cards accepted. 8 Via di Porta Settimiana (phone: 581-8284). Expensive to moderate.

Taverna Flavia – It's been fashionable with the movie crowd, journalists, and politicians for over 30 years. Owner Mimmo likes autographed pictures — one entire room is devoted to Elizabeth Taylor — and the *Sardi's* style survives, despite the crash of "Hollywood on the Tiber" long ago. Near the *Grand* hotel, and open quite late. Good pasta dishes and fine grilled fish. Closed Saturday lunch, all day Sundays, and August. Reservations necessary. Major credit cards accepted. 9-11 Via Flavia (phone: 474-5214). Expensive to moderate.

Taverna Giulia – This reliable old favorite is set in a 600-year-old building. Genoese specialties include pesto served over the traditional *troffie* noodles, and smoked fish. Closed Sundays and August. Reservations advised. Major credit cards accepted. Vicolo dell'Oro (phone: 686-4089). Expensive to moderate.

Vecchia Roma – The setting is truly out of a midsummer night's dream on magical Piazza Campitelli on the fringe of Rome's Jewish quarter. The menu is traditional, the ingredients fresh, the salads pleasing, and the waiters courteous. We love it. Closed Wednesdays and 2 weeks in August. Reservations advised. No credit cards accepted. 18 Piazza Campitelli (phone: 686-4604). Expensive to moderate.

Apuleius – Near Rome's United Nations office complex, this tavern serves seafood in amiable, if kitschy, surroundings. Its Aventine hill location is a plus. *Spaghetti alla pescatore* (fish sauce) is special. Closed Sundays. Reservations advised. Major credit cards accepted. 15 Via Tempio di Diana (phone: 574-2160). Moderate.

La Campana – This unprepossessing, 400-year-old, truly Roman restaurant is favored by everyone from local folk to the stars and staff of RAI, Italian radio-television. Waiters help decipher the handwritten menu, which tempts most with *carciofi alla romana* (fresh artichokes in garlic and oil), *tonnarelli alla chitarra* (homemade pasta in an egg and cheese sauce), and lamb, and truffle-topped poultry dishes. Closed Mondays and August. Reservations advised. Major credit cards accepted. 18 Vicolo della Campana (phone: 686-7820). Moderate.

La Carbonara – On the square where Rome's most colorful morning food market has been held for centuries, this is where *spaghetti alla carbonara* (the sauce is eggs and bacon) is said to have been invented. The windows of the ancient palazzo look out over the scene; indoors is no less authentically Roman, from menu to decor. Closed Tuesdays. Reservations unnecessary. Major credit cards accepted. 23 Campo dei Fiori (phone: 686-4783). Moderate.

Il Cardinale – In a restored bicycle shop off the stately Via Giulia, decorated in a somewhat precious turn-of-the-century style, this popular evening spot specializes in regional dishes: pasta with green tomato or artichoke sauce, grilled eels, a sweetbread casserole with mushrooms, and *aliciotti con l'indivia* (an anchovy and endive dish). Closed Sundays and August. Reservations advised. Visa accepted. 6 Via delle Carceri (phone: 686-9336). Moderate.

Checco er Carettiere – In the Trastevere area — the Greenwich Village of Rome — this eatery has a large and friendly interior, with a garden in a courtyard, and a wood-paneled dining room. A guitarist strolls among the tables, a flower girl proffers blossoms, and a fledgling artist opens her portfolio to display sketches of surrounding landmarks. The food's super. An antipasto made entirely of seafood is a specialty, and there's a unique mixture of tomatoes and potatoes. Closed Sunday evenings and Mondays. Reservations advised in the evenings. American Express and Visa accepted. 10-13 Via Benedetta, Piazza Trilussa (phone: 581-7018). Moderate.

Le Colline Emiliane – With Tuscan inspiration and truffle toppings, an eatery like this is becoming a rarity. Service is prompt, decor simple, and the *maccheroncini al funghetto* delicious. It has a well-deserved reputation for consistency over the years. Closed Fridays and August. Reservations advised. Major credit cards accepted. Near Via Veneto. 22 Via degli Avignonesi (phone: 481-7538). Moderate.

Costanza – For those who prize a bit of history with their supper, these vaulted dining rooms are in a 2,000-year-old entryway to the ancient Theater of Pompey. Now wildly chic, it has an interesting menu and is pleasant in winter; the service in summer is irritatingly slow. Closed Sundays and August. Reservations advised. American Express and Visa accepted. 63 Piazza Paradiso (phone: 686-1717 or 654-1002). Moderate.

Cuccurucù – A garden overlooking the Tiber provides one of Rome's most pleasant summer settings for dining alfresco, while inside it's cozy and rustic. The antipasti are good, and so are the meats grilled on an open fire. Ask for *bruschetta con pomodori* (toasted country bread smothered in fresh tomatoes and oregano), and a *spiedino misto,* a sort of shish kebab bearing great chunks of veal, pork, and sausage, all interspersed with onions and peppers and grilled. Closed Sunday evenings and Mondays year-round, Sundays in the summer, and August. Reservations advised. Major credit cards accepted. 10 Via Caloprati (phone: 325257). Moderate.

Il Dito e la Luna – Sicilian fare and *la cucina creativa* (Italy's answer to France's nouvelle cuisine) are featured at this lovely restaurant with white walls, terra cotta floors, and antique furnishings. Specialties include *lasagnette con scampi, pomodori, e zucchini* (flat pasta with shrimp, tomatoes, and zucchini), *anitra in pasta sfoglia* (duck in puff pastry with an orange sauce), and a good selection of homemade desserts. Open for dinner only; closed Sundays and August. Reservations advised. No credit cards accepted. 51 Via dei Sabelli (phone: 494-0276). Moderate.

Il Drappo – Drapes softly frame the two small rooms of this *ristorantino* run by the brother-sister team of Paolo and Valentina Tolu from Sardinia. They offer delicate dishes based on robust island fare, fragrant with wild fennel, myrtle, and herbs. The innovative menu, recited by Paolo and artfully prepared by Valentina, always begins with mixed antipasti including *carta di musica* (hors d'oeuvres on crisp Sardinian wafers). Closed Sundays and 2 weeks in August. Reservations necessary. American Express accepted. 9 Vicolo del Malpasso (phone: 687-7365). Moderate.

Giulio II – Fish baked in parchment and Sicilian-style stuffed swordfish are the specialties at this stylish new eatery in the Parioli quarter. It is within walking distance of the *Coppede'* fine arts complex, with its lovely fountain and architectural curiosities. Closed Saturday lunch, Sundays, and August. Reservations unnecessary. Major credit cards accepted. 80 Via Arno (phone: 841-5535 or 855-1002). Moderate.

Isola del Sole – A converted houseboat on the Tiber offers a variation on the theme of alfresco dining — with lunches under a welcome winter sun, or candlelit dining with the summer stars as backdrop. Try pasta with eggplant and ricotta, ravioli stuffed with *porcini* mushrooms, or carpaccio (thin slices of raw beef seasoned with olive oil, lemon, and flaked parmesan cheese). Extra-special chocolate mousse. From 11 PM to 4 AM there's a piano bar and dancing. Closed Mondays. Reservations advised (for best service, get there by 8:30 PM). Major credit cards accepted. Between Ponte Matteotti and the *metropolitana* train bridge; walk down to the river from Lungotevere Arnaldo da Brescia (phone: 320-1400). Moderate.

Mario – A Tuscan favorite, with the usual Tuscan specialties such as Francovich soup, Florentine steaks, and delicious game in season, all prepared with admirable care and dedication by Mario himself, but served by only three overworked waiters. Closed Sundays and August. Reservations advised. Major credit cards accepted. 55 Via della Vite (phone: 678-3818). Moderate.

Al Moro – Not far from the Trevi Fountain, this is a quiet, dignified place, very "in" with the theater crowd and the powers-that-be at the nearby Parliament. Traditional Roman specialties and seasonal dishes such as pasta with truffles are a must, as is the *fritta vegetariana,* a mix of deep-fried vegetables and cheeses. Closed Sundays and August. Reservations advised. No credit cards accepted. 13 Vicola delle Bollette (phone: 678-3495). Moderate.

Osteria Picchioni – The most expensive pizza in town, but it could also be the best, and it's a whole meal. Only top-quality ingredients are used in this family-style, old-fashioned trattoria, but the decor runs to plastic flowers. Fortunately, they don't tell the whole story. Watch out for the prices — a plate of spaghetti with truffles can run around $100! Be sure to make reservations — there are only 50 places. Closed Wednesdays. No credit cards accepted. 16 Via del Boschetto (phone: 465261). Moderate.

Osteria Sant'Ana – The locale was a convent in the 18th century, and Elio, the owner, is the third generation to run a restaurant. The vegetable hors d'oeuvres array is admirable, while carnivores will enjoy the charcoal grill; everyone likes the marron glacé ice cream, the location near Piazza del Popolo, the somewhat austere tone, and the moderate price considering the quality. Closed Saturday afternoons, Sundays, and 1 week in August. Reservations necessary in the evenings. Major credit cards accepted. 68 Via della Penna (phone: 361-0291). Moderate.

Otello alla Concordia – A delightful trattoria in the middle of the Piazza di Spagna shopping area, with certain tables reserved for habitués and a colorful courtyard for fine-weather dining. The menu is Roman, and it changes daily, depending a great deal on the season. Closed Sundays, *Christmas* week, and the first week in January. No reservations. Major credit cards accepted. 81 Via della Croce (phone: 679-1178). Moderate.

Pierluigi – The fish is fresh, the piazza is charming, the price is a bargain, and in summer, the dining is alfresco. Reservations, therefore, are necessary at this popular trattoria in the heart of old Rome. Closed Mondays and Tuesday lunch. Reservations advised. Major credit cards accepted. 144 Piazza de' Ricci (phone: 686-1302). Moderate.

Al Pompiere – Visiting firemen and travelers adore this bright, old-fashioned restaurant in an ancient palazzo near the Campo dei Fiori, whose name means "The Fireman." The menu includes deep-fried artichokes and mozzarella-stuffed zucchini blossoms. Closed Sundays. Reservations advised in the evenings. No credit cards accepted. 38 Via Santa Maria Calderari (phone: 686-8377). Moderate.

Su Recreu – Finding this spot isn't easy, but the Sardinian food is worth the expedition. The large buffet antipasto is a "take all you want" affair, and there are about a dozen hot and cold choices. The authentic mozzarella (made with buffalo milk) is marvelous, as is anything cooked on the large wood fire right at the entrance. The fresh fish will add to the price. Closed Mondays. Reservations advised. Major credit cards accepted. 17 Via de Buon Consiglio; one block off the Via Cavour, not far from the Forum and the Via del Colosseo (phone: 684-1507). Moderate.

Shangri Là–Corsetti – In the EUR suburb, it's much favored by American businessmen who like the fresh fish. The public pool alongside can be agreeable despite the loud, loud music. Closed August. Reservations advised. Major credit cards accepted. 141 Viale Algeria (phone: 592-8861). Moderate.

Sora Cecilia – Founded in 1898, this modest trattoria offers homemade *agnolotti* (large ravioli) and good *penne all'arrabiata* (pasta with a peppery tomato sauce). Closed Sundays. Reservations advised. American Express accepted. 27 Via Poli (phone: 678-9096). Moderate.

Specchio Antico – Young people run this 6-year-old restaurant that is decorated with fine antiques from their father's prestigious shop. They have won kudos for the spaghetti with seafood *in cartoccio* (a paper bag), delicious array of vegetable hors d'oeuvres, and grilled meats. Closed Sundays. Reservations necessary in the evenings. Major credit cards accepted. 17 Via dei Pastini (phone: 679-7273). Moderate.

Toto alle Carrozze – It has hardly changed after all these years, but we liked it then and we like it now — a trattoria with a banquet spread of strictly Roman antipasti, good pasta, and Roman fish and meat dishes. This is a *giovedì gnocchi, sabato tripa* (Thursday gnocchi, Saturday tripe) kind of traditional Roman place. Closed Sundays. No reservations. Major credit cards accepted. Just off Via del Corso at 10 Via delle Carrozze (phone: 678558). Moderate.

Tullio – Up a narrow hill, just a few yards from the Via Veneto is this just refurbished Tuscan trattoria that serves superb *ribollita* (Tuscan vegetable soup) and baked beans *al fiasco* (in the bottle). It's a custom to place a straw-covered bottle of chianti on the table — diners pay only for what is drunk — and if you're not planning to visit Florence, this is a good place to try a grilled steak Florentine-style. Closed Sundays and August. Reservations advised. Major credit cards. 26 Via di San Nicola da Tolentino (phone: 481-8564 or 474-5560). Moderate.

Le Volte – Carlo Castrucci ran the renowned restaurant at the *Eden* hotel, and now has struck out on his own, in the 16th-century Palazzo Rondanini. Under its frescoed ceiling, diners can enjoy linguini in a lobster sauce, pizza baked in a wood-burning oven, and wild boar with polenta in autumn and winter. Closed Tuesdays and for 15 days in August. Reservations advised. Major credit cards accepted. 47 Piazza Rondanini (phone: 687-7408). Moderate.

Altrove – A new trattoria in the old Subura quarter between Trajan's Market and the Basilica of Santa Maria Maggiore. In one of the downstairs rooms, there is a patch of original Servian wall from ancient Rome. Open until 1 AM; closed Sundays. No reservations. Major credit cards accepted. 35 Via Cimarra (phone: 474-2923). Moderate to inexpensive.

Il Barroccio – *Pane rùstico,* crusty country-style bread, is made here every day, and beans are baked in a wood-burning oven. On a side street not far from the Pantheon, this is a prime place to try *crostini* in all its infinite permutations, and if you want to sample Roman-style pizza, do it here. Across the street at No. 123 is its twin, *Er Faciolaro,* owned by the same people. One or the other always is open. Reservations unnecessary. Major credit cards accepted. 13 Via dei Pastini (phone: 679-3797). Moderate to inexpensive.

Il Falchetto – Conveniently set off Via del Corso, with a few tables outdoors in fine weather, this might seem a tourist haven. But knowledgeable Romans fill the small rooms even in the gray days of winter. The imaginative game, veal, and fish dishes are delicious. Closed Fridays. Reservations advised. Major credit cards accepted. 12-14 Via Montecatini (phone: 679-1160). Moderate to inexpensive.

La Fiorentina – This favorite Roman pizzeria, with its wood-burning oven and grill, is in residential Prati on the Vatican side of the river. It serves pizza even at lunchtime, a rarity in Italy. Tables on the street in good weather. Closed Wednesdays all day, Thursdays at lunch. Reservations advised. Major credit cards accepted. 22 Via Andrea Doria (phone: 312310). Moderate to inexpensive.

Il Giardinetto – Not far from Piazza Navona is this quiet and charming newcomer with a few outdoor tables. The owner is Tunisian, speaks English, and cooks creditable Italian fare, including the ever-popular *spaghetti alla carbonara* (with egg and bacon), onion soup, and tiny *gnocchetti sardi* (an eggless Sardinian pasta with a sauce of fresh tomato and aromatic basil). A good value. Closed Mondays. Reservations necessary in summer. Major credit cards accepted. 125 Via del Governo Vecchio (phone: 686-8693). Moderate to inexpensive.

Giggetto al Portico d'Ottavia – In Rome's Jewish ghetto, this is the place to sample the delicious and well-prepared fried artichokes that most Roman menus identify as *alla giudia,* "Jewish-style," as well as zucchini flowers stuffed with mozzarella and *crostini* (fried bread offered with an assortment of toppings). But don't take the waiters' occasional lack of attention personally; they ignore everybody. The food is first-rate and the experience absolutely authentic. Closed Mondays. Reservations advised. Major credit cards accepted. 21/A Via del Portico d'Ottavia (phone: 686-1105). Moderate to inexpensive.

La Luna sul Tevere – A river restaurant, the "Moon on the Tiber" brought their chef from the Via Veneto's famed *Café de Paris.* Set on the banks of the Tiber, beneath the Duca d'Aosta Bridge, it has alfresco dining in summer and a rustic barge for indoor meals during inclement weather. Specialties include fettuccine with tuna and wild *porcini* mushrooms, breast of chicken with almonds, and petits fours of *tartufini* and *cremini.* Closed Mondays and the last 2 weeks of November. Reservations advised. Major credit cards accepted. Via Capoprati (phone: 323-6456). Moderate to inexpensive.

Le Maschere – For a taste of Calabria's Costa Viola, fragrant with garlic and devilish with red peppers, try this rustic and charming 17th-century cellar behind Largo Argentina. The fare is not for fragile stomachs: antipasti of tangy salamis, marinated anchovies, and stuffed, pickled, or highly seasoned vegetables of every sort; pasta with broccoli or eggplant, or the traditional *struncatura* (handmade whole-wheat pasta with anchovies, garlic, and bread crumbs); fresh swordfish harpooned off the Calabrian coast, *stoccafisso* (salt cod stew with potatoes), or meats grilled on an open fire; pizzas, southern sweets, 100-proof fresh fruit salad, and *tuma* (Calabrian sheep's milk cheese). Dinner only. Closed Mondays and part of August. Reservations necessary on weekends. Major credit cards accepted. 29 Via Monte della Farina (phone: 687-9444). Moderate to inexpensive.

L'Orso '80 – An old-fashioned trattoria close to Piazza Navona and with good traditional fare such as *spaghetti alla matriciana* (with bacon, cheese, and tomatoes). Meats are grilled over a wood fire. Closed Mondays and August. Reservations unnecessary. Major credit cards accepted. 33 Via dell'Orso (phone: 686-4904). Moderate to inexpensive.

Al Piedone – Tiny and unpretentious, this spot is much favored by newsmen and politicos from nearby Parliament. Try the rigatoni with broccoli, sausage, and bacon, or the Puglia-style *orecchietti* (pasta) with hot red pepper, broccoli, and anchovies. When available, the roast veal stuffed with almonds, pine nuts, and raisins is truly special. A good wine list for a modest restaurant. Closed Sundays and late August. Reservations advised in the evenings. Major credit cards accepted. 28 Via del Piè di Marco (phone: 679-8628). Moderate to inexpensive.

Polese – This is a good value any time of the year, either outside under the trees of the spacious square or inside the intimate rooms of the Borgia palace. A great summer starter is *bresaola con rughetta* (cured beef with arugula, seasoned with olive oil, lemon, and freshly grated black pepper), and the *pasta al pesto* is fine year-round. Closed Tuesdays. Reservations taken reluctantly (come and wait your turn). Major credit cards accepted. 40 Piazza Sforza Cesarini (phone: 686-1709). Moderate to inexpensive.

Ponentino – A pizzeria in Trastevere, it has the ubiquitous wood-burning oven. The youthful owners also serve spaghetti old-Trastevere-style (with tuna, anchovies, and capers), vegetarian antipasto (the best choice), and grilled meat including lamb chops. Closed Mondays. Reservations necessary in summer for tables outside in the piazza. Major credit cards accepted. Off Via della Lungaretta near Tiber Island. 10 Piazza del Drago (phone: 588-0680). Moderate to inexpensive.

Sora Lella – In the heart of Rome on Tiber Island is this trattoria serving authentic Roman dishes such as *penne all'arrabiata* (quill-shaped pasta with spicy tomato sauce), *pasta e ceci* (pasta and chick-peas) with clams, tiny sautéed lamb chops, and beans with pork rind. Closed Sundays. No reservations. No credit cards accepted. 16 Via di Quattro Capi (phone: 686-1601). Moderate to inexpensive.

La Tavernetta – It looks like a take-out pasta shop, but there are actually four narrow dining rooms set one above the other. This is a tiny, tidy spot, barely a block from the Spanish Steps (toward the Piazza Barberini), where the homemade pasta is pretty near perfect and seafood is the specialty. Closed Sundays and August. Reservations advised. Major credit cards accepted. 147 Via Sistina (phone: 679-3124). Moderate to inexpensive.

Trearchi da Gioachino – Among the declining numbers of true Roman trattorie, this one stands out, thanks to Mamma Colomba Giammiuti's loving cooking. She comes from the Abruzzi region and specialties include homemade ravioli, *pappardelle* noodles with hare sauce and lamb, and other pasta made in various delectable ways. Closed Sundays and late August. Reservations advised. Major credit cards accepted. 233 Via dei Coronari (phone: 686-5890). Moderate to inexpensive.

Ettore Lo Sgobbone – A trattoria popular with newspaper and TV journalists, noted for its unpretentious Northern Italian home-style cooking. Pasta and risotto courses are excellent: Try the simple *tonnarelli al pomodoro e basilico* (pasta with fresh tomato and basil sauce) or *risotto nero di seppie* (rice cooked with cuttlefish in its ink). Reservations advised for the few tables outdoors on the rather dreary, typically working class street. Closed Tuesdays. Reservations necessary. Major credit cards accepted. 8-10 Via dei Podesti (phone: 323-2994). Inexpensive.

Da Giulio – Another bargain for budget-minded travelers, on a tiny street off Via Giulia in a historic building. A few tables line the sunless street in the summer, but inside is most pleasant — if a bit noisy — with an original vaulted ceiling and paintings by local artists. Roman family-style cooking. Closed Sundays and late August. Reservations advised in summer. Major credit cards accepted. 19 Via della Barchetta (phone: 654-0466). Inexpensive.

Grotte Teatro di Pompeo – One of several places in this tiny, packed neighborhood that claims to be the place where Julius Caesar met his untimely end. On any chilly day, the *zuppa di verdura* (vegetable soup) can keep one's inner self warm, and the *fettuccini verdi alla gorgonzola* (green noodles in a rich cheese sauce) is a wonderful pasta choice. The colorful but unprepossessing premises don't bother guests. This is the perfect place for cost-conscious visitors to try *osso buco con funghi* (veal shank with wild mushrooms) and *saltimbocca alla romana* (small pieces of veal with prosciutto). Closed Mondays and August. Reservations unnecessary. Visa accepted. 73 Via del Biscione (phone: 654-3686). Inexpensive.

La Sagrestia – Lots of places claim the best pizza in town, and this one is a top contender, with pies fresh from the wood-burning oven. Good pasta, good draft beer, ever-crowded and cheery, with kitschy decor. Near the Pantheon. Closed Wednesdays and 1 week in mid-August. Reservations advised for large groups. Major credit cards accepted. 89 Via del Seminario (phone: 679-7581). Inexpensive.

Lo Scopettaro – On the Tiber River, right near the Porta Portese flea market, is this popular, noisy neighborhood spot that serves traditional Roman fare such as *pasta e fagioli* (pasta and beans) and simple grilled meat. Closed Tuesdays and August. Reservations unnecessary. No credit cards accepted. 7 Lungotevere Testaccio (phone: 574-2408). Inexpensive.

Settimio all'Arancio – Simple but good, right in the heart of downtown Rome, near the old Jewish ghetto. It's always crowded. Particularly noteworthy is the *fusili con melanzane* (pasta with eggplant). Closed Sundays and August. Reservations advised. Major credit cards accepted. 50 Via dell'Arancio (phone: 687-6119). Inexpensive.

La Villetta al Piramide – Near the Protestant cemetery and the marble pyramid, this cheery, large trattoria is run by owner-cook Ada Mercuri Olivetti, who once took first prize over 4,000 other Roman cooks for her *spaghetti all'Amatriciana,* made with special bacon, tomato, and cheese. She serves other wholesome, hearty dishes, including vegetable antipasti. Closed Wednesdays. Reservations unnecessary. No credit cards accepted. 53 Viale Piramide Cestia (phone: 574-0204). Inexpensive.

A novelty for Rome are the less expensive eateries as an alternative to pizza; one such is the *Lucifero Pub* (28 Via dei Cappellari; phone: 654-5536), a fondue-and-beer tavern tucked into a side street off the Campo dei Fiori.

 BARS AND CAFÉS: For lighter meals, Rome's many *caffès* are also well worth trying. The most fashionable spots for the lunch or pre-dinner *aperitivo* are the *Caffè Greco* or the *Baretto* (Via Condotti), *Rosati* or *Canova* (Piazza del Popolo), and *Harry's Bar, Carpes,* the *Café de Paris, Doney's,* or others on Via Veneto. Best for light lunches are *Canova* and *Café de Paris. Babington's* (Piazza di Spagna) is an English tearoom that serves expensive snacks and luscious cakes. Currently *alla moda* is the little *Bar della Pace* (Piazza della Pace behind Piazza Navona), which is frequented by vendors from the nearby market in the morning and pre-lunch period, and then later in the day (until 3 AM) by all types, from artists and filmmakers to punks, poets, and students who, when the little marble tables fill up, rest their drinks and their bottoms on cars parked in the square.

At the tiny, busy Piazza Sant'Eustachio, the *Bar Eustachio* serves what is reputed to be the best coffee in town. It is an Italian-style espresso bar where a quick coffee is downed while standing. In the Jewish ghetto, lovers of sweets stand on line to get pastries fresh from an ancient oven, in the tiny, shabby, and excellent *Forno del Ghetto* (119 Via Portico d'Ottavia), where the production follows the religious holiday tradition.

As rising prices (and the influx of Chinese restaurants) oblige the more inexpensive trattorie either to upgrade to *ristorante* status or simply to disappear, they are being replaced by wine shops–cum–wine bars. In addition to selling the traditional glass, bottle, or case of wine, these establishments also now offer a light lunch of artfully prepared vegetables or pasta and a glass of good wine (from November through March, try the wonders of the *vini novelli*) for $10–$12 per person. They are scattered all over old Rome, and are tiny and dark. Simply look for their sign — *Enoteca*. The shops have only a few tables, do not take reservations, honor no credit cards, and close before 8 PM. Try the *Bottega del Vino da Bleve* (9/A Via Santa Maria del Pianto; phone: 686-5970) in downtown Rome; the tiny *Cul de Sac 1* (73 Piazza Pasquino; phone: 654-1094), which re-creates the atmosphere of an old *osteria; Il Piccolo* (74 Via del Governo Vecchio; phone: 654-1746) near Piazza Navona; and *Spiriti* (5 Via di Sant'Eustachio; phone: 689-2499).

On summer evenings, the after-dinner crowd often moves toward one of the many *gelaterie* in Rome, some of which are much more than ice cream parlors, since they serve exotic long drinks and *semifreddi* (like the famous *tartufo* — a double chocolate truffle — at Piazza Navona's *Tre Scalini,* where they sell 800 a day), and a few have lovely gardens and even live music. *Selarum* (12 Via dei Fienaroli) and *Fassi* (45 Corso d'Italia) have both gardens and music. Perhaps the best-known *gelateria,* however, is the very crowded *Giolitti* (40 Via Uffici del Vicario), not far from Piazza Colonna — try any of the fresh fruit flavors; it also boasts a tearoom (closed Mondays). Others are the sleek, high-tech *Gelateria della Palma* (which is also a piano bar, at the corner of Via della Maddalena and Via delle Coppelle), *Fiocco di Neve* (51 Via del Pantheon), and *Di Rienzo* (5 Piazza della Rotonda), all near the Pantheon; *Gelofestival* (29 Viale Trastevere, in Trastevere); and *Biancaneve* (1 Piazza Pasquale Paoli, where Corso Vittorio Emanuele II meets the Lungotevere dei Fiorentini). Favorites in the fashionable Parioli residential district are *Gelateria Duse* (also called *Giovanni;* 1 Via Eleonora Duse) and *Bar San Filippo* (8 Via San Filippo), both specializing in *semifreddi; Bar Gelateria Cile* (1-2 Piazza Santiago del Cile); the nearby *Giardino Ferranti* (29 Via Giovanni Pacini); and the *Casina delle Muse* (Piazzale delle Muse) for a fabulous *granità di caffè con panna* (coffee ice with cream). In the Jewish ghetto, try *Dolce Roma* (20/B Via Portico d'Ottavio; phone: 689-2196) for chocolate chip cookies and Austrian pastries. *Europeo Gran Caffè* (33 Piazza San Lorenzo in Lucina) is the place for indulging in high-calorie pastries.

DIVERSIONS

For the Experience

Quintessential Rome

 Romans are such *maestri* of pleasure that they consider it foolish to venture very far afield for the thrill of a Kenyan safari or for the peaceful pleasure of a seashell hunt in the Seychelles. Italy is still a country where the smallest unit of time is the "while," and only since the concept of *lo stress* was imported from America have Italians needed the noun *il relax* (pronounced re-leck-e-*say*) to describe the state of being that they have always taken for granted.

Any visitor can savor the quintessence of this city, which has entranced travelers since the Visigoths first applied for a visa, simply by getting away from it all at any one of the suggestions of vintage destinations and diversions that follow. So remember, before you trot off to the Great Wall or sail for Bora Bora, there's no place like Rome.

GRAND OPERA IN THE BATHS OF CARACALLA: In the summer of 1819, the Romantic poet Percy Bysshe Shelley came to the ruins of the Baths of Caracalla to seek inspiration for his verse play *Prometheus Unbound.* Here, seated upon a marble bench shaded by soaring umbrella pines and cypress trees, he wrote Acts I and II.

The monumental baths are still inspiration for poets, artists, and musicians. For more than half a century (with the exception only of the years during World War II) the annual performances of opera held here on summer evenings under the stars have been enchanting Romans and visitors alike. The sumptuous complex of baths begun in AD 206 under Septimius Severus was inaugurated by his son, the Emperor Caracalla, in AD 216. Although the precious inlaid marble floors, wainscoting, statuary, and mosaics were carted away during the 16th century to adorn Rome's palazzi, the ruins — their high walls and sections of the vaulted roof still intact — remain grandiose and evocative.

The first opera ever performed here was a 1914 production of Giuseppe Verdi's *Aïda,* with Pietro Mascagni conducting. Still an all-time favorite, its stirring music and Egyptian setting provide an excuse for a rousing processional in which (depending upon the year's budget) camels and elephants often lumber across a stage that is set amid the ruins of the ancient *caldarium.* The stage is also the setting for other operas, including *Turandot,* and occasional concerts by top-flight musicians. Who can forget the ultimate trio — Carreras, Domingo, and Pavarotti — going aria-to-aria during the *1990 World Cup* festivities? While perennially threatened by eviction, striking singers, and budgetary blues, the season nevertheless endures, and its essence is the same as when La Callas sang here: grand opera in grand surroundings. The only difference is that today's seats are more comfortable.

MORNING MARKETING AT CAMPO DEI FIORI: The soul and belly of modern-day Rome, the market dresses up each day, its stands heaped high with mounds of green artichokes, wild mushrooms, purple eggplant, oranges, and radishes — looking pretty enough to paint and definitely good enough to eat. Presiding over this lively scene are the Roman farmers and merchants, hawking their vegetables, lamb chops, fish, and dried lentils, and happy to help you select the ripest melon or tell you the best way to prepare eggplant. The flower stalls, delicatessen, and butcher shops surrounding this outdoor food *festa* are works of art in their own way: Peek in at the bakery (don't resist a hot-from-the-oven sample of pizza-like dough drizzled with olive oil), the butcher, and the cheese monger to see their displays.

The brooding, hooded statue in the center of the piazza is of Giordano Bruno, the radical Renaissance-era priest who was burned at the stake here in the year 1600. Public hangings were also held in this square until Napoleon's day; today, as the morning winds die down and the stalls are shut for the day, the basalt paving stones are washed down, and recaptured by young boys with soccer balls. In the evenings, the myriad neighborhood restaurants take center stage; by night, Romans like to wander the neighboring piazzas, big and small, to peer into the trattoria windows and to admire the vestiges of Pompey's Theater, whose stadium-like sections survive today in the shapes of the adjacent smaller piazzas and alleyways.

TESTACCIO: "Here lies one whose name was writ in water" is inscribed on the headstone over the grave of John Keats, the Romantic poet who died in Rome and is buried amidst trees and flowers in the meditative stillness of the small Protestant cemetery on Via Caio Cestio in Testaccio, Rome's liveliest — and most recently redis- covered — quarter. Keats lies right next to another signal burial monument: Rome's only pyramid. (It was commissioned by Gaius Cestius, a citizen of ancient Rome who so indebted his children — he left them the bill for the monument — that they were forced into bankruptcy.) The pyramid and cemetery mark the outer limits of Testaccio, which sits directly across the Tiber River from the better-known Trastevere. Testaccio is deceiving: Quiet and workaday until night falls, it comes to life as a host of little trattorie, some of the noisiest pizzerias in all of Italy, and spots for hot jazz and cool sounds throw open their doors. The restaurant tradition dates to the time when the main slaughterhouse was located here (about 20 years ago). Wait until dark to come to Testaccio, and then become part of the throng and drift with the crowd until you find the place that suits you best — but don't dress for dinner: The locals would never dream of wearing a jacket and tie just to go out to eat. Youthful high spirits soar through its alleyways, and it's sort of amazing to realize that this "new kid on the block" is 2,000 years old!

OSTIA ANTICA: There is a desolate sweetness about the ruins of Ostia, Rome's ancient seaport; they offer a portrait of the everyday hustle-bustle world of ancient Rome, and are in some ways more fascinating than the great forums of the Caesars. Here, in what is now many acres of shady archaeological park, businessmen in the time of Julius Caesar maintained offices for managing the affairs of empire.

The sea was closer then, and in this port city ships arriving from distant Egypt, Greece, and Turkey were unloaded, their goods placed on river barges to be moved up the Tiber to the capital. In Ostia's colonnaded main square, the identity of each business office — shipwright, cord and rope dealer, ivory importer, timber salesman — is de- picted in the black-and-white mosaic pavement in front of the shop. On the residential streets, the villas and patrician houses give an understanding of how the hoi polloi lived — down to the private lavatory set under the stairwell on the ground floor of one house. In all, it is a special thrill to walk down Ostia's narrow streets; on either side are its newly restored 3-story buildings, still standing after 2,000 years. The little medieval *borgo* (village) of a few houses within the walls of the impressive Castello (castle), outside the entrance gate, has charm of its own, and the small museum, *Museo Ostiense,* helps make the whole more comprehensible.

TRAJAN'S MARKET: Only 200 yards from the busy traffic hub of Piazza Venezia, Trajan's Market lies nearly 2 millennia away in time. After being closed for years of restoration, this somewhat misleadingly named 3-story office complex with 150 stores — which once housed 170 shops on 6 levels, plus a covered merchandise-mart —

is now open to visitors. Commissioned in AD 100 by the Spanish-born Trajan, the brilliant general and later Emperor of Rome (from AD 98 to 117) who pushed the Roman Empire to its farthest extremes, this is a little-known (but well worth visiting) taste of ancient Rome.

It was Apollodorus of Damascus, Trajan's architect, who revolutionized architecture with his addition of strutted vaults on pilasters under a central, long barrel-vault roof; this made high windows possible, which for the first time in history brought daylight into an enormous interior space. The semicircular complex and its adjacent forum remained in use well into the Middle Ages. Trajan's military prowess is evidenced in the monumental column in the Trajan Forum (the white marble bas relief column scroll details the general's victory over the gold-rich Dacians).

VILLA D'ESTE GARDENS OF TIVOLI: It took Neapolitan architect Pirro Ligorio 20 years to create the gardens for the villa of the ambitious Cardinal Ippolito d'Este (the pope sent the ambitious cardinal here — sort of a papal slap on the wrist — in 1550). The site was an old monastery which the cardinal greatly enlarged and decorated with frescoes; its rear loggia, or open gallery porch, overlooked a steep slope and the plains toward Rome.

Ligorio had an entire medieval village cleared away and terraced to make room for a classical Italian garden and then built a half-mile-long pipeline to bring water from the Aniene River to feed the fountains. A total of 500 fountains were built; ancient statuary was brought from the excavations at nearby Hadrian's Villa to be placed in the new garden setting. It became, said Henry James, "a wondrous romantic jumble." Today you walk beneath the same tall cypresses that both he and Franz Liszt admired, and you can hear, as they did, the music of the waters gushing, dancing, cascading, gurgling, fizzing.

For the best vistas, walk the Avenue of the Hundred Fountains, or stand by the central Dragon Fountain, whose main jet is the finest single fountain. The four dragons surrounding the fountain, versions of heraldic monsters from the crest of Pope Gregory XIII, were put here for his visit in September of 1572. Newly reopened after 2 years of problems over polluted water vapor, these fountains now also show how water itself is utilized as a material, much like clay or marble, to make a moving sculpture. The gardens are located just an hour's drive from downtown Rome, and are best seen in the morning.

ROME AT CHRISTMAS: Spirits soar along with prices, and stores stay open on Sundays during Italy's holiday jubilee, which lasts from early December until the arrival of La Befana, the national answer to Santa Claus, on January 6. A giant *Christmas* tree stands guard at Piazza Venezia. Windows are dressed in glitter and Styrofoam snow (as close as Rome almost ever gets to the real thing). A nearly life-size crèche is built into the steps of Piazza di Spagna, complete with bagpipers and, nearby and playing their pipes, live Abruzzi shepherds in leggings and leather vests.

Shoppers wrapped in showy furs inspect the king's ransom of gold and jewels along Via Condotti, and Piazza Navona is jammed with stalls selling records, toys, ready-stuffed stockings, and the freshly mined hunks of coal-colored rock candy known as *carbone.* The city fathers offer an elegant gift to visitors and Romans — free concerts in selected ancient churches and palazzi, their organs tuned and frescoes brilliantly illuminated for the occasion.

Wear warm clothes, and warm your hands on a fistful of roasted chestnuts from a street-corner vendor, or sip an espresso with whipped cream in the antique *Caffè Greco* (86 Via Condotti; phone: 6-678-2554), aromatic with freshly ground coffee, Diorissimo, Gucci leather, and the sweet smell of prosperity.

FOUNTAINS OF ROME: In the thick heat of a Roman August, flocks of bare-legged tourists (and the few natives who have not migrated to the teeming beaches) converge under the spray of the city's innumerable fountains. Clutching fast-liquefying ice cream cones and soaking their feet in the recently restored Fontana di Trevi, these chill-seekers stare enviously at Neptune riding his marine chariot through cool waves of marble and water, or they enjoy the water, water everywhere, alongside the Four Rivers at Piazza Navona, the Roman bathtubs at Piazza Farnese, the horses at Piazza Esedra, the fish at the Pantheon, or the climbing turtles at Piazza Mattei. Those with the energy to wander find comfort at corner cast-iron fountains spouting drinking water that has been piped from springs outside the city ever since the ancients built the aqueducts. And in the evening, when the temperature has receded to the level of long sleeves and slacks, the fountains provide a soothing background gurgle and a civilized place to rinse off the stickiness of that irresistible watermelon ice cream nightcap.

TRASTEVERE: The people who live in Trastevere, the medieval maze of curving alleys and *piazzette* on the west bank of the Tiber, believe that their neighborhood is the only true Rome — and its inhabitants the only true Romans. Gentrification has set in, but the neighborhood still teems and throbs with life Italian style, particularly on Saturday nights in summer. Visit it then and walk across the river by way of the boat-shaped Tiber island known as the Isola Tiberina. Get there when dusk gilds the medieval mosaics in Piazza Santa Maria, and hunt around for one of the area's base-ment theaters, mini-jazz clubs, and tiny art cinemas, their signs camouflaged by laundry hung out to dry. Then have supper outdoors at one of the chaotic *pizzerie* that appropri-ate sidewalks and parking spaces all summer long.

After midnight, stop at the back door of an unassuming bakery a block from Piazza Trilussa to sate yourself on tomorrow's *cornetti* and hot, cream-filled bombe. And at dawn on Sunday, show up at the immense flea market at Porta Portese, which closes by lunchtime, to comb through piles of early Renaissance Levis, stucco busts of Mus-solini, and priceless and prongless silver forks. You just might find something you couldn't live without haggling for.

MASS IN ST. PETER'S, Vatican City: There is an opulent sense of secrecy and devotion in the penitent hum seeping from the confessionals, the permanent smell of incense, the smoky glow of candles on gilt-framed paintings and glinting baroque statues in St. Peter's Cathedral. Here's where the elegant faithful of Rome share pews with poorly clothed pilgrims from Lithuania, Poland, and Zaire, and stately processions of white-robed men and boys perpetually reenact a ritual that only the initiated can fully understand.

The air undulates with murmured prayers and mumbled chants, the voice of the priest filtered through ancient loudspeakers, the organ's mellow buzz, the harsh treble of the occasional impious baby. Sometimes the dark whispers of the mass are broken by a bright burst of sound as orchestra and chorus deliver the Bach *Magnificat,* the soloists' voices rebounding off the fluted columns and convoluted walls. At the final cadence, the hush sets in again.

Rome's Most Memorable Hostelries

Sooner or later, whenever the world became too much for them, the Greta Garbos and Winston Churchills, Richard Wagners and Liz Taylors of every era slept here.

None of this should come as a surprise to anyone who has ever experi-enced the pleasures of the best Roman hotels. Like one big room with a view, Rome is full of princely villas, Renaissance rooms, and other handsome accommodations lovingly and lavishly ransomed from the past. These historic hostelries supply the perfect excuse to avoid the anonymous glass-and-concrete business domes of postwar Italy.

EDEN: Located on a quiet street a few steps from Via Veneto, this hotel stands in stately isolation, like an oak tree spreading proudly over a jumbly jungle. While not the most famous hostelry in Rome, it is sought out by the sophisticated traveler who expects seamless service, a central location, and a garage in which to park the car (most unusual in the center of this major city). Its panoramic bar, roof garden restaurant, and some of its 116 air conditioned rooms have delightful vistas over the umbrella pines and sprawling gardens of a next-door monastery and the French Academy. Details: *Eden,* 49 Via Ludovisi, Roma 00187 (phone: 6-474-3551).

FORUM: Few hotels anywhere in the world can boast rooms with such views. For Rome this is almost as tall as they come, and the roof garden and adjacent rooftop restaurant, which back up against the wall of a medieval church tower, overlook the Forums of the Caesars. This is not, strictly speaking, a luxury property, but rooms are comfortably sized, if not huge; the service is pleasant, the elevator works, and all around are lively restaurants in the Subura. All this, and it is within walking distance of Piazza Venezia and near a *metropolitana* (subway) stop. Details: 25 Via Tor dei Conti, Roma 00184 (phone: 6-679-2446).

GRAND: This old-fashioned, luxurious property, near the railroad station and the Quirinal Palace, the residence of the Italian president, and not too far from the American Embassy, has a courtly, sober, and somewhat ambassadorial air about it. Still among the proudest links in the CIGA chain, it's oh so chic — the elaborate white ballroom is a favorite setting for haute couture fashion shows and distinguished Roman weddings. Guests here have included opera diva Maria Callas and Hollywood's Elizabeth Taylor — before and after Burton. Rooms and bathrooms are large and well appointed and the mattresses are *comme il faut.* The food served in *Le Restaurant* is considered among the best in Rome. Guests also can enjoy a drink at one of its two supremely cozy bars or relax to the strains of soothing harp music over afternoon tea. Details: *Grand Hotel,* 3 Via Vittorio Emanuele Orlando, Roma 00185 (phone: 6-4709).

HOLIDAY INN CROWNE PLAZA MINERVA: Honest. Any resemblance to US members of this chain begins and ends with its formal moniker; Romans know this early-19th-century hotel with the tongue-twister name simply as "the Minerva." Located on the central piazza of that name in the historical section of the city, adjacent to the Pantheon, it shares the square with Santa Maria Sopra Minerva, Rome's most important Gothic basilica (which is built on and incorporates the ruins of a temple to the goddess Minerva).

After a recent multimillion-dollar renovation under the direction of architect Paolo Portoghese, the lobby has been completely redone in shades of delicate pastels; and *La Cesta* restaurant has been reappointed with stunning fixtures. There are 118 rooms, 13 junior suites, and 3 presidential suites, all with air conditioning, color satellite TV, and electronic safes. The suites are elegantly decorated with Napoleonic period furnishings — and even the meeting rooms have fine frescoes and statues. There's a comfortable piano bar, *La Cupole,* plus a rooftop terrace (building codes have so far prohibited a rooftop café or restaurant) that offers a unique view of the Pantheon and of the ancient city. Details: *Holiday Inn Crowne Plaza Minerva,* Piazza della Minerva, Roma 00186 (phone: 6-684-1901).

LORD BYRON: Members of Italy's automobile aristocracy and such other luminaries as Michael Jackson make this small, elegant, out-of-the-way place in the quiet suburb of Parioli their home away from home. Once a private villa, it has 47 rooms and a small bar, but no swimming pool and no spa — nothing but discreet (with a capital "D") personal attention, subdued opulence, and what very well may be the single finest restaurant in the capital, *Relais le Jardin* (see *Buon Appetito: Rome's Best Restaurants*). The relative quiet and smog-free air make up for the need for taxis or a chauffeur service for the 10-minute ride into downtown Rome. The traditionally-decorated rooms are spacious, though some baths are not. Details: *Lord Byron,* 5 Via Giuseppe de Notaris, Roma 00197 (phone: 6-322-49541).

MAJESTIC: Two years ago, after a costly renovation, this property was reopened under new ownership. The turn-of-the-century dining room and lobbies, including some halls that are richly adorned with frescoes, were restored to pristine condition with sumptuous carpeting and draperies; rooms and baths are well appointed and spacious. The service is professional, and the downtown location across the Via Veneto from the American Embassy and close to airline offices is important in a traffic-bound city where your best chance of making an appointment on time may be to walk there. In any case, underground parking is only a block away. Details: *Majestic,* 50 Via Veneto, Roma 00187 (phone: 6-486841; fax: 488-0984; telex: 622262).

SOLE AL PANTHEON: One of Rome's most venerable old hostelries, this was always among the most convenient because its doorway gives out onto Piazza della Rotonda, the fountain square facing the Pantheon. After a recent renovation, this small hotel is also one of Rome's most sought-after (and pricey). Be sure to ask for a room with a view — a few on the top floor have balconies and whirlpool baths, and panoramas of the spectacular skyline. Though the rooms have limited dimensions, this is a place for a poet soul with a fat pocketbook — though some will wrinkle their noses at the kitschy downstairs lobby. Details: *Sole al Pantheon,* 73 Piazza della Rotonda, Roma 00186 (phone: 678-0441; fax: 684-0689).

Buon Appetito:
The Best Restaurants of Rome

While all those mad dogs and Englishmen are running around in the noon-day sun, Romans are lolling in the shade of a spaghetti tree in a piazza by the banks of a river of Frascati. Every afternoon, they sit happily and hungrily at table for 3 or 4 hours. Almost every evening, dinner is the principal entertainment. The city is full of family trattorie that make the most of their comestible bounties, wonderful establishments that offer a mix of homeyness, sophisti-cation, and generally superb foods made from whatever was in the market that morning (usually written in purple ink in an almost indecipherable scrawl). At places like these, it's great fun to share the Italians' zest in their culinary heritage — those below are just the *crema della crema.*

La cucina creativa — Italy's answer to the nouvelle cuisine of France — is firmly established. Old-fashioned cereal staples like barley and *faro* are new culinary fashions; give them a try. With 5,000 miles of coastline, there are plenty of fish in the Italian seas that are dished out in grand style in Roman restaurants. There are more pasta dishes in Rome than there are forks (see the pasta glossary in USEFUL WORDS AND PHRASES; we suggest making an effort to try them all). Be sure to phone ahead for reservations. And if you overeat, a shot of the pungent little herbal horror known as Fernet-Branca, available in most bars and restaurants, normally will chase away all evil abdominal spirits. *Buon appetito.*

ALBERTO CIARLA: A high priest of the Roman culinary scene, Alberto sets the pace in numerous ways — decor, menu, wines, style — at a time when Italy's topflight chefs continue to experiment with and celebrate their reinventions of Italian regional cuisine. For well-heeled guests who don't have to worry about the hefty bill, dinner in his trendy Trastevere establishment is a must. The black dinner plates in this dimly lit dining place are brightened by Signor Ciarla's inventive ways with fish. He also turns his hand to pasta with herb and vegetable sauces and beautifully served meat and game dishes;

desserts are picture perfect. Dine outdoors in good weather. Open for dinner only; closed Sundays. All major credit cards accepted.Details: *Alberto Ciarla,* 40 Piazza San Cosimato, Roma 00153 (phone: 6-581-8668).

COSTANZA: The narrowest of alleyways leads into a spacious, traditional-looking trattoria that was always a Roman favorite, and is now among the smartest eateries in the capital; its international reputation has not suffered from being next door to *The New York Times* Rome bureau offices. The stuffed homemade pasta — varieties change with the seasons — is delectable; look for ravioli plump with puréed artichoke, or try the wild *porcini* mushrooms (boletus) on pasta; the antipasto offerings are of the highest quality.

The decor is upmarket rustic — terra cotta floors and white walls, the better to show off the back interior wall, a patch of the ruins of Pompey's Theater. Good value for money in terms of both food and atmosphere, but don't bother with the handful of outdoor tables in summer unless you arrive very early in the evening or don't mind a long wait between courses. Closed Sundays and August. American Express and Visa accepted. Details: *Costanza,* 63 Piazza Paradiso, Roma 00186 (phone: 6-686-1717 or 6-654-1002).

GIRARROSTO TOSCANO: The cramped staircase entrance to this popular restaurant (whose name means simply "spit-grilled, Tuscan-style") doesn't prepare first-time guests for the spacious, cave-like rooms around the corner. From Roman *haute bourgeoisie* and movie producers to Middle Eastern yuppies and American cardiologists on convention, the clientele waits patiently at the entrance and then sits down zestfully to enjoy the eavesdropping, the people watching, and the bustle — and to dine excellently on ultra-traditional Tuscan specialties. Waiters automatically serve plattersful of well-aged hams, mortadella, salami, prosciutto, mozzarella, stuffed tomatoes, meatballs, baked eggplant, and other antipasti. Then, right after you've eaten enough to last at least a couple of days, dinner begins. Gigantic Florentine steaks grilled to perfection stand out in any season; spaghetti with fresh tomato and basil is a worthy summer offering. Menus with prices are sometime things at best, and if you don't want antipasto, which costs extra, say so as soon as you sit down. Closed Wednesdays. Details: *Girarrosto Toscano,* 29 Via Campania, Roma 00187 (phone: 6-482-1899).

MARIO: Anyone who came to Rome in the 1950s and 1960s is likely to remember this finest of Rome's traditional Tuscan restaurants; return guests will be pleased to know that nothing has changed since then. The famed *ribollita* (twice-boiled vegetable soup, which depends upon a deep purple cabbage for its special taste), consumed with a mere dab of purest Tuscan olive oil; the pasta with game sauces; the robust game dishes and thick steaks *alla fiorentina* — all still conjure up the sites and scents of Tuscany's hillsides. This is the place at which to eat and to drink Chianti — and then to delight in the reasonably small check. Service is bruskly Tuscan; the decor is dark and old-fashioned; and the location is central to serious shopping around Piazza di Spagna. Closed Sundays and August. All major credit cards accepted. Details: *Mario,* 55 Via della Vite, Roma (phone: 6-678-3818).

RELAIS LE JARDIN: Though this superlatively comfortable and elegant dining room is a bit out of the way, in the Parioli suburb, once there you'll agree that the food deserves the fuss. The menu is dizzying yet engaging: Zucchini flowers stuffed with bean purée, ravioli filled with pigeon, and watercress flan with scallops were among the recent offerings. The service is discreetly attentive and formal. Closed Sundays and August. Reservations are essential. All major credit cards accepted. Details: *Relais Le Jardin,* 5 Via Giuseppe de Notaris, Roma 00197 (phone: 6-322-4541).

ROMOLO: In this famed tavern in the heart of Trastevere, near a particularly picturesque ancient city gate, the painter Raphael supposedly courted the baker's daughter whom he also painted in a portrait called *La Fornarina.* It might have been yesterday, for there is a recaptured sense of Rome as it was then when you dine in the quiet garden in the midday dappled shade of a 450-year-old arbor.

Nothing is nouvelle here: The cuisine and the good wine list cling to the appropriately Roman-traditional, with such hearty fare as spaghetti *alla boscaiolo* (woodchopper-style — that is, with mushrooms and tomato), and mozzarella *alla Fornarina,* melted cheese wrapped in prosciutto and accompanied by a fried artichoke. Reservations necessary in summer especially. Major credit cards accepted. Closed Mondays and August. Details: *Romolo,* 8 Via di Porta Settimiana, Roma 00153 (phone: 6-581-8284).

EL TOULÀ: Completely unlike the plain, brightly lit restaurants so typical of Rome, this one boasts decor that is at once plush and subtle, a clientele that is aristocratic and well traveled, a staff as warm and easygoing as the local trattoria's, and a menu that takes diners through Paris, Vienna, and a score of other European capitals.

Stick to the dishes of Venice, the restaurant's culinary starting place. Try the *radicchio di Treviso ai ferri,* a slightly bitter red lettuce served grilled. Go on to black risotto, a rice dish perfumed with squid and its ink. Try calves' liver with onions or sage butter or the famous *baccalà mantecato* (creamy codfish). And finish up with *tiramisù,* a creamy coffee-and-chocolate-flavored confection whose name means "pick-me-up." Skiers and hikers headed for the Dolomites should look up the sister restaurant of the same name in Cortina d'Ampezzo. Closed Saturdays at lunchtime, Sundays, and August. All major credit cards accepted. Details: *El Toulà,* 29/B Via della Lupa, Roma 00186 (phone: 6-687-3750).

VECCHIA ROMA: The name means "Old Rome," and that is what this restaurant offers, dining in a handsome piazza of baroque churches and Renaissance buildings, only steps away from some of the finest monuments from ancient Rome. The menu leans to Italian classical specialties, with a broad selection of justifiably beloved old favorites like prosciutto and melon, pasta classics, veal in a tuna sauce or grilled baby lamb chops, and fresh country salad greens; there's also an impressive wine list. The setting is classic trattoria: white-washed walls, rustic furniture, and an agreeably old-fashioned air. Tradition reigns here, and reigns well; it's Rome's quintessential summer place at midday or in the evening under the giant market umbrellas. Closed Wednesdays and 2 weeks in August. All major credit cards accepted. Details: *Vecchia Roma,* 18 Piazza Campitelli, Roma (phone: 6-686-4604).

Cafés

Perhaps no other institution reflects the relaxed Italian lifestyle as much as the ubiquitous café (or bar, as it is called in Rome). From small emporia with three tin tables (where locals perpetually argue the Sunday soccer results) to the sprawling outdoor drawing rooms of Rome's *Caffè Greco,* life slows to sit-and-sip. Romans order Campari or cappuccino and put the world on hold. Inside, Roman cafés are for receiving friends and suitors, reading the paper, and writing the great Italian novel. Some regulars even get their mail at their local café. Outside, in summer, the café is for appraising and supervising the passing spectacle. Puccini set a whole act of his opera *La Bohème* in a café.

When you visit those below — a few of the most evocative of the breed — remember that cafés are not necessarily inexpensive. Table prices are usually far higher than what you pay for the very same items if standing at the bar. So when you're charged $5 for an espresso, don't grumble — just think of it as rent.

EUSTACHIO IL CAFFÈ: Among Romans, to say nothing of foreign denizens, the issue of where the best cappuccino can be found is surpassed only by the question of where the best morning *corneto* (a sweetish croissant, not on any list of low-cholesterol food) is sold. The runaway favorite for first prize is this *caffè,* which has been in the same location on the same square near the Pantheon since 1938. Drink your cappuccino where Henry Kissinger and countless others drank theirs. The special taste comes from fine coffee beans roasted over a wood-burning fire; it also depends on the whipping cream, which helps give the foam to the little cap on top. (For one of the best *corneti,* walk across the piazza to the *Bernasconi* café; 82 Piazza Sant'Eustachio; phone: 6-656-1309.)

CARPES: Via Veneto is synonymous with the word "café," and the entire street is a year-round sidewalk sipping and people watching festival; to single out one is to somewhat needlessly belittle the others, each of which has its claim to fame. The newly renovated *Carpes* (which old-timers will recall as *Carpano*) stands out for its turn-of-the-century decor, which lends a sense of Europe as it was in the age of Grand Tourism, before the wannabe Fellini crowd made Via Veneto a sometimes tacky cliché. Light lunches are also available. Closed Wednesdays. 2 Via dei Glincini, Anguillara Sabazia (phone: 6-901-8364).

GRECO: When this café was opened in 1760 by the Greek-born Nicola della Maddalena, its clients were local working people. Later, the tranquil little marble tables in the three back rooms were a place for Stendhal and Schopenhauer to pause and reflect. They prompted Hans Christian Andersen to characterize Rome as the only city in the world that made him feel instantly at home. Casanova mentioned the establishment in his memoirs, Mark Twain loved the place, Nicolai Gogol scribbled *Dead Souls* seated on its austere benches, and the painter Giorgio de Chirico said he couldn't paint without stopping here for his daily dose of the Italian drink Punt e Mes. After World War II, local intellectuals dubbed the narrow elongated room where John Keats, Washington Irving, and Oscar Wilde had taken coffee "The Omnibus."

Today, the place is full of busts and statues of such famous habitués, and the front bar is jammed with expensive furs and suede slippers whose owners are catching their collective breath between jaunts to Fendi and Ferragamo. Couturier Valentino comes here, as do members of the Bulgari clan, whose shop is nearby. *Caffè Greco* has been declared a part of Italy's national patrimony, and even the waiters, who dress in tails, look as if they're being preserved for posterity. 86 Via Condotti (phone: 6-679-1700).

TRE SCALINI: Not surprisingly, this place is a perennial favorite with both Romans and foreigners, particularly in summer, when the cone-seekers are often three deep at the ice cream counter inside. The setting — right at ringside in Rome's beautiful and car-free Piazza Navona, facing Bernini's famous Fountain of the Rivers — is incomparable, the cast of characters colorful. The renowned specialty is the *tartufo,* a grated bitter chocolate–covered chocolate ice cream ball swathed in whipped cream and named for its resemblance to the knobby truffle. 28 Piazza Navona (phone: 6-654-1996).

■ **Note:** Though not a café in its literal sense, Babington's must be mentioned here. A century ago, in 1892, two English spinsters founded a tearoom for their fellow Britishers. Located directly across the Spanish Steps from the small building in which John Keats died (it was then the heart of Rome's artists' quarter), in those years the fairest maidens from outlying villages would come, dressed in elaborate traditional costume, for a day's work posing for the myriad foreign and Italian painters who would then sell their works to the tourists. Painters and pilgrims, art lovers and the artisans who made picture frames in the neighborhood, would then repair to the tearoom for a cheery cuppa. The costumes are gone, but otherwise the neighborhood has retained some of its original flavor; and the many art and antiques dealers of the nearby streets (like Via Margutta) gather here for light lunches and, later, for rich, homemade tea cakes and scones. On a rainy autumn day of gallery hopping and showroom shopping, its welcoming wood fire and skillfully brewed tea afford the ultimate in creature comforts. Closed Tuesdays. 23 Piazza di Spagna (phone: 6-578-6027).

Shopping in Rome

In the beginning, Italians created marble statues, stone palazzi, and alabaster altarpieces. In our era, the national talent has turned from the eternal to the ephemeral, from the permanent to the portable. As a result, the descendants of Cellini and Michelangelo lavish their genius for design, their sure instinct for what is simply beautiful, on the creation of objects for daily use that delight the senses. The result has come to be known as "Italian style."

Most shops practice the Anglo-Saxon rite of *prezzi fissi* (fixed prices). Or at least they claim to. But it never hurts to try for the traditional *sconto* (discount) on the grounds that you're paying in cash, that you're buying in quantity, that the price is outrageous, or that you were sent by the owner's brother-in-law in Buffalo.

For information about the best buys and where to find them, read on.

WHERE TO SHOP

CHAIN STORES: In a nation dedicated to the proposition that boutique is best, the department store and one-stop shopping site are only a minor part of the scene. *La Rinascente* recently has upgraded its collections in its Rome store. *Coin* and *UPIM,* the nationwide major leaguers, both sell middle-priced clothing and household items of decent quality. The former has shops all over the city; the latter has a store downtown, on Via del Tritone, that is a comfortable place to begin conspicuous consuming within the city limits. *Standa* resembles a glorified *Woolworth's* and is here, too. Clothing is a good buy, especially at *UPIM;* prices are fair, and many items are pure cotton or all wool. Housewares are also attractive and inexpensive.

Since all four chains are self-service and have fitting rooms, they're convenient places to figure out your Italian size and get a feel for price or fit — without having to employ sign language with the salespeople.

STREET MARKETS: If shopping is entertainment, Rome's street markets are its best theater. Most of the country's most intriguing goods can be found here. High-quality shoes show up at the city's gigantic Sunday morning labyrinth at the Porta Portese. Forget the four walls and shop as the Italians do — alfresco. For every Roman who goes to mass on Sunday morning, a dozen go shopping with the masses. To join them, stuff a little naked cash in a tight pocket, leave camera and purse at home, and prepare to shuffle through the packed streets. Sundays from 5 AM (the bargain hour) until 1 PM.

The vast clothing market at the daily shops and stands on Via Sannio, near San Giovanni, is the place for good buys and a wide assortment of rough stuff — army surplus, jeans, down jackets, mode-of-the-moment sweaters. Beware of imitation Levis, Wranglers, and such, and be sure to check out Rome's mini-*Macy's* across the street — the *Coin* department store.

The air conditioned shopping mall has finally appeared on the Roman scene. *Cinecittà Due* (Viale Palmiro Togliatti), with over 100 shops, reachable by subway, is open daily except Sundays, from 9 AM to 8:30 PM. Don't expect bargains.

One of the most rewarding Roman experiences is to take the time to pore over new and used books, occasionally authentic antique prints, and modern reproductions of etchings of Rome's monuments — all offered weekdays in the stalls at the Piazza di Fontanella Borghese. Many of the reproductions (some rare booksellers also stock originals) are the work of Giambattista Piranesi, whose first plates of Roman antiquities were printed in 1743. Piranesi was a forerunner of the rediscovery of Roman antiquities in the 18th century. He was followed by other engravers who have left us documents of romantic ruins and the Roman palazzi and piazze as they looked in the Renaissance and baroque eras.

BEST BUYS

CLOTHING: The prospect of picking up an entire wardrobe in Rome is so tempting that some travelers dream of an airline losing their luggage permanently.

Giorgio Armani creates clothing for women in styles not unlike those he makes for men. The star of both shows has always been the broad-shouldered, loose-fitting jacket and slacks that manage to be at once comfortably baggy and elegant of line. The designer's Emporio models can be found in many outlets; his boutiques have exclusive models at triple the price. A shopper's prime destination is 102 Via del Babuino.

Laura Biagiotti's spare, linear clothes in softly offbeat colors, are displayed against a dazzling white backdrop in her shop at No. 43 on the dark, narrow Via Borgognona.

Missoni started with knitwear, but the unexpected fabric and color blends can now be found as shirts, slacks, bathing suits, and even belts for men and women. The all-time classic is a heavy cardigan sweater for men, suitable as outerwear, in sophisticated color mixes. The newest wrinkle: handsome sheets, bedspreads, stunning area rugs, and wall hangings. On a rainy day, it's cheering just to pop into a *Missoni* shop. 38/B Via Borgognona; Missoni Uomo (for men) at 78 Piazza di Spagna.

Luisa Spagnoli offers high-quality, moderately priced clothing for women in the purest cotton and wool — which is why this designer's more than 100 shops are popular in every corner of the country. On the Via Frattina and at 84 Via Barberini.

Valentino has ready-to-wear for men and women with a sophisticated look that is both timeless and elegant. Women's dresses are slim and tailored or full and definitively romantic. 12 Via Condotti and 15 Bocca di Leone for women, 61 Via del Babuino for men, women, and children. If money doesn't matter, bypass the boutiques and go for the *alta moda* (haute couture) at 24 Via Gregoriana.

Il Discount dell'Alta Moda (16/A Via del Gesù) sells last season's high fashions at down-to-earth prices. *Bassetti Confezioni* (5 Via Monterone) also has high fashion ready-to-wear for both men and women at discounted prices and is the best fashion bargain in the Eternal City.

FABRICS: Italy is known around the world for its velvet, linen, silk, and other fabrics.

Cesari has a dizzying selection of upholstery material at 96 Via Frattina, as well as regally impractical lingerie and home linen at the branch at 195 Via Barberini. All stores offer good prices during January white sales.

Bises is another place for fine fabrics. 93 Via del Gesù.

Galtrucco features all kinds of fabrics, especially pure silks. 23 Via del Tritone.

Naj Oleari offers famed cotton fabrics and accessories from bags to lampshades. 25/A Via di San Giamcomo and 32 Via dei Greci.

FOOD: In Rome, there is a wide selection of Italy's finest food products in the shops along Via della Croce or at *Franchi* (204 Via Cola di Rienzo). And when Italians travel around their own country — and they rarely bother with any other — they pride themselves on knowing when and where to find each special food at its golden moment.

Asparagus – A tender white variety, delicately tipped with violet, is grown from March to May. Eat it raw, sliced into salad. In Rome and Sicily, wild asparagus is a fleeting treat, often served in a *frittata* (omelette). The best place to find fresh asparagus in Rome is in the market at Campo dei Fiori.

Cheese – Most shops throughout the city stock gift boxes of *parmigiano reggiano,* the perfect cheese — natural and wholesome — for snacks and grating. Made from pure buffalo milk, fresh mozzarella is delicate and soft — not the rubbery stuff so often seen in American supermarkets. True mozzarella must have a minimum of 30% buffalo milk, the rich ingredient that gives this cheese its unique taste; the rest is properly (and legally) called *fior di latte,* and is cow's milk.

FURS: The youthful look of family-owned *Fendi* became famous around the world when the company introduced the fur-lined raincoat over 25 years ago. Since then, the five Fendi sisters have made squirrel and shearling as sexy as sable, and put their double-F symbol on leather goods of every description, from key chains to suitcases. The whole range of Fendi design can be seen in the firm's six separate shops on Rome's Via Borgognona, near the Spanish Steps.

HATS: To top off any Rome visit, stop off for a hat at the world-famous *Borsalino,* featuring everything from a humble bowler to a fancy, ostrich-feathered creation suitable for an afternoon at Ascot. 157/B Via IV Novembre.

JEWELRY: Italians have been working with precious stones and metals since the time of the Etruscans. So if you make only one Italian purchase, it ought to be a small (but fine) piece of jewelry. Your Gucci shoes may lose their charm, but gold never seems to go out of style. For the prized hand-chased, Florentine effect, be sure to shop at one of the *Buccellati* boutiques in town. A quarter of the Via Condotti's windows glow with gold. Look for *Bulgari* and *Buccellati* (still reigning supreme), *Cartier* and *Van Cleef,* and nearby, *Di Consiglio, Massoni, Merli,* and *Rapi.*

Knowledgeable buyers also seek out the exclusive shops tucked discreetly into corners of the neighboring Piazza di Spagna district: *Capuano,* inside the courtyard of the Palazzo Caffarelli (61 Via Condotti); *Vincenzo Arcesi,* whose contemporary designs are made on the premises (86 Via della Vite); and *Petochi,* which sells imaginative jewelry and lordly old clocks (23 Piazza di Spagna, above *Babington's* tearoom). For irresistibly convincing costume jewelry, stop at *Bijoux de Paris* (27 Via Condotti).

KNITWEAR: The knitted creations of Italian factories are famous for reasons that can be immediately seen in almost every clothing store in Rome.

Benetton is a prime destination for anyone who wants to take home an armload or two of sweaters and skirts. In the last few years, the streets of Rome have sprouted dozens of *Benetton* shops, and their windows are full of the informal, brilliantly colored, inexpensive sweaters, shirts, pants, and accessories for men, women, and children. Remember, *Benetton* is an Italian company.

Albertina hand-finishes glamorous knit clothes in a tiny workroom above her store (20 Via Lazio). The best of her works have been exhibited in the *Metropolitan Museum of Art;* the merchandise is a paradigm of Italian craftsmanship.

LEATHER GOODS: Just as France's Louis Vuitton made his initials the hallmark of luxury luggage, Italy's big G's — *Gherardini, Gucci,* and *Nazareno Gabrielli* — have become synonymous with Italian leather fashion. Each company makes and markets its own lines, emblazoning its initials on boots, briefcases, key rings, umbrellas, bags, and baggage. Since the quality is high (with prices to match), any one of these items is sure to impress. Shops are located on or near Via Condotti.

Bottega Veneta's advertising suggests that your own initials are enough. But the firm's buttery soft, basket-weave leather is their own unmistakable statement, as you can see for yourself in the company shops at 18 Via San Sebastianello.

For less expensive versions of Italy's luxury lines, visit *Armando Rioda* (90 Via Belsiana — on the second floor). You'll find hand-crafted copies of all the greats at impressively discounted prices.

SHOES: You'll find a shoe shop on virtually every corner in Rome, but it's the rare Anglo-Saxon foot that matches an Italian last. Price is generally a clue to what you're getting — as usual, you get just what you pay for. When in doubt about the composition, just sniff. The aroma of real fine leather is unmistakable.

Ferragamo made Italian shoes a byword of elegance in the US when its namesake and founder fitted John Barrymore, Mary Pickford, and Gloria Swanson in Hollywood in the 1920s. Still largely handmade today, the firm's shoes are available in various widths — which makes them a rarity in Italy. Soft and comfortable men's and women's loafers are top sellers despite prices that will take your breath away. (Be aware that the company's main store is in Florence.) 66 Via Condotti.

Raphael Salato offers sparkly sandals, glossy moccasins, and other attention-getters for men, women, and children. 104 and 149 Via Veneto.

Beltrami dresses its windows at 19 Via Condotti with a moneyed gleam every bit as splendid as those of the jeweler *Bulgari* down the street. Sleek and sophisticated women's clothing rounds out the picture.

Spas

In Italy, real water-immersion addicts wouldn't even think about a trip to the Riviera or the Greek Isles when they could wallow happily in the mud of Salsomaggiore. Consequently, Italy's water — and its mud — are the base of one of the country's most lucrative industries. There are *terme* (spas) all over the country. Some flourish on the sites of thermal springs first exploited by the ancient Romans, those imperial water-worshipers, who built baths with great fervor. Others trace their origins to antique legends of healing streams spurting from the warm blood of slain princes and miraculous geysers that gushed forth from the tears of abandoned maidens.

Happily, visitors to Rome who are "taking the waters" can indulge themselves at a spa just an hour away at Fiuggi in Lazio. When Michelangelo felt the need to flee Rome and the rigors of painting the ceiling of the Sistine Chapel — for a breath of clean air and a sip of purifying water — it was to this town (south of Rome and 2,500 feet above sea level) that he came. Carried by papal couriers to Boniface VIII in Rome during the Middle Ages, this water is now bottled and sold all over Italy, but many Italians still consider a summer holiday at the source essential to year-round health. Fiuggi's two springs, each set in a lush garden, are known nationally as surefire cures for kidney disturbances; one is recommended for morning therapy, the other for postprandial (open April through November). During the interval, leave the spa area and explore the Old Town with its high walls, stone staircases, and evocative aromas of wine cellars, wood fires, and grilled meat; one of its charming outdoor restaurants makes a pleasant stop before a tour of the surrounding Ciociara hills. If you decide to stay, hotels range from the simply splendid — Italy's kings summered here — to the simple and economical, with full facilities for the disabled. The splendid *Grand Hotel Palazzo della Fonte* (phone: 6-775-5081) — built in 1913 — recently underwent a $30-million renovation. Italy's kings and queens used to take the waters here. In addition to the usual luxury hotel and spa amenities, there is a fitness center with personalized exercise program, haute weight-watching cuisine, a golf course, riding, and tennis. Details: *Azienda Autonoma di Soggiorno,* 4 Via Gorizia, Fiuggi (Frosinone) 03015 (phone: 775-55446).

Cooking Schools

Until recently, every Italian home's kitchen was a cooking school, *la professoressa* was *la Mamma,* and the student body was restricted to family members. However, Italians have discovered the pleasures of their own nation's regional cooking right along with the rest of the world: Neapolitans now eat Tuscan food at home and Venetians down Sicily's cannoli and cannelloni —

foods that, as often as not, *Mamma's mamma* told her nothing at all about. Enter the cooking school.

One is taught by Jo Bettoja, one of the leading lights of Italian cooking. Both are in English, and are staged in spring and summer; early booking is a must. Here are Rome's best scuole di cucina.

ROMAN COOKING SCHOOL: Run by Audris d'Aragona and Alice Pugh, English-speaking classes are held at a lakeside retreat 16 miles (26 km) from Rome in the former fishing village of Anguillara. The atmosphere is homey and the cuisine is a sampler of specialties from all regions of Italy. Details: *Roman Cooking School,* 2 Via dei Glicini, Anguillara Sabazia (Lazio) 00061 (phone: 6-901-8364).

SCALDAVIVANDE COOKING SCHOOL: After Jo Bettoja, an American from Georgia, exhibited her good taste by marrying into a distinguished Italian family that still cures its own prosciutto and salami, she soon came to realize that other Italians were not learning what she had learned from her new *Mamma*-in-law. So she began combing the countryside for great classic Italian recipes. With this knowledge under her belt, she wrote a cookbook and is now sharing her culinary expertise at her cooking school (*lo scaldavivande* means "the covered dish"). The English-language course is held in a 17th-century Roman palazzo, with a farewell graduation luncheon at the family's 18th-century hunting villa outside the city and lodging in the first class *Mediterraneo* hotel, which her husband's family also owns. Details: *E&M Associates,* 211 E. 43rd St., New York, NY 10017 (phone: 212-599-3994 in New York State; 800-223-9832 elsewhere).

For the Body

Tennis

 It wasn't too long ago that only a select group of Italians donned tennis whites for an afternoon of tennis, 5 o'clock tea, and 7 o'clock cocktails. Tennis was the game of the elite.

Then, after Italy produced a few champions during the 1950s, Italians began viewing tennis through new eyes. Hundreds of clubs were established all over the country and everyone rushed to join. Networks broadcast major international tournaments, and now it's often very hard to find a free court.

Despite the fact that few people come to Rome for the express purpose of playing tennis, several hotels have at least a court or two.

The courts at the *Cavalieri Hilton* (101 Via Cadlolo; phone: 6-31511) and at the *Sheraton Roma* (Viale del Pattinaggio; phone: 6-5453) are open to non-guests for a fee. There are courts occasionally available at the *Foro Italico* (phone: 6-361-9021). Also open to the public is the *Società Ginnastica Roma* (5 Via del Moro Torto; phone: 6-488-5566) which has 5 courts that are open from 9 AM to 9 PM. In the Appica Antica area, the 4-court *Oasi di Pace* (2 Via degli Eugenii; phone: 6-718-4550) also has a swimming pool.

■**INTERNATIONAL TOURNAMENTS:** For those accustomed to the respectful hush of *Wimbledon,* the noisy Roman crowds can strike a jarring note. But if you just think of the noise as heartfelt enthusiasm, attending a tournament in Italy can be a cultural (as well as a sporting) experience. One such tournament at which this very Mediterranean show of excitement takes place is the *Italian Open,* which is held in Rome each May.

For exact dates and information on purchasing tickets, contact the *Federazione Italiana Tennis* (70 Viale Tiziano, Roma 00100; phone: 6-321-9897). For news about the sport in Italy, consult the country's major tennis publications: *Matchball, Il Tennista,* and *Tennis Italiano,* available on newsstands.

Good Golf

The British brought golf to Italy around the turn of the century, but it was another 50 years before the game acquired any degree of popularity — and then it remained an activity of the very social or the very rich.

For complete information about golf in Italy and Italian golf clubs, contact the *Italian Golf Federation,* 388 Via Flaminia, Roma 00196 (phone: 6-323-1825; fax: 6-322-0250).

Below, two close-by golf destinations.

OLGIATA: The preferred Italian venue for most major international tournaments, the *West* course is tough and demanding — particularly for the power golfer who may be short on precision. British course architect C. K. Cotton started with plenty of space, so there's never a feeling of congestion. At the same time, he gave every hole a character all its own, balancing the layout as a whole to challenge every facet of a player's skill and strategic abilities. The large greens have narrow bunkered entrances, the levels change (though never too drastically), and there's scarcely a straight hole on the course. There's also a 3,092-yard, 9-hole *East* course. Closed Mondays; visitors may not play on weekends. Details: *Olgiata Golf Club,* 15 Largo Olgiata, Roma 00123 (phone: 6-378-9141).

ROMA: Rome's golf devotees, from caddies to cardinals, love this undulating 6,344-yard layout near the Acquasanta Springs, 9 miles (14 km) north of Rome. It is probably the most prestigious course in all of Italy. The most strenuous test of shotmaking is posed by the strong winds that normally sweep across its pines, cypresses, and oaks. Accuracy is a must. Closed Mondays; book well ahead for weekends. Details: *Circolo del Golf Roma,* 716/A Via Appia Nuova, Località Acquasanta, Roma 00178 (phone: 6-788-6159).

Best Beaches

Beach lovers should be aware that Rome isn't a sun worshiper's haven (although tanning by the Trevi Fountain isn't a bad hobby). In fact, only one community, at Sperlonga, in nearby Lazio, is worth visiting. Attracting an intensely casual young crowd in June and July, and families with station wagons during the national holiday month of August, this tiny village is a Moorish labyrinth of white buildings, staircases, and alleyways stacked compactly on a seaside ledge, with the beach stretching below in a silken crescent. A few miles away is the Grotto of Tiberius, where the emperor maintained a huge marine theater and his own personal pleasure dome.

A little-known museum there, the *Museo Nazionale Archeologico di Sperlonga,* houses several ancient monumental sculptures pieced together from thousands of fragments found buried in the grotto's pools and sands. Especially note the 2nd-century BC Greek sculptural depictions of Homer's *Odyssey.* Sperlonga itself, easily reached from Rome, has only a handful of modest hotels; the lively, moderately priced *Corallo,* right in town, has a staircase that plummets to the beach. Also in the center is the *Florenza Residence,* a renovated palazzo with modern apartments. *La Playa* at Fiorelle on the beach is well equipped with creature comforts. After you climb back up at day's end, you'll be ready for a swim or a meal at *La Siesta.* Details: *Associazione Pro Loco,* 22 Corso San Leone, Sperlonga (Latina) 04029 (phone: 6-771-54796).

For those into the sport, windsurfing boards and lessons are available at *Castel Porziano (primo cancello,* or first gate); in nearby Fregene at the *Stabilimento La Baia* (phone: 6-646-1647) and the *Miraggio Sporting Club* (phone: 6-646-1802); and at the *Centro Surf Bracciano* (Lake Bracciano, 20 miles/32 km north of Rome; no phone).

Horsing Around, Italian Style

When you begin to believe that Romans are irretrievably wedded to their automobiles body and soul, remember that Italy's equestrian tradition goes back to the *condottieri* — the great mounted warrior-princes of the Renaissance. Notice, too, just how many *Olympic* medals the Italians gallop off with in the four-footed competitions. And when you consider how many fine places there are for a horse-loving visitor to pursue his or her avocation in and around Rome, you may change your mind about Italians and autos.

There are several riding schools and clubs in Rome, and dozens more in the country-side surrounding the city. A regional branch of the *National Association for Equestrian Tourism (ANTE)* arranges special events for riders, and can provide a complete list of local facilities. Better than almost any other Italian experience anywhere, a day trip through woods and vineyards to a tiny Roman amphitheater will help a visitor envision what Italy was like before the Fiat Age. Details: *ANTE,* 5 Via A. Borelli, Roma (phone: 6-444-1179).

Elsewhere in and around Rome, the following establishments also can provide information on equine opportunities:

Centro Ippico Monte del Pavone (Via Valle di Baccano, Campagno, Roma, 00194; phone: 6-904-1378). Organizes summer nighttime rides around the nature reserve of Lake Martignano.

Società Ippica Romana (30 Via dei Monti della Farnesina, Roma; phone: 6-396-6386 or 6-396-5404).

OTHER EXPERIENCES OF EQUINE ROME

In addition to equestrian experiences such as those detailed above, other opportunities should be on every horselover's Rome must-see list:

International Horse Show – Held in the Piazza di Siena in the Villa Borghese park every May, it offers some of Europe's best and most aristocratic jumping competition and ends with a breathtaking *carabinieri* cavalry charge. A real event.

Le Capannelle Racetrack – If you have a free sunny Sunday afternoon in Rome and a couple of dollars burning a hole in your pocket, blow the whole packet here, just beyond Ciampino Airport. The atmosphere is Italy's turfiest.

Biking

The bicycle is the nimblest transportation through a traffic-strangled city, and most foreign pedalers can easily manage the Seven Hills of Rome in low gear. But a word to the two-wheeled: Italian automobile drivers consider cyclists more a nuisance than folks entitled to a share of the roadway. Ride with extreme caution — and a solid helmet.

Few tourists (and fewer Romans) ever see the verdant Rome it's possible to enjoy on the Villa Circuit, which travels 18 miles (29 km) from one major public park to another, all former private estates. Start on the silent residential Aventine Hill, cross the Tiber, and climb up the Gianicolo to the vast Villa Doria Pamphili. Dozens of muskrats, descendants of a single pair brought here as part of an experiment, waddle and paddle around the lake in the park's center. Pass by St. Peter's, cross the river again, and pedal through the Villa Borghese gardens. The Pincio terrace, overlooking Piazza del Popolo, offers the classic view of Rome captured by northern painters in love with the city's unique light. From the Borghese park due north to Via Salaria, it's a short ride to the Villa Ada, wooded and aristocratic — our final suggested stop. *Nino Collati* (82 Via del Pellegrino, Roma; phone: 6-654-1084) has rental bikes, including tandems with two, three, and even four seats. There are also rentals at the entrance to the *metropolitana* at Piazza di Spagna, at Piazza del Popolo, and on Lungotevere

Marzio. Along the Via Flaminia, leading down from the Piazza del Popolo, is the city's first bike trail, with signs, which follows the Tiber.

Walking

Despite the more familiar images of thronged piazze and medieval quarters as compact as a box of stone dominoes, Rome and its environs offer glorious, history- and scenery-rich walking opportunities. For Roman walking itineraries, see DIRECTIONS.

For those serious walkers who have had their fill of monuments and would like to leave town for a while, the Parco Nazionale del Circeo in Sabaudia, Lazio, is only about 49 miles (78 km) south of Rome. A dangerous land of sorcery and spells when Odysseus passed through 3,000 years ago, the scene of Circe's mythical magic is now an enchanting national park on the edge of the Tyrrhenian Sea. In the landscape where Odysseus brought down a deer, the modern visitor can still catch glimpses of wild boar, fox, and hare. An experienced hiker can scramble over the promontory of Monte Circeo, which seems, when seen from the north, to rise from the sea like the figure of a reclining woman. From there, trekkers get to enjoy the fine view of the Pontine Islands, one of which, Zannone, is under park jurisdiction and can be visited by hiring a private boat from the popular resort island of Ponza. The park itself has a dozen or more easy walks through oak forests and low Mediterranean brush, often on trails used long ago by woodcutters and the *carbonai,* who once made charcoal here. The four coastal lakes, part of the park complex, teem with birdlife in spring and fall. Open from 8 AM to 7 PM. Details: *Parco Nazionale del Circeo,* 107 Via C. Alberto, Sabaudia (Latina) 04016 (phone: 773-57251).

Hunting

Whether out of love of sport or from necessity dictated by legendary appetites, the ancient Romans (as well as today's woodlands' lovers) took their hunting very seriously. Special wildlife breeding parks were created to make sure that everyone got his share, and there were no controls or restrictions at all on hunting (an anomaly in a nation that had laws for just about everything else).

Today, things are drastically different. To put the brakes on a situation in which hunting had become wildly popular and game increasingly scarce, all kinds of regulations — both regional and national — are imposed on what can be hunted, how, when, and where (far too many regulations in the opinion of many). If you do decide to hunt, expect to be confronted by a discouraging snarl of red tape. For further information on rules and regulations, contact the *Federazione Italiana della Caccia,* also called *Federcaccia* (Italian Hunting Federation; 70 Viale Tiziano, Roma 00196; phone: 6-323-3779, 6-323-3784, or 6-323-3810).

Lazio is considered very good for pheasant shooting. There also is some wild boar. Details: *Federazione Italiana della Caccia,* 70 Viale Tiziano, Roma 00196 (phone: 6-323-3784); or *Ente Produttori Selvaggina,* 69 Via L. Valerio, Roma 00146 (phone: 6-559-0832).

For the Mind

Twenty-Five Centuries of History: Rome's Museums and Monuments

 Napoleon determinedly exported a significant portion of Italy's art treasures to France, but even so, what remains easily could fill a planet or two. Parochial museums house ancient booty from local excavations. Villas from the 17th century overflow with 16th-century paintings, 1st-century sculptures, and quite a bit from all the centuries in between. The massive state museums have basements stuffed with national artwork from 2,500 years ago.

Faced with all this, a visitor to Rome is well advised to master the fine art of museumgoing. There is something essentially numbing about the means by which we normally view the world's greatest art, so when visiting the giant Italian warehouses of beauty, stop first to thumb through the catalogue or finger the postcards to get an idea of what the collection includes — and where to find it. Determine in advance what you want to see most, and don't try to cover everything. If you attempt a single heroic sweep of the 1,000 rooms of the *Vatican Museums,* for example, you may well develop a case of the dread Titian-fission, where all the Madonnas blend into one polychromatic blur. And when you look at paintings at random, study a picture before you inspect the nameplate — that's the best way to quickly determine what you really like, as opposed to what you're supposed to like. And try to give luncheons and Leonardos equal attention.

Break away from the gargantuan museums in any way you can. Don't forget that single altarpiece in a small church, the grouping of portraits adorning the fireplace of the ancient mansion — art in the environment for which it was originally created.

And visit a gallery or an auction house occasionally, just to remind yourself that once it was *all* for sale.

Note: Most of the opening and closing times listed here should be right most of the time. But museum hours in Rome are often rearranged because of personnel shortages, labor disputes, surprise restorations, and as many other causes as there are cups of cappuccino at a café. Caveat visitor!

CARAVAGGIO COUNTRY: If you wake to a Roman morning too sunbathed and gleaming to spend the day as a museum shut-in, combine some shopping, strolling, and snacking with a treasure hunt for the half-dozen major works by this talented 17th-century painter and street-brawler, a notorious libertine who nonetheless revolutionized religious painting by setting his scenarios in lifelike locales and populating them with realistic — rather than idealized — characters. These are distributed throughout what art historian Howard Hibbard called "Caravaggio Country" — the alleys, markets, and sun-shot piazzas that provided his models during his brief, tempestuous Roman career.

Begin at the Church of Santa Maria del Popolo, just inside the Roman walls. On the sides of a dimly lit chapel are his *Conversion of St. Paul* and *Crucifixion of St. Peter.* After stopping for a cappuccino and a nut croissant at *Rosati's,* across the street, head for the once-suburban estate of the Borghese family. Wander through its huge park, then visit the *Galleria Borghese,* a fine, manageable museum whose roster of Caravaggios includes the dramatic *Madonna dei Palafrenieri* and a roomful of others.

Then on to the virtual geometric center of Rome, Piazza Navona, where the hordes seem oblivious to the proximity of great art just a couple of blocks to the east at the recently restored and pristine mid-16th-century Church of San Luigi dei Francesi, on Via della Dogana Vecchia. Three paintings there portray the life of St. Matthew, among them the *Calling of St. Matthew,* arguably the single most famous of Caravaggio's images, and the *Martyrdom of St. Matthew.* Ten minutes away is the Church of Sant'Agostino, with its *Madonna of the Pilgrims,* a tender painting of a Madonna modeled on Caravaggio's mistress, cradling a round and energetic bambino; note the dirty feet of the pilgrims, a controversial note of realism at the time it was painted in 1604, 6 years before Caravaggio contracted malaria and died. Finish your tour with a pistachio ice cream cone at nearby *Giolitti's* (40 Via Uffici del Vicario). Churches are usually open daily from 7 AM to noon and from 4 to 6 PM.

For other Caravaggio explorations, visit the *Doria Pamphili Gallery* in the Palazzo Doria Pamphili near Piazza Venezia (at 1/A Piazza del Collegio Romano), and the *Palatine Gallery* in the *Vatican Museums,* which houses the famous *Entombment of Christ.*

PANTHEON: Come to this most perfectly preserved of ancient Roman buildings in the morning to witness the column of rain or sunshine that plunges through the giant round oculus in the middle of the roof. Visit again at twilight to sit on the steps of the fountain facing it, and watch the procession of clinging couples, soldiers on leave, families on tour, and the soccer players whose game in the portico has probably been going on since the fall of Rome.

The Pantheon's proportions — its height equals the diameter of the dome — give it an aura of classical calm no matter who is coming or going. The structure was also a remarkable feat of engineering, the magnitude of which is suggested by the fact that the diameter of its dome was unsurpassed in the city until the construction (with prefab concrete) of the *Palazzo dello Sport* for Rome's *1960 Olympic Games.* The bronze doors are originals; the street level has risen since its construction by Hadrian in approximately AD 120 (replacing its 150-year-old predecessor), and the original staircase that led up to its colonnaded entrance has been replaced by a traffic-free piazza that slopes down to it.

Initially a pagan temple to all the gods, the spacious, cylindrical Pantheon became a Christian church in 606; it now holds the tombs of the first two Kings of Italy and of the painter Raphael (whose epitaph reads "Here lies Raphael: While he lived the great mother of all things feared to be outdone; and when he died she feared too to die"). Open Tuesdays through Saturdays from 9 AM to 2 PM, Sundays and holidays to 1 PM; closed Mondays. Details: *Pantheon,* Piazza della Rotonda, Roma 00100 (phone: 6-369831).

MUSEI VATICANI: Occupying palaces constructed by popes from the 13th century onward, the Vatican collections are among the most impressive in the world, comprising works of every epoch. But seeing even a part of them poses a challenge. The pleasures are interspersed with a fair assortment of priceless objects in glass cases with which most people really don't want to bother. And there are not only the usual population of other museum visitors, but also sizable bands of Vatican visitors and other pilgrims vying for space in front of the objects that one does want to see.

The Sistine Chapel, in particular, sometimes seems more like a very tastefully decorated subway during rush hour, especially since its ceiling — Michelangelo's depiction of the *Creation* — now is brighter and more vivid as a result of a 10-year restoration project. Revitalization of *The Last Judgment* is expected to take at least another year. The solution: Visit at 9 AM sharp. Grab a ticket and scurry past what seems like kilometers of papal robes, old maps, and tomb inscriptions until you've left the school groups and Ecuadorian nuns far behind. Your destinations are the *Raphael Rooms;* the *Apollo Belvedere,* the *Laocöon Group,* and other classical statuary in the *Pio-Clementino Museum;* and the works of Fra Angelico, Giotto, and Filippo Lippi in the *Pinacoteca* (Picture Gallery). Open Mondays through Saturdays from 9 AM to 2 PM; around *Easter* and from July through September, Mondays through Fridays from 9 AM to 5 PM, Saturdays from 9 AM to 2 PM; on the last Sunday of every month, from 9 AM to 1 PM (no admission charge); closed on other Sundays. Details: *Musei Vaticani,* Viale Vaticano, Roma 00100 (phone: 6-698-3333).

Theater, Music, and Opera

Italy has been a land of patrons and performers since the flushest days of the Medicis. Noble courts throughout the peninsula maintained private orchestras. Comedians *dell'arte* found the palace gates flung wide open with welcome. Now, where the aristocracy is too impoverished to treat, the government has rushed in, and virtually every fair-size city has its publicly funded concert hall and *teatro stabile* (repertory theater), and some 40,000 subsidized musical events a year crowd the Italian calendar. As a result, ticket prices are far more reasonable than in the US — as long as they are purchased before the familiar *esaurito* ("all sold out") strip is pasted across the poster outside the theater.

In Rome, concerts are definitely a growth industry. Far from keeping audiences away, the widespread ownership of compact disc players and Walkman cassette players has actually brought down the average audience age. Increasingly, venues include not only staid and sterile local auditoriums but also Renaissance palazzi and medieval churches, piazzas, and flower-edged cloisters and courtyards. A recent Roman summer festival offered a strong quartet concert on a barge moored off the tiny Tiber Island. And you've never really heard Bach until you've heard his music reverberating through a baroque basilica.

Long more popular than classical music in Italy, opera continues to boom. Bricklayers really do whistle *Traviata* as they trowel; your loge-mates may hum along with *Madame Butterfly.* Though the days have passed when fiascos automatically ended with a shower of rotten vegetables, there are still lots of lusty boos when the diva turns out to be a dog — and bravos when the tenor hits a string of flawless high Cs.

In the theater, Goldoni and Pirandello are perennial favorites — with Guglielmo Shakespeare a close third. Though theatrical activity is more national than metropolitan (companies usually do a limited run in major cities and then go out on tour), an opening night in Rome can be almost as exciting as one in London or New York City. The stutter-and-mutter traditions that have reigned in much of the US since the rise of the Actors' Studio have no place here. The Italian stage style is definitely declamatory. Just think of it as reflecting the greater melodrama of daily Italian life.

RAI ORCHESTRAS: A household word from the Alps to the Ionian Sea, *RAI* — which stands for *Radio Televisione Italiana,* the state network — is among the most influential organizations on the national music scene, because it sponsors a symphony orchestra and chorus in each of Italy's four largest cities, each with its own full-length season and its own auditorium. The Rome orchestra produces a regular season at the *Foro Italico,* gives a special concert for the pope once a year — either in St. Peter's or in the Vatican's giant Sala Nervi — and premieres many contemporary works at the Villa Medici in an annual festival in September. On the other hand, the parent organizations also break down into pocket-size chamber and choral groups. A chief mission of *RAI* is to keep alive many little-performed works from past centuries. But it also has a virtual monopoly on symphonic pieces by contemporary composers. Tickets are kept at popular prices, and many concerts are televised. Details: *Auditorio del Foro Italico,* 1 Piazza Lauro de Bosis, Roma 00100 (phone: 6-365625; Thursdays through Saturdays only).

ACCADEMIA NAZIONALE DI SANTA CECILIA: Named in dignified Latin style for the patron saint of music and established in 1566 by Pierluigi da Palestrina, this organization serves a host of functions, managing Rome's symphony orchestra in residence, staging its concerts in the Vatican's stark *Pio Auditorium* on Sunday afternoons (with reprises on Monday and Tuesday evenings) from October to June, and orchestrating Bach-to-Berg chamber performances in the academy's own delightful hall on Friday evenings. A guest conductor system brings visiting conductors such as Maazel, Abbado, Giulini, and Sawallisch. Yuppies and university students are swelling the once rather elderly ranks of the city's concertgoers, and large chunks of tickets are sold by subscription, so be prepared to queue to snare a seat. In summer, *Santa Cecilia* moves out into the open and presents evening concerts in the hilltop Piazza del Campidoglio. Since seats here are not numbered, it's wise to find your place an hour or more before the music begins, settle down with a picnic supper, and enjoy the summer sunset in the company of Michelangelo's majestic architecture. During the interval, stroll behind the square for Rome's best overview of the Forum by night. Details: *Accademia Nazionale di Santa Cecilia,* 4 Via della Conciliazione, Roma 00100 (phone: 6-654-1044 or 6-689-3623).

TEATRI STABILI: Italy has no single great national theater. It has instead 15 *teatri stabili* — regionally or municipally sponsored repertory companies that perform in their own theaters in Rome and other major cities, as well as tour up and down the peninsula. In addition to premiering most contemporary Italian plays, they offer at least their share of foreign works — and thereby vary the diet of Goldoni and Pirandello that more traditional Italian companies serve the Sunday matinee crowd. In Rome, be on the lookout for the *Teatro di Genova,* the *Centro Teatrale Bresciano,* and the *Teatro di Roma* at the *Argentina, Valle,* and *Quirino* theaters — splendid historic theater buildings all. Contact the tourist office for details.

Rome's Most Colorful Festas

The Italian delight in gregarious ritual means that hardly a day passes in Rome without some community of even a few hundred souls celebrating some historical event, some traditional food, or some patron saint. As with everything else they do, Romans celebrate in grand fashion. Below, some of the most festive of Roman festas.

EASTER WEEK: The collective passion for ritual has all Italy — and most especially Rome — in its grip during the 4 days preceding *Easter Sunday,* as nearly every village and town throughout the nation stages some special procession or ceremony. Some of these are derived from ancient pagan practices and some from medieval customs. In Rome, the pope walks in a *Good Friday* procession in the ruins of the Colosseum, where Christian martyrs met their deaths.

L'INFIORATA, Genzano, Lazio: On the Sunday after *Corpus Domini* in June, the long street that slopes up to the Church of Santa Maria della Cima in this hill town just outside Rome is completely, fragrantly carpeted with flowers worked into elaborate abstract designs, copies of famous artworks, or biblical scenes. Everyone in town, and visiting Romans by the score, turn out to see the pretty show and then pile into nearby country restaurants to fork down foothills of fettuccine with amber-hued liters of the local castelli wine. Follow their example. And don't leave Genzano without a wheel of the bread that bears the town's name — a dusky, rustic, crusty delight. Details: *Azienda Autonoma di Soggiorno e Turismo dei Laghi e Castelli Romani,* 1 Viale Risorgimento, Albano Laziale (Roma) 00041 (phone: 6-930-5798; fax: 6-932-0040).

SAGRA DELL'UVA, Marino, Lazio: When this town on the slopes just southeast of Rome celebrates its grape harvest on the first Sunday of October, wine actually flows from its Fountain of the Moors. After the sacred thanksgiving rites of the morning (procession, grape offering to the Madonna, and ritual restaurant feasts), the day turns pleasantly pagan, with allegorical floats, roast suckling pigs, garish street stands, and gushing wine (gratis) — the straw-golden dry white of the Alban hills. Meanwhile, the mood builds from merry to mildly wild, and celebrants routinely stagger on until late at night. Details: *Ente Provinciale per il Turismo,* 11 Via Parigi, Roma 00185 (phone: 6-461851).

LA FESTA DI NOIANTRI: For a boisterous week in mid-July, when the richest Romans have fled to the sea or the mountains, the teeming Trastevere quarter becomes one sprawling outdoor trattoria. As night falls and the air cools, streetlights illuminate rows of tables stretching for blocks, restaurant blending with pizzeria melting into café. Merrymakers pack the streets, musicians stroll, garish stands jam the main avenue, piazze become dance floors and open-air cinemas, and — because there is a religious foundation to all this — the Madonna del Carmine Church stays open as late as the watermelon stands. The *noiantri* of the celebration are "we others" — the people of Trastevere who consider themselves the only true Romans and choose to honor their neighborhood when *those* others have fled the heat. Details: *Ente Provinciale per il Turismo,* 11 Via Parigi, Roma 00185 (phone: 6-461851).

An Antiques Lover's Guide to Rome

Though Italy preserves some of the finest collections of antiquities in the world, buying genuine antiques is not an easy matter. Plenty of dealers are willing to sell small relics of ancient Rome or Etruscan civilization, but even if these items were genuine, the strict control on exporting antiquities would make it impossible for foreign purchasers to take them out of the country. At the same time, the kinds of handsome household items of later periods that predominate in the antiques trade of countries like England and Scotland are uncommon in Italy; poorer than other European nations, it never had a large middle class to demand luxury goods in quantity. The objects of value that do exist were almost always made for large noble families who have passed them down — or sold them at prices far beyond the means of the average buyer.

There is a thriving antiques trade in Italy, particularly in Rome. Many dealers trade in non-Italian goods. Many of the moderately priced antiques found here are English; silver is an especially common stock item. And since the antiques market in Rome is generally softer than that in London or New York, such items could well cost less than at home.

WHAT TO BUY

Italian antiques do exist in several categories. Candlestick holders and marionettes, Sicilian puppets, and lamps made from opaline are good finds, as are figurines from the traditional *Christmas presepe* (nativity scene). Also look for the following:

CHINA AND GLASS: There is a lot of Venetian glass about, but it is very hard to tell its age without expert advice (there are some master glass blowers who make excellent reproductions). The original Venetian crystal tended to be of a darker, smoky hue.

COPPER AND BRASS: You don't have to be an expert to find good pieces of domestic copper and brass. These metals were used for domestic utensils and, therefore, no imprints were used. The oldest pieces were shaped with a hammer and are of irregular thickness.

FURNITURE: Most genuinely old Italian furniture is very heavily restored or extremely expensive. What is available is often not nearly as beautifully finished as pieces made in England or France; design was generally considered more important. Renaissance furniture is particularly sought after and difficult to find at reasonable prices. Popular versions of *barocchetto* (baroque) furniture, however, as well as *rustico* (rustic furniture), are still available.

JEWELRY: Though Italy is one of the world's major centers of modern goldsmithing, much antique jewelry sold here is imported. However, the market offers some very beautiful and ornamental earrings — mostly produced in Gaeta in Lazio. Serving as a constant reminder of the beloved, these were traditionally used instead of engagement rings by peasant girls who worked in the fields, where a ring would have been a nuisance. Small mosaics that depict scenes of ancient Rome and are of great value can be spotted by a sharp eye in shop windows on Rome's Via del Babuino and Via della Scrofa, some from the early 1800s. Many shops also sell old cameos.

PAINTINGS: Since Italians are the world's experts at restoration, there are plenty of appealing pictures on the market. But don't automatically assume they'll be as authentic (or as valuable) as they are handsome. Also be sure to ask first about export restrictions.

PICTURE FRAMES: Gilded-and-carved wood-and-glass frames can still be found fairly easily — though you need a very large wall to hang them and a large bank account to pay for those made during the Renaissance. More practical are the little dressing table frames made in mahogany. They are not outrageously expensive and are widely sold.

POTTERY: Production of majolica — the tin-glazed and richly colored and ornamented earthenware pieces Italians know as maiolica or faïence — reached its zenith in the northern Italian towns of Deruta, Faenza, and Gubbio, and in Urbino (the Marches) and Castelli (Abruzzo), during the Renaissance. In the middle of the 16th century, potters in Faenza introduced a lacy, baroque style of "white" pottery, called *bianchi di Faenza,* which remained popular well past the middle of the 17th century. Both types of pottery are much sought after now. There are many clever copies, and antiques dealers tell of colleagues who commission pieces and then have them joined together with copper wire so that the finished vessel looks authentically old. Another trick is to glaze century-old bricks to give them an aged look before turning them into Castelli pottery.

PRINTS: The mapmaker of the medieval world, Italy created maps by the score, beginning in the 14th century. Prints were also widely issued. Many of those available today have been reproduced on old paper or pulled out of old books. However, the stallholders in Piazza Borghese sell the real thing at reasonable prices and are very helpful and knowledgeable.

WHERE TO SHOP

For a comprehensive listing of antiques dealers by region and specialization and of major fairs, consult the *Guida OPI dell'Antiquariato Italiano,* published by Tony Metz, and the *Catalogo dell'Antiquariato Italiano,* published by Giorgio Mondadori. Both are in Italian.

Rome is Italy's major center for antiques hunting, and most of the largest and most-reliable dealers are on Via del Babuino, which runs from Piazza di Spagna to Piazza del Popolo. Among them are the following:

Apolloni – Antiques. 133 Via del Babuino.
Arturo Ferrante – Antiques. 42/43 Via del Babuino.
Di Giorgio – Antiques. 182 Via del Babuino.
Fallani – Sculpture. 58/A Via del Babuino.
Olivi – Antiques. 136 Via del Babuino.

Browse in the venerable shops above, but the *Granmercato Antiquario Babuino* (150 Via del Babuino) is still the best bet for small, guaranteed items, most of which are English. Everything is clearly visible, priced, and explained.

Other good shopping streets are Via Margutta, behind Via del Babuino, Via del Governo Vecchio, Via di Panico, Via dei Coronari, Via Monserrato, Via dell'Orso, and the Campo Marzio area. (Via dei Coronari is especially delightful for strolling during the annual autumn antiques fair, when all the shops are open at night.)

In the ancient Roman suburb known as the Subura, near the Roman Forum between Via Cavour and Via Nazionale, there are a number of small, interesting shops — many of them selling Art Nouveau. The restorers in Via Boschetto are a good source of reasonably priced 19th-century furniture. The following dealers are worth a visit:

Bottega di Montevecchio – Small objects. 15 Piazza di Montevecchio.
Dakota – Small 1950s objects. 494 Via del Corso.
Enrico Fiorentini – Marble. 53/B Via Margutta.
Galleria delle Stampe Antiche – Prints. 38 Via del Governo Vecchio.
Galleria Spada – Small objects. 3 Piazza Capo Ferro.
Giacomo Cohen – Carpets. 83 Via Margutta.
Gussio – Majolica. 27/A Via Laurina.
Luciano Coen – Carpets. 65 Via Margutta.
La Mansarde – Furniture. 202-203 Via dei Coronari.
Pacifici – Bronzes and arms. 174 Via Giulia.
Rosario Lo Turco – Puppets. 173 Via dei Pianellari.
Lo Scrittoio – Furniture. 102-103 Via dei Coronari.
Tanca – Antique jewelry and silver. 12 Salita dei Crescenzi.

In addition, look for good prints, as well as other items, at the stalls in Piazza Borghese, and visit the following auction houses:

L'Antonina – 23 Piazza Mignanelli (phone: 6-679-4009).
Christie's – 114 Piazza Navona (phone: 6-654-1217).
Finarte – 54 Via Margutta (phone: 6-678-6557).
Semenzato – 93 Piazza di Spagna (phone: 6-676-6479).
Sotheby's – 90 Piazza di Spagna (phone: 6-678-1798).

Finally, the Sunday morning flea market at Porta Portese can be fun. However, it's said that anything you see there of real value has probably been stolen. Never pay the first price quoted.

RULES OF THE ROAD FOR AN ODYSSEY OF THE OLD

Buy for sheer pleasure, not for investment. Forget about the carrot of supposed retail values that dealers habitually dangle in front of amateur clients. If you love something, it will probably ornament your home until the Colosseum falls.

Buy the finest example you can afford of any item, in as close to mint condition as possible. Chipped or broken "bargains" will haunt you later with their shabbiness.

Train your eye in museums. These are the best schools for the acquisitive senses, particularly as you begin to develop special passions.

Get advice from specialists when contemplating major acquisitions. Much antique furniture and many paintings have been restored several times, and Italian antiques salespeople, particularly in Rome, are more entertaining than knowledgeable. If you want to be absolutely certain that what you're buying is what you've been told it is, stick with the larger dealers. Most auction houses have an evaluation office whose experts will make appraisals for a fee. Even museums can be approached in some cities. In Rome, two useful contacts are Sally Improta, a member of the *Appraisers' Association of America,* at the *Bottega di Montevecchio* (15 Piazza di Montevecchio; phone: 6-687-0497) and *Art Import* (a British firm specializing in British antiques, but knowledgeable about the trade in general; 2 Piazza Borghese).

Don't be afraid to haggle. Only a few of the large dealers have *prezzi fissi* (fixed prices). The others will decide for themselves how much you can afford and charge accordingly. So the rule of thumb is to bargain wherever you don't see the *prezzi fissi* sign. A word of warning: While most larger dealers take credit cards, smaller shops do not.

When pricing an object, don't forget to figure the cost of shipping. Around 30% of the cost of the item is about right for large items. Italian firms are expensive, so the best idea is to stick to the bigger international shipping firms, which offer a door-to-door service to New York, as well as advice about required export licenses. The following Rome firms could be helpful:

Bolliger – 61 Via dei Buonvisi (phone: 6-655-7161; fax: 6-651-7136).

Emery Air Freight – 48/A Via Passo Buole, Fiumicino (phone: 6-658-1621).

Italian Moving Network – 132 Via del Tritone (phone: 6-690-2009).

Note that the Italian government requires that any object of possible historical interest to the Italian state be declared and levies an export tax on goods exported to the United States.

Churches and Piazzas

Whether it's a sleek designer space ringed with chic cafés or a rustic square sprouting vegetable stalls, Rome's piazzas are the acknowledged centers of local activity. Revolutions are preached there, crowds harangued, heretics burned, confetti sprinkled. Every day marks a new period in the perennial urchin-league soccer match. Every evening, tables and chairs are hauled onto the sidewalk, and a new hand is dealt in some card game that seems to have been in progress since the sack of Rome. And every Sunday, at the end of mass in the late morning, a churchful of the faithful pours out onto the square for a round of gossip before lunch. The church, drawing its patrons from the teeming society just outside its portals and representing a supremely Italian mix of diversion and devotion, is the raison d'être of almost every piazza in Rome. Their styles range from plain to grandiose, from a small church tacked as afterthought onto the dusty piazza of a Roman suburb to St. Peter's, with its oval square designed to allow optimum admiration of the basilica's façade. So when making a list of touristic tasks, put "sloth" and "idleness" very near the top and spend a large, lazy slice of as many days as possible doing as the Romans do — sitting and sipping and stretching and strolling on a glorious Roman piazza in front of a lush Italian church like those listed below. Here, indeed, the *far niente* (doing nothing) for which Italy is well known is truly *dolce* (sweet).

PIAZZA NAVONA: This pedestrian island in the middle of traffic-snarled Rome retains the elliptical shape, and much of the function, of the ancient Roman racetrack whose site it now occupies. But the chariots have been replaced by children on bicycles who cut nimble paths between unsuspecting photographers and rolling soccer balls. In summertime, people cluster to watch the progress of while-you-wait caricature artists or drop coins in the regiments of open guitar cases. Jugglers, fire-eaters, and long-haired bongo players vie for the attention of passersby. Hack artists peddle their watercolor cityscapes. In winter, from *Christmastime* through *Epiphany*, the piazza is crowded with booths full of sweets, toys, crèche figures, and goodies-stuffed stockings. In the middle of it all is the famous Bernini fountain, *Fontana dei Fiumi* (Fountain of the Rivers), which represents as powerful, writhing human figures what the 17th century considered the world's four great rivers — the Nile, Ganges, Danube, and Plata. There was no love lost between Bernini and his former pupil Borromini, who designed the Church of Sant'Agnese on the west side of the square. So the Rio della Plata is shrinking in horror from it, and the Nile has its head covered — some say to avoid seeing the church. (But in fact, it is because the Nile's source had not yet been discovered.)

PIAZZA SAN PIETRO, Vatican City: Since the first basilica of St. Peter's was built in the 4th century by order of the Emperor Constantine (on the site where St. Peter was martyred and subsequently buried), millions of pilgrims have crossed continents by plane, train, car, carriage, and on foot to get to this vast elliptical space, the main square of Christendom. Every Wednesday morning in warm weather, thousands pack between the welcoming arms of Bernini's two semicircular statue-topped Doric colonnades to hear and see the pope on his Vatican Palace balcony. (The best comment on the efficiency of the Vatican is that, despite the hordes, the place is spotless.)

The present basilica, ordered after 11 centuries had left its predecessor somewhat the worse for wear, took a good chunk of the Renaissance to build, and drew on the talents of Bramante, Michelangelo, and others. Among its myriad wonders are Michelangelo's *Pietà* (encased in a bulletproof glass since its mutilation and restoration several years ago); Bernini's *Baldacchino*, a 46-ton bronze altar canopy so elaborate it is really more architecture than sculpture; and the climb through the innards of Michelangelo's cupola for a glorious view into the well-shielded Vatican gardens and out over the entire city. Visits to the subterranean vaults have become increasingly popular.

The whole place is overwhelming; save your first impression for a moment when you're fresh and firm-legged, and don't try to see it in tandem with the vast Vatican museums. For further details, consult *Special Places* in THE CITY.

PIAZZA DI SPAGNA: The thing to do at this picturesque relic of 18th-century Rome can be summed up in a single word: nothing. Refresh yourself at Bernini's gushing, boat-shaped fountain, the *Barcaccia*. Recline on the voluptuous curving staircase. Almost magically, you'll find yourself impelled to stay right where you are. It has been this way for years. The stage-like set of 138 travertine stairs, known to everyone (but locals) as the Spanish Steps (after a palace that housed the Spanish Embassy to the Holy See), climbs to the twin-turreted Church of Trinità dei Monti and the green sprawl of the Villa Borghese park beyond. In the wings at No. 26, with a window onto the staircase, is the house where John Keats died in 1821, now a museum devoted to him and his fellow Romantics. In May, the stairs are covered with red, pink, and white azaleas; at *Christmastime*, the platform midway up is the site of an illuminated, near-life-size crèche. Rome's answer to New York's Fifth Avenue, Via Condotti runs from the foot of the Spanish Steps to Via del Corso and is a favorite spot for window shopping and the ritual evening *passeggiata* (promenade). (Also see *Special Places* in THE CITY.)

Remarkable Ruins

The only museums in the world where picnics and dogs are allowed, and where sightseeing is ideally combined with a sunbath, a game of touch football, or a bottle of wine, historic ruins have always been part of Italian life. In the last century, cows grazed along protruding bits of now-priceless antique wall. The disfigured Roman street-corner torso called Pasquino served under Rome's more repressive popes as one of the "talking statues" on which sometimes witty protesters hung anonymous slogans and insults. And every government since Mussolini's has tried to dig up, fence off, and charge admission to the thousands of ruins peppering the city.

But there are simply more of them than anyone can catalogue. In Rome alone there are so many buried theaters and villas that building the city's skimpy subway system took 20 years — in good part because of the labyrinth of subterranean treasures that had to be dodged.

Each ruin is in its own distinctive state of decay, and the most romantic may not necessarily be the most historically significant. And each complex of ruins has its own particular mood and its own prime viewing time during the year. The spectacular hilltop temples, with views that plummet over rocks submerged 40 feet below the sea, belong to clear, hot summer days. For urban experiences like the Roman Forum, you won't feel crowded, even on Sundays, except during the peak tourist times at *Easter* and midsummer. Whatever you do, by all means make the pilgrimage through the ice cream and soda peddlers at some time during your Roman sojourn to pay homage to these ancient places. Be sure to check schedules in advance; many of the most important sites are closed on Mondays or Tuesdays and on holidays — and many shut down Sunday afternoons as well. And always keep an eye peeled for the unobtrusive yellow signs that point down dusty roads. Together with the handful of superbly interesting destinations sketched below, the moss-covered stumps of column in the middle of the woods that are found in this fashion may turn out to be the best part of the journey.

COLOSSEUM: Every week beginning in AD 80, at a time when Romans supplied free entertainment to their populace on a scale unique in the history of the planet, 50,000 spectators packed this stadium for an afternoon of gory Roman fun. Hundreds of gladiators did battle to the death, and unarmed Christians wrestled hungry lions; on state occasions, the Colosseum was flooded and naval battles staged. Since then, a large chunk of the outer wall has gone — Renaissance construction workers regularly chopped away at the structure when they needed marble for St. Peter's and assorted palazzi. Buttresses were erected by Pius VIII (1800–23) to keep the structure from caving in on itself. Henry James's Daisy Miller came here against her elders' advice, caught Roman fever (as malaria was called then), and died of it. The luxuriant vegetation she came to see by moonlight (the 420 exotic species prompted two books on Colosseum flora and countless rhapsodies by Dickens, Byron, and other Victorians) has been entirely weeded out, a situation "much regretted by lovers of the picturesque," according to the 19th-century writer Augustus Hare. The floor was then excavated to reveal the locker rooms underneath — with separate but equal facilities for lions and Christians. The lions have long been replaced by stray cats, but the allure of the structure is as strong as ever, and visitors instinctively appreciate the genius of the engineers who found a way to erect such a gigantic structure on marshy ground (a challenge even today), and who designed it so that immense and often rowdy crowds could enter, claim seats, and exit with ease through its 80 *vomitoria.* Experiencing its immensity, it's easy to understand how Romans could think that were the Colosseum to fall, so would Rome — and the world itself. Until recently, contemporary visitors always have had to cross a potentially fatal torrent of traffic that promised to be no less lethal than Roman fever to get there, but when the piazza in front finally was closed to cars, this dangerous hazard was eliminated. Details: *Ente Provinciale per il Turismo,* 11 Via Parigi, Roma 00185 (phone: 6-461851 or 6-700-4261). See also *Special Places* in THE CITY.

FORUM AND THE PALATINE: Begin your visit to ancient Rome on top of the first of Rome's seven hills, where Romulus and Remus were supposedly suckled by a she-wolf and where Rome began, because you'll be too tired to get up there *after* seeing the Forum. Bring picnic, kids, dogs, sketch pads, and cameras. The Palatine offers fine views through the framework of pine trees over ancient and modern Rome. Marble columns tower romantically over fields of flowers scattered with carved chunks of marble. Ruins of the luxurious imperial villas that once covered most of the hill — the reason that the Palatine is the namesake of all the world's palaces — stand next to the remains of the mud huts where Rome's founders settled in the 8th century BC. Painters such as Claude Lorrain and Jean-Baptiste Camille Corot created canvas after canvas depicting this ruin-scattered landscape; to judge from their work and that of their contemporaries, all Rome must have once looked like this. Seeing it inspired the English to pioneer a whole new style in landscape gardening.

Following in the footsteps of early Romans, climb down from the Palatine to the low area that grew from a neutral meeting ground of hilltop tribes into the center of downtown ancient Rome to become the Forum. Actually made up of many different fora, it was once an agglomeration of open-air markets, shopping malls, government buildings, temples, and public meeting spots, and their ruins can all be seen. Along its Via Sacra, Julius Caesar returned from the wars in triumphal processions, and at its Basilica Julia, Mark Antony harangued the crowd after Caesar was killed. It was the business center of the empire as well as its religious and political center, and still embedded in the floor of the Basilica Emilia are the coins that melted in fires during the sack of Rome in the 5th century. During the Middle Ages, the Forum was covered with dirt and garbage and called Campo Vaccino (Cow Field); when excavations began in the 19th century, a good deal of it was 20 feet underground. Today, much of the Forum lies beneath the roaring traffic of Via dei Fori Imperiali. What is left is a white, open jungle of fallen columns and headless statues; the detailed plan available at the entrance is a must. Don't miss the Forum of Trajan, which is separate from the rest and the best preserved of all. Keep in mind that this neighborhood becomes danger-ously hot at midday in summer. Open daily at 9 AM to 1 hour before sunset; closed Mondays. Details: *Ente Provinciale per il Turismo,* 11 Via Parigi, Roma 00185 (phone: 6-461851). See also *Special Places* in THE CITY.

BATHS OF CARACALLA: This grandiose tribute to the human body was built on 27 acres by the Emperor Caracalla in the 3rd century AD. Each of the sunken, mosaic-covered floors visible today was the bottom of a single pool. To get an idea of size, follow the curve of an imaginary arch up from one still-standing base; the other side is hundreds of feet away. Each one of these huge pools was heated to a different tempera-ture by an elaborate underground central heating system, and the whole complex was open to the public. For a nominal fee, the citizens of Rome could pass from tub to tub, soaking in the steaming water of the circular *caldarium,* rubbing elbows with friends in the *tepidarium,* and talking brisk business in the *frigidarium.* Changing rooms, dry steamrooms, and gymnasia flanked the pool rooms. Everything about this glorified bathtub of ancient times is big — so it's entirely appropriate that the outdoor opera and ballet performances staged in the *caldarium* in July and August are blockbusters. (A legendary *Aïda,* for instance, was complete with prancing horses and a ponderous pachyderm.) It seems entirely fitting that Percy Bysshe Shelley composed Acts I and II of his *Prometheus Unbound* here. Open 9 AM to one hour before sunset. Closed Mondays. Details: *Ente Provinciale per il Turismo,* 11 Via Parigi, Roma 00185 (phone: 6-461851; for information on summer performances, phone: 6-575-8302).

VIA APPIA ANTICA AND THE CATACOMBS: Somber but refreshingly cool, the 2nd-century Catacombs are miles of underground tunnels where the early Christians practiced their outlawed cult in secrecy, hid when necessary, and buried their dead behind slabs of marble or terra cotta — among them St. Cecilia, St. Eusebius, martyred popes, and others. The Catacombs of St. Calixtus and St. Sebastian, two of the most striking, are both notable for their examples of early Christian painting. Both are on the Via Appia Antica (Appian Way), the former closed Wednesdays, the latter Thursdays.

Back with the sun and the pagans aboveground, explore the rest of the Via Appia Antica, one of the most important of all the roads that led to Rome. From the time of its construction between Brindisi and the capital, beginning in 312 BC, it was the primary link to distant outposts. Now lined with broken columns, headless statues, umbrella pines, and secluded villas, this sleepy haven for lovers and families is still partly paved by the same large, jagged slabs of stone that surfaced Roman roads from Egypt to Gaul during the empire. Off the road stand some of the arches whose sloping tops carried water, gravity-fed, from miles-distant springs to Rome's public fountains and houses of the wealthy. Have dinner at one of the many family-run trattorie that line the Appia as you approach the city walls. Details: *Ente Provinciale per il Turismo,* 11 Via Parigi, Roma 00185 (phone: 6-461851). See also *Special Places* in THE CITY.

OSTIA ANTICA, Lazio: This much underrated and undervisited ruined sprawl at the mouth of the Tiber — in remarkably good condition because the excavations are relatively recent — was once among the most important trading centers of the empire. It had a population of 100,000, was a meeting place for sailors and merchants from all over Europe and northern Africa, and boasted remarkable cultural and religious diversity — obvious today from the remains of its synagogue, several Christian chapels, and the dozen or so temples to the Persian sun god, Mitra. A pile of columns marked with the name of their owner, Volusianus, and lying on what used to be a wharf, is a poignant symbol of its fall from prosperity, brought on by a malaria epidemic and the silting up of the harbor. Open daily except Mondays from 9 AM to 4 PM in winter, 9 AM to 6 PM in summer. Details: *Ente Provinciale per il Turismo,* 11 Via Parigi, Roma 00185 (phone: 6-461851); or *Museo di Ostia Antica,* Ostia (phone: 6-565-0022).

TARQUINIA AND CERVETERI, Lazio: Virtually all that is known of the remote, but hauntingly familiar, Etruscan civilization comes not from excavation of their cities but from excavation of their burial grounds (*necropoli*), virtual cities themselves of underground chambers and dome-shaped tombs. Though their inscriptions are written in a language that still baffles experts, the scenes of elaborate lovemaking and jovial banqueting inside tell a story equivalent to thousands of words. The *Vatican Museums* and the *Villa Giulia* in Rome both have extensive collections of the angular, modern-looking household objects the Etruscans buried with their dead. Equally worthwhile are the more intimate displays in the medieval towns of Tarquinia and Cerveteri, which superseded Tarquinii and Caere, two of the most important cities of ancient Etruria. The cozy museum buildings are so old it's easy to forget that they are 1,500 years younger than the tools, weapons, and pots they contain. Closed Mondays. Details: *Ente Provinciale per il Turismo,* 11 Via Parigi, Roma 00185 (phone: 6-461851); or the *Museo Nazionale Cerite,* Principe Ruspoli Castello, Ceveteri (phone: 6-995-0003); and the *Museo Nazionale di Tarquinia,* Palazzo Vitelleschi, Corso Emmanuele, Tarquinia (phone: 766-856036).

VILLA ADRIANA, Tivoli, Lazio: The sophisticated emperor and amateur architect Hadrian enjoyed this stately pleasure dome just outside Rome for only 4 years before his death in AD 138. But it was a one-man city, and every detail of its two swimming pools, two libraries, gymnasium, theater, thermal baths, courtyards, tree-lined avenues, and dozens of buildings was perfect. Each window in each of the hundreds of rooms was placed for the best possible view of the gentlest of the estate's rolling hills. Jets of water spouted strategically in every corner, statues from all over the empire surrounded the pools, and romantic nooks for secluded contemplation were sculpted out of nature to appear as if they'd always been there. Still standing in a huge, rambling, and somewhat abandoned archaeological park are numerous buildings, including a marine theater — a delightful little island construction accessible by bridges. The villa's sculpture is now in museums all over Europe, and many of the buildings have been replaced by beautiful olive groves, but copies of the statues are set between the Corinthian columns along one of the swimming pools, the Canopo, to suggest the magnitude of Hadrian's vision of home, sweet home; a scale model at the entrance gate reproduces the entire layout. Closed Mondays. Details: *Azienda Autonoma di Soggiorno,* 13 Piazzale Nazioni Unite, Tivoli (Roma) 00019 (phone: 774-20745 or 774-530203).

Genealogy Hunts

Unfortunately for modern-day pretenders to the throne, only a privileged few will find their ancestral roots reverently inscribed in the exclusive *Libro d'Oro della Nobiltà Italiana* (Golden Book of the Italian Nobility), published by the *Istituto Araldico Romano* (Via Santa Maria dell'Anima, Roma 00186) and available in most genealogical libraries. This is just as well. The monarchy was outlawed in Italy in 1946, and having to check if you're listed in the *Libro d'Oro* is like wanting to know the price of a Lamborghini — if you have to ask, it's not for you.

Also, be forewarned that there are no proven extant lines of descent extending back to the ancient Etruscans, Greeks, or Romans, despite many impassioned claims to the contrary. (However, if behavior is any indication of kinship, these claims may have some basis. The ancient Romans were so eager to prove that they had descended from the city's founding fathers that they had their *sacra gentilica* — family tree, Roman style — painted on the walls of their homes, and fake ancestor portraits and spurious pedigrees were not unknown even then. Rather than dusty canvases, though, these parvenus proudly displayed phony portrait busts, and Aeneas replaced the *Mayflower* as the preferred point of ancestral departure.)

Happily for contemporary ancestor worshipers, Italians have kept meticulous records, beginning as far back as the 13th century, and legitimate evidence of Italian forebears — no matter how humble their origins — usually is yours for the searching. With a little digging around, you'll probably at least be able to visit the church where your Great-Uncle Sal married your Great-Aunt Rosa before leaving for America, or the port where your grandfather waved good-bye to the Old Country, or the cemetery where your mother's family has been resting quietly for centuries.

For those who would rather leave the digging to others, reputable genealogical societies in Italy will do it for you for a fee. Among them are *Istituto Araldico Coccia* (Count Ildebrando Coccia Urbani, director; 6 Borgo Santa Croce, Palazzo Antinori, Casella Postale 458, Florence 50122; phone: 55-242914) — write for its "international ready reckoner," which lists six programs for heraldic and genealogical research; *Istituto Storico Araldico Genealogico Internazionale* (Count Luciano Pelliccioni di Poli, director; 5 Via Pio VIII, Roma 00165); *Istituto Araldico Genealogico Italiano* (Count

Guelfo Guelfi Camaiani, director; 27 Via Santo Spirito, Florence 50125; phone: 55-213090); and *Ufficio di Consulenza Tecnica* (Presso Collegio Araldico, 16 Via Santa Maria dell'Anima, Roma 00185).

But if dig you must, try to do as much preliminary research as possible before your trip. For example, check with your local library and state offices for local published records, regional archives, and local history. The US Library of Congress (Local History and Genealogy Room, Jefferson Building, Washington, DC 20540; phone: 202-707-5537) and the New York Public Library (Division of United States History, Local History, and Genealogy, Room 315N, 42nd St. & 5th Ave., New York, NY 10018; phone: 212-930-0828) both have extensive facilities for in-person research, but you may want to call these institutions in advance to find out if they do have material relevant to your search. Also, the *Family History Library of the Church of Jesus Christ of Latter-Day Saints* has more than 10,000 reels of Italian genealogical records on microfilm, available for consultation in person at its headquarters (35 North West Temple St., Salt Lake City, UT 84150; phone: 801-240-2331) or through any of its branch libraries. Using the Mormons' index reels, you can, for a small fee, order from Salt Lake City the microfilm records of any Italian town. Film should arrive at the branch library in about 6 weeks, and loans are renewable for 2-week periods up to 6 months. There is no charge for reviewing a film at the headquarters in Salt Lake City.

The *Italian Cultural Institute* (686 Park Ave., New York, NY 10021; phone: 212-879-4242) publishes an information sheet on how to go about researching your Italian ancestry. Further tips can be provided by two publications: *Italian Genealogist* (published for the Augustan Society, PO Box P, Torrance, CA 90507; phone: 213-320-7766) and *Italian Family Research* (Summit Publications, PO Box 222, Munroe Falls, OH 44062). Look in your library for T. Beard and D. Demong's *How to Find Your Family Roots* (McGraw-Hill, 1977), which contains an excellent list of genealogical resources available in both Italian and English. In Italy, the Ministry of Foreign Affairs (Ministero degli Affari Esteri; 1 Piazzale Farnesina, Roma 00194) has an Office for Research and Studies of Emigration (Ufficio Ricerche e Studi dell'Emigrazione), which also may be of assistance.

Constructing a family tree is a backward process: You need to start with your parents' dates and places of birth, their parents' dates and birthplaces, and so on — as far back as your search will take you. It should be a considerable stretch since it's quite possible to trace Italian families to about 1500, when it became obligatory for baptisms to be registered in parish churches. To obtain the relevant documents, make sure you have the exact names of each ancestor (remember, many Italian surnames were irrevocably, if unwittingly, changed through clerical misspellings at Ellis Island and other ports of entry), as well as the names of any family members closely related to the ancestor you are researching. You can request many different types of documents that contain information about a previous generation: for example, birth and death certificates, marriage licenses, emigration and immigration records, and baptism and christening records.

REQUESTING RECORDS: Before 1865, personal records — baptism, confirmation, marriage, and death — were kept, as a rule, only by parish churches. Thus, to obtain information on your family prior to 1865, you should begin by writing either to the parish priest or to the bishop holding territorial jurisdiction. Since 1865, birth, marriage, death, and citizenship records have been kept by the *comuni* (municipalities), so you must write to the *comune* from which your ancestors came. Address your request to the *Ufficio di Stato Civile* in the town where the birth, death, or marriage took place. While many of the offices have English-speaking personnel, making a request in Italian usually will facilitate matters considerably.

DIGGING DEEPER: Once you've done your basic research, you might want to turn to some older records or even use them as duplicates to verify information you've already accumulated. The following are some of the records most readily available by mail or in person.

Certificates of Family Genealogy – Write to the General Records Office (Ufficio Anagrafe) in the town where your family member lived to obtain a certificate of your family genealogy (*certificato di stato di famiglia*) giving names, relationships, birth-dates, and birthplaces of all living family members at the time of recording. These certificates usually date from about the turn of the century and can go back as far as 1869.

Emigration Records – Write to the prefecture of the province of the emigrant's birthplace or port of departure to obtain documentation of an ancestor's emigration from about 1869 to the present. Addresses of provincial prefectures are available from *Unione delle Province d'Italia,* 4 Piazza Cardelli, Roma 00186 (phone: 6-687-3672).

Draft Records – For draft records dating from 1869 to the present, write to the military district in charge of an ancestor's town of residence (*Distretto Militare,* name of town), giving birthdates and birthplaces. Some conscription records go back to the Napoleonic era (as early as 1792).

Clerical Surveys – To obtain Catholic parish records (*status animarum),* contact the Central Office for Italian Emigration (UCEI, 3 Via Chiavari, Roma 00186; phone: 6-686-1200) for addresses of local parishes. Records of birthdates, marriage dates, and other biographical information exist, irregularly, from the beginning of the 18th century.

Protestant Parish Registers – Write to the *Genealogical Society* in Salt Lake City (address above) for the addresses of 16 Waldensian parishes in the Piedmont district. The parish records include information similar to Catholic clerical surveys and date from 1685.

Roman Catholic Parish Records – Write to the vicar-general of the diocese in-volved (you can get the address from the Central Office for Italian Emigration, above) for permission to consult the records, which usually are written in Latin. Baptism and christening records, as well as marriage records, date from 1545 (1493 in the town of Fiesole) to the present. Death and burial records go back to the beginning of the 17th century.

Tax Assessment or Census Registers – Write to the *Istituto Centrale di Statistica* (16 Via Cesare Balbo, Roma 00184; phone: 6-46731) to locate the old census data *(catasti),* also called *libri di fuochi* in southern Italy and *libri degli estimi* in the north. Often dating from the 14th century, these contain so-called real estate records (actually tax records — census takers were no fools even then) of heads of households, subten-ants, or taxpayers and their residences along with the amount of tax assessed. Most of the records are located in the *Archivio Secreto del Vaticano* in Rome, the *Archivio di Stato* in Florence, and the archives of the Kingdom of the Two Sicilies in Naples.

Ecclesiastical Records – For clerical records from the 13th to the 19th century, write to the *Archivio Secreto,* Città del Vaticano, Roma 00185 (phone: 6-6982).

Notarial Records – Contact the Ispettore Generale of the *Archivio Notarile* (89 Via Padre Semeria, Roma 00154; phone: 6-512-6951) for records concerning wills, donations, settlements, and land sales dating from about 1340. For similar records from Waldensian Protestant archives beginning in 1610, contact the Ispettore Generale of the *Archivi di Stato di Torino* (165 Piazza Castello, Turin 10122; phone: 11-540382).

Other Sources – *Archivio Centrale dello Stato,* the Italian national archives, are located in a central office (Piazzale degli Archivi, Roma 00144; phone: 6-592-6204); more complete records are kept in the various former independent states that existed before the unification of Italy. There are substantial archival centers in Bologna, Flor-ence, Genoa, Lucca, Mantua, Milan, Modena, Naples, Palermo, Parma, Siena, and Venice.

With the above information and a little *pazienza* (patience), you should have a firm grasp for a lengthy climb up your Italian family tree.

A Shutterbug's Rome

 The dramatic interplay of lustrous marble and terra cotta tile, crowded squares and romantic corners, these are Rome's photogenic stock in trade. Even a beginner can achieve remarkable results with a surprisingly basic set of lenses and filters. Equipment is, in fact, only as valuable as the imagination that puts it into use.

Don't be afraid to experiment. Use what knowledge you have to explore new possibilities. Don't limit yourself with preconceived ideas of what's hackneyed or corny. Because the Colosseum has been photographed hundreds of times before doesn't make it any less worthy of your attention.

In Rome as elsewhere, spontaneity is one of the keys to good photography. Whether it's a sudden shaft of light bursting through the crowds climbing the Spanish Steps or an ancient ruin set in between two ultramodern shops along the Via Veneto, don't hesitate to shoot if the moment is right. If photography is indeed capturing a moment and making it timeless, success lies in judging just when a moment worth capturing occurs.

A good picture reveals an eye for detail, whether it's a matter of lighting, positioning your subject, or taking time to frame a picture carefully. The better your grasp of the importance of details, the better your results will be photographically.

Patience is often necessary. Don't shoot a wide-angle view of the Pantheon if a bus suddenly passes in front of it. A TV antenna in a panorama from St. Peter's? Reframe your image to eliminate the obvious distraction. People walking toward a scene that would benefit from their presence? Wait until they're in position before you shoot. After the fact, many of the flaws will be self-evident. The trick is to be aware of the ideal and have the patience to allow it to happen. If you are part of a group, you may well have to trail behind a bit in order to shoot properly. Not only is group activity distracting, but bunches of people hovering nearby tend to stifle spontaneity and overwhelm potential subjects.

The camera provides an opportunity, not only to capture Rome's charm, but to interpret it. What it takes is a sensitivity to the surroundings, a knowledge of the capabilities of your equipment, and a willingness to see things in new ways.

LANDSCAPES: Rome's ancient ruins and abundant architectural styles are compelling photographic subjects. Getting the full sweep of the city's visual effect can be vital to a good photograph.

Color and form are the obvious ingredients here, and how you frame a picture can be as important as getting the proper exposure. Study the shapes, angles, and colors that make up the scene and create a composition that uses them to best advantage.

Lighting is a vital component in landscapes. Take advantage of the richer colors of early morning and late afternoon whenever possible. The overhead light of midday is often harsh and without the shadowing that can add to the drama of a scene. This is where a polarizer is used to best effect. Most polarizing filters come with a mark on the rotating ring. If you can aim at your subject and point that marker at the sun, the sun's rays are likely to be right for the polarizer to work properly. If not, stick to your skylight filter, underexposing slightly if the scene is particularly bright. Most light meters respond to an overall light balance, with the result that bright areas may appear burned out.

Although a standard 50mm to 55mm lens may work well in some landscape situations, most will benefit from a 20mm to 28mm wide-angle. Panoramic views taken of the Capitoline Hill fit beautifully into a wide-angle format, allowing not only the overview, but the opportunity to include other points of interest in the foreground.

To isolate specific elements of any scene, use your telephoto lens. This is the best way to photograph Santa Maria in Cosmedin or get a rare shot of the pope standing on his balcony. The successful use of a telephoto means developing your eye for detail.

PEOPLE: As with taking pictures of people anywhere, there are going to be times in Rome when a camera is an intrusion. Your approach is the key: Consider your own reaction under similar circumstances, and you have an idea of what would make others comfortable enough to be willing subjects. People are often sensitive to suddenly having a camera pointed at them, and a polite request, while getting you a share of refusals, will also provide a chance to shoot some wonderful portraits that capture the spirit of the city as surely as the scenery does. For candid shots, an excellent lens is a zoom telephoto in the 70mm to 210mm range; it allows you to remain unobtrusive while the telephoto lens draws the subject closer. And for portraits, a telephoto lens can be effectively used as close as 2 or 3 feet.

For authenticity and variety, select a place likely to produce interesting subjects. Piazza Navona is an obvious spot for visitors, but if it's local color you're after, visit the Trastevere area, strike out for the Jewish ghetto, or stroll through the produce and fish markets early in the morning. Aim for shots that tell what's different about Rome. In portraiture, there are several factors to keep in mind. Morning or afternoon light will add richness to skin tones. To avoid the harsh facial shadows cast by direct sunlight, shoot in the shade or in an area where the light is diffused. The only filter to use is a skylight.

SUNSETS: The best place to be for a Roman sunset is on any one of its seven hills. Each affords a spectacular ancient backdrop at day's end.

When shooting sunsets, keep in mind that the brightness will distort meter readings. When composing a shot directly into the sun, frame the picture in the viewfinder so that only half of the sun is included. Read the meter, set, and shoot. Whenever there is this kind of unusual lighting, shoot a few frames in half-step increments, both over and under the meter reading. Bracketing, as this is called, can provide a range of images, the best of which may well be other than the one shot at the meter's recommended setting.

Use any lens for sunsets. A wide-angle is good when the sky is filled with color-streaked clouds, when the sun is partially hidden, or when you're close to an object that silhouettes dramatically against the sky.

Telephoto lenses also produce wonderful silhouettes, either with the sun as a backdrop or against the palette of a brilliant sunset sky. Bracket again here. For the best silhouettes, wait 10 to 15 minutes after sunset. Unless using a very fast film, a tripod is recommended.

Red and orange filters are often used to accentuate a sunset's picture potential. Orange will help turn even a gray sky into something approaching a photogenic finale to the day and can provide particularly beautiful shots linking the sky with the sun reflected on the water. If the sunset is already bold in hue, the orange may overwhelm the natural colors. A red filter will produce dramatic, highly unrealistic results.

NIGHT: If you think that picture possibilities end at sunset, you're presuming that night photography is the exclusive domain of the professional. If you've got a tripod, all you'll need is a cable release to attach to your camera to assure a steady exposure (which is often timed in minutes rather than fractions of a second).

For most nighttime situations, a strobe does the trick, but beware: Flash units are often used improperly. You can't take a view of the Colosseum with a flash. It may reach out 30 to 50 feet, but that's it. On the other hand, a flash used too close to your subject may result in overexposure, resulting in a "blown out" effect. With most cameras, strobes will work with a maximum shutter speed of 1/125 or 1/150 of a second. If you set the exposure properly and shoot within range, you should come up with pretty sharp results.

CLOSE-UPS: Whether of people or of details of ancient ruins, close-ups can add another dimension to your photography. There are a number of shooting options, one of which is to use a 70mm or a 210mm lens at its closest focusable distance. Unless you're working in bright sunlight, a tripod will be worthwhile. If you are very near your subject and there is a good deal of reflective light, it may pay to underexpose a bit in relation to the meter reading.

If you do not have a telephoto lens, you can still shoot close-ups using a set of magnification filters. Filter packs of one-, two-, and three-time magnification are available, converting your lens into a close-up lens. Even better is a special macro lens designed for close-up photography.

■**Note:** Standing before some of Rome's most moving Caravaggios, you may feel an urge to capture the painting on film. Don't do it. Besides the fact that many museums and churches do not allow photography, the results are almost certain to be disappointing. In most of the churches, the lighting is so bad or the painting so far away that a flash will not help. If you really want to bring the memory of the painting home with you, buy a prepared slide from the museum gift shop or a book that has the painting in it.

A SHORT PHOTOGRAPHIC TOUR

ST. PETER'S SQUARE: If there were a competition, Piazza San Pietro could vie for the title of Most Photographed Square in the World. Good shots can be had here from almost any angle. Just remember that pictures of buildings are more interesting with people in them — and that doesn't mean taking dozens of pictures of Aunt Julia waving to the folks back home. Try shooting the men and women from religious orders in their individual garb, the pilgrims of all nations and races, the children gazing awestruck at the gigantic columns of Bernini's curving colonnades, or glimpsed through the splashing fountains. Look for the circular paving stone located between the 83½-foot obelisk and one of the fountains, and turn toward a colonnade. From that vantage point it will appear to be a single row of columns. For panoramic views, visitors may reach the dome by elevator, then climb a staircase to the top; from here you can also see the pope's backyard. The very best views of the dome, however, are shot from two vantage points: the Janiculum Hill, from which it is seen at eye level, and from the Ponte Umberto I, a Tiber River bridge near the Palazzo di Giustizia (Justice Building). The pope's famous balcony, from which he addresses the immense crowds in the piazza, is on the right if you are facing the main façade of the church.

ROMAN FORUM: However romantic, the ruins of Rome present a challenge to the photographer, who must work to keep them comprehensible and readily identifiable. In the Roman Forum, as elsewhere, this is best achieved by concentrating on a telling detail: a single broken column, a patch of mosaic. For contrast to the dull gray stone or pale marble of ruins, try to include a spot of life and color: a red poppy, a green acanthus leaf, or a patch of trailing vine. Seek out an exciting detail for a close-up, such as a wet basalt paving stone of the Decumanus Maximus still showing the groove left there by decades of ancient chariot wheels. A young girl seated on a carved column base on the Palatine Hill overlooking the Forum, a lizard poised against the *opus reticulatum* brickwork typical of ancient Roman construction, or a cat dozing on a fallen temple metope will add life to your scenes of ancient Rome. The challenge of making the stones come alive to the viewer is half the fun of photographing in Rome.

OSTIA ANTICA: The ancient seaport of Imperial Rome offers acres of ruins and gardens, which include an open-air theater, taverns, and even an entire ancient Roman street, all bathed in the shade of lofty umbrella pines. One public facility was a marble-topped collective latrine. Photographers may enjoy shooting the small ancient synagogue and, in another mood, the black-and-white mosaics that served as advertisements in front of the places of business around the central forum of Ostia.

CAPITOLINE HILL: For some of the best views of the Roman Forum, climb to the top of the Capitoline Hill. On either side of the central City Hall Building (the Campidoglio) are short streets with vest-pocket parks overlooking the forums. From the overlook (reached at the right side of the Campidoglio) you can also see the ancient Roman records building; built into the foundations of the Town Hall itself it is one of the oldest known office buildings in continuous use. Still atop the Capitoline Hill, in the courtyard of the *Capitoline Museum* (to the right of the Campidoglio) are gigantic marble pieces of statues, including an enormous hand. These are old favorites of photographers in Rome, but your version may be the best ever.

PIAZZA NAVONA: This piazza offers a never-ending variety of photographic possibilities because its character changes so drastically during the span of the day. At dawn, when clouds tend to be showy and dramatic, priests stride through; in mid-morning sunlight or mist, children feed and chase the pigeons. Pretty girls pose for sidewalk portraits in the afternoon and evening, when the crowds surge through the square, and the boys size up the girls while children on bicycles vie for space. Come *Christmas,* the piazza is lined with booths selling toys and crèche scenes; during the pre-*Lenten Mardi Gras* period, Roman children, dressed in gorgeous costumes, traditionally walk here. At any time it is a lively parade of people and people watching people from ringside seats in the four cafés and two restaurants that serve outdoors year-round. This is Rome's outdoor living room, and a photographer's lively atelier. The pigeons know they are supposed to pose on the hand or forehead of the figures in the famous Bernini fountains. Pray for a rainy day: The effect of the piazza is most spectacular then.

TRASTEVERE: Trastevere, the neighborhood across the Tiber, has been crowded and lively since the days of the ancient Romans. Today it is still a crowded, fascinating warren of narrow streets, craftsmen's workshops, cafés where students play chess and sip herbal tea, and foreign and Italian residents from all walks of life going about their lives. The central meeting place of Piazza Santa Maria in Trastevere is the best spot to capture the flavor of life in Trastevere; but don't just stop here: Dive into the narrow alleys all around for often surprisingly calm vistas that have changed little over the centuries.

TIBER ISLAND: The island has two levels, one at nearly water's edge and another at one of the two bridge crossings; both provide stimulating photographic opportunities. Both bridges date from ancient Roman times. From them are views of the low skyline of small temples 2,000 years old, and the medieval bell tower of Santa Maria in Cosmedin. Go down the steps to the lower level (when facing the Church of San Bartolomeo, the steps are to the right) for fine views of rushing water and a third ancient bridge, the Ponte Rotto.

COLOSSEUM: Perhaps you're not the first person to have captured on film this most familiar of all Roman monuments from ancient days, but there are some different angles from which to photograph it. The least familiar view, in which the building appears intact, is from the Oppian Hill (Colle Oppio). Climb the staircase to the right of the *metropolitana* station, and take Via Nicola Salvi west to Largo Agnesi; or continue into the green Parco Oppio, where Nero built his Golden House.

DIRECTIONS

Introduction

Rome is the quintessential city for walking; indeed, a case can be made that it can *only* be seen on foot. The city is small, its monuments — many still within the boundaries of walls left standing from Caesar's time — are close together. Here, in ways the eye may not immediately see, ancient Rome lives on, not only in its splendid archaeological parks and magnificent monuments, but in its particular, intimate, and creative everyday life.

For at least 8 centuries, walking tours have been an essential part of a visit to Rome. In fact, the walking tours described below were in part inspired by Benedetto, a canon of St. Peter's in the 12th century, who designed a tour for pilgrims to the city.

In many ways, today's explorer will find the Eternal City much as it was in Benedetto's time — except for the cars (though many areas are off-limits to automobiles). The results of an ambitious cleanup project are beginning to be felt; many structures are emerging from their plastic restoration shrouds, and at no other time in recent memory have Rome's monuments, palazzi, and churches been in such pristine condition. Marble façades are newly scrubbed to their original creamy white splendor, and stuccos have been meticulously repainted in gorgeous pastels.

A wanderer may see some signs of this general cleanup, coming upon a group of white-coated restorers painstakingly brushing the grime away from cherubs and angels or bent over the street replacing some *sanpietrini,* paving stones made of volcanic rock that were used to pave St. Peter's Square.

Don't be intimidated by the labrynthine streets and lack of sidewalks. Rome's famous seven hills may loom large in history, but many of them are in fact smaller than a city block. In 390 BC, the Servian Wall surrounding the city and its seven hills stretched a mere 6½ miles. The Emperor Aurelius expanded the walls another 5 miles. Now a 582-square-mile metropolis, Rome encompasses all the seven hills, plus Trastevere, the area across the Tiber, and the Campus Martius, or Martian Fields, the flat area just inland.

The areas between the hills were once narrow valleys traversed by spring-fed streams. These small valleys, marked today by street names like *clivo,* or gap — rather than "street" — were marshy, unhealthy areas, rife with malaria. The patricians of the city lived on hilltops; the plebeians lived down below.

The physical and social complexity of Imperial Rome grew as the Empire expanded, and monuments were raised to emperors and gods, and large structures such as the Pantheon were built on the flatlands.

The forums were the places where business was conducted, and bathhouses, libraries, courthouses, theaters, and sports arenas began to fill more and more of the once marshy valley areas.

A city that is 3,000 years old was not designed for automobiles, and a walker may find them a hostile presence. When to walk? Avoid long walks during the afternoon hours, when the pollution hangs heavy in the air. Early morning is best, but lunchtime is good, too; it's the sleepy hour when Romans — and their cars — snooze, and a visitor can savor the streets in the dusty sunlit silence.

The following ten walks aim for variety. They are short and long, citified in downtown Rome and countrified on the Appian Way. Two of the walks are tailored for history and art buffs: *Medieval Rome — Pilgrims and Perils* and *Masterworks of Architecture Through the Ages.* For relaxing strolls designed to soak up the atmosphere, consider the walks around the Pantheon and Campo dei Fiori neighborhoods, or the tour of *The Bridges.*

Our walks go through the Subura, where gladiators once lived, through the old Jewish ghetto area, and Trastevere. In addition to pointing out things that meet the eye, we'll also introduce a subterranean Rome of hidden rivers and ancient ruins that lie below street level. But regardless of which paths you choose, keep reminding yourself to look up: at the glorious cupolas and domes and bell towers; at the secret gardens on the rooftops; at the flocks of swallows and Rome's newest feathered visitors, the cormorants and sea gulls; at the billowing clouds above the low Roman skyline, especially after a northern wind has swept away the grime.

Walk 1: From Kings to Countesses — Pantheon and Piazza Navona

A perfect first day may well begin at Piazza della Rotonda, the "rotonda" being the Pantheon, the best preserved of all Rome's ancient monuments. Originally dedicated to the seven planetary gods, it was built in 27 BC by Marcus Agrippa; it was burned down in AD 80 and rebuilt by the Emperor Hadrian around AD 120, then restored by the emperors Septimius Severus and Caracalla; and in AD 606 it was christianized as Santa Maria ad Martyres. A Barberini pope had its original bronzed portico moved to make the great *baldacchino* (canopy) over the altar at St. Peter's — hence the Roman bons mots, *Quod non fecerunt barbari fecerunt Barberini* (What the barbarians didn't do, the Barberini did.)

Approach this monument from the west to enjoy the natural chiaroscuro of the narrow Via Giustiniani in early morning, when ancient walls and paving stones (they're washed early each morning) send up swirls of chilly air to mix with the warming rays of the sun. At the corner is the sun-drenched, open Piazza della Rotonda — people-size, and free of automobiles. Rival cafés have staked out their sides of the square with tables and chairs; they'll do a brisk business all day and evening. *Café di Rienzo,* the neo-baroque temple of plastic, marble, and Venetian glass on the Piazza della Rotonda (see *Bars and Cafés* in THE CITY), has a plush tearoom, perfect for a rainy day. On a sunny morning, linger outdoors over a first or second breakfast of cappuccino and a *cornetto,* a slightly sweet crescent roll. Locals gravitate to *Café Tazza d'Oro* (no tables, however) for the sinfully rich iced coffee–and–whipped cream confection called *granita di caffè.*

All around, people go about their daily business, with casually affectionate disregard for the majestic 2,000-year-old Pantheon, a temple to the gods — and final resting place of Raphael and the first two Kings of Italy. Today, children have roller skate races around it and tourists sunbathe on the steps of the fountain in front. Designed by Giacomo della Porta and erected by Pope Gregory XIII, the fountain's base supports a 20-foot-tall Egyptian obelisk dedicated to Ramses II.

This is a neighborhood of shops, restaurants, parliamentary office buildings (identified by the glass-cage guard posts outside), wonderful coffee bars, and

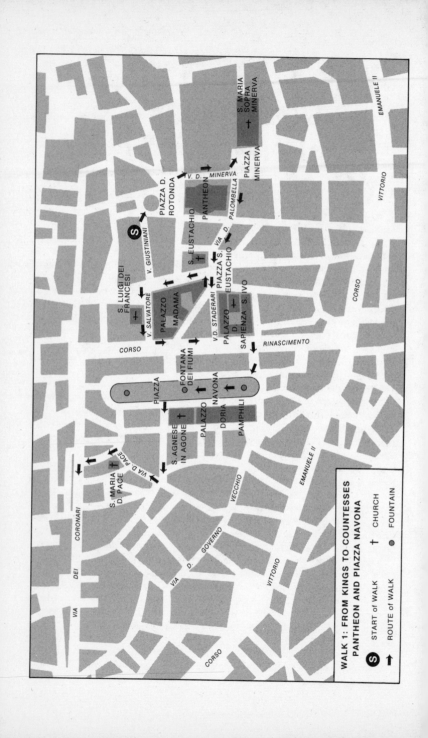

WALK 1: FROM KINGS TO COUNTESSES
PANTHEON AND PIAZZA NAVONA

Ⓢ START of WALK
† CHURCH
● FOUNTAIN

↑ ROUTE of WALK

S. MARIA SOPRA MINERVA †
PIAZZA MINERVA
V. D. MINERVA
PIAZZA D. ROTONDA
PANTHEON
V. D. PALOMBELLA
V. GIUSTINIANI
S. EUSTACHIO †
S. LUIGI DEI FRANCESI
VIA D.
PIAZZA S. EUSTACHIO
V. SALVATORE
PALAZZO MADAMA
V.D. STADERARI
PALAZZO D. SAPIENZA S. IVO
CORSO
RINASCIMENTO
FONTANA DEI FIUMI
PIAZZA NAVONA
PALAZZO DORIA PAMPHILI
S. AGNESE IN AGONE †
VIA D. PACE
S. MARIA D. PACE †
DEI CORONARI
VIA
VIA D. GOVERNO VECCHIO
VITTORIO EMANUELE II
VITTORIO
CORSO
CORSO

some ornately decorated ice cream parlors. After paying the *conto* (bill) for your cappuccino, which will be higher if you sit at a table than if you sip it Roman-style, standing up at the bar (or *all'Americano,* as the Romans say), take the Via della Minerva to the small Piazza Minerva, directly behind the Pantheon (one square leads directly into the other). In this adjacent square, amid a crush of ingeniously parked cars, stands a charming marble elephant wearing an expression that may be whimsical or wearisome, depending on the eye of the beholder. On its back is another Egyptian obelisk brought to Rome in ancient days.

The work of sculptor Gian Lorenzo Bernini, the pachyderm was a rarity in Rome at the time. So why did he sculpt one? His friends explained that he was fresh from an unsatisfactory period of work in Paris, and wanted to express his sense of holding the weight of the world on his back. Others have said that it is a reference to Pope Alexander VII's reign and is supposed to symbolize intelligence, as the basis of all wisdom.

The somewhat plain-looking Church of Santa Maria sopra Minerva was built on top of an ancient pagan temple to the Roman goddess. It is Rome's only Gothic church, and has some fine stained glass windows. Among the many treasures inside are two versions of Michelangelo's *St. John the Baptist;* in a side chapel look for the first version, which was carved of imperfect marble and was, therefore, discarded. The finished masterpiece stands to the left of the front altar. On a more mundane level, to the right of the main door, note the high-water marker, a reminder of Rome's notorious floods.

Loop around to the west by threading along on the narrow Via della Palombella, behind the Pantheon. This route offers a chance to see some vestiges of the original white marble that once covered the entire building. The zigzagging Via Della Palombella leads to Piazza Sant'Eustachio, a square that is in itself a lesson in the history of architecture. To study it in comfort, take a seat at one of the two cafés, the famed *Bar Eustachio,* whose coffee is celebrated (see *Bars and Cafés* in THE CITY), and the no less excellent *Bernasconi.*

Starting with the oldest part of the square is the Church of Sant'Eustachio, built on top of a pagan temple. At the height of the Middle Ages it was given a brick campanile; then came a pure baroque façade, and at the top, a deer with horns: St. Eustace was a pagan Roman soldier who saw a deer with Christ's face while he was out hunting, and instantly was converted.

This whole neighborhood, or *rione,* is named for Sant'Eustachio (St. Eustace); here, during the Renaissance, were many shops that sold spices and essences. Today, the area is still filled with numerous shops, most notably those selling hams and cheeses; the shops are called *Norcineria,* for the owners' farm homes in Norcia in Umbria. Another mainstay of commerce here are religious articles; this was, after all, a temple area and later an enclave for churches, and life-size plaster saints, tailors serving the priesthood (including Gambarelli, tailor to the popes), and shops selling chalices are all around. In fact, this is probably the best place in all of Rome to buy a *Christmas* crèche.

Looking clockwise, from the Church of Sant'Eustachio, there is a small, dainty, and exquisite Renaissance family palazzo with a painted façade. Continue clockwise, and note the stunning, elaborate white marble corkscrew campanile atop the dome of Sant'Ivo alla Sapienza. Right underneath is an immense, round, red granite fountain that recently was found buried in the basement of the adjacent Senate building when workers were building a computer center.

This is one of two fountains on the small Via degli Staderari (the name comes from the makers of scales who had workshops here). The other is the tiny, attractive Fountain of the Book, so named because this area was home to the University of Rome from 1303 to 1935; in fact, the whole *rione* is still rife with bookstores and stationery shops selling fine fountain pens and notebooks. Take a sip of the water from the fountain; like the other fountains in central Rome, it is fed by mountain springs, which arrive by ancient Roman aqueduct. Its purity and freshness are at least part of the secret of the sublime Roman coffee you've been sipping.

Retrace your steps on Via degli Staderari, and note the heavily guarded (on all sides) entrance to Palazzo Madama, a large Renaissance palace, now home to the Italian Senate. Built over the medieval residence of the once powerful Crescenzi family, it was enlarged by the Medicis of Florence, who liked it enough to buy it. In 1740, Pope Benedict XIV purchased it and transferred the government here; the street running past it is Via del Governo Vecchio (Street of the Old Government).

Just a few steps down Via del Governo is the Church of San Luigi dei Francesi, beautifully restored outside and filled with masterpieces inside. This is the national church of France, and contains two magnificent Caravaggio paintings — *The Calling of St. Matthew* and *The Martyrdom of St. Matthew* (said to be among his finest works) — which can be properly floodlit if you drop a few 100-lire coins into the box outside the chapel. (Most of the artworks in churches are hard to see by natural light, so always hunt for the possibilities of additional illumination.)

Now take Via Salvatore, the street between the church and the Senate, and turn left onto the broad Corso Rinascimento and the ceremonial entrance to the Senate, with its silken-caped, spear-carrying honor guards outside.

A block south is the entrance to the Palazzo della Sapienza, whose spiral campanile by Borromini we saw earlier from the Piazza Sant'Eustachio. If you're lucky (and it is unlocked), the austere scholars' courtyard (*sapienza* means knowledge) designed by Borromini, with the Church of Sant'Ivo at the end, is well worth a look.

Before crossing the Corso Rinascimento, note the storefront marked Cambio, a commercial moneychanger. Changing money in a Roman bank can be tedious — lines can seem endless. This little Cambio, however, manages to be clean, prompt, courteous, and uncrowded; open regular business hours, it generally offers a good exchange rate.

Across the Corso are two short lanes that lead into Piazza Navona. There isn't time in any single morning to do more than walk through this elegant long ellipse, but even taking a leisurely stroll is to experience its charm. As time permits, return at different hours of the day to study the myriad elements of the square, affectionately dubbed "Rome's outdoor parlor." There are pleasant shops to visit as well, including a china and pottery shop at the corner of Corsia Agone, with fair prices and a wide selection of utilitarian and decorative items; at either end of the piazza are two shops for toys, stuffed animals, and fabulous dolls (Italy is a major toy and doll manufacturer). The best toy stores are *Al Sogno Giocattoli* (No. 53) and *Bertè* (No. 108).

Far less appealing are most of the works of the artists who set up their easels in the middle of the square. Choose carefully if any of these canvases attract you; most are tasteless hokum, but one or two of the artists are actually professors of fine arts who supplement their teachers' wages by moonlighting.

You'll also have to work hard (though why resist?) to keep from buying a devilishly delicious and calorie-laden *tartufo,* a chocolate-covered ball of ice cream filled with chocolate and rolled in more chocolate nuggets. It's a late-night favorite, usually enjoyed alfresco; but it's equally scrumptious on a rainy day on *Tre Scalini*'s charming first-floor (second-floor to Americans) indoor tearoom.

Seated here or on one of the outdoor benches, look out at the bustling Piazza Navona — site of Bernini's Fontana dei Fiumi and Borromini's Church of Sant'Agnese in Agone. The square is built in the shape of a racecourse (that's what it was in the days of the ancient Romans), and today kids race each other on bikes (there's a rental stall in the piazza itself); their forebears raced each other in horse-drawn chariots. These ancient *agonale* games (the word "agonistic," or competitive, is derived from this), or races, were held here in the days of the Emperor Domitian, and so it is often called Domitian's Stadium. It was here that Domitian organized his Roman version of the *Olympic Games.* Until 500 years ago the ruins of that stadium could still be seen. From 1477 to 1877 the piazza was used as an outdoor market, which only then transferred to Campo dei Fiori.

From early December through January 6 (*Epiphany*) toys, crèches, candies, gift items like belts and wallets, and *Christmas* tree decorations are sold beneath the benign gaze of the two saints of the Italian *Christmas,* Santa Claus — a US import — and the native good witch of *Christmas,* La Befana (her name comes from *Epiphany*), who brings children presents on January 6. In the past, if they were naughty they received lumps of charcoal, so among the candies on sale during the yuletide season are chunks of black candy that look like coal.

Romans frolicked here during the Renaissance, with games and tournaments and *Mardi Gras* parties; to this day, just before *Lent,* Italian children — wearing gorgeous costumes that have been passed down from one generation to another — parade here. During the time of Pope Innocent X (he was Bernini's patron) the piazza was intentionally flooded every August by blocking the drainage ditches for the *Feast of the Lake.* Carriages shaped like gondolas were drawn into the water by horses, whose slipping and stumbling were considered part of the merriment.

It was this pope of the Doria Pamphili family who gave the piazza its present look. Three fountains for watering horses already existed. He commissioned improvements of all three, including the central fountain which was by Bernini (when touring this pontiff's own nearby Palazzo Doria Pamphili, look for his mockup of the fountain in the entry hall to the private apartments). Bernini gave his fountain the theme of four great rivers, representing the four corners of the world: the Nile, whose source was unknown, the Plata, the Danube, and the Ganges. It has marvelous horses and arched-backed sea creatures leaping out of waves; a 54-foot-high Egyptian obelisk sits at the top.

The idea that Bernini covered the face of the Nile to block the view of the Church of Sant'Agnese in Agone (designed by his rival, Borromini) persists, but isn't true; in fact, the face is covered to show that the source of that river was unknown.

To the left of the church is the Brazilian Embassy, originally the splendid palazzo (in 1650) of Pope Innocent X's dowager sister-in-law, Donna Olimpia Maidalchini Pamphili. Since that was the period when the pope was also King of Rome, her position made her its queen. She commissioned so many works of architecture that she was also in effect the queen of baroque; just look around this piazza to see the impact of her "reign." If it is unlocked, visit Sant'Agnese in Agone, with its spectacular frescoes. Occasional masses are said in English here; the hours are posted on the door.

Across the piazza is the seemingly more humble Church of San Giacomo degli Spagnoli, built in 1450, with a hospital serving the Spaniards in Rome. Popes and potentates would come to an upper floor here to watch the summer flooding of the piazza. Its pretty doorway dates from the Middle Ages; every morning at 7 a verger emerges from it to feed the pigeons.

Now walk through the passageway of Via di Sant'Agnese by the *Café Tre Scalini* (see *Bars and Cafés* in THE CITY). After passing the handsome Torre Millini, a 14th-century tower whose name is written on its Guelph battlements, this pathway leads into a fascinating warren of shops of all kinds. Here you can watch craftspeople at work weaving, sculpting marble, gilding picture frames, and restoring furniture. The ivy-covered *Bar della Pace* (see *Bars and Cafés* in THE CITY) is a gathering place for young travelers; its marble tables are busy all day. Forget the restaurants right here; most look inviting, but are disappointing.

The Via della Pace near the café leads, however, to one of Rome's baroque masterpieces, the tiny half-moon of the Church of Santa Maria della Pace, attached to such neighboring buildings as Palazzo Lancellotti with stones that seem to have wings and movement. The church is under restoration; upon its completion, the Raphael fresco of the Sibyls housed inside will again be visible.

Passing to the right of the church, under the arch, don't be startled by the gun-toting soldiers. The small cobbled lane leads to Largo Febo, another piazza, and the small, elegant *Raphael* hotel, where former Italian Premier Bettino Craxi always stays when in Rome; the guards are posted here to ensure his safety.

Continue on past the *Raphael* and the unrelated garden trattoria and turn left to the Via dei Coronari, a long, straight street, the center of one of Rome's antiques districts. Legend has it that the name came from the Countesses of Rome having to sell their *corone* (crowns or tiaras) in shops here. The real story is slightly different. The street was laid out by Pope Sixtus IV around 1480 as a perfectly straight 1-mile-long line. Pilgrims to St. Peter's walked it from the Trevi Fountain to the Vatican, and so it came to be lined with shops selling medals and religious trinkets and "crowns" (which also refers to rosary rings). Raphael lived at No. 124.

The antiques dealers here have a festival every summer, a sort of open house showing their best wares. Don't hesitate to walk inside the shops, even if just to admire their treasures. Smile a pleasant "Buon giorno" at the proprietor, look around, and then depart. Nobody will insist on helping you unless you truly wish to discuss the merchandise. Some of the dealers here have authentic pieces from the Renaissance, while others are selling Liberty and Art Deco — very beautiful, very expensive.

There are some good trattorias, pizzerias, and a few restaurants with real charm in this neighborhood (our choice is *Pino e Dino,* located in a secluded, minuscule piazza just off the Via dei Coronari).

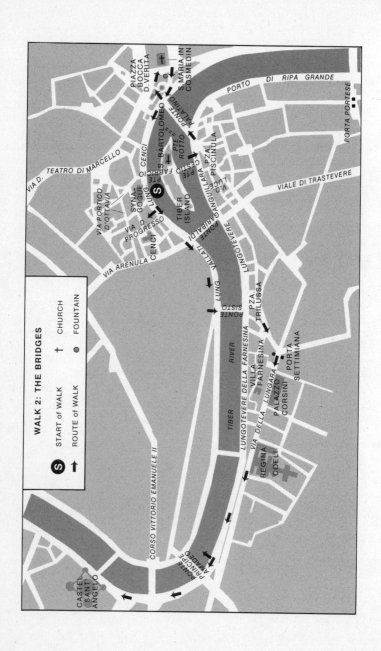

WALK 2: THE BRIDGES

S START of WALK

↑ ROUTE of WALK

✝ CHURCH

● FOUNTAIN

Walk 2: The Bridges

What could be nicer on a sunny morning than walking along the Tiber River — *il Tevere,* to Romans — to admire the vistas from its bridges? A good choice for a Sunday morning stroll, when the automobile traffic is the least bothersome; two of the bridges on this tour are always closed to traffic: those on either side of Tiber Island, the Ponte Fabricio and the Ponte Cestio.

The Tiber is the artery coursing through Rome, and the city itself exists on seven hills overlooking it. In its earliest days, Rome was a trading post; the waters of the Tiber were shallow enough around the island for people to have their flocks wade across. Under Imperial Rome, important docks were built and booty and goods from the far-flung empire were unloaded from river barges arriving from Ostia, the seaport. Picture scores of slaves on these banks unloading cargoes of grain from Sicily in terra cotta jars, or precious blocks of yellow marble from what is Libya today, or immense obelisks brought in from Egypt. Until the early part of this century, boats brought goods down here from as far north and inland as Perugia, transporting them nearly 250 miles down the Tiber.

The river overflowed so regularly — enveloping the great piazze like the one in front of the Pantheon (look at the Church of Santa Maria sopra Minerva for one of the many high-water marks that appear around the city) — that it eventually had to be dammed. Because of this, Rome lost its importance as a riverfront city, and the river, no longer navigable, became an adjunct instead of a vital part of Roman life. Gradually, the mills that lined the river banks, whose waterwheels had for centuries ground flour for bread, disappeared. In our own day, industrial waste has turned the Tiber into an open sewer, and woe betide anyone who swims in it. (Even so, a few do every year, at considerable health risk.)

Today's Romans are rediscovering the Tiber and its banks for other pleasures; numerous private rowing clubs are moored here and a few raft cafés and colorful floating restaurants (*Canto del Riso* is one of our favorites) are popular. The new riverboats help the rejuvenation; the owners of the first of these personally cleaned long-neglected banks about a dozen years ago. Now, every summer, *Expo Teverean,* an exhibition with displays of books, handicrafts, and assorted artworks, is a dockside event.

For an exploration of the Tiber as part of Roman life, start at what is in a way the heart of Rome: the 900-foot-long Tiber Island — Isola Tiberina — which also used to be called the Sacred Island. It's reached by crossing the Ponte Fabricio, which the Romans call the Ponte dei Quattro Capi because of the four faces of Janus adorning the two marble markers. Although the kindly god Janus was supposed to protect people entering and exiting, the bridge here — at one time made entirely of wood — collapsed in 179 BC. The current bridge dates from 62 BC.

Tiny Tiber Island is a special part of ancient Rome. The Romans have a legend that the island grew from a seed of grain tossed in after the Etruscan kings were kicked out; even then, politicians spread the notion that things prospered only after they took office. It is assumed that the first building on the island was a refuge for followers of the god of healing. After a plague in 291 BC, the Romans sent a delegation to Greece to seek advice from a sybil, and were counseled to avoid further trouble by building a shrine to Asclepius, the Greek god of healing. They did, placing it here. Adjacent to the shrine was a spring where pilgrims slept. Gradually, the shrine was improved into a temple; by the time Rome was an empire stretching from Asia to England, the entire almond-shape island was composed of different temples, swathed in white marble, taking the shape of a large white boat with a central obelisk floating in the river. (Old prints by Piranesi show the ruins on the high prow.) Most are gone, but if you stroll downriver just a short way along the embankment, to the left are some vestiges of marble decorations, such as Asclepius's symbol, the serpent, which represented his healing powers. (A serpent sheds its skin and hence restores and renews itself.) Walk down some stairs onto the island's downriver "prow," and, on the Ponte dei Quattro Capi side, look for a patch of marble wall with a small snake carved on it.

Amazingly, the sacred spring remains. Look at the steps leading to the altar of San Bartolomeo, which stands on the site of the earliest original temple; there is a well covered with a grate. Deep below this, the spring still flows. Across from the church is a busy hospital. During the plague, victims were left here in a hospice; today the island remains a place of healing. Peek into the drugstore in front of the hospital: The cupboards and painted big ceramic jars are copies of ones that used to be in an old-fashioned pharmacy, and the painted 18th-century ceiling is original.

To the right, after exiting the pharmacy, and to the left of the church, at No. 20, is the new *Museo Storico dell'Isola Tiberina,* a small historical museum devoted to the island; almost complete as we went to press, it is scheduled to open this year. Make a note that if you are in need of refreshment, adjacent to the museum is the *Antico Caffè dell'Isola,* which has two rooms inside with tables for snacks. Next door is the popular Roman trattoria, *Sora Lella.* If dining alfresco suits you, look downriver, at the small park on the marble-paved point of the island — a good spot for stopping to read or, later, to return to for a picnic.

Off the southern tip of the island is an immense carved white marble arch from the first stone bridge ever built across the Tiber. It was used for about 1,500 years, until it finally collapsed in 1598 after a major flood; it has been known as the Ponte Rotto (the Broken Bridge) ever since. When the arched iron bridge was taken down after a new bridge was built just beyond it, a medieval tower that stood facing it and a nearby 15th-century church also were torn down.

An odd legend had it that a seven-branched golden candelabra that the Romans seized from the temple in Jerusalem (you can see it on a carving under the Arch of Titus) was buried under the Ponte Rotto. Was it? Well, archaeologists have found a signal number of ancient treasures buried in the river sludge right here.

Continuing across the river on Ponte Cestio (built beween 62 and 27 BC and totally rebuilt in AD 368) you emerge on the Lungotevere Anguillara. From here, look down at the bridge; its travertine surface was ripped off the façade of the Theater of Marcellus, which was already partially in ruins in the 4th century AD. The bridge has two small side arches and a huge central arch. Just ahead, down a few steps, lies Piazza in Piscinula, a good place to stop for lunch or a snack. We recommend *La Cornucopia* (see *Eating Out* in THE CITY), *Comparone,* and a small outdoor café that serves homemade ice cream; just down the Via della Luce are more trattorie. After looking in for a moment to the Piazza in Piscinula (see *Walk 8*), head downriver along the banks to the Ponte Palatino, past La Scarpetta, an ancient children's hospital.

Passing the Ponte Palatino, walk along the raised passage by the river; this is the Porto di Ripa Grande (*ripa* means "quay"). After 1692 this was Rome's main river port; below, it's still a port for a riverboat, and there's also a café. Don't forget to look across the river for the opening of the Cloaca Massima, the large sewer (originally a natural brook and then a canal from early Roman times) draining from the originally marshy Roman forums. Like so much of ancient Rome — aqueducts and fountains — this sewer system beneath the forums is still in use; it passes approximately under Santa Maria in Cosmedin, the church whose spire stands out across the river.

The long building on the right is the freshly restored Istituto Romano di San Michele, a Victorian-era children's home now used for city offices and an occasional art exhibit. Beyond is the city gate and the Porta Portese, a bit of ancient wall that on Sunday mornings is the entrance to an enormous labyrinthine market for antiques (real and fake), clothes, raincoats, umbrellas, leather handbags and wallets, potted plants, chandelier dangles, watch faces, shoes, and puppies. Some of the best buys are from the stands manned by Eastern European immigrants, who live in refugee camps at Ostia; they sustain themselves by selling goods from home.

Walk back to the Ponte Palatino, cross it, and you're walking straight into earliest Rome. There is a trove of interesting buildings right off of the bridge, around a grassy park with a sculptured fountain and banks of oleander. This is the Piazza della Bocca della Verità — the mouth of truth. The piazza is named for the masked bearded man (no one knows whether it is intended to be a god's face or a satyr's) whose face is carved on a huge stone disk-like object that was perhaps once used as an oversize manhole cover, or, more likely, as a rolling doorstop or an object that was slid over a pit into which offerings were made to a god. Since 1632, the Bocca has been a fixture of the portico of the Church of Santa Maria in Cosmedin. Legend has it that if you put your hand inside the stone object while you tell a lie, you'll lose your hand. (This legend may date from the late medieval era, when the threat was used as a warning to children about lying). The church is a bit inland, opposite a riverside group of two temples and a fountain. The broad intersecting avenue is Via del Teatro di Marcello.

The Piazza della Bocca della Verità was first cleared and redesigned in the early 1700s to allow a more picturesque view of the nearby Roman temples. The Fountain of the Tritons was designed by the architect Carlo Bizzaccheri and sculpted by one F. Moratti in 1715 — it only looks like a Bernini work.

(If you could block out the incessant flow of traffic for a moment, imagine this area in Roman times. You are standing between the old city wall and Dock Street, the busiest port in town (and remember that aside from mule, donkey, or horse-drawn wagons on rough roads, *all* merchandise was borne by waterway then).

The two temples before you are the circular so-called Temple delle Vesta (140 BC) and the rectangular so-called Temple of Fortuna Virile (1st century BC, but atop at least one built much earlier). These were actually both built atop considerably raised hillocks, out of piety, but also doubtless to protect them from the notorious floods of the Tiber, no less frightening to the ancients than to all who lived in Rome until about a century ago, when the Tiber was dammed to stop them.

Both temples are intimately involved with the life of the river. Right under where the long, ugly modern building called the Anagrafe (Hall of City Records) stands was the main ancient port area of early Rome. Astride the docks here — which stretched along the riverbanks for hundreds of yards — stood warehouses. In the middle was a temple to the god Mithra. (The temple is still here, in the basement of the Anagrafe.) Mithra was an interesting god, and caught the fancy of the Roman troops in Alexandria, Egypt. He was connected with Babylonian astrology; after someone died, it was Mithra who assigned him or her a place in hell or heaven.

This site, just north of the temples, was the first real approach to Rome before one reached its walls; it was an area filled with foreigners, many of them Greeks, perhaps sailors or those who had fled Turkish Constantinople in the late Middle Ages. The area was known as Little Greece in early Rome (the city then also had an Etruscan quarter and a Jewish quarter — in Trastevere, across the Tiber). To this day, each Sunday morning at 10:30 AM a Greek rite mass is held in the Church of Santa Maria in Cosmedin.

Religion was part of daily life in ancient times; the rich businessmen of the export-import trade dutifully raised temples to honor the protecting deities. The Temple to Fortuna Virile, which faced the port, was in fact once called the Temple of Portuno, after the divinity who protected maritime commerce and the port. The Temple delle Vesta was dedicated to Hercules Olivarius (this was the Hercules who looked after the interests of the rich port merchants' associations; the Olivarius refers to oil, a mainstay of trade).

Built on the ruins to what was once a high altar to the Greek god Hercules, the Church of Santa Maria in Cosmedin is an outstanding feature of this area. Construction began in AD 772 by Pope Adrian I and continued for 2 decades. This being the neighborhood (*schola*) of the Greeks, the quay on which the church stands is called the Ripa Graeca; the church was originally called Santa Maria in Schola Graeca.

The church's elegant campanile is one of Rome's oldest and most beautiful; its original bell, made in 1289, still rings. Its vault rests upon four mighty ancient Roman columns of granite and marble. And in the front portico, with its seven arches, is the Bocca della Verità mentioned earlier — the mouth of truth. Take a moment to look inside the church. The splendid flooring of colored stones, called cosmatesque style, looks amazingly like an Oriental carpet.

From Piazza Santa Maria in Cosmedin, walk a few steps toward the river and turn right; beyond the Ponte Fabricio to Tiber Island, this is called Lungotevere dei Cenci, the riverside drive named for the family of the tragic Beatrice Cenci. Here stands the Synagogue, built in 1874, with its small and interesting museum. The ritual articles from the Renaissance housed here were made by some of Rome's finest artists and craftsmen.

An interesting detour at this point may be a walk to Via del Progresso, just around the corner, to Palazzo Cenci, Beatrice's family home. Shelley wrote about Beatrice in his poem *The Cenci*. She and her brothers killed their brutal and tyrannical father, who had imprisoned her in a castle in the Abruzzo. When the deed was discovered, she was put to death by Pope Clement VIII, who promptly confiscated her considerable wealth (no one seemed to know where the money went).

On Via del Portico d'Ottavia, the old ghetto street that runs parallel to the riverside road, there are several restaurants, a couple of cafés with outdoor tables, and myriad shops that offer good bargains. *Limentani,* a huge warren of a place selling everything from housewares to fine china, is the largest in the area. All of the merchants in this former ghetto area keep their prices competitive, and have a reputation of fair dealing.

Continue along the Tiber, heading upriver toward Ponte Garibaldi; make a note to visit *Da Evangelista,* a fine old-fashioned trattoria on the corner (phone: 6-687-5810).

Look across the Garibaldi Bridge at a medieval tower, one of the last remaining of the many that once guarded the Tiber crossings (and where customs duties were collected). Upon its completion in 1888, this was the world's third-longest river crossing: Only two over the Seine in Paris were longer. Designed by architect-engineer Angelo Vescovali, it was built on three massive pilings faced in travertine marble. There used to be swimming clubs for men only, on the banks below; even today, you can still sometimes see men fishing from the bridge with huge square nets.

Proceed upriver in a northerly direction; the riverside drive becomes Lungotevere Vallati, which leads to the Ponte Sisto, a pedestrian bridge built as a shortcut to St. Peter's during the *Jubilee Year* of 1475. Pope Sixtus IV personally went by boat to lay the first stone for this bridge, erected on the ruins of the Aurelius, a prior Roman bridge, built more than a century before Christ. An inscription reads, "You who pass because of the kindness of Sixtus IV, ask Divine Providence to keep this great Pontiff in good health, and you too who make this prayer, go in good health, whoever you may be."

Crossing it (preferably prayerfully), you're in Trastevere again, at Piazza Trilussa. Trilussa was a popular and witty poet of the 19th century who wrote in the Roman dialect, called Romanesco; there is a statue of him in a corner to the right of the square. The delightful tiny streets of Trastevere are perfect for aimless wandering. Walk past the statue and bear right to enter the Piazza San Giovanni di Malva; walk toward the Porta Settimiana, an ancient and picturesque gate, and follow the long Via della Lungara, which runs under the gate. To the left is the 15th-century Palazzo Corsini, which is not normally open to visitors. For a time, the Catholic convert, Queen Christina of Sweden, lived within these august halls, and after 1800, Madame Letizia,

Napoleon's mother, made her home here. In 1883, when some of its fine artworks were removed to the museum at *Palazzo Barberini,* it became the official Italian Accademia dei Lincei, a scholarly academy. Inside is *Narcissus,* a famous painting by Caravaggio.

Across the street is the Villa Farnesina, built for the Renaissance banker Agostino Chigi; its gallery of splendid paintings has a fresco of *Galatea* by Raphael. Chigi is said to have been so wealthy that, after he dined, he threw his silver plates from the terrace (no longer extant) into the Tiber; fortunately, his servants, with the aid of a big fishnet craftily stretched underwater, saw to it that the silver would live to shine another day.

Continue upriver on the riverside drive, now called Lungotevere della Farnesina. On the left is Regina Coeli (Queen of Heaven), the notorious Roman prison where presumed offenders are held while being charged. On the hill behind the not so heavenly prison, relatives of the imprisoned called up greetings, family news, and other messages to Peppe, Mimmo, and Sor Giovanni locked inside.

Here you have a choice: Walk back across the next bridge (Ponte Principe Amadeo) and return to the city center in the general direction of the busy Corso Vittorio, or continue along the river as it swings around toward the beautiful Castel Sant'Angelo. The bridge of the angels is Rome's prettiest; two of the angels that adorn it are reproductions of the originals by Bernini. At river level is a restaurant; the grassed-in castle moat is a park well suited to a picnic. Bring along an extra scrap or two — this is the favorite run for Roman Rovers — and you'll share your paths with some of the city's finest mutts, who like to chase the cats who are the moat's permanent and most legitimate residents.

Walk 3: The Campo

If the Town Hall on top of the Capitoline Hill, the Campidoglio, is the thinking head of Rome, the old market square of the Campo dei Fiori is its belly, its heart, and — as you'll soon hear from the cheerful shouting — its lungs as well. And just beyond the *campo*, the most plebeian, raucous, and lively of squares, stroll down a sober and silent street of aristocratic townhouses, the splendid (and now traffic-free) Via Giulia. Walk here in the morning (morning, because the *campo* market shuts down at 1 PM) from the Piazza Venezia, ending up across the river and at the peak of the Janiculum, one of Rome's hills that provides a stupendous view of the city, or in the gardens of the Orti Botanici, Rome's botanical gardens, a green oasis of luxuriant plants and shade trees in the very center of town.

From Piazza Venezia, facing Via del Corso, take the street to the left, the Via del Plebiscito, with its uninterrupted flow of buses, along a narrow sidewalk to the Piazza del Gesù. In a massive silver casket inside the ornate, late-16th-century Chiesa di Gesù are the remains of the Spanish soldier Saint Ignatius, the founder of the Jesuit order. This splendid church, an expression of the Counter-Reformation and the revival of Catholicism after the Council of Trent, was intended to show the Christian world the continuing power and glory of the Roman Catholic church, as opposed to the teachings of such heretics as Martin Luther. Across the street is today's Christian Democratic party headquarters — hence the well-armed *carabinieri* guards and, when the powerful and glorious of the party meet, a small fleet of dark blue Alfa Romeo limousines.

Continue on Via del Plebiscito to Largo Argentina. In the center of this busy square is a fenced-off area where there are the ruins of four small ancient Roman buildings; three of these used to be temples. (The area is slated to be turned into a park.) Despite the traffic, the piazza is lovely: A medieval porticoed building bravely stands its ground at one corner, and on another side is the *Argentino Theater;* dating from 1780, it still features nightly performances. Take the continuation of Via del Plebiscito (the road on which this walk began), which becomes Corso Vittorio Emanuele II, and proceed in a straight line to the newly restored Church of Sant'Andrea della Valle at 6 Piazza Vidoni.

Art lovers will know this church for its second chapel on the right of the entrance, believed to be the work of Michelangelo; opera lovers will know it as a setting for *Tosca,* one of Puccini's most popular works (in this most Roman of operas, Tosca's lover is contentedly working on the frescoes in the church in Act One, but is executed in Castel Sant'Angelo by Act Three).

At 168 Corso Vittorio Emanuele II, just beyond the church, on the left side of the street, is the Piccola Farnesina dei Baullari, a pretty Renaissance building, home of the *Barracco Museum.* As we went to press, this small

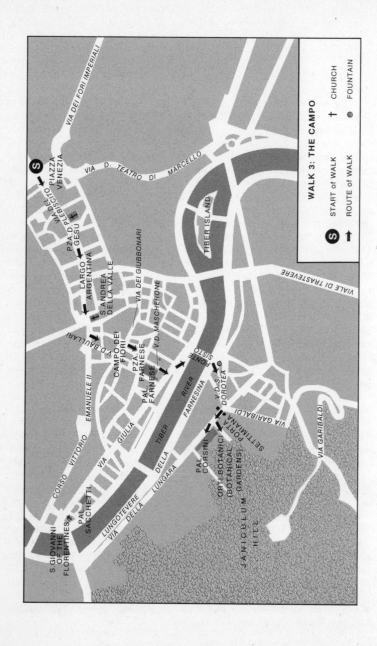

WALK 3: THE CAMPO

S START of WALK   ✝ CHURCH

↑ ROUTE of WALK   ● FOUNTAIN

museum, boasting a private collection of fascinating pre–Roman era sculptures, was due to reopen after being closed nearly 4 years for restorations. The artworks belonged to the Baron Giovanni Barracco, who donated it to the city in 1904. Two famous German archaeologists, Wolfgang Helbig and Ludwig Pollak, helped assemble the collection, which includes a sphinx uncovered near Santa Maria sopra Minerva (near the Pantheon), on the site of a temple to the Egyptian god Isis, ca. 43 BC.

Turn left at Via dei Baullari to the festive, almost circus-like setting of the Campo dei Fiori, Rome's most fascinating open-air food market. In 55 BC, Pompey built Rome's first arena-like stone theater here; the little streets all around follow the curves of the theater and its entrances.

Campo dei Fiori literally means "Field of Flowers," and there are various explanations for the name. By one account, Pompey was in love with a woman named Flora: hence the name, Flora's Field. In another version, the historian Gregorovius explained that the name pertained to certain wildflowers, or to the springtime revels that took place in the neighborhood. Appropriately, the area still has a small flower market, and an atmosphere of revelry.

Somewhat out of place is the brooding statue overlooking this colorful scene: the solemn figure of Giordano Bruno, a troublemaking, heroic, and puritanical priest who was burned at the stake here in the year 1600. Since this also was the site of numerous other public executions, the statue was put here a century ago in memory of all the victims; at that time the piazza's original basin fountain was moved to the square in front of the Chiesa Nuovo, on Corso Vittorio Emanuele.

Around dawn every day (except Sunday) dozens of stands are set up here. Under the traditional square white awnings are mounds of burnished eggplant, bright strawberries, zucchini blossom bouquets, and huge globes of artichokes; in one corner is a display of seafoods of all kinds and shapes, resting on big wet fig leaves laid over cracked ice — fresh today, to be eaten today.

Stroll through the aisles to see the exuberant, dramatic way Romans carry on their daily shopping. Impassioned discussions precede selection. Are these yellow peppers the best you have, or are you keeping the box beneath the counter for the restaurant down the street? Were these really grown in your garden, or did they come here in a truck from Calabria? The *carciofi:* Are they the real Romanesque ones — can you eat the whole thing — or are they the inferior Tuscan stuff? And how can you charge $2 for an artichoke; aren't they in season? I can get it cheaper at the next stall over . . .

One of the joys of the Italian housewife is to be able to buy (and haggle over) fresh vegetables, and she has an unerring instinct for the right stall. You can watch the old grandmothers, seated on stools, as they pluck off the outer leaves and pare artichokes. One delightful stall has an artist's array of dried beans and lentils. Elsewhere, skinned carcasses of whole lambs and rabbits may be hanging from rafter hooks; poultry may come plucked, though a few feathers may be left on a chicken to show it is barnyard raised and not battery-bred, or else to show it is a guinea hen, a popular Roman Sunday treat sometimes found in restaurants.

At 1 PM or so the market is whisked away, as if it were the circus leaving town. The black square paving stones called *sanpietrini* are swept with twig brooms and sloshed clean; the cars and kids with soccer balls and the strollers move back in, and the square assumes its alter ego for the remainder of the day.

Once the daily spectacle is over, try one of the area's restaurants. Half a dozen are right in this piazza, beginning with the popular trattoria *La Carbonara* (see *Eating Out* in THE CITY), whose tables fill one corner of the square. Inside are high-ceilinged, wood-beamed rooms that overlook the piazza — try for a table near the window. This was a posting house in the 19th century, and is in a building hundreds of years old.

If the shops are still open, take a few minutes to wander the little shopping streets like Via dei Giubbonari; it begins just beyond the fish stalls at the southeastern corner of the piazza. (The street name means "street of jackets," and clothing is still sold here at very competitive prices.) Continue down any one of the three short lanes leading south to the majestic Piazza Farnese, an adjacent piazza with an utterly different quality. The *Café Farnese* (facing the Palazzo Farnese on the corner) is a fine place for a postprandial cup of espresso; it has real flowers on fake marble tables outside.

The grand piazza was largely the work of Antonio da Sangallo the Younger and Michelangelo, by then (the 1550s) an octogenarian, but busier than ever as an architect. The Palazzo Farnese, which today houses the French Embassy, is usually considered the finest Renaissance building in Rome. It can't be visited, but anyone is welcome to sit outside on the long stone bench that stretches in front of the façade. The palace was built for Alessandro Farnese, a cardinal from one of Rome's great noble families, who later was elevated to the papacy as Paul III. The two huge bathtub-shape fountains are made of Egyptian granite, and used to be in the Baths of Caracalla.

Take Via del Mascherone, the small street to the left of the Palazzo Farnese; it leads past a handsome, apricot-colored baroque building toward the beautiful, half-mile-long Via Giulia. Here sits an amusing statue: a man's face with water dribbling out of the corners of his mouth. Turn right and walk under the arch to admire the buildings and the six 16th-century churches on this street, one of Rome's most coveted addresses. Fine antiques shops display their exquisite treasures in the front windows; there are also a few small, funky shops. Along the side streets are enjoyable restaurants, including the small *Il Drappo* (see *Eating Out* in THE CITY). As you stroll, be sure, too, to look up from time to time. You'll catch glimpses of the secret rooftop world of fabulously decorated garden terraces.

It was Pope Julius II (Via Giulia was named for him) who asked the architect Bramante to improve the street, which he did so well that Giorgio Vasari proclaimed it the finest street in all of Rome during the high Renaissance. Before then, it was called Via Florida, for the large number of Florentines who had settled here; they made it famous for its shops even then. Among them was Benvenuto Cellini, the master goldsmith of the Renaissance, who wrote in his famous autobiography, "I had a little house on Via Giulia. . . ." Cellini had his brother Francesco buried in the Church of San Giovanni of the Florentines, built by Jacopo Sansovino during the plague of

1448. This church (2 Via Acciaioli) is near San Biagio della Pagnotta (66 Via Giulia), whose façade is by Sangallo the Younger; it is adjacent to the 16th-century Palazzo Sacchetti. In an early reclamation project, the apse of this church was actually built out into the Tiber River, which runs parallel to this road only a block away.

The Church of San Biagio della Pagnotta (in English, Saint Blaise of the Bread Loaf), named for the bread traditionally dispensed to all comers on his liturgical feast day, stands atop a Roman temple to Neptune, appropriate perhaps because of its proximity to the Tiber.

Retrace your steps back down the Via Giulia until, after the arch, you come upon a small flight of steps that lead to the Tiber. Across the street is Ponte Sisto, a narrow Roman pedestrians-only bridge (see *Walk 2*) which incorporates the original ancient Roman bridge built by Caracalla. Look for its "eye" marking on the arches; this is a high-water mark, which when reached warned that bad flooding was coming.

Cross the bridge and face the fountain known universally to Romans as "Er Fontanone," the big fountain. Under the little statue of the 19th-century poet Trilussa (to the right of the fountain square) is a bitter political verse by this beloved Roman penman, with his signature below. Rome was famous for its so-called "talking statues," including the one to Pasquino (see *Walk 5*), to which irreverent political and sometimes anti-religious verses would be attached, like wall posters. Trilussa's famous verse dedicated to Pasquino translates loosely as:

> *As I wuz readin' my usual paper,*
> *Lyin' on the grass under a shade of straw,*
> *I saw a pig an' said hey you swine,*
> *I saw a donkey an' said hey you jackass.*
> *Maybe the beasts here miss the sense,*
> *But at least I have the fun*
> *Of being able to tell it like it is*
> *Without the fear of goin' to prison.*

Veer slightly to the right past the *Orient Express* restaurant (open only in the evening) — this is Trastevere now, and there's one good trattoria after another — and walk up Via di San Dorotea. On the right is the Porta Settimiana, a gate with a medieval aspect, which was once actually part of the wall built by the Emperor Aurelius. Just before it is the house (No. 20) where Raphael's beautiful mistress, La Fornarina, supposedly lived — this is one of several in Rome to make the claim.

At this point the hardy will head upward, along the winding Via Garibaldi leading to the Janiculum Hill, with its great views of Rome (there's also a children's puppet theater). Or continue along the Tiber to the right, along Via della Lungara. This road, parallel to the Tiber's Lungotevere della Farnesina, goes past the Palazzo Corsini on the left (No. 10), which has a small museum open most days until 2 PM, with a superb collection of Renaissance and baroque-era paintings. This also was Queen Christina's home when in Rome.

On the right is John Cabot, an American college in Rome, and the prestigious Italian Academy of dei Lincei, founded in 1603 and similar to the French Academy or the American Academy of Arts and Sciences (not open to the public); its home is the early-16th-century Villa Farnesina, which also has a fresco by Raphael in a ground-floor gallery. Continue to the left, behind Palazzo Corsini, to the lovely Orti Botanici (botanical gardens), with its rare trees and plants. It is an oasis at the end of the Via degli Orti D'Aliberti.

Walk 4: Memorable Monuments — From the Colosseum to a Keyhole

Hopefully, this is one of those Roman days when the northern breeze (*la tramontana*) is blowing, the sky is a nearly purple blue, and puffy white clouds make a picture-postcard background. But even if the weather doesn't cooperate, don't despair: Our journey, which stops at the Colosseum, an arch built by an emperor, an 1,800-year-old house, the earliest Jewish cemetery in Rome, and the world's most famous keyhole, is one of the most memorable in any weather.

Begin at the Colosseum, easy to reach by bus or subway (*la metropolitana* — the stop is Colosseo.) This walk will cross two hills, the Monte Celio and the Aventine, before ending close to another subway and bus stop, the Piramide. Bring a picnic to be enjoyed when hunger strikes (though there will be some restaurants, but not a great many, along the way); stop where you can for a refreshing drink; there are, alas, few cafés nearby.

Begun by the Emperor Vespasian in AD 72, the Colosseum is continually being excavated by archaeologists trying to reconstruct it as it was from the one-third that is extant; what they have been turning up is, literally, garbage: peach pits, grape seeds, and nut shells from snacks, probably discarded by the 50,000 or so spectators who nibbled as they watched the gladiators battle wild animals — or each other — to their deaths. Historians tell us that the arena's proper name is the Amphitheater of Flavius (this was Vespasian's family name), and that it was inaugurated by his son, the Emperor Titus, with a wild orgy of 100 days of feasting and fighting. More than 1,000 lions were killed and 3,000 gladiators took part. Many of the gladiators probably walked to battle from their huts in the Subura, today's lively, gentrified Monti quarter, above the forums on the opposite side of the Aventine. After the gaudy, blood-drenched combat, those who were able would walk home, some to say prayers of thanksgiving at the nearby temples — perhaps Jove-of-the-Beech-woods, or the temple to Igeia near Via del Serpente.

The chariot races and gladiator combats that took place here and that may have sent some Christians to their deaths (historians dispute this tradition), continued until AD 404, when a monk named Telemacus ran into the arena and tried to halt the spectacle. He was murdered by the crowd, but the

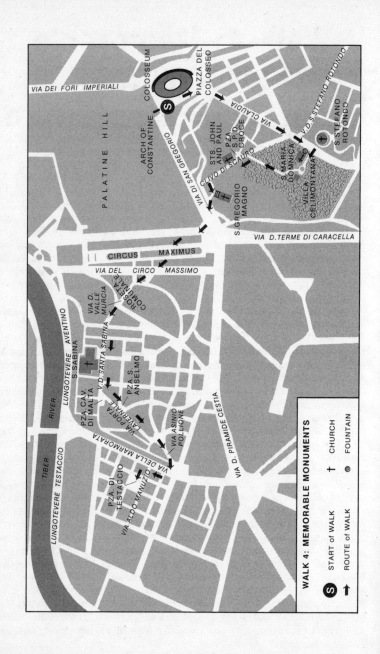

WALK 4: MEMORABLE MONUMENTS

S START of WALK   † CHURCH
↑ ROUTE of WALK   ◉ FOUNTAIN

incident marked the beginning of the demise of the famous fights to the death between man and man, though their fights with wild beasts did go on until 523. By the Middle Ages, the building was damaged by an earthquake and abandoned until it was converted into a military fortress by the Frangipane and the Annibaldi families. The games were briefly revived in 1332, and young men with fancy Roman names, some descendants of emperors, organized Spanish-style bullfighting; 19 heedless aristocratic youths and 11 blameless bulls died, and for Rome at least, that was the real end.

On a grassy knoll just behind the Colosseum rises the magnificent Arch of Constantine, stunningly restored and pristine white. Constantine the Great (that is, Flavius Valerius Constantinus) was a Roman emperor born on Feb. 27, ca. 280, to Helen, who was canonized as the discoverer of the True Cross. In 313 he defeated Emperor Maxentius, partly because poor Maxentius's troops, hoping to ambush Constantine's from the Tiber River north of Rome, drowned when their boats sank. This arch, erected 2 years afterward, celebrates the victory.

With the Edict of Milan that same year, Constantine proclaimed the tolerance of Christianity, paving the way for it to become the official religion of the empire. Constantine was baptized on his deathbed, and is thought of as the first Christian ruler of the Roman Empire. He always claimed his success was due to his Christian conversion; it certainly helped the church, which prospered under his patronage. The paleo-Christian basilicas of Rome, starting with St. John Lateran and then St. Peter's, Santa Maria Maggiore, and St. Paul's Outside the Walls, all date from his reign.

The arch celebrating his military prowess is something of a collage, for it incorporates segments from other and earlier stone sculptures, including a frieze showing Trajan's triumphs over the Dacians. There are hunting scenes with sacrifices from yet another older monument, and eight reliefs from a monument to Marcus Aurelius, including one showing a triumphal procession into Rome.

From here, follow the Colosseum by walking uphill, on the far side of the Piazza del Colosseo (to avoid crossing the traffic lanes more than necessary), and go right along the old wall on Via Claudia. The bustling neighborhood on the left, consisting of small shops, restaurants, and an unbelievably large number of auto repair shops, is near the original site of the Porta Capena, an old city gate. Outside the gates, teams of mule skinners stood ready to transport goods, in an active area where there were a lot of taverns, inns — and a tough-looking crowd. Today, the area, surrounded by magnificent umbrella pines, is quiet — save for the barbarian car drivers. It was here, during the days of Imperial Rome, that various foreign legions of barbarian soldiers were quartered; the soldierly tradition is still in evidence by the Celio military hospital on the left, the same one from which Herbert Kappler, a notorious Nazi war criminal held by the Italians for decades, mysteriously escaped in 1972.

On the right once stood a temple to Claudius (Via Claudia is named for him), built by his fourth wife, Agrippina. When you reach the hilltop, pause a moment to admire the little fountain, the Navicella. It's a Renaissance copy of an ancient Roman votive statue, perhaps connected to a nearby temple to

Jove, and probably put there as thanks for a safe voyage; it's thought to have been offered by some foreign legionary. Incidentally, the tradition of the ex-voto (votive offering) continued in Italy until fairly recently; at the Porta Portese market on Sunday mornings you can still buy silver "eyes," "livers," and other organ oddments from nearly our own age, which were similarly tacked up around a statue of a favored protective saint or madonna. Just beyond, past the hospital, at the intersection of Via Claudia and Via Santo Stefano Rotondo is the imposing, round Church Santo Stefano Rotondo, which dates from the 5th century. Inside is a throne that purportedly belonged to Gregory the Great. Near the Navicella fountain is Santa Maria Domnica (10 Piazza di Santa Maria Domnica), a smaller, not quite as ancient church, standing on the highest point on the hill; it dates from the 9th century and was erected over ancient ruins. Over its altar is a 9th-century mosaic. To the right of the fountain is the gateway to the large and lovely 16th-century park of the Villa Celimontana (one pathway is named for the late Francis Cardinal Spellman of New York City). In a city of rare beauty, this is one of Rome's quietest and loveliest corners — it's only a few minutes from the city center, and yet here time seems to stand still, car noises seem remote, wisteria bloom by the wayside, and the imagination takes wing. Shaped like a four-cornered handkerchief draped over the hill, the park is literally dotted with picturesque Roman ruins, including remains of a temple to Jove and an Egyptian obelisk, toward the bottom right-hand corner of the handkerchief. Walk through the exit that leads to the Piazza San Paolo della Croce.

Dominating this small square is the magnificent Church of Saints John and Paul, built over, and partially incorporating, a 4th-century Roman house. These two early Christians were Roman officials martyred in the time of Julian the Apostate (he came after the Christian convert Constantine, and contested the new religion). The doorway is Romanesque, and two magnificent Roman columns soar upward on either side of the central door inside the colonnaded portico. Dating from the 5th century, the portico was discovered during excavations encouraged in the early post–World War II period by the abovementioned Cardinal Spellman. Inside the Roman house below the church are some outstanding frescoes — if the church is open, be sure to see them. Outside, across the piazza, is an exceptionally fine medieval bell tower, considered the most elegant of the period.

From the piazza, the Clivo di Scauro lane leads downhill beneath the buttressed arches of the church. On the left are more Roman ruins and the Romanesque Oratories (chapels) of Saints Andrea, Barbara, and Silvia; if the latter is open (as with every second church in Rome, or so it seems, it is under restoration at this writing), don't miss the opportunity to see the Guido Reni painting of the *Concert of Angels* (the entrance to the chapels is to the left of the steps to San Gregorio).

The Church of San Gregorio Magno, devoted to Pope Gregory I (called Gregory the Great), stands high atop an imposing flight of steps. It was first a Roman temple, then an early Christian basilica that incorporated 16 columns to support the temple roof; in 1630 it was given its present baroque façade. Gregory actually lived here, in his father's house, near the early basilica, which was dedicated to St. Andrew. After Gregory's death in 604, the church was dedicated to him; inside is his episcopal throne.

It is stirring to realize that from this doorway in the year 596, St. Augustine and 40 monks set out to begin their mission of converting the English to Christianity. The church is open from 9 to 11 AM and again from 3 to 6 PM; vespers are held at 12:40 and 6:30 PM.

From here the Palatine Hill lies directly across the broad and busy Via di San Gregorio. Leaving the church, take the passageway bearing left that runs above the street, heading in the direction of the Circus Maximus — visible from here as a swath of green grass, shaped like an enormous bathtub. The squat modern building across the sea of cars is the Food and Agricultural Organization (FAO) of the United Nations. Steps from the overpass lead down to street level. Cross with the traffic lights, then walk a few yards alongside the Circus Maximus on Via dei Cerchi; hop over the low wall and walk right across the circus, on the paths.

This may be the spot where the poet Catullus, looking enviously at a handsome jockey racing along on a mighty steed, was inspired to write one of his poems. Poor Catullus was seated next to a lovely young woman, who was obviously smitten with the jockey. In his poem, Catallus confesses his envy; but he acknowledges that if he were on the horse and realized she was admiring him, he'd probably have become whoozy, grazed a post, and lost his mount — and his girl.

After walking across the width of the circus, take the stairs at the other end up to the Aventine Hill, yet another of Rome's seven hills. The climb to the top is rewarded by an overlook that affords a fine view of the Palatine Hill and its stretch of magnificent buildings. (The Palatine was home to patrician families and their princely palaces.) Directly across the hill — unmistakable with its high arches still extant — stood the Domus Augustana, the imperial palace built by the Emperor Domitian.

A total of seven emperors lived here, each expanding upon the others' ambitions. Augustus had a compound of three buildings here, facing the Circus Maximus. He was succeeded by Tiberius, then by the dread Caligula, and (after Claudius's reign) by Nero himself, whose palace here burned down in AD 64 (Nero cleared out, moving over to the Appian Hill). However, Domitian (the sixth emperor — in 13 years — after Nero), rebuilt on the Palatine on a grand scale, adding to the original compound of the Domus Augustana until the imperial palaces practically blanketed the hilltop. He was succeeded on the hill by the competent General Trajan, and finally (76 years after Trajan) by Septimius Severus, who ruled from AD 193 to 211. By then the hill had become so overcrowded that when Septimius Severus wanted to put in a swimming pool (bath), he had to cantilever it from the hillside as if it were a deck; the great brick arches directly ahead were erected for support.

Domitian's palace, designed by the famous architect Rabirius, was a compound of three buildings constructed between AD 81 and 96 — the Domus Flavia, for formal entertaining and state audiences; the Domus Augustana, or private apartments; and the Stadio, for games and races (not to be confused with the public-access Circus Maximus below). Among the embellishments of the Domus Flavia were a great hall (about 110 feet long) with marble statues in niches in the walls, and a lofty ceiling 3 stories high; a basilica; a *lararius* (guardhouse); a Greek library and another for works in Latin; a huge portico overlooking the Circus Maximus; and a fabulous marble-paneled dining room with central heating. From the great hall and the dining room the emperor could distract himself from political issues by relaxing in the fountained interior courtyard.

Once rested, turn away from this splendid scene to cross Via del Circo Massimo carefully (walk on the white stripes; they don't guarantee that drivers will stop for you, but they are at least an encouraging factor). This leads to Piazzale Ugo La Malfa, named for an esteemed postwar political leader of the Republican party. Follow the semicircle of marble benches where cats and old folks like to sun themselves, and go left onto Via di Valle Murcia. On either side of this sloping ground is the Roseta Comunale, the city rose garden; it is open to visitors for most of May and June. At the highest point in the garden — entered on the left — buried beneath ground is the oldest Jewish cemetery in Rome (the city has the oldest Jewish community in Europe).

Continue uphill to the Giardino degli Aranci — the Orange Garden — a small, romantic orange grove, bordered on one side by a stretch of ancient Roman wall. This is a peaceful place, where children play and lovers embrace. There is a balcony here that overlooks a curve of the Tiber Island and offers a panoramic view of some of the city's monuments. In this vista, from left to right, is the Janiculum Hill, with a lighthouse more or less straight ahead; the dome of St. Peter's Basilica; the Monte Mario in the distance to the right; the white corkscrew baroque campanile of Sant'Ivo alla Sapienza; and next to it the flatter dome of the Pantheon (half is visible). The impressive building to the right on the hill is the French Academy at Trinità dei Monti, above the Spanish Steps. Then there are the white "wedding cake" or "typewriter" (the ugly, intrusive monument to Victor Emmanuel II, of 1911), the Campidoglio (designed by Michelangelo), and the medieval fortress, the Torre delle Milizie.

Return to Via di Valle Murcia, where the church adjacent to the garden is the Romanesque, 5th-century Church of Santa Sabina, so austere and ancient it seems almost otherworldly. This is the only example of Ravenna-style architecture of that century in Rome. The first chapel was built in 460 on the site of the home where Sabina, a Roman matron, is said to have received Christian instruction from her friend Serapia. Both were murdered for their faith. The sweet apron garden to the side is public, and has been tended for almost 1,000 years by the monks of the church. Nearby, not surprisingly considering the lovely site, was a Roman temple to Juno.

Via di Valle Murcia now becomes Via di Santa Sabina; continue on for 1 more block, until you come to No. 3 Piazza Sant'Anselmo, site of the world's most famous keyhole. It is located in a building that now belongs to the Knights of Malta, and three countries are visible through this keyhole: Malta, an independent territory, represented by that country's patch of cypress lane; Italy; and *dulcis in fondo,* the dome of St. Peter's Basilica, representing the extraterritorial Vatican City. At about this time the whereabouts of a café or restaurant will be pressing. Best bet is the lively Testaccio quarter. Here are several blocks of neighborhood-type restaurants, ice cream shops, and small coffee bars around a central market square. To reach Piazza di Testaccio, walk downhill from Piazza Cavalieri di Malta, using Via Porta Lavernale and its continuation, Via Asinio Pollione; turn right on Via della Marmorata and walk 2 blocks west. Turn left onto Via Aldo Manuzio; it leads directly into the piazza. Also be aware that the No. 94 bus line passes through the Aventine Hill in the direction of Piazza Venezia. On the Via della Marmorata, the No. 95 bus also goes to Piazza Venezia, Via del Corso, and on to Via Veneto and Piazzale Flaminio, via Piazza del Popolo.

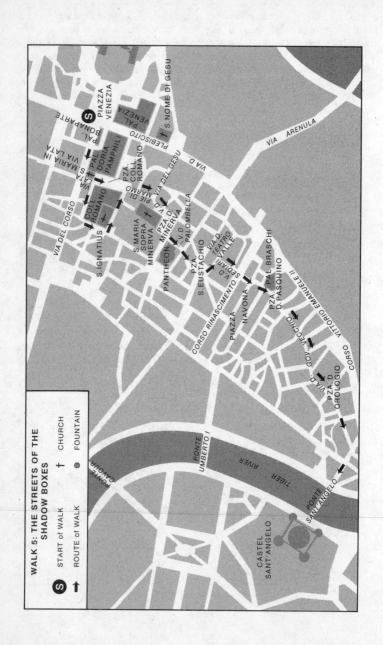

WALK 5: THE STREETS OF THE
SHADOW BOXES

S START of WALK

↑ ROUTE of WALK

† CHURCH

● FOUNTAIN

S PIAZZA VENEZIA

PAL. BONAPARTE

PAL. VENEZIA

S. NOME DI GESU

PAL. DORIA PAMPHILI

PZA. COLL. ROMANO

VIA MARIA IN LATA

VIA LATA

VIA DEL CORSO

VIA D. PLEBISCITO

VIA DEL GESU

VIA ARENULA

COLL. ROMANO

S. IGNATIUS

PIE DI MARMO

S. MARIA SOPRA MINERVA

PANTHEON

PZA. D. MINERVA

V. D. PALOMBELLA

S. EUSTACHIO

VIA D. SEDIARI

VIA D. TEATRO VALLE

CORSO RINASCIMENTO

PIAZZA NAVONA

PAL. BRASCHI

D. PASQUINO

VIA D. GOV. VECCHIO

VITTORIO EMANUELE II

CORSO

PZA. D. OROLOGIO

PONTE UMBERTO I

PONTE CAVOUR

TIBER · RIVER

PONTE SANT'ANGELO

CASTEL SANT'ANGELO

Walk 5: The Streets of the Shadow Boxes

Ancient Rome survives all around — in broken bits of worked marble that have been tucked into a wall, in a sarcophagus utilized as a fountain, in a bit of ancient Roman wall still standing next to a bus stop, in the roots of an acanthus plant thriving in the ruins beneath a column bearing an ancient carving of its jagged leaves.

This walk follows a slightly zigzagging line from Piazza Venezia to the Ponte Sant' Angelo over the Tiber, and gradually to the majestic Castel Sant'Angelo.

When facing Via del Corso from Piazza Venezia, the building on the left corner with its pleasant bar is Palazzo Bonaparte, where Letizia Bonaparte, Napoleon's mother, lived for 20 years; from her chair on the corner balcony, she kept track of the goings-on every day. She would have enjoyed the famous arm-signal ballet of today's white-gloved traffic policeman on his pedestal below her balcony, now a favorite photo opportunity for tourists (see *A Shutterbug's Rome* in DIVERSIONS).

The Corso, as everyone calls it, is almost a mile long. At its far end is Piazza del Popolo and the beginning of the Via Flaminia, the ancient Roman road. The Rome of 2,000 years ago had no proper city planning, but even so the Corso existed as Via Lata (Broad Street). It was drastically improved during the Renaissance, and became Rome's most prestigious neighborhood of important palazzi.

This happened basically because Paul II, the Venetian pontiff who built Palazzo Venezia, had a liking for foot, water buffalo, donkey, and chariot races; he wanted to see them, and so needed a straight stretch of track (*corso* means "run"); even today, the street is blocked off for an occasional Sunday jogging marathon or mass bike outing through the ancient city. It was paved in 1736, and given gaslights only in 1854; Michelangelo walked down this road in the dark, to call on Vittoria Colonna, a noted poet who lived nearby and whom he admired.

The dark stone Church of Santa Maria in Via Lata (306 Via del Corso) is the first church on the left, immediately past Palazzo Doria Pamphili. Here, crossing the Corso, was Diocletian's arch of triumph, and just 100 or so yards ahead was an altar to Claudius, celebrating his soldiers' victory over the English in AD 43.

It is thought that St. Paul lived for a time on the site of this church, in the home of the centurion who had brought him to Rome; there are Roman ruins beneath the structure. The present church — with a façade by Pietro da Cortona — dates from 1660; when Donna Letizia Bonaparte gave up watching the crowd from her corner perch she came to vespers at this church. Some of the Bonaparte family are buried here.

Turn left at the short Via Lata (the original Roman name of the Corso survives only here), and take a ritual sip of water at the humble but beloved Fountain of the Delivery Man (*Facchino*). This is one of six "talking statues" in Rome (the most important of these is farther along on this walk); in fact, they served as message centers during the 17th and 18th centuries. People would write anti-government slogans and attach them anonymously to the statue. If the slogan rhymed (which they often did), and was controversial (they often were), it would be all over town within an hour. But since the Mayor-King of Rome during the time of the talking fountains was also the pope, the protesters had a problem. One political poet who got caught was one Abbondio Rizzi, a delivery man carrying a wine barrel — the hero for whom the fountain was named. Some say that Michelangelo himself made the sketch for the whimsical fountain after the popular Rizzi's death. The fountain honoring him has just been painstakingly restored, but is already in poor condition because of the pollution from the buses along the Corso.

Via Lata leads into the Piazza del Collegio Romano, where an Egyptian obelisk once stood at its center. On this site is the L-shaped Palazzo Doria Pamphili, the largest private palazzo in Rome. The present owner, Princess Orietta Doria Pamphili, is a descendant of Admiral Andrea Doria, who ruled Genoa in the mid-16th century. Earlier, the Dorias also helped bankroll Christopher Columbus; a portrait of the explorer hangs in the museum at No. 1/A (open on Tuesdays and Friday through Sunday mornings). Also on display here are this papal family's impressive collection of Renaissance paintings and sculpture. Inside the private apartments (which can be visited with a separate admission charge), you can see the Columbus portrait, as well as a 6-foot-tall structural model of the enormous Fountain of the Rivers by Bernini (in Piazza Navona), commissioned by the Dorias.

The palazzo, built in 1445 upon solid Roman foundations, was given a new façade in 1660 by Antonio del Grande; the rococo Via del Corso façade came a century later. It was home to the Doria Pope Innocent X, whose portrait by Velazquez that hangs in the little museum is noted in most art history books. Facing the palazzo is the Collegio Romano, originally a seminary. Innocent X was the first Jesuit pope, and this former seminary (it's a public high school now), which shares a roof with the Church of Saint Ignatius just behind the school, was an early seat of Jesuit power.

Look up at the seminary roof to see one of Europe's oldest observatories. Since Galileo's day, astronomers have monitored the weather from here. To maintain measurements perfectly comparable with the unique records of the past, the scientists still use centuries-old instruments, including a long and undyed strand of blond human hair.

Walk around the seminary and start down the narrow street, Vicolo Doria, to see the Church of Saint Ignatius, which was designed by Carlo Maderno, among others. The baroque apron piazza by Filippo Raguzzini is often described as an opera set. Take a moment to step inside to admire the ceilings, a stunning exercise in perspective painted by a monk named Brother Pozzo. Sometimes free concerts are performed here (including at *Christmas*), when visitors have an opportunity to hear its famous organ.

Saint Ignatius himself, former soldier-founder of the Jesuit order, lived nearby, at 45 Piazza del Gesù. If you would like to detour and visit the rooms where he lived, (open from 9:30 AM to 12:30 PM weekdays), turn left off of Via del Piè di Marmo until you reach Via del Gesù. The Church of S. Nome di Gesù (Holiest Name of Jesus), which the Romans called "La Chiesa di Gesù," was built in 1626 to celebrate the canonization of Saint Ignatius. It stands on the site of an earlier, smaller church.

Leaving Sant'Ignazio, go left and continue to circle around so that you return to Piazza del Collegio Romano, under an arch built 125 years ago to connect the school to a library. Along here is *Il Buco,* one of Rome's better Tuscan restaurants; several other good trattorias can be found to the right on Via del Piè di Marmo. The big marble foot perched on the pedestal at the beginning of the road is a remnant from a colossal, 24-foot-tall statue, whose origins are a mystery. It could be the remains of a statue of a Roman emperor, or a surviving relic from a temple that once stood at this spot. Whatever its origins, today's art students love to paint its toenails red.

On Via del Piè di Marmo, there are some fascinating shops to the right, beginning with *Fioravanti* (No. 19), which sells minerals; ask to see the *pietra paesina,* a Tuscan stone that uncannily resembles a landscape. Painters used to add a few green leaf clumps and grass to heighten the effect, and it was once a popular souvenir from Italy: left plain, it still is. A few steps farther along is *Akka* (No. 21), a dealer of African antiquities.

This little street leads through the Piazza della Minerva, past the new *Holiday Inn Crowne Plaza Minerva,* situated in an old hotel (entirely renovated and elaborately refurbished) where Stendhal used to stay (see *Rome's Most Memorable Hostelries* in DIVERSIONS). It's built on top of — and incorporates some of the ruins of — the Baths of Agrippa, which extended almost to the Pantheon. Cut diagonally across the piazza. The building beside the newsstand is the one in which Galileo Galilei was tried for heresy by the Inquisition. Ironically, the building now houses the Ministry for Scientific Research. Dominating the center of the piazza is the famous Bernini elephant (the Romans jokingly called it "Minerva's chickie"), holding up an Egyptian obelisk.

Adjacent to the Ministry on the right is the Church of Santa Maria sopra Minerva (so named because it is built on the foundations of a temple dedicated to that goddess), Rome's only church dating from the Gothic period. It was built in 1280 from plans drawn by the same monks who designed Santa Maria Novella in Florence. Fra Angelico is buried here, and there are sculptures by Bernini and Michelangelo, plus outstanding paintings, including those by Fra Filippo Lippi. There's also an inscription with good advice: "So as not to be killed by the bad air of Rome, take a weekly enema, don't get tired, don't suffer hunger or cold, give up fruit and love, and take hot drinks."

The church also was the meeting place of the Archconfraternity of Matchmakers from 1460 on through the Renaissance. To help poor girls find a husband, this charitable institution provided them with a dowry of 30 *scudi* each, a white dress, and a pair of wooden clogs. (If she'd enter a convent, however, the ante was upped to 50 *scudi.*) On a more sober note, Rome's first auto-da-fé religious heresy trials were held here.

Outside, marble plaques indicate how high the Tiber River rose during the disastrous floods that tore away whole sections of some of Rome's historic bridges. Proceed on Via della Palombella, the narrow street behind the Pantheon that passes over the ruins; on the other side are *botteghe,* or small shops, built over ruins of an ancient Roman public library. Passing through the Piazza Sant'Eustachio (see *Walk 1*), turn left after the *Bar Eustachio* (a good spot for cappuccino) onto Via del Teatro Valle, named for a marionette theater (now a regular working theater with fine productions). Built in 1854 in the former courtyard of Palazzo Capranica, the theater's lovely façade was designed by Sangallo. (Shoppers should make a note to explore *Bassetti,* the labyrinthine men's and women's quality discount clothing store at 22 Via Monterone, south of the piazza.)

Now turn right onto Via dei Sediari, the street of the chairmakers, instantly recognizable by the chairs and straw furniture sitting outside the *botteghe.* Some are new, some are valuable antiques being repaired — often right in the street, where you can watch.

Walk straight ahead on Via dei Sediari, cut across Corso Rinascimento, and continue through to the far end of Piazza Navona to Via del Pasquino, a short road leading into the Piazza del Pasquino. Here is Rome's most important "talking" statue. The homely artwork, believed to be a copy of a Greek original, depicts Menelaus holding the body of Patroclus, who was slain by Hector during the Trojan War. For centuries this statue group lay buried in rubble on Via Leutari, a tiny street nearby, and was used as a handy stepping-stone over muddy puddles. It was raised onto its pedestal behind Palazzo Braschi (see below) in the early 16th century. But instead of calling it Menelaus, the locals called it "Pasquino," supposedly after a hunchback tailor with a tart tongue who lived in the neighborhood. Since the neighborhood was filled with cafés, and popular with students from nearby Rome University, the originally amusing epigrams left on the statue quickly turned into witty diatribes called *pasquinades* against the court of the pope-king, *il Papa Re.* These epigrams were so provocative that Adrian VI, the pope of the time, wanted the whole statue dumped into the Tiber. He was warned against this action by his councillor, the Duke of Sessa, who told him that the frogs from the river bottom would croak out the message anyway. "Burn it then," the pope grumbled. "No, the rabble will have a martyr and celebrate his anniversary with speeches," said the duke. The statue was saved. Even today, there is always Pasquino-inspired graffiti.

Before exiting this square, peek into *Cul de Sac 1,* an old wine shop with a handsome marble serving bar (see *Bars and Cafés* in THE CITY). Directly across the street, on the tiny wedge-shape Piazza del Pasquino where Via del Governo Vecchio begins, is the small Church of the Confraternity of the Agonizzanti, so named because it was the place where the names of those sentenced to death were listed, a tradition that continued until the early 19th century. Built in 1692, it counts among its treasures the diaper supposedly worn by the infant Jesus. (The church's other, more traditional, name is the Church of the Nativity.)

The serious Rome aficionado may wish to make a detour around the block to visit the *Museo di Roma* at Palazzo Braschi (10 Piazza San Pantaleo; see also *Museums* in THE CITY), whose permanent collection includes landscape and cityscape oil paintings that afford fascinating views of 18th-century Rome. On the ground floor is the interesting tiny papal train (two elegant cars) in which the pontiffs rode when they went to visit their flocks in the vicinity of Rome.

Walk back around the block to the Via del Governo Vecchio, the street of the old government. It's a straight street laid out just 1,000 years ago as the Via Pontificalis, which leads to the Vatican, and quite intentionally makes a direct route to the ancient Roman bridge, the Ponte Sant'Angelo. In fact, the government was run for a time out of Palazzo Nardini (its façade was designed by Bramante). On either side of the palazzo are townhouses dating from the 15th and 16th centuries. Keep an eye out for No. 48; this is another house that claims to be the one where Raphael's beloved La Fornarina (the baker's daughter) lived.

During the Renaissance, historians noted with displeasure the large number of junk dealers and old clothes mongers who inhabited this quarter, though there were also book dealers serving the university crowd. It is the same today. Along this street are dozens of *botteghe* selling secondhand clothes, books, funky 1950s plastic jewelry, antique marble fireplaces, beautiful old furniture, and clocks. There also are plenty of good restaurants, cafés, pizzerias, and wine shops; choose any one of these — you won't go wrong.

Don't be alarmed by the assembly of parked police cars; there hasn't been an accident. On the right (at No. 28) is a tiny, old-fashioned *pizza al taglio,* where you can buy squares of plain pizza dough that has been baked on a wood-burning oven (one of the last of its kind in Rome). Point to the topping you prefer and pour yourself a glass of wine from the Castelli. A favorite among *caribinieri* (the *pizzettari* always serves them first), the pizza is worth waiting for.

From here, either take your pizza back to Piazza Navona to eat on a marble bench or keep walking ahead, through Piazza dell'Orologio — the Clock Square (in the 17th century, this was the Justice Building), making a beeline toward the Bridge of the Angels. Crossing the bridge, you come to Castel Sant'Angelo and a grassy park in what used to be the castle's old moat: a good spot to relax at the end of this walk.

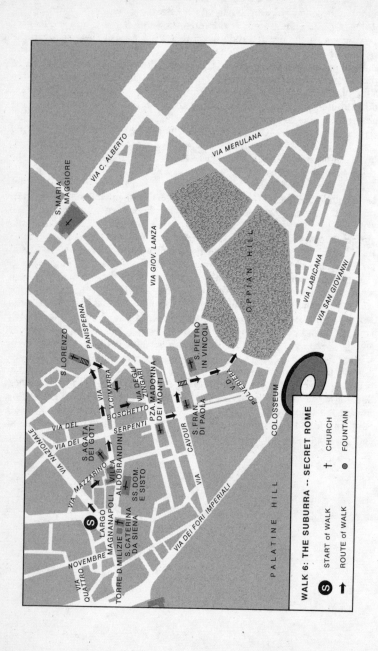

WALK 6: THE SUBURRA -- SECRET ROME

S — START of WALK

↑ — ROUTE of WALK

✝ — CHURCH

● — FOUNTAIN

Walk 6: The Subura — Secret Rome

This walk goes into an ancient Roman suburb, or, literally, through the elongated valley below the settlements on the hills. The area was once traversed by a river, which curved its way through three of the seven hills of Rome — the Quirinal, Viminal, and Palatine — all the way to a fourth, the Esquiline. The Colle Oppio (Oppian Hill), one of the three small summits of the Esquiline, is a large archaeological park with a view overlooking the Colosseum — an ideal spot for a picnic.

The word "Palatine" comes from *pallatium* (as does our word "palace"); in fact, the Palatine was a place of patrician palaces very early on in ancient Rome. The wealthy lived on the hilltops, far from the malaria-ridden lowlands.

The low ground just beyond the shopping plazas and business squares (forum), also situated in the unhealthy valleys, was home to the riff-raff of early Rome — innkeepers, gamblers, thieves, fugitive slaves, and the boxing stars of the time: certain popular gladiators whose physical prowess scandalously titillated even a few of the aristocratic ladies. The playwright Plautus wrote that the residents of the Subura were "money changers and usurers . . . bakers' boys covered with flour, river longshoremen, butchers, fortune tellers, and prostitutes or their managers."

This was not entirely accurate, for along with the rickety and unhealthy lower hillside dwellings were a few important temples and some patrician homes as well. The well-born Julius Caesar lived here for a time early in his political career, perhaps as a canny ploy to win the support of the plebeians.

Though the only gladiators these days are kids on motorbikes, some of the lively atmosphere of the Subura can still be captured: There still are colorful taverns and amusing restaurants, small art galleries, crafts shops, ancient temples — and even a good pastry maker.

Start from Largo Magnanapoli, just uphill from Piazza Venezia on Via Quattro Novembre. At this hectic crossroads, in the midst of a triangular patch of grass, is a relic of Roman stone wall dating from the 4th century BC. Tradition has it that the wall was built by Servius Tullius (the legendary king, who actually lived 2 centuries earlier); in any case, the city once was contained within this walled area, extending more or less along the route of this walk, and then down to the Tiber. The walls kept the city very small, thus the overcrowding of the Subura.

The huge tower that dominates this triangular crossroads of Largo Magnanapoli is the Torre delle Milizie — the Tower of the Militia, so called because that area was near the forums; after they were sacked and vandalized, this became a logical place to build the fortresses typical of Rome in the Middle Ages. This is the largest of the 20 medieval fortress towers left in Rome today (originally there were 200). Next to it is the 17th-century Church of Santa Caterina da Siena, now under restoration.

The palm trees on the terrace above this small square are part of a park surrounding the late-16th-century Villa Aldobrandini; the villa can be reached by walking around the block, along the shopping street of Via Nazionale and turning right on Via Mazzarino. Once a splendid private mansion, the villa now belongs to the Italian state and is used for office buildings (the villa is now closed to visitors, but you can still see vestiges of this magnificent ancient structure through the wrought-iron grill).

On the left, just before the corner of Via Mazzarino and Via Panisperna, is the entrance to one of Rome's oldest and most curious churches: the beautifully restored, tiny Sant'Agata dei Goti. The Germanic people called Goths were among the invaders of Rome in the early centuries after Christ, and they plundered Rome in AD 410, setting up their stronghold just above the Trajan Forum — that is, near where you're standing. They were Arians, followers of Arius, a pre-Protestant Christian; the Nicene Creed exists to contradict the Arian heresy. This small church was the Goths' Arian church, the only one ever in Rome. When their power ebbed, the church building was left to deteriorate for a century. In 592, however, Pope Gregory the Great reclaimed it for Roman Catholicism. Inside, admire the four marble columns holding up a 12th-century canopy topped by what looks like a miniature Roman temple, situated over the altar in the apse. The courtyard is small and elegant, with a well in the center. The original twelve columns, one for each apostle, are still intact. The cosmatesque floor (the name comes from the Greek word for "decorated," and really refers to the Byzantine influence) is from the 15th century.

At the intersection of Via Mazzarino and Via Panisperna, look diagonally across the street. At 1 Largo Angelicum is the graceful Church of Santi Domenico e Sisto. It was built on the site of a famous temple to Diana that dated from the 1st century AD, and it has been a church since the year 1000 or so. The current structure was designed by Giacomo della Porta and built between 1587 and 1593; it was completed by another outstanding architect, Carlo Maderna. Inside are splendid artworks and a high altar designed by Bernini in 1640.

The neighborhood was once called Gallinae Albae — White Hens — and the street name is believed to be a corruption of the phrase *panis et perna* (bread and ham), which the Clarissan nuns in the adjacent monastery distributed to all comers on the feast day of San Lorenzo (Saint Lawrence) until the 1920s.

Walk uphill to the Church of San Lorenzo on the left. It was closed for restoration as we went to press, but its peaceful courtyard is lovely; on the right stands a charming medieval house with an exterior staircase. For a time the body of Saint Brigid was placed in a Roman sarcophagus inside the church, an event marked by the small modern statue of her in the churchyard.

Lorenzo is an especially popular saint in Rome; 34 churches are dedicated to him. This church is located on the site where Lorenzo was said to have been burned on a grate in the year 258. In the 4th century, a church honoring him was built here, and 1,734 years after his death the present church stands in the very same place, albeit on a higher level than the original. Inside are works by Francesco Romano and Michelangelo's student Pasquale Cati, among others.

Return to Via Panisperna, then look left; at the end of this street is the enormous early Christian basilica called Santa Maria Maggiore. Cross Via Panisperna to the Via Cimarra, a small, L-shape road that veers downhill, past a small restaurant, *Altrove* (see *Eating Out* in THE CITY).

Turn left at the intersection of Via Cimarra and Via del Boschetto. This is a street of small shops and restaurants. Make a note that at the far end (going in the opposite direction) is the justly famed *Picchioni Pizzeria* (open only in the evening, however). Walk toward the small (nameless) café at 115 Via del Boschetto, where a few outdoor tables offer a view of the fountain square called Piazza della Madonna dei Monti.

This is the very heart of the ancient Subura quarter, whose modern name, the Monti, comes from its hilly landscape. The short Via degli Zingari (Street of the Gypsies), which runs into the tiny square, leads past the Ukrainian Catholic Church (No. 3). Just ahead (at 52 Via Baccina, on the corner of the piazza) is a small pastry shop with fine cakes and tartlets baked on the premises — your nose will guide you there.

The much-loved Church of the Madonna dei Monti is on the square, and just past it (on a wall on Via dei Serpenti) is a somewhat garish mosaic madonna stomping on a serpent. Historians say they don't know why this was called Serpent Street, and theorize that the area was once woods with a stream cutting through it, so there probably were snakes here. But it's also a fact that a block from here was yet another ancient temple, this one dedicated to Igeia, the daughter of Asclepius, the healer. Like her father, to whom a temple on Tiber Island was dedicated, she too symbolized health (hygiene, that is), and is traditionally shown holding a cup of healing potion in one hand and a serpent in the other. The myth goes that the serpent would drink the medicine in the cup, change his skin, and be renewed and young again. The serpent, in short, was quite at home in this neighborhood as a symbol of the temple.

Walk straight ahead in the direction of the Colosseum, and cross Via Cavour; go left for half a block. Here is a steep staircase leading uphill toward the Colle Oppio; a yellow sign indicates the Basilica of San Pietro in Vincoli (St. Peter in Chains). At the top of the steps, to the right at the end of an overlook, is the Church of San Francesco di Paola, and a convent similarly dedicated to the patron saint of Calabrians and seafarers. Plunge ahead through the tunnel-like archway of Roman wall, to come out at the square by St. Peter in Chains (open daily from 7 AM to 12:30 PM and 3:30 to 7 PM).

This church began as an oratory in the 5th century after Eudoxia, the daughter of Theodosius II and wife of Valentinian III, received from Juvenal, the Bishop of Jerusalem, the chains that had bound the Apostle Peter during Herod's reign. Michelangelo's marvelous statue of Moses is inside; it is so lifelike that supposedly when the maestro finished it he tapped it on the knee with his hammer and said, "Why don't you speak?"

Two medieval towers can be seen from this square: One serves as the bell tower for the Church of San Francesco di Paola; the other stands astride a palazzo that belonged to the infamous Borgias. When you leave the church, take the first street to the left, passing (on the left) the School of Engineering of Rome University. At Largo della Polveriera, named for the munitions depot that once was here, look down the street for a glimpse of the forum and Palatine Hill across the way. The Emperor Vespasian lived near here as a young man; he probably would have walked this way en route to the Colosseum, perhaps to oversee the massive construction project. This is also near the site of the sprawling Domus Aurea (Nero's palace) and the later Baths of Titus — some of the ruins of which are worked into the walls here.

Walk along the ancient Roman walls to the park of the Oppian Hill. This spot affords the finest view of the Colosseum. From this vantage point, the arena still has all its original marble facing, barely marred by time, barbarians, and the earthquakes, whose toll is all too apparent on the other side. (For more information on the Colosseum, see *Walk 4* and THE CITY.)

As you wander through the confusion of impressive ruins, you'll encounter, in the middle of the Parco Oppio, the lane called Via degli Orti di Mecenate; down this road, on the left, is a delightful early Renaissance house built over and incorporating ruins of the Trajan baths.

Visitors to this park are safe — most likely you'll see engineering students reading their notes between classes and art students sketching — but be aware of the vagrants who live in some of the duskier corners. This is an area where only a few innocuous homeless congregate, but there are drug addicts as well. The graffiti are the work of local neo-Fascist diehards (the Italians call them *i nostalgici* — nostalgic for Mussolini to this day).

Don't let these mild admonitions inhibit you from basking in the sun on the grass or sitting on the benches, surrounded by the ruins of the bath complex and the spectacular view of the Colosseum. Another spectator was here before you: the despised, egomaniacal Emperor Nero. Here stood his Domus Aurea, or Golden House, his enormous palazzo with great vaulted ceilings, designed by the architect Severus. Built after the fire of AD 64 burned down his palace on the Palatine, this vast new compound and gardens sprawled from here over many scores of acres. Where the Colosseum is now was once his gardens and a small lake. Just beyond, on a spot still marked by the travertine slabs of a pedestal, Nero erected a nearly 100-foot-high statue of himself in bronze, and gilded it as if *he* were the sun god; it took 24 elephants to roll it into place.

Much of the Golden House compound was destroyed after Nero died, and Trajan had *his* architect, Apollodorus of Damascus, build baths right on top of the ruins. Nevertheless, inside Nero's residence there are some rooms with paintings said to have inspired Raphael when he worked on his frescoes for St. Peter's. Unfortunately, some of the most interesting parts of what is left of the Domus Aurea lie underground today (the little roofs over excavations show where). Excavations are continuing, and these cannot be visited, so visitors will have to be content with just imagining the Emperors of Rome, with Nero delighting in the vision of his own shiny image as tall as a 10-story building, reflected in the little lake.

If you haven't brought a picnic, the area across from the busy Via Labicana and Via San Giovanni has plenty of trattorias and a few nice restaurants worth trying, including the pleasant *Al Gladiatore,* overlooking the Colosseum.

Walk 7: Medieval Rome — Pilgrims and Perils

With the collapse of the Roman Empire in the early centuries after Christ, the great marble temples, theaters, baths, palaces, and city walls were smashed and sacked by northern invaders generically called "barbarians." In the 6th century the Goths destroyed the aqueducts, and in 1084 the walls were breached and Rome was devastated by Robert Guiscard's Normans; much of the city was rebuilt as a fortress. Fear ruled; not even the popes were safe, and by the 13th century they had to flee to Viterbo, north of Rome, and then to Avignon in France.

But at the same time, this world of brutality, which is mirrored in Roman architecture, was also a world of faith and of the spirit. Barbarians or no, pilgrims braved the highway vandals to come to pray in the already venerable basilicas and shrines sacred to Christianity; some of the houses of worship bore plainly Byzantine influence from the Eastern Roman Empire.

Both sides of early Rome, the sacred and the profane, temple and fortress, have survived not only those early waves of devastation, but also the arrogant builders of the 1930s and the frantic traffic and pollution of the 1990s. To see those vestiges of early times is a serendipitous experience. There's a special pleasure in gazing at the complex Roman skyline, and suddenly to be able to single out an earlier period of time; it allows the present to disappear for a while and makes medieval Rome come alive.

Modern-day pilgrims should be aware that much of this walk was designed in 1140 by Benedetto, a canon of St. Peter's. Like Benedetto, we focus on the Trajan Forum, the Church of the Aracoeli, the Theater of Marcellus, and Tiber Island.

As the empire collapsed, and Rome sank into lawlessness, the buildings where the great Roman patrician families and their retainers lived and worked were adapted to parry the danger. Palazzi were no longer sprawling and open as they were in Imperial Rome; they were raised tall, and secured, so that the Roman landscape seemed spiked with as many as 200 lofty towers. The windows of these small family fortresses were kept small and high above street level to minimize danger; the interiors were dark and airless. On street level were open porticoes that served as market stalls by day. All around the entire city an expanded ring of stout walls, with 24 fortified towers, was built by order of Leo IV, who became pope in 847 and rebuilt the city after it was sacked by the Saracens.

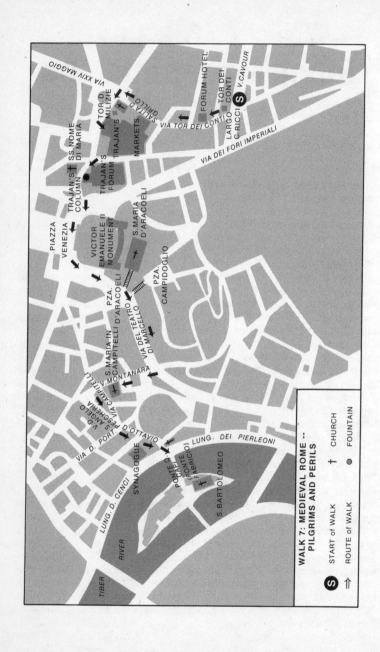

WALK 7: MEDIEVAL ROME --
PILGRIMS AND PERILS

S START of WALK
⇑ ROUTE of WALK
† CHURCH
● FOUNTAIN

Most of Rome's medieval towers were built after Benedetto's day, but they are plainly marked on a 1323 city map; now in the Vatican Library, it's believed to be a copy of one made a half century earlier.

Start from Largo Corrado Ricci, at the corner of Via dei Fori Imperiali and Via Cavour. This area, in the midst of the forums, so bristled with towers in the Middle Ages that it was called Campotorrecchiano — the Field of Towers. Here, magnificent with its yard-high horizontal striping of dark brick and white "bricks" hacked out of marble rubble from the forum, is a glowering fortress and tower, Torre dei Conti. This small castle, standing in the center of a Roman forum, was built in 1207 by Riccardo dei Conti di Segni, whose brother was Pope Innocent III. It is built over a pagan temple atop gigantic blocks of soft ruddy brown tufo stone from Albano, removed from the buildings of the sacked forums nearby. Its tower, loftier than we see it today (part tumbled during an earthquake in 1348), was the tallest in Rome, and the poet Petrarch was quite taken by it when he visited. Walk on Via Tor de' Conti, which begins about 10 yards up Via Cavour, at the intersection of that street with Via Fori Imperiali, and walk toward the *Forum* hotel. Just past the tower there's a small house and, under a leafy trellis, a few benches and tables, home to street people, young lovers, and older neighbors; today, part of the tower is a social center for the elderly.

Now walk past the *Forum* hotel, following the old wall. You may want to drop in at the hotel for breakfast on its geranium-filled rooftop terrace. A graceful window from the late Middle Ages and a small tower (campanile) from the Church of Saints Quirico and Giulitta make up one wall of this terrace. From here there is a sweeping view of the forum and close-ups of the Torre dei Conti. Have a seat on the wrought-iron chairs to meditate a moment on the ebb and flow of history — and the ebb and flow of traffic on a road Mussolini had ordered cut right through and over the ancient forums. From here you can also reflect on Mussolini arranging a military parade on this very avenue for Hitler, literally with "tanks" of papier-mâché.

At the *Forum* hotel, take the road uphill; continue along the Salita del Grillo, walking beside a wall built between the Forum of Augustus and what had been an earlier shanty town, the Subura. The impressive and newly restored building on the right is the Renaissance-era Palazzo del Grillo. Connected to it by an arch on the left is another tall medieval tower, the 13th-century Torre del Grillo; it's now only two-thirds of its original height but in pristine condition.

Continue uphill; on the left are three houses of the Middle Ages. You then pass the Casa dei Cavalieri di Rodi, the 13th-century building of the Knights of Rhodes, also called the Knights Hospitalers, Knights of St. John, and the Knights of Malta (it's now used as a chapel). Constructed over Roman buildings — it incorporates the colonnaded atrium of one — and, typical of medieval constructions, it leans right into the firewall for strength. At the top of the hill, look back to see the perfect crenellations of the 13th-century Torre delle Milizie.

Turn left at the church onto Via Ventiquattro Maggio. Here is the entrance to the Trajan Markets — the semicircular ancient Roman building complex of 3-story buildings tucked into the hill. The building — in use well into the

Middle Ages (though for just what use is uncertain) — is in excellent condition. It's worth taking a half hour for a walk inside. Tourists have always loved these markets: Emperor Costantius II, visiting Rome from Constantinople in 356, was duly impressed, according to historian Ammianus Marcellinus, who brought the emperor sightseeing here. Like him, walk down into its half-moon of a piazza. Cutting across it is a Roman road, paved (like the Appian Way and other Roman city streets) with black lava rock. This is the Via Biberatica, and on each side are 3-story buildings with marble doorways; only an occasional pane of glass is a reminder that you're not in the year 356. Early in the 4th century the sacking of the area had already begun, and some of the marble from the markets went into the building of the Arch of Constantine. By 1232, Roman life had degenerated; the need for fortification in the area was filled by the construction of the Torre delle Milizie right atop these markets.

Continue downhill on Via Ventiquattro Maggio; next to a small pseudo-Venetian palazzo (the color of orange sherbet) is a small medieval building tucked in between larger ones. From around the year 1000 through the 15th century, this area of the forums acquired ten churches and abbeys and five medieval fort-like buildings and towers.

Take the broad staircase that descends between the buildings. At the bottom of the stairs you'll be standing in Trajan's Forum, the biggest of all the forums, literally at the foot of the stunningly restored Trajan Column, a white marble corkscrew-shape structure with a comic book–like narrative carved in bas relief portraying Trajan's achievements. His statue stood on the top of the column until 1587, when it was replaced with one of St. Peter.

Born in Spain, Trajan was a beloved emperor who ruled from AD 98 to 117. He was an outstanding general and governor, builder and conqueror — he extended the Roman Empire to its farthest reaches — who moreover showed clemency toward Christians. Well into the Middle Ages, therefore, the cult that developed among Christian followers in Rome was so strong that many were buried at the foot of his column. A legend of the time had it that at the base of his column Trajan's skull was found with his tongue intact; believers said this proved that thanks to a prayer for his soul by Gregory the Great, he had not been sent to hell as an unbaptized pagan. And perhaps Trajan's connection with Christianity explains why the column was used during the late Middle Ages as the steeple for the long since disappeared Church of San Niccolò de Columna — Saint Nicholas of the Column.

On the left is the fine *Taverna Ulpia* restaurant, overlooking a forum, and on the right, the splendid Church of Santissimo Nome di Maria, in full baroque splendor. Weave your way carefully across the busy Piazza Venezia and its Victor Emmanuel II Monument (the so-called white "wedding cake" or "typewriter"), with a Tomb to the Unknown Soldier; cross over to Piazza d'Aracoeli.

At the piazza, stand in front of Palazzo Colonna, at No. 1 (once the home of a princely Roman family, today it houses the Syrian Embassy, among other offices); look across the street. At the top of the Capitoline Hill is the Campidoglio, whose impressive square was laid out by Michelangelo in the High Renaissance. During the Middle Ages, after the long sleep of a collapsed economy, Rome revived in the mid-12th century, and a commune was established with free institutions once again; its brief, glorious Senate met here (brief because it eventually boiled down to exactly one senator).

Across the street from the embassy, to the left of the Town Hall complex, is Santa Maria d'Aracoeli (the name means Saint Mary of the Altar of Heaven), the church built on the spot where a sibyl told Emperor Augustus of Christ's coming birth. During the 13th century, Franciscan monks rebuilt the original paleo-Christian church into the Gothic-Romanesque–style one that stands today. The strong of heart can climb the 122 steps leading to the church; the stairs were built in 1348, and are one of the great feats of architecture of the period. In the years preceding the Roman commune, men who demanded greater civil liberties rallied by this church. Today, Romans gather here — especially on *Christmas Eve* for its midnight mass, when a Christ child of olive wood is placed in the manger. So venerated is the Bambin Gesù figure that it is usually draped in gifts of jewels, and schoolchildren still bring it letters on *Epiphany*. (During the 1930s, while Mussolini was haranguing from his balcony in Palazzo Venezia, the figure was taken out of the church — transported by its personal carriage — to make a sickbed visit; the entire crowd turned its collective back on the Duce to kneel for the passage of the Holy Infant. Inside the church is the tomb of Pope Honorius IV, a sculpture by Arnolfo di Cambio, one of the greatest medieval artists to leave his mark on Rome.

After exiting Santa Maria d'Aracoeli, walk down the steps, cross the street, and turn left, to Via del Teatro di Marcello. Continue on this street past the small, elegant *Cometa Theater,* and notice the ancient Roman Theater of Marcellus, dating from the golden age of Augustus Caesar. It was one of the earliest monuments to fall into ruin in early medieval Rome, and part of its travertine façade was used to face the Ponte Cestio, which links Tiber Island to Trastevere.

During the mid-12th century, the Fabii family built a fortified mansion right on top of the imposing mass of the theater, which was already collapsing into ruins; its arches were turned into defensive bastions. In later centuries these same arches served to shelter the workshops of the wine bottle cork makers, and in the 18th century the little street nearby came to be called Corkers Alley.

Nearby (on the right) are other important ruins: two ancient Roman temples, one to Bellona, another to Apollo Sosiano, of which three magnificent columns still stand. To arrange to visit the temple and theater excavations as well, ask at the nearby offices of the Ripartizione X of the Fine Arts Commision, 29 Via Portico d'Ottavia (phone: 6-671-03819).

Turn right onto Via Montanara off Via del Teatro di Marcello. At No. 4 look up to see a medieval arch tucked into a row of small, hunkered-down, fortress-like buildings from the late Middle Ages. Notice a gap between the church and the palazzo; walk through it to a little balcony that offers a charming view of an ancient Roman street and of the Theater of Marcellus, whose exterior façade from this vantage point is intact, giving an idea of its original splendor.

The Via Montanara is a short road that leads directly to Piazza Campitelli, where there are two Renaissance-era palazzi — both built by the outstanding architect Giacomo della Porta — flanking the Church of Santa Maria in Campitelli. The pale blue hue of the newly restored palazzo at No. 10 is typical of the recent decision by Rome's city-fathers to promote the use of the lighter colors that were used in Rome earlier in this century; the decision is slowly changing the face of the city as the dark red and ochre colors of Mussolini and early postwar Rome fall into disuse. In the corner is *Vecchia Roma,* a favorite old Roman restaurant, situated on a far corner to the left as you leave the church (see *Buon Appetito: The Best Restaurants of Rome* in DIVERSIONS). It is especially pleasant in summer, when tables are set up outdoors.

Turn left onto Via della Tribuna di Campitelli. At No. 16 is Palazzo Caetani-Loveatelli, a mansion belonging to one of the more prestigious families of the Renaissance; above Trajan's Markets we've already seen their earlier fortress, the Torre delle Milizie, at Largo Magnanapoli. With the new wealth and security of the Renaissance, homes were more spread out. And at No. 23 are ancient columns of varying sizes, removed from the ruins and recycled into mundane palazzi.

Following around the apse of the church, walk down Via della Tribuna di Campitelli, an alley that leads to another small balcony offering another unusual close-up view: This time it is of the trio of magnificent columns still standing from the Temple to Apollo Sosiano of 435 BC; below is a litter of column drums in marble, and a few standing columns, solitary and melancholy, as cats prowl around them and preen in the sun.

Walk back into the alley and look up to see some tantalizing glimpses of terraces on modern Rome's rooftops. Above the window at No. 9 is more evidence of ancient Roman temple cornice fragments embedded into modern buildings for decoration. To the left on Via di Sant'Angelo in Pescheria is still another unusual view: the more or less intact back of the Portico d'Ottavia, with a medieval building actually attached to it for support. Walk right through the little alley — it leads straight through two giant columns, to emerge on Via del Portico d'Ottavia, the far end of what was once Rome's Jewish community, the main street of the old, once-walled ghetto. The big, square-domed Synagogue is on the right. On the left (9 Piazza Montesavello), just before reaching the intersection with Lungotevere dei Pierleoni, is the small Church of San Gregorio Magno, with its Hebrew and Latin inscriptions. Built for St. Gregory the Great (the son of Senator Gordiano and his wife Silvia, who was canonized), its elegant chapel has a painting showing Gregorio feeding the poor.

Across the Lungotevere drive is the Ponte dei Quattro Capi (the Street of the Four Heads), so named because its markers on either side are decorated with four faces. Built by one L. Fabricius in the year 62 BC, its proper name is Ponte Fabricio. During the Middle Ages, Rome's large Jewish community lived on both sides of the Tiber in this area, and on the island itself, and so at that time the bridge was also called the Bridge of the Jews. From here, look across at the low skyline: to the left, the bell tower (campanile) of one of Rome's loveliest medieval buildings, Santa Maria in Cosmedin, stands out. (Cosmedin comes from the Greek word for decorated or adorned, and during the 12th and 13th centuries churches had typically cosmatesque floors of porphyry or other round or oval-shape colored plaques inserted among stones.)

The tower at the end of this bridge was formerly part of an 11th-century fortress. Just beyond it is the 10th-century Church of San Bartolomeo, erected on the site of a temple to Asclepius and a related healing spring so sacred that, even at the time of the Crusades, the builders of the church left the spring open right in the altar steps, where it remains today.

Steps lead down to the end of the island, where there is a park area for a rest and a picnic. To the right in the tower complex is *Sora Lella,* a pleasant old-fashioned trattoria (see *Eating Out* in THE CITY); next door is the small, recently modernized, wood-beamed *Antico Caffè dell'Isola,* with table service in the back and snack tables on the floor above. Whether you choose to picnic or dine, this is a perfect spot to stop.

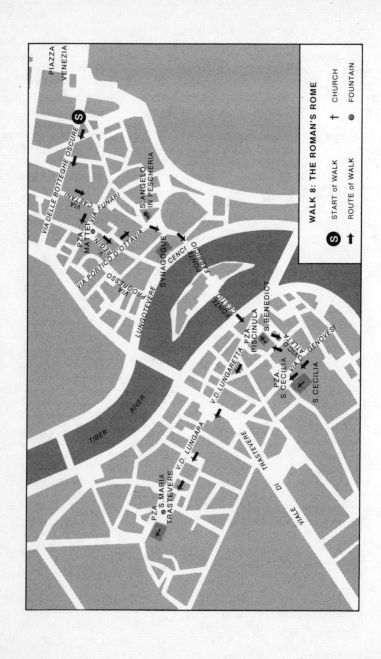

WALK 8: THE ROMAN'S ROME

S START of WALK   † CHURCH

↑ ROUTE of WALK   ● FOUNTAIN

PIAZZA VENEZIA

VIA DELLE BOTTEGHE OSCURE

VIA CAETANI

VIA FUNARI

PZA. MATTEI

S. ANGELO IN PESCHERIA

VIA D. REGINA

VIA PORTICO D. OTTAVIA

VIA PROGRESSO

LUNGOTEVERE

SYNAGOGUE

CENCI

PONTE FABRICIO

PONTE CESTIO

V. D. LUNGARETTA

PZA. PISCINULA

S. BENEDICT

VICO D. ATLETA

VIA D. GENOVESI

PZA. S. CECILIA

S. CECILIA

TIBER RIVER

V. D. LUNGARA

V. D. LUNGARA

VIALE DI TRASTEVERE

VIALE DI TRASTEVERE

PZA. S. MARIA TRASTEVERE

Walk 8: The Romans' Rome

There's hardly an area in Rome that doesn't recall its ancient past. It is demonstrated by the coexistence, almost everywhere one looks, of buildings, artifacts, and oddments from more than 2 millennia of civilization. Even so, the old Jewish ghetto of Rome, and Trastevere, the artisans' quarter, also once inhabited mostly by Jews, are particularly compelling. Even though the cruel walls of the ghetto have come down, the neighborhood still seems connected to its history, especially in the relative silence of the early afternoon, when shops are closed for the lunch break and few people are walking about.

Begin at the Via delle Botteghe Oscure — the Street of the Dark Shops — not far southwest of the Piazza Venezia beyond Via San Marco, and step back in time in the streets of the old ghetto.

The Street of the Dark Shops is home to what used to be called the Italian Communist party. Its name has recently been changed to Partito Democratico della Sinistra (PDS, or Democratic Left party). These are national headquarters, but in recent years Rome has had two Communist mayors, one of whom was the authoritative art historian Giulio Carlo Argan. In ancient times, an old circus (theater) stood here, and in the gloomy protection of its abandoned arches people set up little shops and workshops.

Via delle Botteghe Oscure intersects with Via Caetani; at that intersection, turn left. A few steps down is a memorial plaque to Aldo Moro on the left. A former Premier of Italy and president of his country's majority Christian Democratic party, Moro was Italy's most powerful politician. He was running for president when he was kidnapped by the terrorist Red Brigades in 1978, and it was here, after 55 days of captivity, that he was found murdered.

On the right (32 Via Caetani) is the entrance to the Antici Mattei, a handsome building from the Renaissance. Today it houses libraries, including the Center for American Studies, where Italian university students and their professors conduct research. Its courtyard is a fascinating scrapbook of ancient Rome in stone — walk in and look around; no one objects if you climb the staircase, which will give you a chance to see the insides of a true palazzo.

Go right onto Via dei Funari (a typical old Roman Jewish name) to Piazza Mattei, to see one of the most delightful of the Roman fountains — the Fontana della Tartarughe — the turtle fountain, designed by Giacomo della Porta, chief architect of Rome around 1580. (He also worked to complete some of Michelangelo's projects, including the dome of St. Peter's; some believe the turtles were added subsequently.)

A few centuries back, this little piazza was headquarters for a clothing merchants' association of glovemakers, furriers, and wool and silk dealers.

Even today it is a fascinating warren of small wholesale and retail shops. Although they're fighting to survive the competition from the big stores on the outskirts of the city, they have a policy of maintaining competitive prices. Generally speaking, considering the current exchange rate of the dollar, this is a good place to shop. Don't try to bargain with the sales clerks, though — those days are mostly gone. (You might politely ask if a discount — *uno sconto* — is offered, but it is better not to insist; in most cases the prices already are discounted.)

Walk straight across the small Piazza Mattei, and turn left onto the narrow Via Reginella to Via del Portico d'Ottavia. This broad, short avenue, ever vivacious and crowded, is known by the real *romani di Roma,* the Romans of Rome, as Piazza Giudia — the Piazza of the Jews. Nothing special happens here, except that it was once the heart of the old, very poor, walled ghetto. In it are two churches: Sant'Angelo in Pescheria, named for a medieval fish market here, and San Gregorio, at the end of Via del Portico d'Ottavia to the right, where Jews were obliged to come Saturdays to hear a sermon delivered by a Catholic priest.

According to one old book on Rome, the Jews listened "seraphically," but had stopped up their ears with wax in order not to hear a word spoken by the priest. Says this old book, "Not a Jew was converted, with but one exception." Another text relates that during the obligatory Saturday afternoon sermon pontifical soldiers kept watch over the 100 men and 50 women (which represented the entire community) obliged to attend, to make sure no one dozed off or appeared inattentive.

The small area compressed the population into an increasingly unhealthy neighborhood of high, overcrowded tenements. In the mid-19th century the walls came down, but it took 20 years to be rid of them, and with their demise also came the destruction of a number of old buildings. Those that remain seem vestigially decrepit due partly to the fact that for centuries, all property inside the ghetto belonged to slum landlords, who did not bother to maintain them. Centrally located, and with real estate being what it is today, this area is enjoying a renaissance of sorts.

Rome's Jewish community is the oldest continuing one known to be living in Europe. At the time of the first persecution, Jews as well as Christians were victimized. In the Middle Ages (around the year 1000), Jews lived in Trastevere (see below), near the port of the Tiber River. Persecuted by Torquemada, Spanish Jews immigrated here in 1483 and again in 1492, the year of America's discovery, when Ferdinand and Isabella expelled 200,000 Jews from Spain.

This area was known for centuries as the "Sant'Angelo" quarter or district, after its church, and with the imposition of a number of restrictions in 1556, Jews were ordered to live only here. It's estimated that perhaps 3,500 Jews were living here at the end of that century; perhaps twice that number at the end of the 17th century; and just under 10,000 at the end of the 18th century. During World War II, Nazi soldiers rounded up hundreds of Jews and shot them in the Fosse Ardeatine outside Rome. Today's 15,000 or so Roman Jews live scattered all over the city, but the Synagogue is here on the Lungotevere Cenci by the Tiber. (There is an entrance to the Synagogue on Via del

Progresso, which intersects with Portico d'Ottavia.) Next door to the Synagogue is the small synagogue museum, always guarded by armed police since a terrorist attack in the early 1980s in which a child was killed.

One of the favorite spots on Via del Portico d'Ottavia is *Forno,* the tiny bakery about midway down the piazza, at the intersection of Via del Portico d'Ottavia and Via Reginella — it's little more than a dark doorway, and inside there are just two small counters. But don't be misled by its humble appearance: The pastries are first-rate. There are also kosher (here it's written "kasher") restaurants, a kosher butcher, and several cafés. Jews and non-Jews frequent restaurants such as *Giggetto al Portico d'Ottavia* (see *Eating Out* in THE CITY) to enjoy traditional Roman Jewish cooking, which has nothing to do with American ideas of Jewish food. Here you eat, in season, the famous deep-fried artichokes and a so-called "mixed fry" of codfish, mozzarella, and bite-size zucchini or zucchini blossoms stuffed with a bit of cheese and a taste of anchovy. Also consider the friendly, reasonable *Al Pompiere,* housed in an ancient Renaissance palazzo (see *Eating Out* in THE CITY).

The portico at the end of the street was built in 149 BC by Quintus Metellus, and rebuilt 126 years later by Augustus, who named it for his sister, Octavia. There was a walk between a double row of columns, temples, some public rooms, and libraries. It was used in connection with the huge circular Theater of Marcellus, which still stands to the right of the portico. And then it became the fish market: so much for the glory that was Rome.

The old market that sold fish brought daily from the Tiber lasted until 1870; a marker attached to a column of the portico shows a large fish. Underneath is a Latin inscription saying, "The heads of the longest fish in this picture right up to the first set of fins go to the magistrates (*conservatori*)." (The heads, being the most delectable part, went to the political bigwigs.)

This and Trastevere, the next stop across the Tiber, are areas of innumerable good, small dining places. Romans have always been excellent cooks, and the ghetto area and Trastevere are the places to try the real thing. The most famous of the early Roman cooks was Apicius, who wrote a cookbook explaining how to make certain sauces, how to cook chopped or stuffed meats (or even game) in a pizza-dough crust to tenderize it, and how to prepare the wonderful green vegetables from the Roman countryside. (Apicius's classification of poultry included peacocks, parrots, and flamingos; fortunately, he never wrote down his recipes.) Fish, especially cod and tuna, was popular with everyone; both are still on restaurant menus today. The fish was brought up the Tiber from Ostia, off-loaded at the docks just a few hundred yards south of here, and brought to the fancy dining rooms of the rich or to the local taverns.

Walk south on Via del Portico d'Ottavia in the direction of the colossal group of ancient ruins and turn right down any street to reach the Lungotevere, the road that runs along the Tiber. Cross the river at the ancient Ponte Fabricio; continue across the tiny Tiber Island (see *Walk 2*), and cross a second bridge, Ponte Cestio. You are now in Trastevere.

Until 20 years or so ago, Old Trastevere was a place where the horses for the tourist carts were stabled, where pickpockets and police were on a first-name basis, and where artists had their studios. Trastevere is often considered the most Roman part of Rome, and in some ways it is: You may find it hard to keep to a map here because of the intricacy of the little streets, but if you don't follow this route, invent your own — eventually you'll find your way out again; meanwhile, you'll have had a wonderful time being lost here.

From the Ponte Cestio, walk away from the river to the charming Piazza in Piscinula. No one knows the reasons for the name — there may have been a fish market here — but in this charming piazza, a medieval complex of house and tower can be seen — the 14th-century Casa dei Mattei, and the venerable St. Benedict, Rome's tiniest church. Founder of the Order of the Benedictines, which did so much to help preserve scholarly and intellectual life in the darkest times of the Middle Ages, St. Benedict lived in a small cell inside the church while he was in Rome. There are two popular restaurants in the piazza — *La Cornucopia* and *Comparone,* plus a café; all three set tables alfresco in good weather.

Pass through the Piazza in Piscinula to Vicolo dell'Atleta. Make a note of *Cul de Sac 2* (No. 21); officially an *enoteca* (wine shop), it serves good food as well. Nearby (No. 11) is *Luna de Carta,* a delightful small shop that carries on the Trastevere crafts tradition by serving as a showroom for artisans and artists who work in paper: sculpture, papier-mâché construction, and inexpensive notebooks. It's open from 10 AM to 6 PM daily except Sunday. Just across the street (No. 14) is a medieval building that stands on top of the foundations of the first synagogue in Imperial Rome.

Continue south on Vicolo dell'Atleta and turn right at Via dei Genovesi. Named for the Genoese sailors who lodged at the Hospice of the Genoese after their ships had put in at the nearby Porta di Ripa Grande, this street opens onto the larger Piazza di Santa Cecilia. The ancient church here honoring Saint Cecilia, the patron saint of musicians, was built before the 5th century; the basilica has been restored at various times so that its interior is a stylistic patchwork; its serene cloister is a delightfully romantic setting.

Retrace your steps to Piazza in Piscinula, and turn left on Via della Lungaretta. Continue to Viale Trastevere, a major artery for buses, motorbikes, cars, bicycles — anything that moves. Cross the street with care, and continue walking straight ahead: the continuation is now called Via della Lungaretta. Here Trastevere is more bustling: Students flock here for the less expensive restaurants, pizzerias, little bars, and cafés to play chess and drink coffee. But it's the street scene that makes it all special.

Then unexpectedly the narrow Via della Lungaretta opens wide into Piazza Santa Maria in Trastevere, and one of Rome's earliest churches comes into view. Its foundations are more than 1,700 years old, but it was completely rebuilt early in the 12th century. The 13th-century mosaics in the apse are by Pietro Cavallini, and show the life of the Virgin; others from the same period glow from a panel of the façade; the artist Domenichino painted the wooden ceiling and the painting of the Assumption from 1610.

The square is dominated by a lively fountain and is filled with cafés that are hopping from dawn till midnight. Take a chair and enjoy the scene: the fountain splashing, the voices calling, the busy life of Rome around you. Here you're part of the picture.

Walk 9: Masterworks of Architecture Through the Ages

Aside from the geography of a city of hills overlooking a sinuous river, Rome's architecture and ruins are an integral part of its beauty and its mystery. This walk, a survey of Roman architecture, is laid out not geographically, but within specific time frames.

The ancient Romans were great engineers and designers whose theories of architecture were laid down in a treatise written by Vitruvius Pollio in about 25 BC. As builders for the public weal, the Romans, perhaps improving on techniques learned in the eastern Mediterranean, mastered the making of cement (which the Greeks did not use), the building of the arch (which enabled their roads to span great rivers and allowed water to run along aqueducts), and the construction of the vault (which could enclose a huge gathering place; until the Romans, all roofs were flat).

The route begins at Trajan's Column, designed by Apollodorus. We'll take a look at an ancient Roman office building, a grand staircase from the Middle Ages, and a square laid out by Michelangelo that epitomizes the Renaissance. Then it's on to see some examples of the baroque style typified by Bernini. At the Quirinal Palace you'll see Napoleonic-era, French-style city planning in action. En route is an amusing example of Italian Liberty style (as Art Nouveau is known here), and those interested in the modernists can end up at famed architect Pier Luigi Nervi's central railway station, still avant-garde after 60 years. Along this walk we'll continue to focus primarily (but not exclusively) on outstanding buildings, each of which is representative in a special way of the architecture of its era.

Trajan's Column (see *Walk 7*), beautifully and recently restored, stands just to the east side of the Piazza Venezia. It's believed that the sculptured depiction of Trajan's military accomplishments against the Dacians (that is, modern Romanians), illustrated on a twisting scroll with 2,500 figures carved in marble bas-relief like an endless comic strip, was made in AD 113 from drawings by Apollodorus, who also designed Trajan's multi-storied, semicircular shopping and business mall next door (the *Mercate Traiani*) and the Ulpian Basilica, a temple within the Trajan Forum, which is in the area all around you. Just 4 years later, in 117, Apollodorus was banished from Rome and then executed by Hadrian, Trajan's invidious successor. Trajan was the brilliant military leader who forced the Roman Empire to its farthest reaches in the world, and his ashes are buried in a golden urn at the base of the

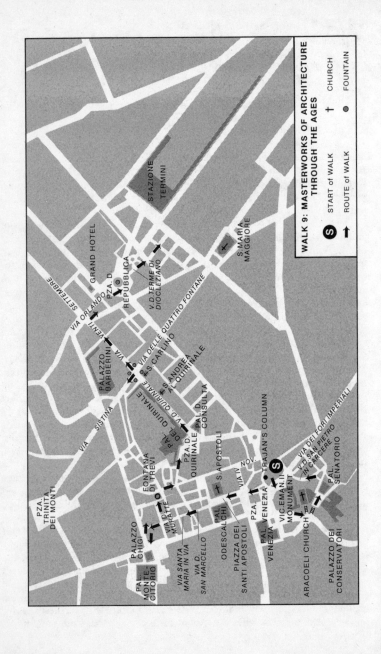

WALK 9: MASTERWORKS OF ARCHITECTURE THROUGH THE AGES

Ⓢ START of WALK
↑ ROUTE of WALK
✝ CHURCH
● FOUNTAIN

VIA ORLANDO
GRAND HOTEL
SETTEMBRE
VIA
PZA. D. REPUBBLICA
V.D. TERME DI DIOCLEZIANO
STAZIONE TERMINI
VENTI
VIA
VIA DELLE QUATTRO FONTANE
PALAZZO BARBERINI
S. CARLINO
S. ANDREA AL QUIRINALE
S. MARIA MAGGIORE
VIA SISTINA
PZA. TRINITA DEI MONTI
V.D. QUIRINALE
PAL. DEL QUIRINALE
PAL. D. CONSULTA
PZA D. QUIRINALE
FONTANA DI TREVI
VIA D. MURATTE
PALAZZO CHIGI
PAL. MONTE-CITORIO
VIA SANTA MARIA IN VIA
VIA D. SAN MARCELLO
PAL. ODESCALCHI
PIAZZA DEI SANTI APOSTOLI
S. APOSTOLI
VIA IV NOV.
TRAJAN'S COLUMN
VIA DEI FORI IMPERIALI
V.D. SAN PIETRO IN CARCERE
PZA. VENEZIA
PAL. VENEZIA
VIC. EMAN. II MONUMENT
ARACOELI CHURCH
PAL. SENATORIO
PALAZZO DEI CONSERVATORI

column. For lunch or dinner amidst the ruins, reserve a table at *Taverna Ulpia* (2 Via Foro Triano; phone: 6-678-9980).

From here, cross the broad Via dei Fori Imperiali to stand in front of the ghastly "White Elephant of Architecture," the Victor Emmanuel II Monument by Giuseppe Sacconi. It was begun in 1885 and completed in 1911 at great expense (and unheeded objections from other contemporary architects). Consider how the small Capitoline Hill must have looked only a century ago, before the construction of this overwhelming, tasteless, and even pointless building, which dwarfs its neighbors. Until it was built, there was nothing on the hillside but trees and shrubs in a park-like setting.

As you walk, watch out, first for cars (don't take chances — cross with the lights!) as you circle around the monument, until you come to a V with a staircase on the left and a ramp on the right. The long staircase leads up to the Church of Santa Maria d'Aracoeli; built from donations given in thanks for delivery from the plague in 1348, it also marked freedom from centuries of barbarian invasions. With the collapse of the empire and the city's destruction by Goths and Normans, urban chaos had long reigned: It was every clan for itself. Apart from the small churches, defensive walls, and dark fortresses built into and over the tumble of abandoned great Roman construction, few attempts were made to build monuments in medieval Rome; curiously, the city is devoid of any important public secular building from that time. The construction in 1348 of these 122 stone steps leading up to the Aracoeli Church on the Capitoline Hill heralded changing times. It showed that life and commerce were returning to Rome again. In fact, it also marked the start of a modest building boom.

Climb the Capitoline Hill, using the broad ramp to the right of the church. It was designed by Michelangelo, who was commissioned by Pope Paul III to build a walkway for a triumphal procession honoring Charles V, the visiting Holy Roman Emperor. On this, the lowest of the Roman hills, important temples once stood during ancient Roman times, but were left to fall into ruin. During the darkest Middle Ages this cradle of ancient Roman civilization was so abandoned that sheep and goats grazed on this hillside, which came to be known by the slightly insulting name "Monte Caprino" — Goat Hill. (It was used as a market square, and some buildings faced in quite a different direction: toward the forums.)

It was Michelangelo, who went on working as an architect into his 80s, who gave the hill its present aspect and major features: the ramp, three palazzi, and the central 12-pointed geometric web design in the pavement, where a pedestal was erected to display the rare, gilded bronze equestrian statue of Marcus Aurelius from classical Rome. After centuries of exposure to the elements, the statue was just restored, and now stands inside the *Capitoline Museum,* to the left, for protection from pollution (for more on the museum, see below).

The rediscovery and new appreciation of antiquities typified the Renaissance; classical statuary no longer would be burned, as it was in medieval times, but raised on pedestals for public delight. Encouraged by their princely patrons, spurred on by the earlier Renaissance in Florence, the architects brought grandeur back to Rome. Streets were straightened, the aqueducts that were smashed by the Goths in the 6th century were repaired, and fountains and palazzi were built. Conscious efforts were made by farsighted popes, like Paul III and Sixtus V, to improve Rome's appearance and functionality.

The little door on the right in the piazza, with the flock of photographers and nervous-looking people standing about in their best clothes, is the entrance to the wedding chapel; here, with considerable pomp and circumstance, His Honor the Mayor's representative performs marriage ceremonies. Afterward, some of the couples will go down into the forum below to be photographed amidst the romantic ruins.

Straight ahead is Rome's City Hall, where after 900 years the city fathers still meet in the Palazzo Senatorio. Originally, it looked into the forums; Michelangelo turned its façade around, to face outward. Part of it is built on top of strong arched vaulting from an ancient Roman office building, the Tabularium (see below).

To the right of City Hall is the entrance to the *Capitoline Museum* in the Palazzo dei Conservatori. If you stop at the museum, don't miss the Hall of the Emperors, with its busts of 65 of them on view in chronological order; you might want especially to look for Apollodorus's patron, Trajan. There is no admission charge to browse in the lovely courtyard, which has bits and pieces of a colossal statue of Constantine: two giant feet, a giant hand, an elbow with veins beneath the marble skin; there is an admission charge to the museum.

In the lane to the right of the central building is the Palazzo Senatorio; the three main buildings arranged in a U-shape have little roadways slicing between them; these small lanes lead to pocket parks with scenic overlooks. Walk out to the overlook to see the vaulting in the Tabularium, a huge corridor-like building right under the palazzo. The consul Quintus Lutatius Catulus had it built in 78 BC as a place to store the government's files. Its arched portico (by an anonymous architect) is the oldest in existence, and never having been pillaged or destroyed, the old city archives building is today in nearly mint condition: It is an architectural rarity. The Tabularium is a reminder, too, that the Roman architectural concepts and engineering skills served the needs of the governors, soldiers, and businessmen managing an empire. A wealthy, vigorous society needed offices and large assembly spaces for the conduct of public affairs — the colonnaded forums, the Pantheon, the temples and tribunals, the baths (with their libraries for reading and gyms for a workout). The perhaps otherwise restive plebeians needed to be entertained, and so there also were theaters (just down the street is the Theater of Marcellus), the racecourses like Piazza Navona, and the big chariot tracks, or circuses.

From here, look down at the forums. Spread out before you is a dense complex of temples and markets, basilicas and triumphal arches. This vantage point affords a sense of Imperial Rome perhaps better than any other single site, although the forums are not easily understood, since they were sometimes built on top of one another. If time allows, take a half day to study them. From here you can also admire the vaulted arches built to celebrate military triumphs, a setting that has inspired so many poets and philosophers.

The hilltop across from here is the Palatine. Here the great emperors had their state apartments and private mansions side by side. In those buildings (whose ruins overlook the forums) they indulged their taste for elegance. They had elaborate entertaining requirements, plenty of money, fine architects, and refined tastes. On the pragmatic side, they had central heating; on the aesthetic, they liked colored decorations: frescoed dining rooms, for instance, and halls paneled with precious marble brought from the far reaches of the empire; mosaic designs enlivened their reflecting pools.

All this was abandoned during the Middle Ages, when the forums and the emperors' dwellings were sacked for building materials for forts, needed for protection from the barbarians (forts and medieval towers were built right below here in the forums). No piece of stone was safe, and it is a miracle that we see what we do. Even the marble statues that had adorned the pagan temples were burned so that their mineral content could go into the making of cement. The kiln to burn the statues was right here, in the forums. One of the archaeological treasure troves of all time was the discovery of more than 20 statues that now stand in the Temple of the Vestals, at the Piazza della Bocca della Verità (see *Walk 2*). They were stacked like logs waiting to be tossed into the flames; no one knows what event intervened to save them.

A second sacking came in 1930, when Via dell'Impero (now Via dei Fori Imperiali) was sliced through at Mussolini's urging. Piazzas and streets from the Middle Ages were cleared away to bring the archaeological sites to the surface, but then instead of leaving the entire area as an archaeological park (as Roman urban planners continued to request), a broad strip of concrete was poured over them.

Leave the overlook and return to Piazza Venezia again by descending the small road to the left of the Palazzo Senatorio — it's called Via di San Pietro in Carcere. Bear right so that you are across the square from the Palazzo Venezia, a former papal palazzo. The building, which was home to the Venetian pontiff Paul II, is one of the finest examples of 15th-century Roman architecture, though its architect is unknown. These days it is better remembered as the location of Mussolini's balcony; the Duce had his office here, and entertained Claretta Petacca, his lover, inside it.

At the corner where that building recedes, becoming Palazzetto Venezia, there used to be a tower and a house where Pietro da Cortona, the prolific painter and architect, lived after 1649. Giulio Romano, a disciple of Raphael and another architect-painter, also lived here in the mid-16th century. Past the modernish insurance company building is the site of the house where Michelangelo died in 1564, at age 89; look for the little plaque commemorating him.

This square was called the Platea Nova (New Piazza) in the Middle Ages, and from the 15th century on it was a place of gaiety and partying at *Mardi Gras* time.

Turn right onto Via Quattro Novembre at the end of the square, and you're at the *Ricordi* store, which has a rich collection of classical music compact disks, tapes, and records. Now cross the street into the Piazza dei Santi Apostoli.

On the left, occupying one entire side of the square, is the immense Palazzo

Odescalchi, still home to the princely family that also owns (and rents for weddings and balls) the fabulous family castle at Lake Bracciano. The palazzo's elongated façade was designed by several 17th- and 18th-century architects, including Luigi Vanvitelli of Naples (who completed it) and Gian Lorenzo Bernini (who began it). There were two Berninis: Pietro, born near Florence in 1562, and his far more famous son Gian Lorenzo, born in Naples in 1598. Pietro began as a painter and became a sculptor in Rome; his son was a sculptor, painter, and architect, who helped create the baroque style. One of his most famous works is the *baldacchino* (the decorated canopy over the altar) in St. Peter's; he also designed the two curving portico "arms" extending out as if to embrace the pilgrims in that square, and the fountain in Piazza Navona. We'll see more of his works farther along.

Inside Palazzo Odescalchi is an elegant courtyard completed in 1623 by Carlo Maderna, the architect who designed the façade of St. Peter's. The palazzo typifies the Roman mansion of the Renaissance: to the street side is a closed façade with windows in orderly tiers, and inside, a garden-like space, usually with a fountain. The typical Renaissance palazzo housed the family, all the relatives, plus the retainers, bookkeepers, lackeys, coachmen, baby-sitters, tapestry repairers, floor waxers, and footmen; and indeed until the early 1950s a top-hatted footman would stand outside such doors as these to open the door for his prince and princess.

Across the street is the splendid Church of the Santi Apostoli, built on foundations from the 6th century. Rebuilt by Carlo and Francesco Fontana in the early 18th century, it was given a new façade by Giuseppe Valadier in the early 19th century. Valadier, born in Rome in 1762, also won the commission to lay out the square of Piazza del Popolo, which is bordered by an ancient Roman gate, the park area overlooking the piazza (the Pincio), and a number of other Roman palazzi and buildings. He was the first modern architect involved in the planning of the city. Inside the church are important artworks, and there is an adjacent cloister; just beyond it are the gardens of the Colonna family, one of the papal families who helped to bring about the Renaissance.

Proceed the length of the piazza and keep walking straight. You may run into young men (or they may run into you) late for classes at Gregorian University, just up the hill to the right. Its street and piazza are called Pilotta, named for pelota, similar to basketball, which has been played here since the early 16th century. If you take a detour up to see that square, look down the lovely street to the right, under the arches: It offers a pretty view. And behind the tiny red door to the left is *Moriondo e Garigli* (2 Via della Pilota), the last of the hand-dipped chocolate shops in Rome.

If you're thinking about lunch, note *Abruzzo,* the old-fashioned trattoria on the corner of Via della Pilotta and Piazza dei Santi Apostoli (phone: 6-679-3897). Otherwise, exit the piazza by continuing straight ahead on Via di San Marcello, past the *Peroni* brewery dating from the early 20th century; it's a popular — and noisy — student hangout. (In its own way, the brewery is a historic building — Rome has few such old breweries left.)

Continue straight down Via di San Marcello, which leads directly to the

Galleria Sciarra, with its stunning polychrome marble floor and painted ceiling with a double-tiered panorama dating from the end of the 19th century. The ceiling celebrates that era's idea of female virtues. The paintings are charming, and the gallery has recently been lovingly restored. This building, the home of Prince Matteo Sciarra, was the work of the architect Giulio de Angelis, and the painter was Giuseppe Cellini (no relation to the more famous Benvenuto Cellini). It was built just 20 years after Italy was unified as a country. (Rome became the capital of united Italy, after Turin and Florence, and so few important buildings were erected.) Other examples of the Roman Liberty (Art Nouveau) style of architecture can be seen at the Quartiere Coppedei, in the nearby suburb of Parioli, at Piazza Buenos Aires (east of Villa Borghese). Florentine-born Gino Coppede's odd neo-Gothic quarter is within this gallery, the best of the Roman Liberty style.

When you exit the Galleria, you'll be on what is the continuation of Via di San Marcello, a street called Via Santa Maria in Via. Continue straight ahead to another gallery of the same era, the 150-year-old Galleria Colonna, which opens on the left. The open-arched gallery is also newly restored, and is replete with café tables in the cool shade. It hardly rivals Milan's fabulous Galleria for splendor, but it is an amiable oasis on a hot day. From a café table you can see, across the rush of buses and official cars (no private cars are allowed on the Via del Corso), the Renaissance Palazzo Chigi (now the Italian premier's office), designed by architect Carlo Maderna for the princely Aldobrandini family. The Council of Ministers has met here since 1961; the building next to it is the Italian Parliament, in the Palazzo Montecitorio. In the middle of the piazza is a tall column; in marble detail it relates the life of Marcus Aurelius, perhaps Rome's most beloved emperor (he thought of himself as a citizen among equals, refusing to be considered a god, as had most of his predecessors). This is the traditional heart of Rome. The fountain, by Giacomo della Porta, dates from the 1560s, and is a favorite rendezvous spot.

From the Galleria Colonna, retrace your steps back to Santa Maria in Via, which intersects with Via delle Muratte. Turn left onto Via delle Muratte and continue to Piazza Fontana di Trevi. Along this route are simpler, less expensive cafés with and without tables, inexpensive pizzerias, and several good restaurants. These shops, by the way, often offer good buys in shoes and handbags (for more information see *Shopping* in THE CITY). The street scene is always lively, with Romans as well as tourists, and in the midst of this rather cheery bustle is the majesty of the Trevi Fountain.

After 7 years of restoration, the 2,000-year-old fountain is again in fine form. The Acqua Vergine aqueduct had been built in 19 BC by the consul Agrippa to carry water from the hills 14 miles (22 km) east of Rome, passing over the Pincio and into the Campo Marzio. During the Middle Ages, when Rome lapsed into chaos and the barbarians were not *at* the gates but *through* them, this aqueduct, like all the others, was not maintained; it still supplied water, but in ever-dwindling amounts. (An early-15th-century drawing shows that the outlet of this aqueduct was a modest half-moon basin into which poured three gushing spouts — not the big fountain that dominates the piazza today.) At that time, the piazza also housed the stunningly beautiful Church of Saints Vincent and Anastasio (facing the Trevi Fountain), and overlooking it at a benign distance, a square tower on the Quirinale Hill, shown in an uninterrupted view; today the view is blocked by the other buildings.

When Pope Martin V was remodernizing Rome in the early-15th century, he restored the aqueduct and ordered a new fountain built. Wanting to improve it, Pope Urban VIII, who reigned from 1623 to 1644, commissioned the fountain-master Bernini to make one "big enough to be seen from the Quirinal Palace" (which sat on the hilltop just above here). Bernini had thought of ravaging Cecilia Metella's mausoleum on the Appian Way, so it was fortunate that his plans were never executed. Finally, in 1732, Nicola Salvi, another great baroque architect, won the commission. And his is the version seen, with the present fountain — its theme taken from the old Acqua Vergine — making up one whole wall of the Palazzo Poli behind it.

The most recent restoration of the fountain is from our time. Its consultant was the American sculptor Peter Rockwell, who has called the complex restoration work "a manual in stone-cutting techniques," because many different types of stones were used to achieve the dynamic effect of crashing waves and snorting horses.

Leave the Piazza di Trevi to climb the Quirinale Hill; walk away from the fountain along Via San Vincenzo for 1 block before taking a left turn onto Via della Dataria. Here a broad travertine stairway leads to the Piazza del Quirinale, with its awesome views of Rome; come back at sunset for a treat — though it's also worth visiting around 4 PM, when a band sometimes plays, and there is a changing of the guard.

Monte Quirino is one of the seven original hills; before Rome was a city, the Sabines lived here. They erected at least four temples to the Sabine gods, the most important of which was Quirinius, their version of the war god Mars. Some of the stones from that original temple were removed to build the medieval grand staircase to the Aracoeli. Centuries later, to enlarge the square, Pope Urban VIII had what was left of one of the temples carted away.

The building where Italy's president lives today was the popes' summer residence before they transferred to Castel Gandolfo. Gregory XIII acquired the original building from Cardinal Ippolito d'Este in 1572. After the Risorgimento and unification of Italy in 1860, it became the Palazzo Reale, home to Italian royalty. After World War II Italy became a republic, and since then the Italian head of state has resided here. The famous gardens of the palazzo have an ancient fountain that provides power for a hydraulic organ. Guests enter through the main doorway, designed by Bernini.

In the piazza center are two enormous statues of the Dioscuri dominating wild horses. These are ancient copies of the 5th-century BC Greek original depicting the twin deities Castor and Pollux, often inaccurately attributed to Praxiteles. Originally they stood in the Baths of Constantine, which were located near what is today Via Ventiquattro Maggio. Also found with them were the two statues we saw in front of the Palazzo Senatorio in the Campidoglio square, the reclining Tiber and Nile.

The 45-foot-tall obelisk in the middle of the square had been brought from Egypt and was originally placed in front of the mausoleum to Augustus by architects. The big granite fountain came from the Roman Forum; for centuries, until 1818, it was used for watering horses. This fountain group was a challenge for architects. The giant ancient Roman statues were placed at various angles before this final arrangement was determined, and architect Domenico Fontana added the marble basin below the granite fountain.

The result is the urban project laid out by the French administrators of Rome when they ruled here in the early 19th century. They aimed for what some critics consider a forced symmetry of buildings. In 1860, under Pius IX, architect Virginio Vespignani had the piazza further expanded by leveling everything, which meant knocking down still more ancient buildings. Across the piazza from the president's palace is another palace, Palazzo della Consulta; built in 1739, it now houses Italy's high court offices. Ferdinando Fuga, born in Florence in 1699 and for 20 years chief architect to the papacy in Rome, won the commission for this building and for the papal horse barns across the street. That building, from which there is a splendid view of Rome, is believed to be the real site of the Roman tower from where the Emperor Nero watched Rome burning.

Down the street the palace stretches with what is called "the long arm," passing two vest pocket parks; on the way to the intersection of Via del Quirinale with Via delle Quattro Fontane is a church of special architectural interest. The little Church of Sant'Andrea al Quirinale was built by Bernini between 1658 and 1671; he considered it his masterpiece. At the above-mentioned intersection is San Carlo, or San Carlino, a church that was designed in 1634 by Bernini's rival, Francesco Borromini; it is regarded as a jewel of baroque architecture, and was Borromini's first commission after 20 years of working as an assistant to others, including Bernini. Borromini then went on to create his masterpiece: Sant'Ivo alla Sapienza.

The four fountains at that intersection (try to ignore the traffic) have recently been restored. Standing at the center of this crossroad, you will be able to see the three obelisks at once: the one at the Piazza del Quirinale, and those at Trinità dei Monti at the end of Via Sistina. From this vantage point, you will also be able to see the Basilica of Santa Maria Maggiore. A left turn from Via del Quirinale onto Via delle Quattro Fontane leads to the enormous *Palazzo Barberini,* a national museum. Architecturally, the U-shape building, designed by Carlo Maderna, was an inspiration to Bernini's colonnades, which stand in front of St. Peter's Basilica. Indeed, the young Bernini took over Maderna's work after the elder architect's death. If a tour of the museum is not in order, continue instead directly ahead from Quattro Fontane (Via del Quirinale now turns into Via Venti Settembre) for 3 blocks and turn right onto Via Orlando. Here, at the *Grand* hotel (see *Checking In* in THE CITY), which takes up the entire block, a stop at one of the quiet bars is a pleasant experience. Admire the full Liberty style of the lobby. In the afternoons, a harpist plays while Roman matrons quietly sip tea.

Exit the hotel, turn left, and continue to Piazza della Repubblica, a large, round piazza with a century-old fountain depicting Leda among the swans. From here continue ahead on Via delle Terme di Diocleziano, where the large white marble awning of the central train station can be seen. The station was designed in the middle of the century by Pier Luigi Nervi, the pioneer of modern architecture, who also designed three Roman stadiums, including the *Palazzo dello Sport.*

For those who want souvenirs of this walk, Rome has a wealth of small shops selling antique prints and attractive reproductions of etchings depicting its monuments; one of the most rewarding Roman experiences is to take time to pore over these prints and maps. In addition, there is an outdoor book market at the Piazza di Fontanella Borghese. Many of the reproductions — and in some shops, a few originals — are the work of Giambattista Piranesi, whose first plates of Roman antiquities, *Prima parte di architettura,* were printed in 1743. Piranesi was a forerunner in the 18th century's rediscovery of Roman antiquities, and he was followed by other engravers who have left us documents of Rome's ancient palazzi and piazze of that time. This last stop is an appropriate coda to this architectural walk.

Walk 10: The Appian Way

If you like to dream, indulge your fancy by walking out of Rome along the Appian Way. You'll pass ancient baths, walk through (and under) the walls that once guarded the old city of Rome, and then wander through what seems a country lane beneath magnificent umbrella pines and cypresses, to a beloved church of Christianity, the place where Peter asked Jesus, "Quo vadis?" Beyond are catacombs that can be visited (bear in mind that one catacomb is closed Wednesdays, the other Thursdays). This is a long walk, so wear sturdy shoes, bring a sun hat or umbrella, and if possible, a picnic: there are restaurants and cafés, but not many.

Begin at the Baths of Caracalla, on Via delle Terme di Caracalla. The Romans loved their baths: A daily bath in one of the city's more than 800 bathing establishments was a regular habit for nearly everyone, from patrician to plebeian. These baths were one of the eleven magnificent *thermae* or free public baths. Much like our version of a downtown athletic club, they had a little pro shop, tennis court, swimming pool, sauna, and gym. The ancient ones were far grander, however, and had space for 1,600 men and women (Diocletian's Baths, by today's modern train station, could serve nearly twice that many). The complex had hot and cold water pools, a library, a shop or two, a lecture hall, a place to walk and talk under a portico, and a gymnasium for ball games and wrestling (even women wrestled and worked out). The baths were begun by Septimius Severus in the year 206, but were inaugurated by that emperor's son Caracalla a decade later. Heliogabalus and Alexander Severus expanded the baths, and Aurelian restored them.

These days, they can be visited from 9 AM to 6 PM in summer and to 3 PM only in winter. A summer season of grand opera starring top performers is held here. The acoustics are excellent, and watching the opera in such a splendid setting can be an extraordinary experience. The favorite opera heard here is *Aïda,* which some audiences remember best for the elephants that sometimes clump across the stage in cadence with the triumphal march (see *Quintessential Rome* in DIVERSIONS).

At the end of the long road is a convent church and school dating from the Middle Ages, and a major traffic junction. Continue straight ahead, across the junction, taking the Via di Porta San Sebastiano. This becomes an almost magical walk as the buildings disappear, and the street narrows to a cobble-stone country lane. On either side are high walls; a bower of trees overhead gives shade, and on the right are gates opening into a pleasant children's park. With a little imagination the sound of the cars becomes the sound of the chariots and covered wagons leaving for the south of Italy, for this was the

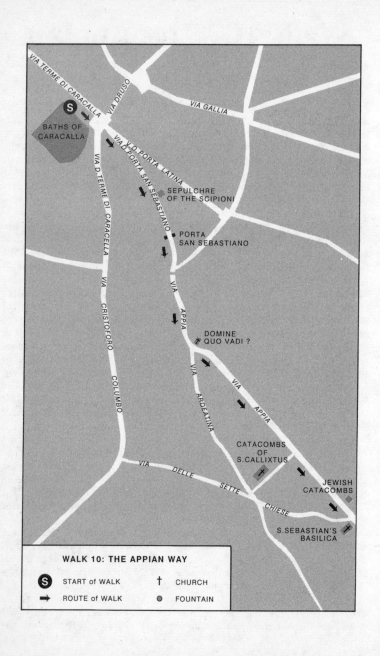

VIA TERME DI CARACALLA

VIA DRUSO

VIA GALLIA

S

BATHS OF
CARACALLA

VIA D. TERME DI CARACELLA

VIA D. PORTA LATINA

VIA D. PORTA SAN SEBASTIANO

SEPULCHRE
OF THE SCIPIONI

PORTA
SAN SEBASTIANO

VIA CRISTOFORO

COLUMBO

VIA APPIA

DOMINE
QUO VADI ?

VIA ARDEATINA

VIA APPIA

VIA DELLE SETTE CHIESE

CATACOMBS
OF
S.CALLIXTUS

JEWISH
CATACOMBS

S.SEBASTIAN'S
BASILICA

WALK 10: THE APPIAN WAY

S   START of WALK   †   CHURCH

→   ROUTE of WALK   ●   FOUNTAIN

beginning of the Appian Way. You're passing the Sepulchre of the Scipioni (also knows as the Tomb of the Scipios), discovered in 1780 and restored in 1926. It was a family mausoleum, with a columbarium and catacombs dating from the 3rd century. It can be visited in summer from 9 AM to 1:30 PM, and on Tuesdays, Thursdays, and Saturdays from 4 to 7 PM (no afternoon visits Sundays, when it closes at 1 PM, or in winter; closed Mondays; 9 Via di Porta San Sebastiano; no phone).

Ahead looms the Arco di Druso (Arch of Drusus) just before the Porta San Sebastiano, which was the ancient Appian Gate built in the late 3rd century by the Emperor Aurelian. (The older wall, with its Porta Capena, was not far from the Circus Maximus.)

Inside the gate is the small and interesting *Museo delle Mure* (Museum of the Walls; 18 Via di Porta San Sebastiano; phone: 6-757-5284). It's open weekdays from 9 AM to 1:30 PM and on holidays from 9 AM to 1 PM; on Tuesdays, Thursdays, and Saturdays, from 4 to 7 PM as well; closed Mondays. Your entry ticket will allow you to walk right onto the walls.

From Porta San Sebastiano the road runs downhill somewhat. This was called the Field of Mars because a sanctuary to the god of war was known to be nearby (foot soldiers left from here for their expeditions in the south).

Continue south on the same well-built Appian Way that soldiers marched, to Capua and to Brindisi, a seaport on the Adriatic Coast. The Regina Viarium (Queen of Roads) was inaugurated in 312 BC by Appius Claudius. On either side of the road are impressive monuments; these surviving ruins are set in one of Rome's most evocative landscapes, with magnificent umbrella pines silhouetted against the sky. These are maritime pines, broad at the top, quite different from the skimpy, swaying loblollies of the American South. Their great pine cones have tiny kernels inside which, when cracked, yield pine nuts (*pignoli*), a favorite treat; if you find a cone, crack the kernels with a rock as the Roman children do. Respighi wrote music to honor the pines of Rome, and the Belgian poet Maurice Maeterlinck penned the following tribute: "He who has seen and understood them will never forget them, and would know them readily among similar trees in a less sacred land. They served as an adornment to the incomparable events they witnessed, and are inseparable from the scattered aqueducts, bare mausoleums, ruined arches, and heroically broken columns which confer such majesty upon this country-side. They have taken on the form of the eternal marbles which they envelop in reverent silence . . . they are Roman, and feel Roman."

Ahead is an overpass. Before reaching it, look to the right; there are tombs dating from the centuries just before and after Christ's birth. There's also a copy of the ancient Roman milestone that was here — it tells you you've completed Mile 1. (The original has been moved to the Campidoglio.) Next, past the ruins of a large brick sepulchre, is a bridge over the little Almone River, one of the tributaries of the Tiber. A goddess's statue was traditionally washed in it by priestesses in ancient Roman days.

Don't forget to look back as you walk; the view of the old walls circling around the city is better from here than from anywhere else. Immediately after the little bridge (about 80 yards away, on the left) is the Sepulchre of Geta, who was murdered by his brother, the Emperor Caracalla. The monumental tomb, which today looks like a tower, was in antiquity a series of ever smaller cubes faced in marble. The elaborate marble decorations, of which only traces remain, must have been at one time very impressive. What is here now is just the central cemented core of the once taller and larger original. Right over it, an indifferent Roman built himself a little house, like a turret.

As you approach the turnoff for the Via Ardeatina, look across the street to the small church with the plain façade that everyone calls Domine Quo Vadis? (Its real name is Saint Mary in Palmis). It is a 9th-century chapel, rebuilt during the Renaissance. It sits on the spot where tradition says that St. Peter spoke to Christ. Peter was escaping from Rome and the Emperor Nero's persecution of Christians; on this road Peter had a vision of Jesus walking toward Rome even as Peter fled. To his Lord, Peter said, *"Domine, quo vadis?"* ("Lord, whither goest Thou?") and Jesus answered reproachfully, *"Venio iterum crucifigi"* ("I come to be crucified again"). Peter turned back, to face his martyr's fate.

A pre-Christian *ex voto* showing an impression of two feet in a marble slab, which stands in the center of the church, was later considered a sign of Christ's passage (this is a copy of the original, which is housed in the nearby Basilica of San Sebastiano).

Across the street from the church is a small tomb from Roman times, with a medieval circular tower added on top. This was the sepulchre of Priscilla, the wife of Flavius Abascantus, a powerful politician in Domitian's reign.

Here the Appian Way continues toward the Alban Hills and then, going slightly inland, curves around mountains to the Tyrrhenian coast at Terracina, a charming seaport village. You can continue on the Appian Way toward the Catacombs (ignore the sign at the juncture with the Via Ardeatina; the little road is for cars and buses). Along the way there is a small café, and a restaurant; one or two more restaurants are farther ahead.

Inside the walls on the Via Appia are the private villas of the well-to-do. These homes were sometimes rented to the Hollywood stars who relocated here to work at Cinecittà in its heyday in the late 1950s and early 1960s, when Rome was called Hollywood on the Tiber. The movie sets were full of fake chariots and papier-mâché Roman buildings for the making of such "epics" as *Ben-Hur, Spartacus,* and *Cleopatra.* In a wedding gown designed by the Sorelle Fontane, Linda Christian wed Tyrone Power, and, bedecked in diamonds, Liz married Dick.

By the time the walk begins to seem interminable, you'll reach the entry on the right to the Catacombs of St. Callixtus (visiting hours are from 8:30 AM to noon and from 2:30 to 6 PM in summer; to 5 PM in winter; closed Wednesdays). Inside is the "Crypt of the Popes," where several popes and bishops were buried in the 3rd century. The word catacomb comes from the Greek *kata kymbas,* or "near the caves" — hence, underground cemeteries.

Across the street from No. 103 is a copy of the stone marking the second mile. Farther ahead are Jewish Catacombs of Vigna Rondanini, which include a synagogue (at this time they cannot be visited without special group arrangements; for information about arranging a tour, contact Roberto Cereghino, 1 Piazza Finanze, Roma 00185; phone: 6-718-3004 or 6-483617). They are located on the left just before the intersection with Via delle Sette

Chiese. On the right, just after the intersection, is St. Sebastian's Basilica, where the original marble slab with the two footprints said to mark Christ's passage is on view. This church dates from the early 4th century and was rebuilt in the 17th century. Its original name was Memoria Apostolorum — in memory of the Apostles Peter and Paul; after the 9th century it was rededicated to St. Sebastian, who was martyred during the persecution under the Emperor Diocletian and is buried in the catacombs here.

Of the original four layers of catacomb galleries at the basilica, usually the second level is the deepest one visitors are allowed to see. They are open in summer from 8:30 AM to noon and 2:30 to 6 PM; in winter, to 5 PM; closed Thursdays.

Continue along Via Appia; on the left are the evocative ruins of the Circus of Maxentius and the Tomb of Romulus; for visits, make special arrangements beforehand with the City Hall fine arts office, the Ripartizione Antichita' e Belle Arti del Comune di Roma (phone: 6-671-03613). There is also the imposing Tomb of Cecilia Metella, and a restaurant or two; about here the cold-drink vending wagons are a welcome sight.

From here, a bus will take you back to the center of Rome; hardy walkers, however, can continue along the Appian Way for a stretch. At this point, the walls drop away, the view across the fields suddenly opens up to reveal small churches, burial markers from Roman times, and the ever evocative landscape with the broken arches of the aqueducts in the far distance. Indeed, you can walk a long way on this road — all the way to Brindisi.

INDEX

Index

BIRNBAUM TRAVEL GUIDES

Order by phone, toll-free: 1-800-331-3761

Name_____Phone_____

Address_____

City_____State_____Zip_____

Discover the Birnbaum Difference
More Details and Discounts Than Any Other Travel Guide

Get the best advice on what to see and do and where to stay while benefiting from money-saving information from America's foremost Birnbaum Travel Guides.

Country Guides—$17.00 Each

☐ Canada   ☐ Great Britain   ☐ Portugal
☐ Caribbean   ☐ Hawaii   ☐ South America
☐ Eastern Europe ☐ Ireland   ☐ Spain
☐ Europe   ☐ Italy   ☐ United States
☐ France   ☐ Mexico   ☐ Western Europe

New Warm Weather Destination Guides 1992—$10.00 Each

☐ Acapulco   ☐ Bermuda   ☐ Ixtapa &
☐ Bahamas   ☐ Cancun/Cozumel/Isla   Zihuatanejo
   (including Turks   Mujeres (including Playa
   & Caicos)   Del Carmen

New City Guides 1992—$10.00 Each

☐ Barcelona   ☐ London   ☐ Paris
☐ Boston   ☐ Los Angeles   ☐ Rome
☐ Chicago   ☐ Miami   ☐ San Francisco
☐ Florence   ☐ New York   ☐ Venice

Business Guides 1992—$17.00 Each

☐ Europe 1992 for the Business Traveler
☐ USA 1992 for the Business Traveler

Total for Birnbaum Travel Guides	$
For PA delivery, please include sales tax	
Add $4.00 for first Book S&H, $1.00 each additional book	
Total	$

☐ Check or Money order enclosed. Plase make payable to HarperCollins Publishers.
☐ Charge my credit card ☐ American Express ☐ Visa ☐ Mastercard

Card no._____Exp. date_____

Signature_____

Send orders to:
HarperCollins Publishers, P.O. Box 588, Dunmore, PA 18512-0588